POVERTY AND UNDERDEVELOPMENT IN TRIBAL AREAS

About the Author

Suvendra Jenamani, Head, the Department of Geography, Government Girls College, Durg-Bhilai, Chhattisgarh. After completion of his M.Phil. and Ph.D. from Delhi University, he was selected as Assist. Professor (Geography) by the Madhya Pradesh Public Service Commission. He is life member of various institutions and organisations. Dr. Jenamani has contributed to the academic world of Geography in his capacity as a researcher, teacher and organizer.

POVERTY AND UNDERDEVELOPMENT IN TRIBAL AREAS

(A Geographical Analysis)

SUVENDRA JENAMANI
Head, Department of Geography
Government Girls College,
Durg-Bhilai, Chhattisgarh

CONCEPT PUBLISHING COMPANY PVT. LTD.
NEW DELHI-110059

ISBN-13: 978-81-8069-169-0

First Published 2005

Published and Printed by

Concept
Since 1974

Concept Publishing Company Pvt. Ltd.
A/15-16, Commercial Block, Mohan Garden
New Delhi-110059 (India)
T: 25351460, 25351794, *F*: 091-11-25357109
E: publishing@conceptpub.com, W: www.conceptpub.com
Editorial Office: H-13, Bali Nagar, New Delhi-110 015, India.

Cataloging in Publication Data--Courtesy: D.K. Agencies (P) Ltd. <docinfo@dkagencies.com>

Jenamani, Suvendra, 1964-
Poverty and underdevelopment in tribal areas : a geographical analysis/ Suvendra Jenamani.
p. cm.
Originally presented as the author's thesis (Ph. D.)—University of Delhi.
Study conducted at the Kalahandi District of Orissa, India.
Includes bibliographical references (p.)
Includes index.
ISBN 9788180691690

1. Kalahandi (India : District)—Economic conditions. 2. Poverty—India—Kalahandi (District). 3. Tribes—India—Kalahandi (District)—Economic conditions. I. Title.

DDC 330.954 13 21

Dedicated

to

My most beloved (Supreme) Father

Who explains me how Indians are living in misery

and want due to poverty of ethical values.

PREFACE

Development related poverty, though not directly considered a part of the 'mainstream' Geography topic, is emerging as a new frontier of research among social geographers, at least in the developing countries.The aspects of social justice, territorial equity and human morality, important concerns in human geography, make this topic attractive and of social relevance to many human geographers. There is absolutely no reason why the topics such as poverty, hunger, deprivation be left to the economists alone, when their domain is too wide and interdisciplinary. It is also realised that tools and techniques, that are exclusively economic, are not adequate to understand the multi-dimensional nature of poverty.

Barring a few studies such as spatial and socio-economic factors of poverty in USA by Morril and Wohlenberg; structural poverty in rural Peru by R.H.T. Smith; identification of intra-urban deprivation in the cities of England by Johnson and others; Peet's explanation of rural American poverty and Misra's work on rural poverty in U.P., Geographic studies on poverty are rather scanty.

The most remarkable deficiencies with non-geographical studies are that : (a) they overlook ecological and saptial dimensions; (b) they fail to throw away the straight jacket of disciplinary compartmentalization to take a holistic view on poverty, and (c) they have not moved away from subsistent concept of poverty.

In contrast geographres have tried to explain poverty and deprivation in entirely spatial terms. They ignore underlying structural mechanisms. Development geographers have done many micro level studies. Development economists share this mistake too.

The present study entitled '*Poverty and Underdevelopment in Tribal areas: A Geographical Analysis*' attempts to fill these gaps by reshaping the concerns and approaches of social sciences to escape both the insular conviction of non-geographical disciplines and excessively subjective nihilism of geography. This is different from previous approaches in the following ways.

Firstly, poverty sub-micro region is seen in the framework of geographic underdevelopment. Secondly, the focus is on differential accessibility to resources by social groups in varied micro-ecological settings. Thirdly, socio-economic correlates of poverty have been analysed in spatial context. Fourthly, local adaptive methods to cope with the conditions of food scarcity are examined. Fifthly, the policy aspects of governmental programmes have been examined from spatial perspective. As a whole, poverty is analysed from a multidisciplinary framework. The study strives to merge primary statistics, abstract thought and grim realities with equal dexterity. It sharply brings out the fact that Development Geography has got more to do with micro level regional welfare than obviously with the growth calculus of economics.

SUVENDRA JENAMANI

ACKNOWLEDGEMENTS

I would like to record my profound gratitude to Prof. R. P. Misra, the then Head, Department of Geography, Delhi University, Delhi, under whose initial supervision and inspiration this project was conceived and executed. Despite numerous pre-occupations and busy schedule he was good enough to accommodate me as one of his last disciples in the fag end of his academic life.

I am equally obliged to my new supervisor Prof. S. K. Aggarwal for extending his kind consent to look after my work on the retirement of Prof. Misra, and under whose supervision the thesis was concluded. He made thorough comments on the chapters and remained warm and considerate throughout. I am proud of the previlege.

I am highly indebted to late Prof. Moonis Raza, the then Vice-Chancellor of Delhi University, Delhi; Prof. S. D. Tendulkar, Development Economist, Delhi School of Economics, Delhi; Prof. Nilakanth Rath, the then Director of Gokhale Institute of Politics and Economy, Pune; Prof. Manoranjan Mohanty, Department of Political Science, Delhi University, Delhi; Prof. B. Mishra, the then Professor, School of Planning and Architecture, New Delhi; Late Prof. Bikram Nanda, Department of Sociology, Jamia Milia Islamia, Delhi; Prof. D. K. Singh, the then Professor, P. G. Department of Geography, Utkal University, Bhubaneswar; Dr. H. Ramachandran, Ex-Reader, Department of Geography, Delhi University, Delhi (who provided the guidance for empirical analysis); Luis L. Esperza, Lecturer of Geography, Mexico University; Felix Padel, D. Phil., Oxford University; for providing intellectual sustenance to the research work.

My thanks are due for Mr. Bhakta Charan Das, Ex-Union Minister and social activist of Kalahandi, Mr. Fanimdam Deo, researcher of history (Kalahandi), Jawaharlal Nehru University; Mr. Anant Giri, researcher (Sociology), John Hopkins University,

U.S.A.; Mr. Raju J. Das, Researcher, Department of Geography, Ohio State University, Columbus, U.S.A.; Mr. Arup Mitra, Reader (Economics), Institute of Economic Growth; Mr. Samarendra Jenamani, Town Planner, BDA, Bhubaneswar; Mr. D.D.R.R. Pattanaik, Civil Engineer, Bhubaneswar; Mr. William Robinson Wolf of Harvard University, U.S.A.; for holding valuable discussions and extending concrete suggestions at different stages of the thesis work.

I am truly grateful to staff of Ratan Tata Library, Delhi University; Systems Research Institute, Pune; Orissa Remote Sensing Organisation, Bhubaneswar; National Informatics Centre, New Delhi; Voluntary Organisations of Kalahandi (LOK DRISTI, FARR, VIKALPA, VISWAS, AWARE, CARE, AGRAGAMEE, GRAMVIKAS etc.) Gandhi Bhawan, Delhi; Architects Consulate, Bubaneswar; Medical, Forest and other Government offices of Kalahandi, Orissa; Members of royal families of Bhawanipatna, Madanpur, Rampur and Khariar; many generous persons and hospitable people of Kalahandi.

I also thank U.G.C. for providing me Senior Research Fellowship to carry out the study. Finally, I express my humble obligation towards my parents, family members, friends, colleagues and above all divine family members of Brahma Kumaris Godly University for their constant encouragement which strengthened me mentally and spiritually to complete this thesis.

SUVENDRA JENAMANI

CONTENTS

LIST OF TABLES

LIST OF MAPS

LIST OF FIGURES

Frontispiece Map

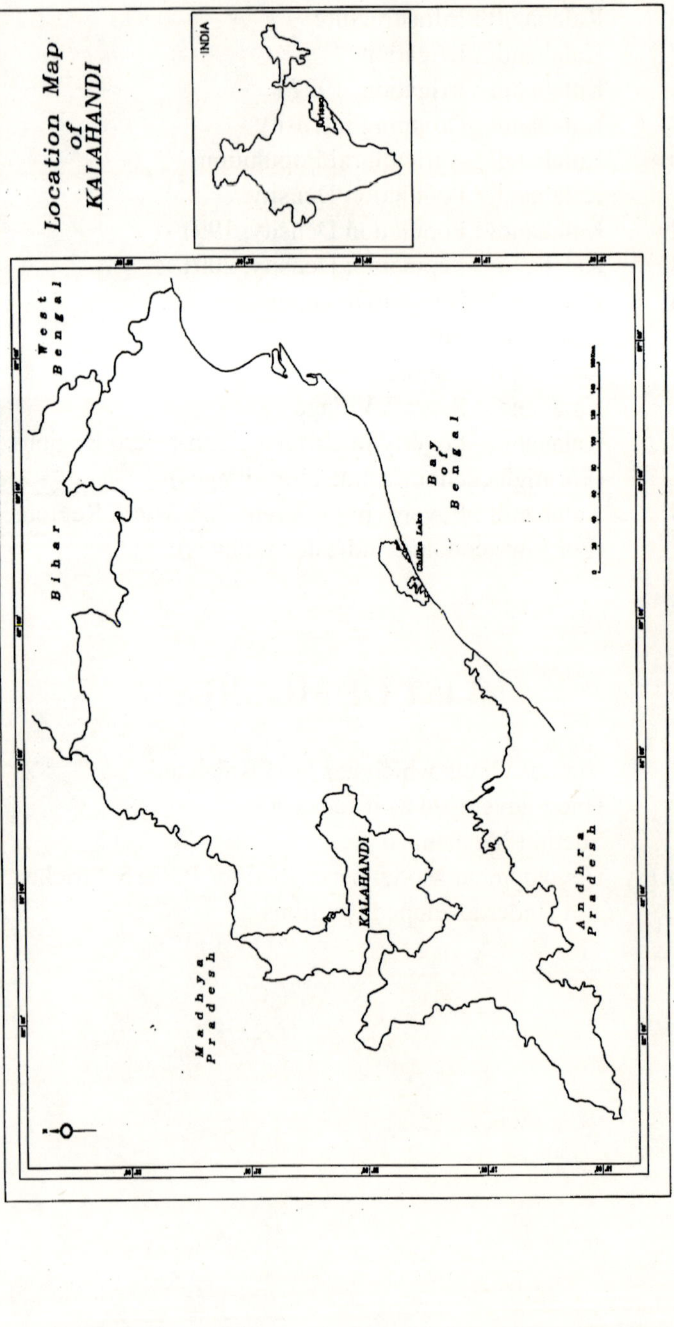

Location Map of Kalahandi

1

INTRODUCTION

India has undergone a substantial demographic and economic transformation during the last five decades or so. The index of agricultural production shows an increase from 58.5 in 1950-51 to 182.7 in 1988-89 (Foodgrains production has gone up four times from 50.8 million tonne in 1950-51 to 208.9 million tonne in 1999-2000). Index of industrial production has risen from 18.31 to 181.1 during 1950-51 to 1988-89 and from 100 to 106.5 during 1993-94 to1999-2000. The service sector has expanded enormously. Much of this improvement has been blunted by rapid increase in population (*i.e.* 2 per cent per annum). In terms of absolute number, the total population is 996.7million in 2000-01 whereas it was only 361.1 million in1950-51, the economy has nevertheless grown faster than the population. As such the incidence of poverty (measured in terms of persons below poverty line) has declined from 48.4 per cent in 1979-80 to about 26.8 per cent in1999-2000.[1] Every effort is being made to make India a welfare Nation.

Realising that great majority of the people of India live in rural areas. Community Development Programme was launched in early fifties to help people help themselves. This programme was later followed up by a number of special anti-poverty programmes such as Small Farmers Development Agencies (SFDA), Marginal Farmers and Agricultural Labourers Agencies (MFALA), Tribal Area Programme (TAP), Hill Area Programme, Drought Prone Area Programme (DPAP) in the seventies. The Projects gave financial assistance to target groups by way of institutional loans and for land development, soil conservation, minor irrigation and rural industries etc. These were further backed by programmes like IRDP, NREP, RLEGP etc. launched in late seventies, eighties and nineties.

Not withstanding these efforts, a large section of Indian population is poor and there are regions which continue to remain in the grip of poverty for decades with frustrating hope of amelioration in near future.

Joshi[2] demonstrates very sharp inter-state variation in the levels of economic development and infrastructure in India. The range of index of economic development varies from 70 to 151 during 1985-86 and the index of infrastructure ranges from 66 to 217 during the same year. States like Andhra Pradesh, Gujarat, Haryana, Himachal Pradesh, Karnataka, Kerala, Maharashtra, Punjab, Tamil Nadu and West Bengal had attained very high developmental index. If the all India average composite index is 100, Orissa's index is only 70 (the lowest among the states) and the Punjab's index is 151, the highest. So far as positional changes in infrastructure are concerned Maharashtra and Gujarat have improved considerably, but Orissa apart from UP, Bihar, Rajasthan and Madhya Pradesh has more or less remained unchanged. In economic development Orissa experienced similar unaltered or little altered situation.

It is evident Orissa continues to be one of the most backward states of India even after fifty years of economic planning. There is gross disparity in resource allocation, infrastructure and development in the state. The Western Orissa comprising mainly the districts of Sambalpur, Bolangir and Kalahandi has been neglected by the powers of the state capital. The following evidences support this statement. West Orissa produces bulk (90%) of the Kendu leaves, one of the major income generator of the state. However, the region gets only six per cent of the total grants, which is decided by the Chief Minister and Pancahayati Raj Minister. And rest of the Orissa, which produces only ten per cent of Kendu leaves takes away the large chunk of the grants.

Sambalpur, Bolangir and Kalahandi together produce more than 50 per cent of the state's total rice. Still because of the inadequate number of governmental purchasing agencies and their distant location, poor farmers are compelled to sell their product at much lower prices than the declared support prices.

Illiteracy is a criterion for the measurement of the neglect and backwardness. The Fifth Education Survey Report brought out that the rate of absenteeism and stagnation among school children was much higher in Western Orissa than in Coastal districts of Orissa.

Low representation in the ministry and the state legislative assembly also indicate the backwardness of the districts of Western Orissa. Since allocation for economic development are guided by the political strength of the area, Western Orissa suffers on this account as well. The Biju Pattanaik ministry had only two ministers from Kalahandi (one cabinet, the other state cadre), one each from Sambalpur and Bolangir. They were assigned less important portfolios compared to their coastal counterparts.[3]

Hierarchical Position of Kalahandi in the Socio-Economic Structure of Orissa

The total geographical area of the district is 11.58 lakh hectares (7.45% of that of the state) of which gross cultivated area is 7.62 lakh hectares. The total population of the district is 15.92 lakhs in 1991 which is 5.05 per cent of the total population of the state. The district has a high proportion of SC and ST. They constitute 47.04 per cent of the total population in contrast to 37.4 per cent for the state as a whole (1981). The population density of the district is 135 per sq. km., that of the state is 202 per sq. km. The sex-ratio is found higher of the district compared to that of the state (972 females per 1000 males). The literacy rate is 40.95 per cent in 1991. Female literacy is relatively much lower in Kalahandi district (12.44%) compared to that of the state (29.10%). Thus the district in terms of the general indicators presents a very low level of development compared to the state average and obviously the developed districts of the state.

Land utilisation pattern in the district reveals predominance of forest area (41.19%) compared to (35.93%) of the state. However, the scope for extension of cultivated area is much limited in the district. The net area shown constitutes 48.70 per cent of the geographical area in contrast to 40.41 per cent in case of the state. The district remains primarily agricultural with 73 per cent of workers (in 1991) depending on agriculture (the figure is 74.07 per cent for the state).

The district has an irrigation potential of 30.65 per cent of net sown area in 1996-97 compared to 30.65 per cent in 1988-89. In spite of low level of developmental efforts the agricultural performance of the district seems to be relatively very high. In 1989-90, the per capita food grains production is Rs. 348 compared to Rs. 256 for the state. The crop pattern of the district reflects lower importance of rice (37.66%) in total cropped area, but relatively higher food crops production (78.45%) compared to 48.01 per cent and 76.88 per cent for the state. The difference in rice area is mainly substituted by production of pulses and oilseeds. Relative predominance of cash crops serves rich farmers interest. The crops showing higher productivity are small mllets, wheat, rape and mustard, cotton, chillies, tobacco. However, only rape and mustard and small millets have relatively higher importance in the crop pattern, compared to the state. The productivity of the dominant crop rice is much lower for the district (7.01 qtls. per hectare) compared to 12.37 qtls. per hectare for the state. The combined index for agricultural development as worked out by the state planning machinery ranks the district in 10th position.

The industrial development of the district is one of the lowest, the rank being 12th next only to Boudh Kandhamal. Per capital consumption of electricity is found to be 47.11 ml. unit in 1996-97 compared to 541.8 ml. unit in the state. The state intervention to evolve small scale industries during 1986-87 to 1990-91 has contributed a share of the district of 4.80 per cent in number of units, 3.07 per cent in total capital invested and 4.89 per cent in the employment generated. Importance of mining remaining at a very low level in the district with the district having a share of only 0.96 in total mining workers of the state, 0.18 per cent in total mining output and 0.07 per cent in total value of minerals. The rank of the district in terms of infrastructural development also remains 12th, next only to Boudh Kandhamal. The district registered 2.16 banks per lakh of population in contrast to 3.12 in case of the state. The number of post offices are 25 per lakh of population in 1990, which compares

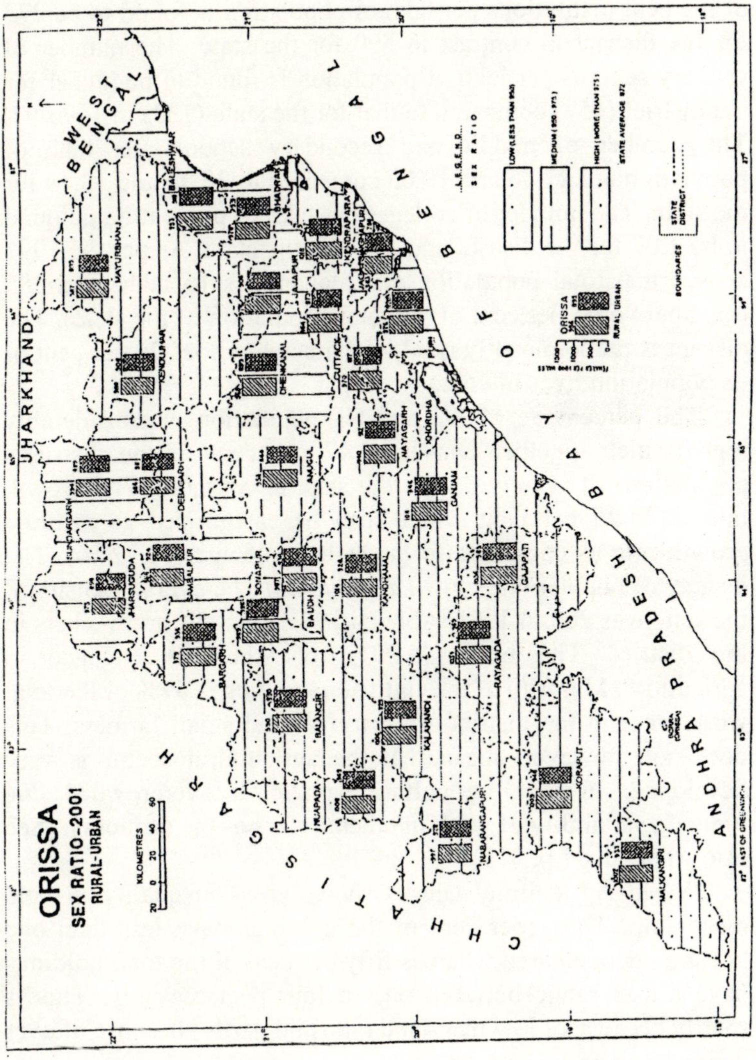

Map 1 : Orissa : Sex-Ratio-2001 Rural-Urban

with the state position. The average road length for 100 sq.km. is 153 for the district, whereas 168 for the state in 1996-97. The district registered 50.92 per cent of villages as electrified compared to 64.02 per cent for the state in 1989-90. The number of medical institutions per lakh of population is found to be 272 for the district in contrast to 590 for the state. The number of primary schools per lakh of population is found to be higher for the district (157) compared to that for the state (133) in 1996-97. The number of middle and secondary schools per lakh of population are 21.86 and 10.05 compared to 28.94 and 13.44 for the state. The number of colleges per lakh of population is found to be 1.07 for the district and 1.37 for the state. As per the 1991 census that total population of Kalahandi is 16 lakhs and 385 (*i.e.* about 5.05 per cent of the total population of the state). The district is predominantly rural in character. About 94 per cent of its population lives in villages.

The percentage of SC and ST population is considerably high (which together constitute 47 per cent of the district's population). It is only 37 for the state as a whole. The growth rate is 14.26 per cent which may be categorised as medium growth rate as compared to the state's average (19.72 %). The density of population is low *i.e.* only 135. The overall density of the state was 203 in 1991. About 4.79 lakh people are workers in the district. The bulk (96.09%) of which is engaged in agriculture. Majority of the cultivators (which is 51% of the total workforce) in the district are marginal and small farmers. This does not, however, mean that the agricultural sector is very developed. In fact, agricultural sphere is overcrowded due limited availability of work in other sectors of the economy. [See also Appendix 1 p. 319]

World Agricultural census shows gross inequality in land ownership. Thirty per cent of the holdings have less than one hectare operated area whereas fifty per cent of the total holdings have a size range between one to four hectares only. This is (partly because of low man-land ratio and partly) because of over dependence on agriculture.

A study by Mallasamanta[4] (1971) shows that Kalahandi falls in low to very low category of levels of development in Orissa. Cuttack, Puri (Bhubaneswar) and Coastal Ganjam have high to very high levels of development. Even within Western Orissa, Sambalpur and Bolangir are better placed in the development index as compared to Kalahandi.

Physical Background of the Problem Area

Though the Kalahandi district is located under the rainfall zone of 100 to 200* centimetres, it is a drought affected area. The climate of Kalahandi is extreme type. It is characterised by very hot summer and extreme cold winter. The hot season follows February, continues till mid-June, when monsoon sets in and lasts till middle of October.

The average annual rainfall of the district is 1378 mm. Out of which rainfall between 1st June to 31st October averages around 1259 mm. About 69 per cent of the rainfall is between July and September. Rainfall in the district is mostly erratic and punctuated generally with long dry spells. Due to scanty erratic and uneven distribution of rainfall the district suffers from frequent drought and almost the entire district is considered to be drought prone. So famine is a common phenomenon here.

The district has some of the very rich natural resources like fertile valleys, high water table, numerous perennial streams, rich mineral reserve and abundant forest cover. However, economically it is one of the least developed districts of India. There have been frequent reports of starvation deaths in the district. No matter how one measures, it is one of the poorest districts of the country.

The district occupies the western portion of Orissa and is situated between 19°11′35″N and 21°8′35″N latitude and 82°25′58″E to 83°45′37″E longitudes. With a population of 1,339,192 persons in 1981, it is divided into 3 sub-divisions, 6 *tehsils* and 18 CD blocks.

The district may broadly be divided into two distinct natural divisions, the hilly tracts and the plain country. The former chiefly comprises the ranges of hills, which run from the northeast to the south-west of the districts and the western

---

* Average rainfall of Kalahandi is 1304 mm. per annum (District Statistical Handbook, 1997).

portion of the Nawapada sub-division and the later constitutes the river valleys of the Tel and its tributaries, and the Jonk valley. The Tel, Indravati and Jonk which form the major tributaries of large river like the Mahanadi and the Godavari constitute the drainage system of the district. Most of the hill streams of the district are perennial. The Tel, Sagada, Hati, Ret and the Utei are almost reduced to tiny streams in their lower reaches from February to June. On the other hand the Raul throughout its whole length, most of which lies inside the forests holds a fair flow of water even in the month of May. The Sagada, Ret, Indravati, Badanala carry a strong stream of perennial water in the upper and middle reaches. The villagers in the open tracts scoop water holes in the sand during the summer months and manage to provide themselves with exiguous supply of drinking water. These rivers are scarcely subjected to high floods. The Tel is the longest and most important river of Dharamgarh *tehsil*. Through out the hill tracts of Kalahandi are met numerous perennial hill streams.

The one time densely wooded tracts on the high hills of Kalahandi is reduced to mere Bamboo and dry mixed scrub in no time through denudation brought about by shifting cultivation. The forest covers almost half of the geographical areas of Kalahandi. It can be broadly divided into three categories : Sal forests, Dry mixed forests, Bamboo forests and Teak.

The climate of Kalahandi district is in many respect similar to that of main Deccan plateau. The year may be divided into four seasons. The hot season from March to May is followed by the South West monsoon season from June to September. The average annual rainfall in the district is 1378.3 mm.*

The variation annual rainfall is not large. In the 48 year period from 1902 to 1950 the highest annual rainfall occurred in 1919 when it amounted to 13.9 per cent of the normal 1923 was the year with lowest rainfall which was only 66 per cent of the normal. There were five years in this period when the rainfall was less than 80 per cent of the normal, at Bhawanipatna there

* Average rainfall of Kalahandi is 1304 mm. per annum (District Statistical Handbook, 1997).

were two such occasions. In 34 years out of 46 the rainfall was between 1100 and1600 mm. On an average there are 65 rainy days (*i.e.* days with rainfall of 205 mm – 10% or more) in a year. This number varies from 59 to Nawapada to 69 at Bhawanipatna. May is the hottest month when the mean daily maximum temperature is about 41°C and mean daily minimum temperature is about 28°C.

The district has had 800057 males and 800328 females in 1991. The decennial population growth rate during1981-91 was +19.50 as against +20.06 of the state as a whole. Density of population is 135 (while it is 203 for the state). The sex ratio is higher than the state. It is 1,000.3 for the district and 971 for the state.

Literacy rate of Kalahandi is 29.3 which is much less than the average literacy of entire Orissa (*i.e.* 49.09). Percentage of SC and ST population to total population are 15.05 and 32.4 respectively. Out of the total main workers about 44 per cent are cultivators, 29 per cent are agricultural labourers, and only 0.3 per cent are engaged in other activities (forestry, mining etc.)

The economy of the district is essentially agricultural. Seventy-three per cent of its main labour force depends on agriculture (Statistical Outline of Orissa, 1999). This is not because agriculture is well developed in the district but due to the fact that opportunities for gainful work outside agriculture is extremely limited. The rate of total irrigated area to net sown area is only about 29.8 per cent (in 1996-97). Although normal rainfall is 1,378 mm, its erratic nature and uneven distribution has been the cause of crop failure for several years in the past. The total net sown area of the district was 396738 hectares during 1976-77, out of which 100260 hectares was irrigated in the Kharif season and 18350 hectares in the Rabi season. The rest had to depend upon rainfall.

The plains of the district are inhabited by some big progressive farmers who have introduced a mechanisation in farming. In hilly areas, inhabited by tribal people, agricultural practices are primitive and shifting cultivation is prevalent on a large scale. Manure is scarcely used and hardly there is any artificial irrigation.

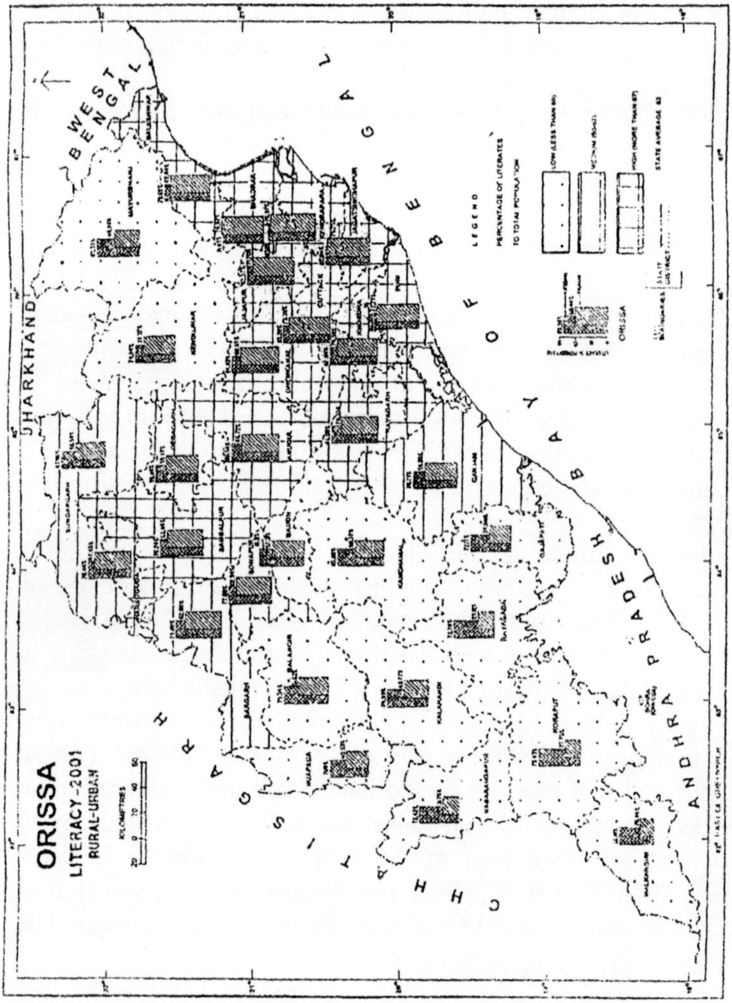

Map 2 : Orissa – Literacy – 2001 Rural-Urban

Natural calamity history of Kalahandi shows that there were famines in 1897, 1899, 1919-20, 1922-23, 1925-26, 1929-30 droughts in 1922-23, 1925-26, 1929-30 and 1965-66 and floods in 1927 and 1977. More recently droughts and food scarcities have been reported almost every year since 1980. Areas most susceptible to drought conditions are Nawapara tehsil, Madanpur and Narla blocks of Lanjhigarh tehsil and Golamunda block in Dharamgarh tehsil. Natural calamities and institutional rigidities have joined hands to keep this district at starvation level with continued acute poverty, pestilence, malnutrition and diseases.

Identifying the Problem

The question that comes to the mind of any student of Development Geography is why is Kalahandi so poor? Is it because the nature is niggardly here? Is it because the people are mentally or physically incapable of improving their lot? Is it because the policy interventions to generate development have not been well conceived and/or implemented? Or, is it because a variety of factors have joined together to create an exploitative spatial system keeping Kalahandi underdeveloped? There are another set of questions which comes to ones mind even before the above questions are answered. What is the future of the people of Kalahandi? Is there any hope for them? If nothing has been worked so far, what is needed to be done in the years ahead? Can we learn anything from the past experiences? And so on. Answers to these questions can be found only when there is scientific, diagnostic and prognostic study of the area and when the style of development followed so far is subjected to vigorous empirical, theoretical and ethical analysis. The aim of the study is to seek answers to these questions with the following objectives in mind.

Objectives

- To measure the spatial incidence of poverty in Kalahandi district.
- To correlate the physical and environmental factors such as access to land, water, forest etc. with the incidence of poverty.

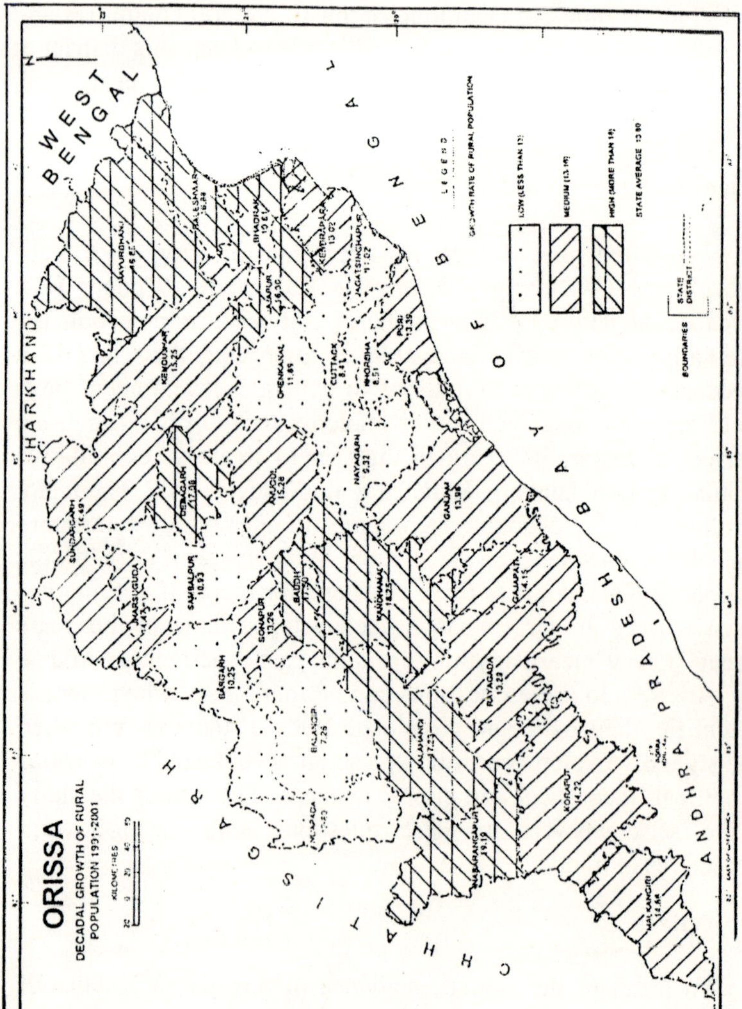

... - Decadal Growth of Rural Population 1991-2001

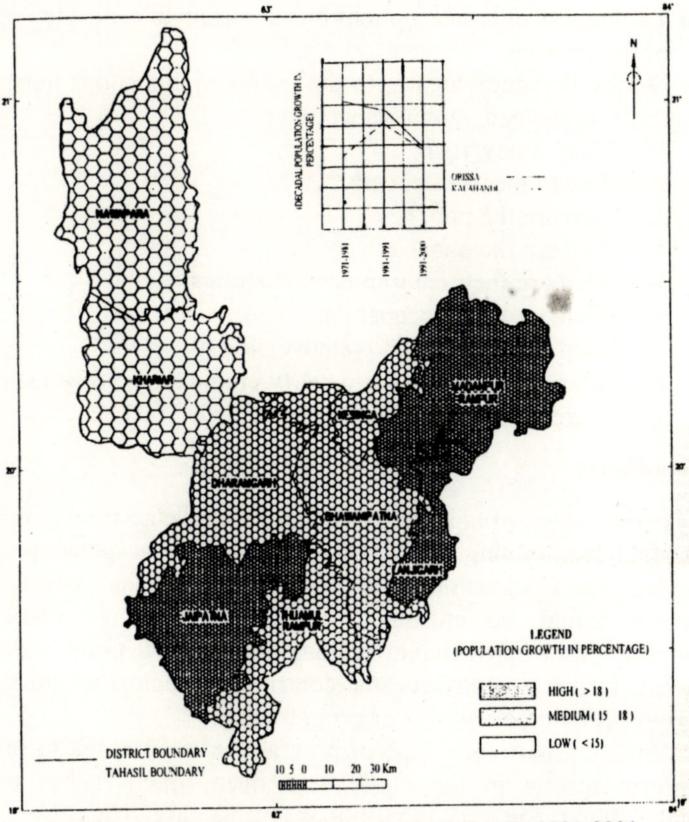

Map 4 : Kalahandi : Decadal growth of population, 1991-2001

3. To analyse the institutional* and social relation of production in understanding the persistent poverty in the area.
4. To examine the rationale, relevance and efficacy of various developmental policies such as Integrated Rural Development Programme (IRDP); National Rural Employment Programme (NREP); Rural Landless Employment Guarantee Programme (RLEGP); Integrated Tribal Development Programme (ITDP); Drought Prone Area Programme (DPAP); Public Distribution System (PDS); Integrated Child Development Scheme (ICDS); Area Development Approach for Poverty Termination (ADAPT); towards eradication of poverty in the district.

---

* To analyse the role of institutions (both internal and external) as mediators between man and nature in socio-economic development.

5. To suggest alternate options for a sustainable development of the district.

During the study answer to the following questions must be sought from the geographic viewpoint :

1. What is poverty?
2. How to measure poverty?
3. Who are the poor?
4. Why are the poor?
5. What are their environmental settings?
6. What are their occupations?
7. What is being done to remove poverty?
8. Policy alternatives for poverty eradication. (Suggestions or prescriptions)

Hypothesis

If same category of households (identified and classified in terms of size, landholding, caste etc.) from different geographical regions, show variation in their poverty, then the geographic factors would be attributed to it. Similarly if organised communities from different regional units (areal units) exhibit varied intensity in poverty, the contributing factor behind such variation could be regional or geographic.

Again, a particular type of programme is expected to bring uniform results in the entire area over which it has been implemented. But very often this is not the case. The difference in the impact of the programme could be due to certain geographic factors, which facilitate or hinder the success of governmental programmes. Geographical or natural factors such as resource base of an area cannot be altered easily. Obviously, there can be two approaches to correct this condition. Either the programmes are to be modified or changed or institutions are to be reformed to facilitate the implementation of the programmes and overcome the geographic obstacles. Taking economic, social, cultural, ecological cost benefit ratio into account, it can be suggested as to what would be a better or easier alternative.

Turning to another point, lack of resources is a geographic factor, whereas access to it is purely socio-economic or institutional factor. Infrastructural resources which partly help to use natural resources through governmental intervention are provided at two levels –

1. Community Level Infrastructure,
2. Household Level Infrastructure.

The former provides community based infrastructure and later helps further to reduce poverty. The community level resources people have differential accessibility. It may bring down inter-village or inter-regional disparity, but not interpersonal disparity. Integration of household level perceived needs, basic needs of the community, and local or regional resource base is essential. For this purpose bottom up approach is a prerequisite.

Considering these aspects there can be two hypotheses, one dealing with diagnostic part and the other with prescriptive part :

1. Incidence of poverty is a function of not merely community and household (*i.e.* socio-economic) characteristics but also that of regional (geographic) characteristics.
2. Difference in impact of various programmes are associated with community, household and regional characteristics.

   Community : Caste, Literacy etc.;
   Household : Landholding, Labour etc.
   Regional : Topography, Soil, Rainfall (Water Availability), Forest, Accessibility etc.

In other words, the hypotheses would be :

(a) That there is spatial variation in consumption expenditure and purchasing power (entitlement) along with distribution of means of production. And this variation across sub micro regions is a function of not merely household (economic) and community (social) characteristics but also regional (geographic) characteristics.
(b) Difference in increase of purchasing power due to implementation of anti-poverty programmes are associated with regional characteristics, apart from household and community characteristics.

NOTES

1. *Economic Survey,* 1989-90, p. S-1 and Mid-term appraisal, Planning Commission, 30-9-2000.
2. Joshi, B. M., *Infrastructure and Economic Development in India,* Concept, New Delhi, 1991, pp. 120-21.
3. Nair, J., "Neglect issue in Orissa", *The Hindustan Times,* 19-4-1994.
4. Mallasamanta, B. S., *Spatial Profile of Development and Patterns of Change in 1961-71 : A case study of Orissa,* dissertation submitted to CSRD, JNU.

2

CONCEPTUALISATION

There is no single universally accepted meaning of "poverty". It varies from place to place and time to time. According to David Sills,[1] poverty has always had several, not entirely separable meanings and is always defined in terms of conventions of the society in which it occurs.

Concept of Poverty

In economic sense, if basic needs are not met man is poor. Singh defines poverty as a state wherein an individual cannot satisfy his minimum wants for healthy living in a given social environment. In other words, it is partial or total inadequacy of 'resources' for the fulfilment of ones needs. This state can be measured in terms of income and assets.

Poverty as perceived by an outsider is different from that of an insider who assesses his poverty in his own terms. In the former sense poverty is of two types, *e.g.* absolute poverty and relative poverty. And in the later sense poverty is rather subjective.

Similarly, human needs are also relative to a great extent and hence cannot be quantified in absolute terms. But there are certain obvious needs which, whether seen subjectively or objectively, are almost the same. Maslow categorised human needs hierarchically. He holds that higher needs are automatically generated as lower ones are satisfied. According to him the lowest type of need is 'survival' required food, clothing and shelter. It is the basic human need everywhere. The second level need is physical and environmental safety or 'security'. The third category need is 'belongingness' and love – the need for affection, pleasure, happiness, fulfilment of interpersonal relationships, conformity to group norms and so on. Fourth important need is 'esteem' or the need for recognition, prestige, status and dominance. And finally, 'self fulfilment', *i.e.* living up to ones full potential is the ultimate need. Need increases over time.

Thus the need can be of various types physical, biological, economic, psychological, socio-cultural or spiritual. However, physical or biological needs of survival are most important. Rowntree emphasises that lack of nutrition or starvation is the worst type of poverty. So minimum nutritional requirement would be a very useful indicator of poverty, provided data are easily available.

Absolute *Versus* Relative Poverty

Absolute poverty provides a clear-cut idea of poverty as it is objective, numerical and precise in nature. It is expressed in absolute terms of food, clothing, shelter, education, health and security conditions. To define absolute poverty, usually minimum level of diet which can provide 2,250 calories per day is fixed. For this purpose the quantity and quality of cereals, pulses, ghee, milk, vegetables etc. are calculated. Most measures of poverty are concerned with establishing the quantity and quality of not only food but also clothing and shelter deemed necessary for a healthy life. Absolute poverty is often known as subsistence poverty (being based on minimum subsistence requirement). It is usually measured by pricing the basic necessities of life and drawing a poverty line in terms of that price. Drewnoweski and Scott in their "Levels of Living Index" define and operationalise basic physical needs in the following way, nutrition (measured by factors such as intake of calories and protein), shelter (measured by quality of dwelling and degree of overcrowding) and health (measured by rate of infant mortality and quality of available medical facilities). In broadened sense absolute poverty includes basic cultural needs. Drewnoweski and Scott include education, security, leisure and recreation in their category of basic cultural needs.

The arbitrariness involved in choosing the criteria for the measurement of absolute poverty, has often been a matter of criticism. Scholars have started thinking of poverty in relation to richness, prevailing living standards, norms and attitudes of society, absolute standards, developed regions or resources. Thus poverty has now been widely accepted as relative concept.

Bengalis spend less on food and more on travel and recreation. They are an art and scenery loving people (like to have aesthetic pleasure). Accordingly, those people who fail to satisfy their travel and recreational needs are considered poor by Bengalis.

If we compare income of an average Indian with that of an average American certainly the later would be much richer than the former. Again an American poor often leads an equal or even a better standard of living than the so called Indian rich.

Within a single nation a comparison of relative levels of income of the top 10 to 20 per cent of population is sometimes made to show the relative poverty.

In the festivals like *Nuakhai* tribes of Kalahandi spend lavishly on food (including meat) clothes and drinks. Those who cannot afford for these are regarded as poor no matter what they eat and wear, other days of the year.

Once upon a time bullock carts and a healthy pair of bullocks were a symbol of status for village farmers. Now-a-days tractor is a farmer's prestigious possession. Earlier it was radio now it is television which marks the richness of a family.

Thus relative poverty is based on certain standards which are relative to particular time and place. It is measured in terms of judgement by members of a particular society of what is considered a reasonable and acceptable standard of living and style of life according to conventions of the day.

Peter Townsend argues that individual families and groups in the population can be said to be in poverty when they lack the resource to obtain the type of diets, participate in the activities and have the living conditions and amenities which are customary or at least widely encouraged and approved in the societies they belong. According to him, any definition of poverty must be related to the needs and demands of a changing society. Within a particular society ethnicity, class, age, religion, region and a variety of other factors can vary judgements about reasonable living standards.

Socio-Cultural Definition of Poverty

Poverty has its socio-cultural dimensions too. Materially poor person may also suffer from lack of recognition, belongingness, achievement and opportunities which has a direct and indirect impact on individual personality and society. In his study Shamugam found that most of the anti-social activities are committed by people of lower economic strata. It may so happen that, unless the poor people overcome these social and psychological depression, poverty, will pass on from generation to generation and become a culture by itself.

Again Saberwal opines that poor is poor because he is incompetent to protect his socio-political and economic interests. Subjective poverty refers to whether or not individuals or groups feel they are poor. This concept of poverty is important since to some degree people act in terms of the way they perceive and define themselves.

Though the above definitions of socio-cultural and subjective poverty are neither quantifiable nor measurable they do provide valuable insights into the perception of the people and non-economic factors influencing well-being. Thus, poverty is of three types, namely : Normative (norms fixed by some agency); Subjective (as conceived by the poor or the researcher) and Relative (status in relation to others).

Production Relation

Poverty never occurs in isolation. It must be looked within the structure of prevailing social relations. Interpersonal or inter-group interaction with respect to use of natural resources can help us to analyse it. Since man-man interaction and quantity and quality of natural resources are different in various geographical settings, the intensity and nature of poverty arising out of those factors are also different geographically.

The very presence of rich among poor is a sign of accumulation of wealth in few hands. But why accumulation takes peace at all? This raises other related questions – who produces wealth? Who distributes it? And who consumes it? Again when, where and how wealth is produced, distributed and consumed? The answers to these questions would lead one to learn about the distribution processes and underpinning causes of poverty. Here few aspects are to be kept in mind. Poverty may be a static condition but the processes generating and maintaining it are essentially dynamic. Again resultant poverty changes when its processes change. And to change processes, first institutions are to be changed. In such attempt revelation of the fundamental factors (not the visible or triggering factors) are important.

Taking all these aspects into account poverty can be defined as : A condition of relative deprivation, measured in terms of assets, income, food intake (nutrition), housing, education, health, infrastructure and social participation, which arise within a static geographic unit of unequal resource distribution and due to a dynamic process of social relation of production, supported by strong institutional foundation.

Measurement of Poverty

There are varied approaches to measurement of poverty.

Level of Living Index (LLI) : The definition of LLI was first given by UN Committee of Experts on International Definition and Measurement of Standards of Living. According to the Committee (which was headed by Prof. V.K.R.V. Rao) LLI is the actual condition of life with respect to nutrition, shelter, health, education etc. Each component has been divided into number of indicators. Composite index is estimated by aggregating the indicators. The only drawback of this method is the selection and assignment of weights of various indices.

This index as an alternative method of poverty measurement was first presented by Overseas Development Council. It basically includes three indicators, i.e. infant mortality, life expectancy (at age one) and literacy with equal weights. Physical Quality of Life Index (PQLI) may help the policy-makers to determine the extent to which their policies do actually benefit different sections of the society. GNP may provide the total or per capita output. But it does not fell much about quality of life since there is no positive correlation between GNP and improvement in life expectancy, death or infant mortality rates or literacy. Moreover, economic comparison between two or more countries on the basis of GNP is not an easy task. In less developed societies (where production, consumption and distribution take place in a small scale and where social structure is more complex and worthwhile comparisons of economic performance is also difficult), GNP can measure growth but not development (which is a comprehensive process of social, political and economic aspect)[2].

There are two general types of "welfare indicator". One involves the use of subjective measures, how people feel about economic growth, happy, more secured or less secured? The other type seek to measure welfare objectively. This type is known physical quality life index.

Various UN agencies including UN Research Institute for Social Development, a number of private groups and individuals have throughout attempted to measure development or under-development and welfare by using hundreds of indicators. Excluding indicators of poverty political and economic development only three criteria – infant mortality, life expectancy and basic literacy seems, to be vital for measuring welfare (PQL) aspects of socio-economic performance because of the following reasons :

(a) None of the three indicators assumes any particular pattern of development or economic organisation.
(b) They do not reflect the cultural values of any particular society.
(c) They reflect results not input (number of hospitals or expensive medical facilities may not be the only cause of reducing death rates).
(d) The three indicators pose little difficulty for cross-cultural comparison.
(e) They show the distribution of social results. (An infant either lives or dies, a person is either literate or illiterate so improvement in these two criteria means there is more equitable distribution of social results.)

(f) The indicators are easy to devise and understand (Gathering the data on these items is not expensive).

(g) The indicators can help exactly to locate the position of region on international development scale.

(h) The indicators are unit free (have no common numerals). Instead a simple index system (0 to 100) is used for showing welfare performance.

(i) A composite indicator can be calculated by arranging the three indicators after assigning equal weight to each of them.

(j) The index can show not only the spatial variations but also temporal change of poverty and underdevelopment. (PQLI is designed not to give emphasis on inputs or efforts or pious pronouncements. By focusing on result the index can identify countries or regions that have used simple inexpensive means of obtaining welfare gains. This would help us to exactly think of alternative development strategies).

(k) Life expectancy or infant mortality are the ultimate result of varied socio-economic processes (such as social relation, nutritional status, public health, family environment, income calorie intake etc.).

(l) The literacy indicator provides information about potential for development and the extent of penetration of developmental effort.

Why other indicators are not included?

Crude death rates can lead to very anomalous results because of differences in age compositions of populations. Birth rates not only suffer from some defect but it is not clear what direction of movement should be called an improvement, since the problem of defining illness is a difficult one. Morbidity rates may not be included in PQLI measure.

Nutritional measurements, e.g. calorie intake posed complex problems of what standards should be taken, how to measure consumption. The benefit of nutritional inputs are substantially affected by personal characteristics, and environmental health considerations. The direct impact of food intake is revealed through infant mortality rates, life expectancy and other socio-economic indicators do not provide information about individual well-being. They also pose problems of cross-cultural comparison. To say that "employment" is a good or satisfactory quality of life index is subjective.

The PQLI do not incorporate socio-psychological characteristics like security, justice, freedom and human rights etc. Composite index requires assignment of weights to its components. All the three indicators (infant mortality, life expectancy and literacy) are independent of each other. Each represents a vital part indicator of poverty and under-development. Since no indication is more important than other equal weightage is to be a assigned to each indicator.

The index shows where a country is placed in relation to the ultimate objective (PQLI = 100) and the advancement of country or region. Equal weighting has the advantage of limiting the influence of any indication.

1. PQLI do not measure economic growth. It complements GNP or SDP.
2. Economic development is not measured by PQLI specific PQLI results can be achieved with various socio-economic structures and levels of GNP. Basic research task is to explain why and how some areas of India which by most development standards would be classified as badly underdeveloped have been able to achieve relatively high PQLI levels (*e.g.* Kerala).
3. PQLI does not measure effort. It measures results of social, economic and political policies. PQLI is deliberately designed to shift attention away from the expenditure side of the policy to its consequences. In this way it can encourage greater concern with efficiency, with how to get superior results from scarce resources.
4. PQLI does measure those desired life quantities that reflect best the extent to which the society is benefiting those that other indexes tend to neglect – the poor and women.
5. PQLI is an index of 'macro' performances. It does not measure micro (project) performances.

Larson and Wilford employing simple averaging and principal component analysis techniques have demonstrated that a simple regression of both PQLI indices thus arrived has yielded indistinguishable results since the correlation between the two PQLI is +999. Based on statistical evidence especially provided by the principal component analysis, they have concluded that PQLI, however, constructed, captures very little about that quality of life that is not already included in GNP per capita. The tests show that a linear combination of the three component variables are unimportant. They have established that (i) linear combination by simple averaging, (ii) assignment of arbitrary component weights, and (iii) generating weight through principal component techniques will all produce essentially the same PQLI for 150 countries. Further their analysis suggests that, PQLI is closely associated with GNP per capita especially when 'a typical' countries are excluded. For instance, thirty countries have been classified as a typical either due to flow of substantial foreign assistance in recent years or due to rise in GNP due to oil price hike. The authors, therefore, concluded that the use of PQLI as welfare measure does not significantly change the results obtained when GNP per capita is used as an indicator. Per capita income according to them remains the more accurate measure of welfare.

The above discussion clearly shows the inappropriateness of measuring levels of living employing PQLI.

Poverty Line Measure

The most familiar and widely used method of estimation of poverty, living below a certain level of living is commonly defined as the poverty line. Here the method is to define the poverty line in terms of a specific level of a consumer expenditure and to reckon the population below this cut off expenditure class as poor. Poverty line approach was initially developed by Charles Booth (1989) and Seebohm Rowntree (1901) in their pioneering works on poverty. While Booth's work was elaborative, Rowntree was more precise and pin-pointed to find an income necessary for 'physical efficiency', as a line between poverty and non-poverty.

The concept of subsistence poverty as Rowntree and Booth suggested allowed expenditure only on food, shelter and basic household implements necessary to keep people physically in order. Later on poverty line approach has been widely used in poverty studies though the basic of the poverty line differed very much.

However, there is lot of controversy about the definition and estimation of poverty line due to differences in the criteria employed for the specification of the level of living expressed in terms of certain expenditure level. It may be noted at the outset that whatever is the criteria employed, poverty line is defined in terms of a specified level of expenditure which is taken as a proxy for the minimum level of income. The following four criteria have been mainly employed for specification of the poverty line.

Proportion of Expenditure on Food

One such criterion employed for poverty line estimation is the proportion of expenditure taken up by essential items, which may be defined as the level of consumer expenditure at which certain proportion such as 80 per cent or 85 per cent is devoted to food and fuel. This presupposes an Engel's Function which shows decline proportion of expenditure goes up. According to Dandekar and Rath this is a much stable function exhibiting good indicator of the level of living. The method is to adopt the proportion of average food expenditure at the national or state level as threshold value.

Calorie Requirements

The second criterion is the average or minimum energy requirement expressed in terms of certain calorie norms. In this method poverty line is defined as : the level of expenditure required to satisfy the minimum calorie requirements for the normal physical functioning of the people of different age groups after adding some allowances necessary for other essential needs like clothing. This method was first employed by Charles Booth and Seebohm Rowntree in their pioneering works on poverty. For instance, Rowntree adopted 3500 calories for a man doing moderate muscular work based on the estimates of 2700 and 4500 calories for men with little physical exercise and men with active muscular work. Apart from the expenditure required to realise this level of calories, Rowntree also made some allowance for shelter and basic household implement.

This method was popularised in India by Dandekar and Rath, followed by many others. Dandekar and Rath defined the per capita calories requirement per day equal to 2250 calories and estimated that in 1960-61 annual per capita expenditure of Rs. 170 was essential to give a diet adequate at least in respect of calories. One important weakness of Dandekar's method is that he had estimated the poverty line as the level of per capital consumer expenditure at which a diet with 2250 calories is attained. For estimating the proportion of the population below poverty line they have taken into account half the population lying in the monthly per capita expenditure class in which 2250 calories have been realised together with the population falling in lower classes. Thus Dandekar in this analysis is confusing between undernutrition and poverty though he has made a clear cut distinction in his later article in *Economic and Political Weekly* in 1981.

Poverty has been identified with undernutrition is conceptually incorrect. As pointed out by Dandekar himself in a later article, when population is classified on the basis of certain income or expenditure, howsoever defined, provided it is sufficiently low, we are defining poverty and sorting out poor and not poor so defined. On the other hand, when we classify population by food intake, we are trying to identify under-nutrition by calorie intake.

The minimum or average norm could be employed for directly estimating the cost for realisation of the defined level of nutrition, which may be taken as the minimum food expenditure irrespective of the fact how the food expenditure has been already spent. It must show the minimum estimated consumer expenditure on food adequate enough to realise the specified level of calories under the assumed general behavioural pattern.

Basic Needs Criteria

Instead of confining the estimation of poverty line to the cost of balanced diet this criterion employs the cost of essential to tolerable human existence as the basis for estimation of poverty line. Rao is the chief exponent of this approach, who remarks that, poverty has to be identified with deficiency in the level of living. It needs no emphasis that level of living includes not only energy requirements but also balanced diet needed for health and other basic needs essential for human existence at a tolerable level.

While this approach seems to be the most comprehensive one, Rao himself admits that this exercise for identification of poverty has still to be undertaken in India.

Government of India Definition of Poverty Line

The Sixth Plan (1980-85) defined poverty line on the basis of nutritional requirement, *i.e.* 2400 calories per person in rural areas and 2100 calories per person in urban areas. In money terms, the estimates were derived by using Rs. 76 per capita per month at 1979-80 prices in rural areas and Rs. 88 per capita per month for urban areas. At 1984-85 prices the cut off lines were revised to Rs. 107 for rural and Rs. 122 for urban areas.

The present definition of poverty, formulated by the Planning Commission, defines the poor as those above per capita consumption expenditure was below the mid-point of the monthly per capita daily calorie intake of 2400 in rural areas and 2100 in urban areas.

In monetary terms and at 1984-85 prices that amounted to Rs. 107 for rural and Rs. 122 for urban areas. Poverty estimated using the above criteria, in 1984-85 there were 273 million (or 37 per cent of total population) poor in India. In 1989-90 the figure is about 211 million. World Bank estimation shows the poverty of India has reduced to 27 per cent.

1. Apart from updating (required on the basis of current prices), inclusion of social consumption also appears as a problem in the calculation of income. (Social consumption in marriages, festivals in rural areas forms

substantial part of rural household expenditure).

2. There is also the question of bringing the norm of the calorie intake, in line with the definition, adopted in the need based minimum wage at 2700 calories. Specific Biological factors like age, sex, and occupational factors apart from rural urban differences should be taken into account while calculating nutritional requirement for (specific) groups or community.
3. Dr. A. N. Khusro, noted economist, while commenting on the very basis of consumption data (which is made available through NSS) says that this index of poverty is one sided. The reasons are :

   (i) When people's income increases, their food consumption does not increase proportionately,
   (ii) Account should also be taken of abatement of other aspects like literacy, education, health, housing industrial consumer goods.

4. Since income distribution data is skewed standard deviation (*i.e.* dispersion around mean) not the mean itself should be considered for measuring poverty. Otherwise absolute value or average has no meaning. Analyses disaggregate data, examine whether there is real improvement in the condition of bottom 10 per cent of poverty.

Previous Studies

Seebohm Rowntree conducted one of the earliest studies on poverty. Using a concept of subsistence poverty he surveyed York in 1899. His poverty line was based on minimum weekly sum of money which was necessary to enable families to secure the necessaries of a healthy life. Although, afterwards he made some alteration in his list of 'necessaries' to account for changing standards and circumstances from 1899 to 1950, his concept of poverty still may not be regarded as relative poverty.

Brian Abel Smith and Peter Townsend (1942) in their book *The Poor and the Poorest* mention that the extent of poverty depends upon the concept of poverty adopted and the measuring instrument employed. They defined poverty, or 'low level of living' as less than 14 per cent of the basic national assistance scale plus rent and other housing costs. Their measure of poverty was more sensitive to judgments of reasonable living standards according to the conventions of the day and as such it was closer to a concept of relative poverty.

Ken Coates and Richard Silburn (1976) look upon poverty as a positive feedback system. In their study in Nottingham they argue that poverty in reality constitute a interrelated network of deprivations. Once trapped poor find it very difficult to escape out of the trap. However, one drawback in this theory of positive feedback is that instead of answering the question, 'why poverty'? The theory directs itself to the question, 'Once poverty exists, how is it maintained?'

Another theory on poverty, was given by Oscar Lewis, an American anthropologist. He developed the concept of culture of poverty from his fieldwork among the urban poor in Mexico and Puerto Rico. Lewis argues that the culture of poverty is a 'design for living' or a set of responses to poor circumstances and problem, which is transmitted from one generation to the next. But the actual existence of a culture of poverty has been questioned. Kenneth Little's study of West African Urbanisation, William Margin's research in the Barriadas of Peru cast some doubt on Lewis thesis.

In his paper on 'Concepts and measurement of poverty' Scott[3] presents empirical data showing the arbitrary nature of poverty lines and the imprecise and relative nature of the concept itself. He makes several suggestions on how data on poverty could be improved. "Profiles of Rural Poverty" (1979) a popularised version of "Poverty and Landless in rural Asia which was published by ILO in 1977 aims to quantify the level of and trends in rural poverty by discussing the major correlates and causes of poverty in some eight Asian countries. The booklet presents a comparative analysis of poverty of Asian countries with that of African and Latin American countries.

Visaria[4], in his report on 'Some Aspects of Relative Poverty in Sri Lanka, 1969-70' highlights the importance of the criteria used to rank households (per capita *versus* total household expenditure or income) for the estimates of the level of inequality as well as for different categories of consumption items. A multivariate analysis of per capita expenditure, income of households and of the earnings of employees has been presented.

A study on 'Fiscal measure for poverty alleviation in the United States' was conducted by Heish[5]. It focuses on the income transfer approach in U.S.A. It describes the magnitude, trends and profile of poverty in U.S. It gives a systematic review of the fiscal expenditure on poverty alleviation and detailed analysis of the effects of public income transfers on poverty alleviation and income redistribution. It finally restates some of the important findings on poverty alleviation and makes a few observations on future.

Rakesh Mohan and others[6] in their paper on 'Measuring Urban Malnutrition and Poverty : A case study of Bogota and California, Columbia' attempts to determine lower bound estimates of the proportion of people who simply do not have incomes adequate to cover the barest minimum of conceptual and empirical difficulties in such estimates have been outlined. Two methods of estimating calorie consumption are suggested. The exposure to nutritional deficiencies at an early age can be expected to impair the schooling of these children and, hence, their future earning potential, locking them in a vicious cycle of malnutrition and poverty. Spatially, the pattern of malnutrition is found to be more distinct than income patterns; the low income area suffer from malnutrition more than might be expected.

Dadabhai Noaroji[7] (1870) was the first Indian genius who worked on Indian poverty and pointed out that genesis of Indian poverty was due to two aspects. One arising from the remittances by European officials of their savings to England for their various expenditures or wants or both there and India and second that arising from similar remittances by non-official Europeans. Earlier Marx[8] has pointed out that the genesis of Indian poverty was in the destruction of self-supporting entire framework of the pre-colonial period without any attempt to build a new one.

After Dadabhai, Dutt[9] (a member of the Indian Civil Service) analysed the poverty of Indian society. He emphasised the inequality of land tenure system (under the British Rule) accompanied by heavy taxation of the impoverished agriculture resulting in permanent poverty of the Indian people (Dutt, 1950). According to Rain[10] the concept of poverty must be seen in the context of the society as a whole. To understand the poor we must study the affluent. Externality is concerned with the rest of the society rather than in terms of the needs of the poor.

Geographic works on poverty are scanty. Misra[11] revealed three types of poverty in his study of Deorea district. He shows social, economic and cultural dimensions of poverty. The results have shown that about 71 per cent of the population lives under conditions of poverty amongst whom the largest section belongs to the class of absolute poverty. Misra has suggested different possible ways for tackling poverty. Radical changes in the structure of development council in order to create a new people's development council has been proposed by him.

Morrill[12] and Wohlenberg have identified geographical, *i.e.* environmental, spatial and regional factors to explain the prevalence and distribution of poverty in U.S.A. Starting from simple correlations they have proceeded for more complex analysis and exceptional cases of poverty. How relative location and population density have influenced the spatial pattern of poverty in the city have been discussed in the end. A part from other ways, strong farm organisation, metropolitanisation (locating a set of new metropolises scattered over countryside), bringing all rural territories and people within reasonable distance of metropolis providing employment to the excess population leaving countryside, have been suggested by the two geographers to eliminate poverty. The earlier non-geographical studies are relatively less ecological and less spatial. On the other hand, the geographical work are relatively weak in their theoretical exposition.

Taking these aspects into account, the present study would analyse poverty in the framework of geography of underdevelopment. The focus would be on differential accessibility to resources by man in varied ecological and spatial settings. The research, above all, would attempt to identify different gaps in institutional and administrative systems which are required to be plugged, to find possible solutions for removal of poverty.

Poverty and underdevelopment often considered synonymous. Some use the two terms interchangeably. Here in the following section, it has been described how 'underdevelopment' like 'poverty' has an entirely different connotation and both the terms have distinct interrelated meanings in the context of Kalahandi.

Concept of Underdevelopment

It is widely held that, countries in which most of the national income is generated in primary sector (*i.e.* agriculture, forestry, animal husbandry, etc.) are underdeveloped. But sectorial distribution of national income and occupational distribution of population at best are indicators of the direction of economic change, they may not always correctly indicate the level of development achieved in a particular country.

The UN experts have defined an underdeveloped country as the one in which per capita real income is low, when compared with the per capita real income of the US, Canada, Australia or Western Europe. However, development or underdevelopment of a country or a region may not always be reflected in its per capita income or the average living standard. According to P.T. Bauer and D.S. Yamey (1969) in underdeveloped countries there is no large scale application of the fruits of scientific and technological advances to agriculture and industry. Subsistence production is generally important and markets comparatively narrow, and manufacturing industry is usually comparatively unimportant.

Underdevelopment, in some respects is a poverty based concept. It is a situation characterised by the worst kind of deprivation. Todaro (1974), while defining underdevelopment in terms of poverty goes beyond narrow economic criterion when he states, "Underdevelopment is a real fact of life for over two billion people of the world, a state of mind as much as a state of national poverty." Davis Goulet (1973) provides a forceful portrayal of underdevelopment in terms of poverty. He states underdevelopment is shocking : the squalor diseases, unnecessary deaths and hopelessness of it all. No man understands if underdevelopment remains for him a mere statistics reflecting low income, poor housing, premature mortality or unemployment. The most emphatic observer can speak objectively about underdevelopment only after undergoing personally or vicariously, the 'shock of underdevelopment'. The unique culture comes to areas he is initiated to the emotions, which prevail in the 'culture of poverty.' The reverse shock is felt by those living in destitution when a new self-understanding reveals that their life is neither human nor inevitable. The prevalent emotion of underdevelopment is a sense of personal and societal impotence in the face of disease and death, of confusion and ignorance as one gropes to understand change of servility towards men whose decisions govern the course of events, of hopelessness before hunger and natural catastrophe. Chronic poverty is a cruel kind of hell, and one cannot understand how cruel that hell is merely by gazing upon the poverty as an object.

According to Jacob Viner (1980) development potential of a country is a much better criterion to judge the extent of its underdevelopment. Therefore, he defines an underdeveloped country as the one which has the potential prospects for using more capital or more labour or more available natural resources, or all of these, to support its population on a higher level of living or if its per capita income level is already fairly too high to support a larger population on not a lower level of living.

To a great number of economists, who believes that underdevelopment is just lack of development Jacob Viner's approach is logical and scientific. Viner focuses his attention on basic characteristics of underdeveloped countries, *i.e.* their development potential. Technically this approach may be correct framework to analyse problem of underdevelopment in third world countries.

Definition of underdeveloped country given by Indian Planning Commission is akin to the one given by Jacob Viner. The Planning Commission defines "An underdeveloped country as one which is characterised by coexistence, in greater or lesser degree, of unutilised or underutilised manpower on the one hand, and of unexploited natural resources on the other." Precisely, underdevelopment is a state which is characterised by low GNP per capita and widespread poverty, scarcity of capital, rapid population growth and high dependency ratio, low levels of productivity, agrarian economy, technological backwardness, high levels of unemployment and underdevelopment, wide income inequalities, smaller participation in (foreign) trade and dependence.

Differential distribution of natural resources is one of the fundamental factors of regional inequality. When cultural (socio-economic) factors fail to correct this inequality developmental disparity becomes aggravated. Sundaram (1975) defines spatial inequality as the uneven development in space which is characterised by a certain pattern of association of different variables (including space, environmental, developmental and socio-economic) in an area contributing to a syndrome of inequality.

Analysis of developmental issues to be realistic must be concerned with economic variables (such as income, saving, investment) as well as non-economic variables like land ownership and tenure system, social stratification and class relations, credit structure, education, health, voluntary organisation, motivation of bureaucracies, economic and political elites and socio-cultural attitudes and values of the people.

In a socio-economic system the knowledge about interacting economic and non-economic factors is important. The dominance dependence relationship between poor and rich, between economically deprived and political weak masses and numerically small elites (in both national and international sphere) must be stressed.

Approaches to the study of economic development :

1. The "Stage of economic growth"
2. The "Structural internationalist" models.

The stages of economic growth are the theories of the 1950s and early 1960s. These economic theories of development maintain that there are a series of successive stages through which all countries do pass. Basing on these theories Marshal Plan (having the provision of massive U.S. technical and capital assistance for Europe after World War II) was formulated. The plan was successfully implemented there, since the European countries had the required institutional and structural foundation upon which higher economic growth was possible within a short period of time. But the theory may not fit the Third World (underdeveloped) countries as the socio-cultural-technological and economic conditions are relatively different from that of developed nations. As a result the second major approach on the "structural internationalist" models gained popular acceptance. These theories explain underdevelopment in the third world countries in terms of institutional rigidities and dependence and dominance relationships between rich and poor nations.

Two models usually come under this school of thought. The "New colonial dependence model" and "False paradigms model". The former one is somewhat a Marxist model which views underdevelopment a consequence of historical evolution of international capitalist system. Few groups of ruling elite of the developing countries (comprising landlords, merchants, businessmen, *zamindars,* bureaucrats etc.) because of their vested interest try to protect and maintain he international capitalist system. Theotonio Dos santos of Latin America, a strong supporter of Neocolonial dependence model argues "underdevelopment, far from constituting a state of backwardness prior to capitalism as rather a consequence and a particular form of capitalist development known as dependent capitalism...dependence is a conditioning situation in which the economics of one group of countries are conditioned by the development and expansion of others, the basic situation of dependence causes these countries to be both backward and exploited. Dominant countries are endowed with technological, commercial, capital and socio-political predominance varying according to the particular historical movement and can, therefore, exploit them and extract part of the locally produced surplus." This leads to inappropriate policies which serve only ruling elites.

As mentioned already underdevelopment or relative backwardness arises out of spatial inequality. It is defined in terms of developmental standards adopted at a particular point of time. Development is not simply material growth. It is also a progress of state of mind. Professor Seers puts three pertinent questions, the answers of which can determine whether a country is developed or not. These questions are :

1. Have general levels of living expanded within a nation to the extent that absolute poverty (*i.e.* deprivation of life sustaining goods); and the nature and quality of educational health and other social and cultural services improved?
2. Has economic progress enhanced individual and group esteem both internally *vis-à-vis* one another and externally *vis-a-vis* other nations and regions?
3. Finally, has economic progress expanded the range of human choice and freed people from external dependence and internal servitude to other men and institutions, or has it merely substituted one form of dependence (*e.g.* economic) for another (*e.g.* cultural)?

Economically more developed nations may not be developed in social, political and cultural sense if people feel inferior to others, and if their freedom of choice is extremely limited. Keeping the above (already mentioned) concept of development in mind let's proceed for a comprehensive and scientific meaning of underdevelopment, which can be well understood through Todaro's model... In Todaro's model of under-development there are basically three components :

1. Low Levels of Living,
2. Low Self-Esteem, and
3. Limited Freedom.

The first component is the economic aspect and the other two components are the non-economic aspects of under-development. However, all of them are interrelated.

Todaro defines 'Low Levels of Living' as insufficient life sustaining goods and inadequate or non-existent education, health and other social services. It is related to low incomes which are the consequence of low average productivity of the labour force. Supply side factors like poor health, nutrition, poor attitudes, high population growth and high unemployment and underemployment and demand side factors like inadequate skills, poor managerial talents, low worker education, labour saving techniques result in low labour productivity. High labour supply and low labour demand lead to high unemployment or underemployment. Again job availability becomes limited due to low income, low saving and low investment. Moreover, low income is also related to large family size and high fertility.

In the model, we find a number of vicious circles. One element leads to other. Once underdeveloped or poor, an area or region remains so far quite a long time without any easy escape, this is evident from the schematic diagram. Low levels of living seems to be a vital component of underdevelopment, society holds the poor at low esteem because of later's low levels of living which affect attitude towards work, cleanliness, punctuality and self-improvement.

Low levels of living means low bargaining power and less economic freedom. Political freedom (or freedom to take decision) is meaningless unless there is economic freedom. In other words low levels of living very often force one to depend both economically and politically upon others. As a result rich people and developed regions dictate terms and hence dominate poor people and underdeveloped regions. Thus low levels of living is perpetuated and exploitation continues.

So, in order to impart high self-esteem and wider range of freedom first 'levels of living' is to be improved. Then only a region or nation can be considered developed. Because of this very reason economic factors particularly poverty (related issues) must be analysed for any fruitful study of underdevelopment.

Previous Studies

Numerous studies on 'underdevelopment' have been undertaken both at national and international level from various angles, taking different components. Keeping in view the peculiar case of Kalahandi three vital spheres of underdevelopment studies have been revealed herewith. These are :

(a) Dependency Theory,
(b) World System Approach,
(c) Theory of International Division of Labour.

Dependency Theory

The theory rests on the analysis of capitalist process of production, which results in economic stagnation of the third world. The central idea of the scholars of this theory lies in the premise that the growth of industrial countries and that of the underdeveloped countries are not separate but opposite phases of the same process.

Frank[13] (1967) is one of the pioneers of the dependent theories on Latin America. His work marks the beginning of international political economic approach. Frank opines capitalism, whether national or international produced underdevelopment in the past and generates underdevelopment in the present.[14] He views, 'The world is dominated by a single economy such that all people are integrated into spheres of capitalist production. They are linked to by a series of metropolis-satellite chains which draw towards the centre. A surplus, produced at each stage of production. The result is that the periphery-satellites are impoverished, whilst the centre accumulates and grow[15]. At global level capitalism produces a metropolis and underdeveloped periphery. At national level a domestic metropolis, surrounded by satellite cities and regions are also produced in exactly the same way[16].

Problems of international (foreign) penetration in the political economies of Latin America are the main issues of interest of dependent theorists who explain the Latin American underdevelopment is a direct consequence of foreign political influences. In the Caribbean, Cross[17] (1979) points out that the society was not influenced Europe but was actually created by it.

'The dependence of peripheral countries on developed countries' had its genesis during the colonial period and since then it has taken different forms. The dependence theorists have distinguished three forms of dependency, *viz*. colonial, financial, industrial and technological industrial. Colonial dependency is based on trade, characterised by the relations between the European countries and the colonies. The second category is characterised by the domination of capital in hegemony centres at the end of the nineteenth century. The technological industrial dependency is the stage of 'neo-colonialism' which is basically economic and political. The penetration of peripheral countries by the core nations in the form of trade, aid and investment has profoundly influenced the socio-economic structure of the former countries.

Current studies show that dependence increased urbanisation by stimulating the rural urban migration. It is said that foreign investment reduces the amount of land available to the farmer forcing the migrants to urban areas[18]. Evans and Timberlake (1980) in their empirical works showed that the greater the degree of economic penetration, the greater is the relative growth of the tertiary sector.[19]

Overurbanisation and consequent economic regress in the Third World has also explained by economic dependent theorists. Timberlake and Kentor (1985) demonstrated that the greater the degree of economic penetration of foreign capital into the less developed countries, the greater is the degree of overurbanisation, the less the economic growth.[20]

World System Approach

The economic dependence according to world system approach is considered to be greatest in the periphery and semi-periphery and least in the core.[21]

The theorist of this approach view that underdevelopment is functional necessity of the capitalist economy. In the three-tired hierarchical system of world economy, Wallerstein[22] notices semi-periphery is a heterogeneous category of countries between core and periphery. A transitional belt is a zone of mixture of both capital and labour intensive production and a high level of class conflict. Core countries export capital, technology along with finished products to the peripheral countries. Timberlake[23] argues that the world system perspective allows us to see how some urban processes at the local and regional level are shaped, in part, by global structures and processes. It sees cities as part of the larger world economy.

World system theorists emphasise that the dependence on aid and investment has a significant impact on urbanisation. They assert foreign investment promotes urbanisation and expands the informal sector labour force. There has been a growing expansion of financial capital from the core to the semi-periphery and periphery, which has profoundly transformed the labour structure of the economies and in turn that of urban systems. As a result peripheral nations are undergoing a process of dependent development.[24]

Theory of New International Division of Labour (NIDL)

NIDL, according to Cohen[25], a system for production on a world scale in which a greater number of people are integrated into activities on by large international producers of goods and international firms which serve these producers.

The world economy (especially, service or tertiary sector), due to increase in capital investment, has been transformed into a system known as World Spatial Division of Labour or New International Division of Labour (NIDL). Its structural change is because of expansion of "internationalisation of capital" (export of capitalist relations of production) and proliferation of multinational corporations[26] who forming an alliance with peripheral elites promote both economic growth and modernisation in poor countries. Such a process tend to excerbate inequality (both economic and political) within peripheral areas which in turn produces conflict and turmoil directed against the elite dominated national state. The capitalist relations of production now created through multinationals, give rise to corporate related services including multinational banks, advertising firms etc. all organised on capitalist lines.[27]

The third world countries are the source of not only raw material but also cheap labour. The core countries have, therefore, shifted their points of production into the cities of these countries. NIDL theorists formulate that unskilled and labour intensive processes have been located in the periphery to take advantage of cheap labour whereas skilled and technologically advanced processes have been retained in the core economies.[28] The migration of international capital and shift of production points to the third world is primarily due to availability of cheap labour as a result of accelerating rural-urban migration. This has led to the development of numerous industrial enclaves which manufacture goods primarily for export (in the form of 'export processing zones' in Caribbeans, Central and Latin America, Africa and Asia).

Atkinson (1997) and others in their recent study discuss on the theory and practice of sustainable economic development. It focuses on implications of sustainability for the development policy. The authors jointly argue that the traditional analysis of savings and investments at macro economic level can be greatly enriched by integrating the environment into the macro-economic picture. They regard environment as capital and its neglect would destroy the humanity. Running the environment down or 'mining' natural capital is a sure recipe for sustainable development. Everyone (including governments, international agencies and developmental banks) hardly care this dimension.[29]

The work, therefore, suggests how to measure sustainability in a micro economic context with the hope that the decision makers can be more alert to underlying genuine trends in the economy and the economic policies. The critical concept here is true savings, a notion of savings in the economy that nets out the depreciation on all forms of capital (including natural capital). To the authors, the productivity of savings matters all investments is not equally valuable and investing in natural capital is contrary to so much of the prevailing development paradigm, quality investment.

Gooneratne and Obudho (1997) in their study on contemporary issues in regional development policy focus on the revitalisation of regional and local economics which form the major plank of any programmes for economic recovery and long-term growth in the countries of Sub-Saharan Africa. They emphasise on democratisation (especially greater participation and representation of grassroots) at different sub-national levels. There is a need for regional economic planning and cooperation in view of the growing importance of changing political and economic alliances on various geographical scales. Resource mobilisation and development efforts at local and regional levels are called for because of the mounting pressure of the debt burden and debt servicing and the structural adjustment programmes. They also feel the growing need by the business corporations and NGOs for regional locations and direct dealings among communities for a more effective organisation and regional management. Finally, private sectors role has been highlighted for more effective local planning. The current globalisation has a direct as well as indirect impact on local and regional development. Various geographic regions are to be flexible and should improve their competitiveness to survive in the fluctuating global economy. In order to ensure sustainable development the development policies must confirm to environmental norms.[30]

Kirkpatrick and Lee (1997) in their work on sustainable development in developmental world examine the different ways in which the integration (of environmental assessment, economic and social methods of appraisal to guide the development process) might be achieved in practice using a variety of countries as case studies.

The authors evaluate to present that there is no single integration model which will be universally applicable. Therefore, they provide a variety of policy solutions to remedy the present deficiencies. They are making aware of lack of integration with those involved in decision-making and consultation activities promoting a more interdisciplinary approach to policy-making and the provision of guidelines reinforced with training programmes on how to undertake integrations sensitive to different contexts and the expansion and improvement of research on the environment, social and economic factors in development processes and improvement of data for integrating appraisal and decision-making.[31]

After conceptualising and presenting literature review let us examine whether poverty and underdevelopment are interrelated and if so what is the exact nature of relationship between them. The term 'poverty' and 'underdevelopment' are often considered synonymous and are used interchangeably. This is both technically incorrect and practically confusing. An area may be poor but not necessarily be underdeveloped. For example Kerala which has higher percentage of literacy and health awareness but poor in its economy. Conversely stating, an underdeveloped area may not be poor, for instance middle east countries. The area here is underdeveloped primarily due to poor resource base (barring petroleum), insignificant indigenous technology and few skilled manpower and hence backward in the overall industrialisation. However, the people are not poor here because of their higher per capita income and modern amenities, which is again due to inflow of large foreign exchange with the export of petroleum.

When Underdevelopment is a State (Condition)

Kalahandi is rich in soil, water wealth and forest resources and it is prosperous in agriculture, generating surplus. It implies that in 'Primary economic sphere' Kalahandi is not underdeveloped, though there is temporal fluctuations in net agricultural production and change in mode of irrigation (*i.e.* from conventional tank, stream etc. irrigation to present well or lift irrigation).

When one looks in terms of infrastructure (road, power, irrigation) high yielding variety seeds, fertilizer application, industries, transport and communication, *i.e.* in 'Secondary economic sphere' Kalahandi is underdeveloped. In Tertiary economic sphere (hospital, school, bank facilities), village level political and administrative organisation Kalahandi is also backward.

When Underdevelopment is a Process

When underdevelopment is looked upon as a dynamic condition it has probably a different connotation for Kalahandi. Then in that case even in primary economic criterion, Kalahandi is not developed. Because the surplus products are siphoned off the district through the outside agents.

Relationship of Poverty and Underdevelopment

The relationship varies according to the fact whether development is a state or a process. It is both positive and negative, direct and indirect, strong as well as weak depending upon the conceptual approach one adopts with respect to underdevelopment to explain poverty and the sub-regional nature of it. For example, the relationship between underdevelopment and poverty is positive (or direct) when one sees poverty against the above secondary and tertiary criteria of the district and also when we analyse poverty as a resultant process of under-development (i.e. siphoning off of the primary products). Elaborating, higher underdevelopment arising from low development of secondary and tertiary sector of the economy and/or exploitation or plundering of natural resources and/or agricultural products will show greater poverty.

The correlation is again positive when we take physical background (relief, soil, drainage, altitude etc.) of certain agriculturally unfavourable regions of it. In other words, higher underdevelopment resulting from higher altitude, sloppy and rugged terrain, poor soil, water logging condition or low water holding capacity of land etc. are likely to have a bearing on poverty (raise poverty) directly by providing scarce natural resources and indirectly by reducing agricultural production.

The underdevelopment and poverty relationship is negative (inverse), when we take exploitation process of the area and increasing impoverishment of larger inhabiting population into account. Again similar relationship between the two is evident, if the area is underdeveloped due to more population is engaged in primary sector, which itself is less developed. If the area is overpopulated, the poverty would be more there.

Suppose a hypothetical region which is relatively free of outside interaction (onslaught or intervention), have different sub-micro regions of different resource population ratio, this would reflect nothing but natural capacity of land, with no sub-micro region showing over or under population. The subsequent migration that takes place shows the imbalance in resource population ratio, with onset of outside economic interactions.

Studying the nature of migration (inter- or intra-regional), time and duration of migration : one can thereby assess the exact magnitude of imbalance caused to the man land ratio. Measuring the transfer of goods, resources within and outside the region, we can learn the volume of resources transported outside or imported inside. The identification of outside agencies in the transfer of goods and resources can give the idea of the groups engaged in underdevelopment process.

Poverty is nothing but the resultant consequence of all these processes.

Underdevelopment is a Process

Poverty is merely its consequence : The analysis of 'Production Relation' encompassing the issues of : who produces wealth? Who accumulates and distributes it? And who consumes it? Again why, how and where this production, accumulation, distribution and consumption takes place? The temporal assessment of net resource flow of a region show a concrete shape and direction of backwardness. Poverty is the natural outcome of this process.

Poverty is a Causative Factor

Underdevelopment is subsequent to it : When people of one resourceful area is poor they would be weak in their bargaining power. This would facilitate the entry of outside exploiters to plunder resources, both natural and human. Whatever development in infrastructure if at all be initiated there, that would solve mainly the exploiters' interest, the area gradually plunging down the scale of underdevelopment. Poor people are not just financially weak, but also physiologically inferior, because of which they have low purchasing power, they can ill-afford education and medicine when they fall sick.

Conclusion

Poverty never occurs in isolation. It must be looked within the structure of prevailing social relations. Inter-personal or inter-group interaction with respect to use of natural resources can help us to analyse it. Since man-man interaction and quantity and quality of natural resources are different in various geographical settings, the intensity and nature of poverty arising out of those factors are also different geographically.

The very presence of rich among poor is a sign of accumulation of wealth in few hands. But why accumulation takes peace at all? This raises other related questions – who produces wealth? Who distributes it? And who consumes it? Again when, where and how wealth is produced distributed and consumed? The answers to these questions would lead one to learn about the distribution processes and underpinning causes of poverty. Here few aspects are to be kept in mind. Poverty may be a static condition but the processes generating and maintaining it are essentially dynamic. Again resultant poverty changes when its processes change. And to change processes, first institutions are to be changed. In such attempt revelation of the fundamental factors (not the visible or triggering factors) are important.

Taking all these things into account poverty can be defined as a condition of relative deprivation measured in terms of assets, income, food intake (nutrition), housing, education, health, infrastructure and social participation which arise within a static geographic unit of unequal resource distribution and due to a dynamic process of social relation of production, supported by strong institutional foundation.

NOTES

1. Sills, D.W., *International Encyclopaedia of Social Sciences,* The MacMillan Company, Pule, 1986, p. 398.
2. *Profiles of Rural Poverty : A popular version of poverty and landless in rural Asia, with additional material on 'Africa and Latin America',* International Labour Office, Geneva, 1979.
3. Scott, W., *Concepts and Measurement of Poverty*, Report No. 81.1, UN Research Institute on Social Development, Geneva, 1981.
4. Visaria, P., *Some aspects of relative poverty in Sri Lanka,* Washington D.C., the World Bank, 1981.
5. Heish, D., *Fiscal measures of poverty alleviation in the United States,* International Labour Office, Geneva, 1979.
6. Mohan, R. *et al., Measuring urban malnutrition and poverty : A case study of Bagota and Cali Colombia,* the World Bank Staff Working Paper No. 447, Washington, 1981.
7. Noaroji, D., *Poverty and Un British Rule in India,* The Adline Press, 1883, London, p. 38.
8. Marx, K., *Articles on India,* Mumbai, 1943.
9. Dutt, R.C., *Economic History of India in the Victorian Age,* Vol. II, Routladge and Kengan Paul, London, 1950.
10. Rain, M., *Problem in Definition and Measurement of Poverty in Towns end,* 1953, p. 46.
11. Mishra, A.P., *Rural Poverty in India Problem in Planning and Strategy for Poverty Alleviation,* Deep and Deep Publication, New Delhi, 1988.
12. Morrill, R.L. and Wohlenberg, E. H., *Geography of Poverty in United Staes,* McGraw Hill, NY, 1971.
13. Frank, A.G., *Capitalism and Underdevelopment in Latin America,* Pelican, London, 1967.

14. Chilcote, R.H., "Dependence : A Critical Synthesis of the Literature" in J. Abu Lughad and R. Hay, eds., *Third World Urbanisation,* Maqurofua Press, Chicago, 1977, p. 131.
15. Forbes, D.K., *The Geography of Underdevelopment : A Critical Survey,* Select Book Service Syndicate, New Delhi, 1985, p. 67.
16. Chilcote, R.H., *op.cit.* p. 135.
17. Cross, M., *Urbanisation and Urban Growth in the Caribbean,* Cambridge University Press, Cambridge, 1979, p. 9.
18. Bradshaw, Y.W., "Urbanisation and Underdevelopment : A Global study of Modernisation, Urban Bias and Economic Dependency", *American Sociological Review,* Vol. 52, No. 2, April 1987, p. 226.
19. Evans, P. and Timberlake, M., "Dependence, Inequality and the growth of tertiary : A comparative analysis of less developed countries", *American Sociological Review,* Vol. 45, 1980, pp. 531-52.
20. Kentor, J., "Economic Development and the World Division of Labour", M. Timberlake ed., *Urbanisation in the World Economy,* Academic Press, Orlando, 1985, p. 197.
21. Bollen, K., "World System Position, Dependence and Democracy : The Cross National Evidence", *American Sociological Review,* Vol. 48, Agusust 1983, p. 470.
22. Wallerstein, I., *The Politics of the World Economy,* Cambridge University Press, Cambridge, 1984, p. 110.
23. Timberlake, M. ed. *Urbanisation in World Economy,* Academic Press, Oralndo, 1985, p. xiii.
24. Bradshaw, Y.W., Urbanisation and Underdevelopment : A Global Study of Modernisation, "Urban Bias and Economic Dependency", *op.cit.* pp. 26-27.
25. Cohen, R.B., The New International Division of Labour, Multinational Corporation and Urban Hierarchy, in M. Dear and A. J. Scott, (eds.), *Urbanisation and Urban Planning in Capitalist Society,* Methuen, New York, 1981, p. 288.
26. Thrift, N., "The Geography of International Economic Disorder", in R. J. Johnston and P. J. Taylor (eds.) *A World in Crisis : Geographical Perspective,* Basil Blackwell, New York, 1986, pp. 15-25.
27. Bradshaw, Y.W., *op. cit.*, p. 195.
28. Henderson, J., "The New International Division of Labour and Urban Development in the Contemporary World System" in D.D. Smithy (eds), *Urbanisation in the Developing World,* Croom Helm, London, 1986, p. 70.
29. Atkinson, G., Dobourg, R. *et. al., Measuring Sustainable Development: Macro Economics and Environment,* Edward Elgar Publishing Limited, Cheltenham, UK, 1997.
30. Gooneratne, W. and Obudho, R.A., (eds) *Contemporary Issues in Regional Development Policy,* Ashgate Publishing Limited, Aldershot, Brookfield, US, 1997.
31. Kirkpatrick, C. and Lee, N., *Sustainable Development in a Developing World : Integrating Socio-Economic Appraisal and Environmental Assessment,* Edward Elgar, Cheltenham, UK, 1997.

3

AREA OF STUDY AND METHODOLOGY

Kalahandi district is situated in the forested uplands of Western Orissa. It extends from 19° 11′35″N to 21° 8′ 35″N latitude and 82° 25′ 58″ to 83° 45″ 37″E longitude. The geographical area of the district is 11,772 square kilometres, which covers about 8 per cent of the total area expansion of the state. With 15.92 lakhs population (*i.e.* 5.05 per cent of the total population of the state in 1991), the administrative unit has three sub-divisions, nine tehsils and eighteen community development blocks.

Kalahandi was known as *Mahakantara* (*i.e.* great forest) in the history of ancient India. It was a feudal estate during British period. In 1936, Khariar *Zamindari* was transferred to this estate of newly formed Orissa. The district however, became an integral part of Indian Union in 1948.

Physiographically, it has two clearly identifiable natural regions, plains (especially river valleys) and hilly tracks (including plateaus and forested uplands). The plains occupy the eastern part of Nawapada* sub-division and extends southwards upto Bhawanipatna and then run westwards through Junagarh and Dharamgarh right up to the district boundary. Almost half of the total area (*i.e.* 11,772 square kilometre) is covered by this physical unit. The hilly undulating topography with well marked elevations, depressions, wide forest clad plateaus on the other hand, covers the western Nawapada sub-division and south

---

* Recently, Nawapada sub-division has been carved out of Kalahandi as a separate district. But, wherever the term Kalahandi has been made use of in this study, the author refers it to the 'undivided district of Kalahandi'.

eastern part of Bhawanipatna sub-division. These form part of the main line of Eastern *Ghats* which rise sharply on the eastern side, gradually lower on the west. To the east of the sharp edged Bastar plateau extends the Kalahandi Plateau which range from 250 m to 300 m in elevation. Drained by the Tel, the Udanti etc. the plateau tappers into the Tel valley towards the north-east.

Dongerla hilly area is thinly populated. Tribals mostly inhabit the hilly tract along with a very small percentage of non-tribals. Tribal population of the division account for about one-third of the total population.

The plain region encompasses the Tel valley (of Kesinga, Narla, Karlamunda and eastern Khariar, Northern Bhawanipatna and part of Golamunda); the Tel-Hatti basin of (Dharamgarh, Junagarh, Kalampur, Jaypatna and Koksara).

Dharamgarh and Junagarh are bounded by hills on the western and eastern side. The northern side is opened towards Udanti Basin and the southern side towards the wider Tel-Hatti basin of Kalampur, Jaypatna and Koksara. The blocks are devoid of any kind of forests.

The undulating plains of Kesinga and Karlamunda are located to the south of river Tel in northeastern Kalahandi. They are separated by intervening Narla block. The region pedologically is the most fertile part of Kalahandi.

Depending on the surface configuration soil types differ. The plateaus and hill slopes contain rocky soil with thin veneer of loam, whereas the peak areas is devoid of any soil or vegetation. The valleys and plains are filled with fertile alluvial soil. Cultivable parts on the Eastern Ghats contain black and red soils, deficient in humus, nitrogen, phosphoric acid, potash and lime. (See Appendix 3 p. 349)

Red soils of these uplands are rich in iron content and are formed mostly due to weathering of metamorphic rocks. These soils are poor in humus, light coloured and thin while valleys have more fertile, fine dark and deep soil. Reclaimed agricultural lands meant for distribution, suffer from humus deficiency consequent upon the frequent practice of burning the undergrowth by the tribal people for centuries.*

---

* Report of Agriculture Experts Team on Dandakaranya Project, Unpublished, pp. 6-7.

Whether due to deforestation or overgrazing or faulty cultivation, erosion of soil is definitely an acute problem of Kalahandi over hills, gullies, rills and wastelands. Though most of the people depend on agriculture, infrastructural facilities (especially irrigation) are hardly available. The percentage of irrigated area to total cultivated area has remained static (mere 9.5, it is 22 for the state as a whole). And there is wide gap between Net Area Sown and Net Area Irrigated (See Map 5). Most of the rivers including important ones like the Tel and the Jonk, the Ret and the Udanti are perennial though highly fluctuating flow. The local *nalas* and streams are seasonal and so

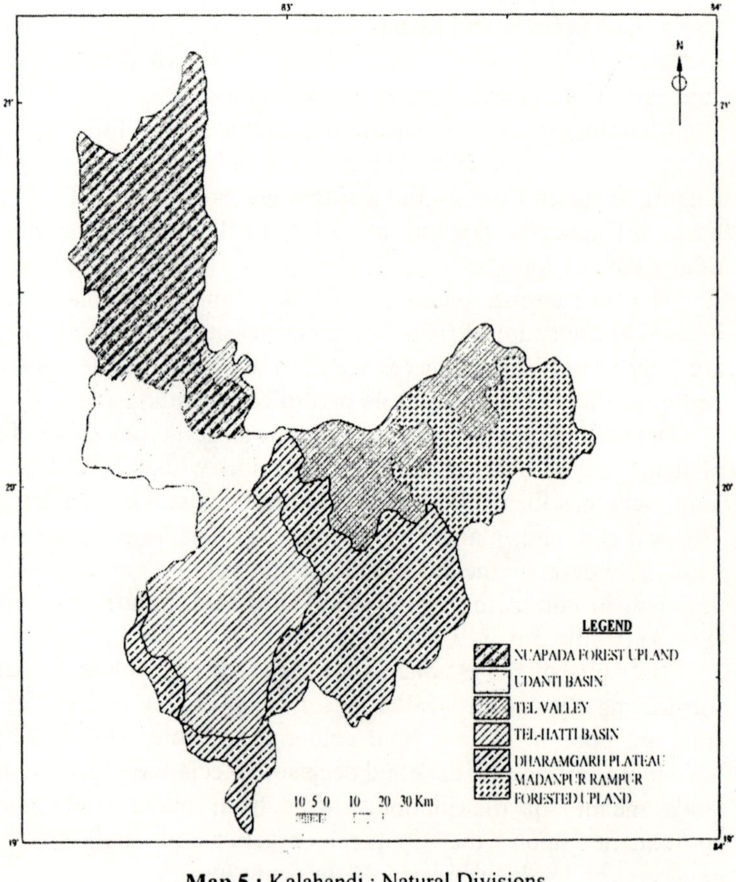

Map 5 : Kalahandi : Natural Divisions

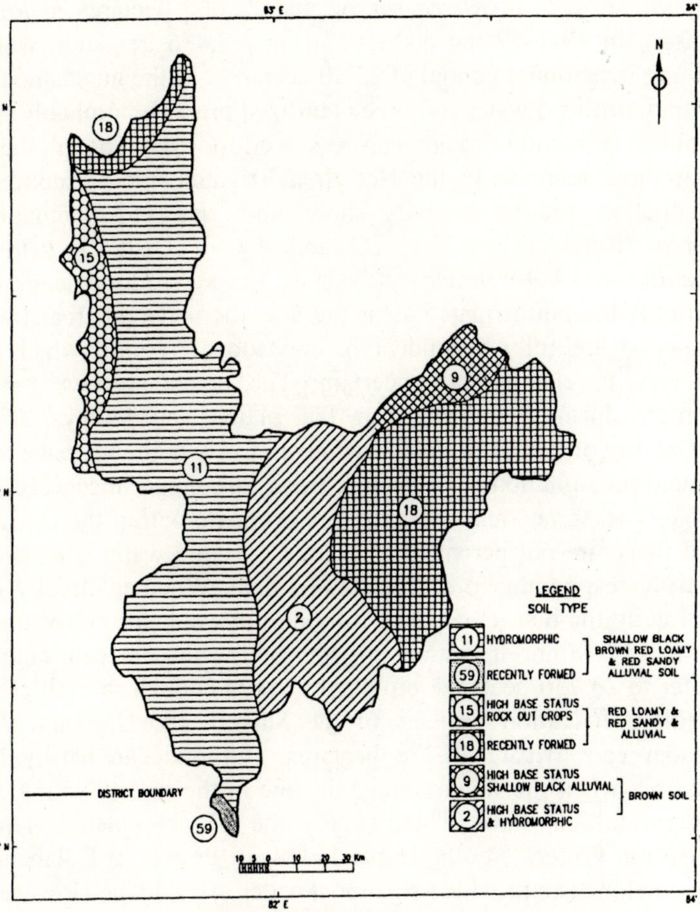

Map 6 : Kalahandi : Soils

dry up as soon as monsoon is over. Certain tracts are deficient in underground water resources. The irrigation potential of the major projects (Jonk, Sandul, Indra, Sagada, Raja, Udanti, Uttei, Indrawati) is 92,930 hectares and 45,750 hectares in *Kharif* and *Rabi* seasons respectively. However, total area actually irrigated by all major projects is only 51.92 thousand hectares in *Kharif* season and 23.79 thousand hectares during *Rabi* season.[1] Similarly annually restorable groundwater potential has been estimated to be 203.56 thousand hectare metres which can sustain installation to create irrigation potential for more than

47,370 hectares in *Kharif* season and 25,660 hectares in *Rabi* season. In 1976-77 the district had only 7,436 irrigation wells having irrigation potential of 2,500 hectares.[2] If the huge amount of underutilized water resource is utilized properly, probably the problem of natural drought can be solved for ever. Though there is gradual increase in the Net Area Irrigated, the agricultural production and productivity show slow rise and fluctuating trends (Refer Tables 7.1, 7.2 and 7.3 of Distt. *Statistical Handbook,* 1989-90). This is because the agricultural lands of not only the non-irrigated areas but also the irrigated areas (and projects) are fully dependent on monsoonal rainfall which is uneven, unreliable and uncertain. The upland receive more rainfall during summer, than the plains and valleys. The variability of rainfall from normal is relatively high, but since the annual precipitation is fairly high floods are bigger menace than drought in some areas. Many rivers originate within the district and these are not perennial. Moreover, ground water fluctuates sharply responding to seasonal rains data. Whether directly or indirectly the district depends fully on rainwater for cultivation. Total 117 Minor Irrigation Projects of the district can supply water to 25,736 hectares, provided there is enough rainfall. The Medium Irrigation Projects of the Saikeli, the Utei and the Sundar can irrigate 14,278 hectares. But this can hardly be possible when the water storage decline in the reservoirs due to low rainfall condition. There is only one fully completed Major Irrigation Project, *i.e.* the Upper Indrawati Project in Kalahandi which alone can provide irrigational water to 3,840 ha. However, its downstream canals of the project are still under construction. (See Appendix 3 & 4 p. 348).

The fate of Lift irrigation points is no way better. These have the capacity to irrigate 6,235 hectares. The total number of such irrigation points (including both public and private) is 544 at present. But the power (electricity) situation in Orrisa and especially in Kalahandi is (precarious) unsafe because of transmission loss, theft and improper management. So, dependence on lift irrigation is not without problem. (The condition of dug wells numbering 1876 is rather worse.)

Even if all the existing irrigation projects, lift irrigation points and dug wells are successfully able to provide irrigation and their capacity is utilised completely, not more than 64,066 hectares of agricultural land would get the requisite water for different crops. The total agricultural land of the Kalahandi is, however, 6,62,000 hectares. Thus nearly 6 lakh hectares of cultivating lands would be left with no irrigation facilities and could be threatened by droughts every year. This high degree of dependence on monsoonal rainwater (which is usually scanty and irregular) is one of the most important (natural-man made) cause of under-development of Kalahandi. Although the normal rainfall is 1,378 mm, its erratic nature and uneven distribution has been the cause of crop failure for several years in the past and even today.

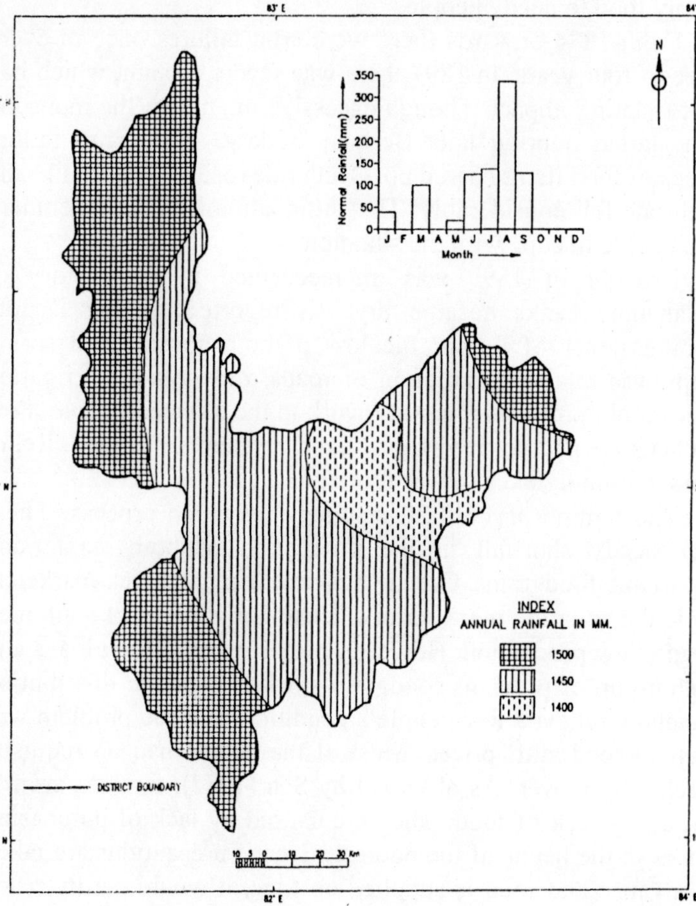

Map 7 : Kalahandi : Rainfall

The entire district is drought prone but areas experiencing frequent drought are the Nawapara *tehsil,* Mandanpur-Rampur and Narla blocks in Lanjigarh *tehsil* and Golamunda block in Dharamgarh *tehsil*. Drought condition prevailed in each blocks except Lanjigarh and Thuamul Rampur during 1991. (*The Sambad*, 11.7.91, p.1)

Kalahandi District Gazetteer (1981) mentions the following years of drought and the subsequent impact and measures (collected from reports of Chhatisgarh of which Nawapara sub-division was an integral part till 1936). Monsoon was untimely in 1868. Paddy crop was damaged. Relief centres were opened to supply food to needy people.

From 1884 onwards there were crop failures once in every three to four years. In 1897 there was severe drought which had a devastating impact. Though excessive in amount the monsoon rain started pouring late. Because of large scale crop failure prices of food items soared up. Death rate rose to 81 per mile and birth rate fell considerably. The entire administrative machinery was unable to cope with the situation.

Drought of 1899 was unprecedented in the history of Kalahandi. Tanks became dry. As reported by the Deputy Commissioner of Raipur the loss of both autumn and spring crops was total. Construction of roads, railways and irrigation tanks could provide temporary work to the affected people. Free kitchens opened up in villages. Land revenue suspended. Relief work was undertaken in war footing.

The famine of 1919-20 resulted in a chain process. There was steady shortfall in the production of both staple and exportable foodgrains. Greedy businessmen and black-marketers made the situation more serious. Unauthorized export continued despite low production. However, provision of *taccavi* loans and opening up of previous foodgrain stocks for public distribution somehow relieved few people's condition. But the problem was spurt in food stuff prices. Most of the people had no requisite purchasing power. As observed by Sen (1982), famines are not caused by lack of food. They are caused by lack of purchasing power in the hands of the poorest. Even if precautions are taken in advance and food is supplied on time, it would hardly reach the hungry unless they are given specific entitlements to food, [entitlement can take the form of free rations from Public Distribution System (PDS), or right to work in public employment programmes][3]. The price rise was followed by cholera, influenza, epidemic, malnutrition and starvation deaths. It was estimated that the rise in death rate was about 80 per mile in 1919.

Droughts of 1954-55 and 1965-66 and 1985 had also similar horrid impacts. The rich people could manage to overcome the problem. But poor people (like landless agricultural labourers) were the real sufferers. And the landed gentry could neither harvest nor could they do manual labour. More recently, 1109 villages in 1987 and 864 villages in 1987-88 were affected by drought in Kalahandi. The calculated crop loss was almost 50 per cent in each of these villages. Though Kalahandi is known for its drought flood is not uncommon here. The 1977 flood was sudden. All the rivers of the district including the Tel and the Sundar and their tributaries experienced steep rise in their water level following heavy rainfall on the catchment areas. The crop loss of Rs. 104.16 lakhs worth, loss of human life and severe damage to transport and communicational lines were reported. Regarding the flood of the river Indravati, 1991 it was mentioned, "But following heavy floods this year district administration fears agriculture might suffer as a result of large scale migration to neighbouring states. The loss due to flood last year was estimated at Rs. 700 crores. This year floods have already affected the population. About 8000 acres of farmland has been sand cast".[4]

The farmers of the district are usually accustomed to cultivation of monocrop and long duration variety of paddy which can only grow under favourable weather conditions. The productivity of different crops is low because of poor soil conditions, erratic and uneven distribution of rainfall, lack of enough irrigational facilities, primitive method of farmings, low literacy and poor socio-economic condition of most of the farmers.

Cowdung, leftovers from crop refuses of the cattle-shed, oil cake, tank-silt are still used as farm manure in most areas. The ash obtained after burning forest cover is used as fertiliser in shifting cultivation. In 1976-77, 5,06,110 tonnes of compost and

12,063 hectares of green manure of sunhemp and daincha were prepared.[5] Leaves, barks and ash of specific plants are used as pesticide while storing grains.

All these, however, does not mean that no effort had been made in Kalahandi for the improvement of agriculture. There is gradual adoption of various inputs. Chemical fertiliser of 9,430 ml. tonnes was consumed in 1996-97. The increasing use of modern inputs is reflected in growing agricultural production and productivity during the recent past despite decrease in NSA. (Refer Tables 7.1, 7.3, and 7.5 of *District Statistical Handbook*, 1989-90). 'The district incidentally, produces surplus foodgrain. The best variety of rice is grown here, of which a record 18,000 tonnes was given into the government (state) pool recently. The districts output of pulses by and large meets the requirements of the entire state. Besides, Kalahandi produces the highest quantum of cotton in Orissa".[6] To some these may seem to be exaggeration of facts. But if we divide the total food production of a year, say 1986-87 (which experienced worst monsoonal season during 80s) with the total population of Kalahandi, the average per capita per day food availability comes nearly 716 grams.* This amount of food is enough for healthy living. However, reality betrays this theoretical estimation. Field observation and various reports show how acute poverty, malnutrition, disease and starvation deaths are common incidents in todays Kalahandi. As mentioned by a newspaper article as many as one thousand starvation deaths have occurred in the last one decade in the state (most of such deaths have been reported from the district itself[7]. This may be mere journalistic presentation or political distortion of facts. But there is definitely some truth in it.

Mishra** Commission Report confirms deaths due to hunger. Such a paradox (when we find rampant poverty even if food production is more than enough) can be explained when we

---

* See Table 7.4 Page 36 of *District Statistical Handbook*, 1989-90. In 1986-87 total Kharif + Rabi products of food crops was i.e.(345.48).(1000).(1000)kg. This is divided by 13.39 lakhs population and then by (12).(30).

** Justice Baidyanath Mishra, a retired judge presented his report to the Orissa High Court. He was the Chairman of the Commission which was set up to investigate into the cases of starvation death and implementation of Poverty Alleviation Scheme in Kalahandi.

analyse poverty in other chapter. But it obviously proves that there is not equitable distribution of food among the people of the district. The surplus food is probably produced by a handful of rich farmer of favourable geographical pockets. Officials admit that almost 80 per cent of the total five lakh hectares of agricultural land is under the *benami* control of the big landlords who corner most of the agricultural produce. And these landlords include many politicians. (S. Roy, 1990-91)

The process of deforestation explains the state of underdevelopment from different angles. Going back to history, one finds contractors who were engaged by the ex-zamindars are responsible for felling trees (especially valuable timbers) recklessly. Under the C.P.L.R. Act, 1917 they were enjoying the monopoly to cut trees above a girth of 4 feet. Through this system of giving contract (which has been adopted for several years) many recruitments were made to the Estate forest staff, who turned into exploiters instead of being protectors of the forest (In fact, indiscriminate cutting of trees by estate contracts is one of the important causes of decline in forest area). In spite of the implementation of Agriculture Extension Programme and resulting deforestation due to that the region was exceptionally rich in moist deciduous forests (*sal* being the most dominant species in Eastern *Ghats*) and teak forests on the upland rims of Northern Kalahandi.

Earlier the northwest Kalahandi and the Tel valley had a rich forest cover of teaks which is commercially one of the most valuable species. After June 1948 villagers were granted the right to standing trees on their private holdings. Since then lot of destruction took place. At present few patches of good quality teak forests possibly exist in the northwest of the Udanti valley.

The governmental policy of 1954-55 allowing leases of bamboos for a period of nine years to Orissa Paper Mills led to gradual deforestation. In the plains the village forests were grossly exploited by local tenants for fuel and agriculture. The "Grow More Food" campaign by the government after World War II diverted more forest lands for non-forest use. Still then 70 per cent of the total geographical area was filled with tropical dry deciduous forest at the time of independence. Official estimation puts the present cover at 46.38 per cent (*i.e.* about 83,000 square kilometre of the total area of the district). However, satellite imagery shows that not more than 10 per cent of the forests is left today. Impact of deforestation on the geography of Kalahandi would be discussed at a later section. Here, who makes use of the forest? 'Why', 'where' and 'how' question are analysed further.

Drought is both a cause and consequence of deforestation. Once there is drought local inhabitants with their only asset labour look upon the forest as their immediate and only source of livelihood (in absence of anyother alternative). They have thorough knowledge of geographic distribution of valuable species, like sandal wood, teak, *resum* (rosewood), *sal*, *bija, haldee, gamban* and bamboo. They are more efficient in collection of firewood, *mahua* flower and *mahua* seeds, *kendu* leaves, *sal* seeds, *neem* seeds, broom grass, tamarinds; fruits such as *harida, bahada amla,* lac, *antia* bark, *sabai* grass, honey, hide, horn, catechu, tamarind, arrowroot etc. So long as forest is used for local need the problem of deforestation does not arise. But once there is commercial exploitation, profit motivation and large scale felling of trees for industrial and domestic needs of the rich city dwellers entire environment starts deteriorating, local people's miseries begin. After independence smuggling, illicit felling and timber trade are carried on more vigorously by corrupt forest officials, greedy businessmen and contractors, sometimes with the help of cunning and influential politicians. Since in a tropical dry deciduous forest species are diverse and mixed it is often not easy to use machines for tree felling especially when valuable species of trees are sought for. Taking advantage of acute poverty, labour (which is cheaply and easily available especially after drought and crop failure), local geographic knowledge and probably lack of environmental awareness of the illiterate people of Kalahadi, timber traders, forest officials and contractors employ them for tree cutting and collection of minor forest produces. And surprisingly enough, the very transport lines (the expansion of which has always been demanded and supported by the believers of so called development as a prerequisite for economic advancement of relatively inaccessible Kalahandi) have been used as channels or outlet for exporting out valuable resources (especially forest tree and forest products). In the name of providing relief and imparting progress in the western Orissa in general and Kalahandi in particular laying down of rail lines and road building were taken up during the colonial period. To quote *District Gazetteer of Kalahandi* (during the famine of 1899).

"The government started road construction work to provide employment to labourers... Earth work and collection of ballast for Raipur-Dhantari feeder line and the proposed Raipur-Visakhapatnam railway line were carried on." The Raipur-Visakhapatnam (or Raipur-Vizianagaram line) which was actually opened in 1931 accelerated the timber trade. The Kalahandi teaks and other woods can now reach well within the far off metropolises of Mumbai, Delhi, Kolkata and Chennai. The J & K Paper Mill, Rayagad which is located on the Raipur-Vizianagaram rail route, draws about 60 per cent of its bamboo requirements from this forest. Similarly, paper mills of Brajarajnagar and those of other districts import lot of sabai grass and bamboo from Kalahandi. In addition to teak and bamboo, timber, firewood and kendu leaves exported out of the district in large quantities. Following Table 3.1 presents the revenue earned by the State Government after selling out different forest products from the district during 1976-77.

Table 3.1 : Revenue from the sale of forest products, Kalahandi, 1976 -77

Items exported	Revenue Earned
Timber	58,34,422
Firewood	6,39,037
Bamboos	9,35,486
Kendu Leaves	56,22,447
Minor Forest Produce	6,87,727
Other Sources	3,86,218

Source : Revenue Department, Government of Orissa. (Also refer Kalahandi forest plan.)

This partly explains why in spite of huge forest wealth, the economy of the district has not improved significantly by it. One may point at the presence of saw mills and carpentry units. But compared to the geographical extent and density of the forest, those industries are small not only in number but also in their annual output. Again sawn timber, timber because of their low local demand and low purchasing power of the local people, are mostly exported.

About ninety-nine per cent of the timber exported are in the form of round logs, timber in the district amounted to 11,184 cft, 83,662 cft and 87,304 cft respectively (*District Gazetteer*, 1981, p.173). Only except providing meagre wage for temporary work of collection of minor forest cutting of bamboos and timbers and plucking of kendu leaves no other considerable economic contribution the forest makes for the toiling masses of Kalahandi.

In 1997, as mentioned in the *District Statistical Handbook*, 1997, out of total forest cover of 4,387.7 square kilometre, 1,449 square kilometre were Reserve Forest, 1992.51 square kilometre were demarcated protected forests and rest were undemarcated, unclassified and protected forests. Administrators are of the view that small proportion of reserve forests is the main cause of deforestation. But the field survey of Indian Social Institute explores that protected forests (over which the local inhabitants have their right) are preserved much more than the reserve forests (which are indiscriminately felled for trade and industrial purposes).[8] The survey has established that protected forest had vanished after they were categorized as reserved in the district. And official data shows area classified as Reserve Forests in which local people have very limited rights has been increasing steadily in the past few decades. (For instance an additional area of 2,077 square kilometre was reserved by the Orissa forest department during 1971-72 to 1977-78. If we follow the established arguments of ISI more deforestation would have already been occurred because of this increasing reservation.

Recently hundreds of hectares of forest land have been leased out to big industrialists for tea, coffee and rubber plantations under the pretext of land reclamation and anti-erosion measures. For example, coffee plantation in Thuamul Rampur and 400 hectare tea project at Gopalpur have been undertaken already.[9] The tea project is launched by the state-owned

Industrial Development Corporation of Orissa Ltd. (IDCOL) and Bajrang Tea Manufacturing Company Private Ltd. Outside private companies like Tata and Brook Bond have already acquired large tracts of forest land for similar purposes. No doubt, these projects when completed would provide livelihood to few hundred local people. But the precious forests which have been destroyed and the invaluable land (large estates) which have been taken possession of would deprive several thousands of people of their age old right over forest land, the very basis of their subsistence. The profit and export motivation of the big companies would hardly improve the district's overall economic condition.

People of Kalahandi are probably caught in a vicious circle. Because of scanty irregular and uneven rainfall drought conditions have prevailed several times during the last one hundred years or so. As mentioned earlier, due to drought and consequent crop loss a large number of local inhabitants fall back upon numerous species of fruits and roots obtained from the forest as the immediate and probably the only source of subsistence. They with their lone asset "labour" often search for alternative means of livelihood. Contractors and forest officials take advantage of this situation. They employ them for the felling of trees and collection of minor forest products. Many villagers stick to wood selling in nearby towns. So, forest exploitation becomes higher during drought period than the normal period. Massive forest cutting for satisfying commercial demand of traders and sustenance of local inhabitants lead to increasing irregularity and decreasing occurrence of rainfall. Low or untimely rainfall results in drought. This is evident from the current rise in frequency of drought. More crop failure and so more food shortage (famine). This ultimately render people poor and workless which in turn force (drive) them into forests for greater exploitation. Thus, whether the problem starts from man-made deforestation or nature made drought a chain of processes (each following the other consequentially) sets in and continues indefinitely. A diagrammatic representation of the vicious circle which explains Kalahandi's perpetual backwardness is presented below :

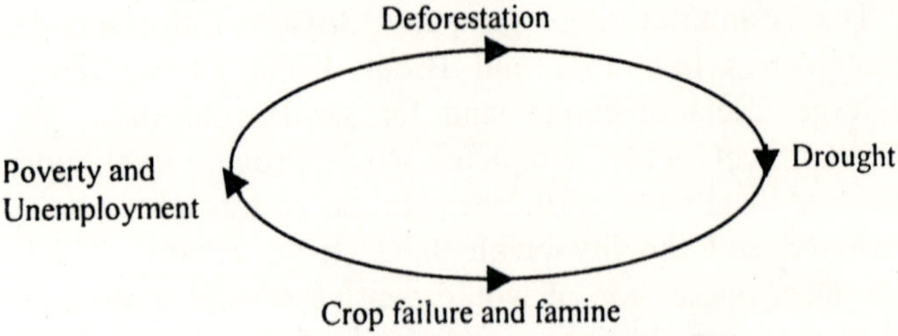

Fig. 3.1 : Vicious circle which has kept Kalahandi underdeveloped as if for ever

It also explains that plausibly there is a link between deforestation and poverty, especially in an underdeveloped economy (like that of Kalahandi). This is already established by Walter Fernandes etc. in their work on "Forest, Environment and Tribal Economy – Deforestation, Impoverishment and Maraginalisation in Orissa."

The environmental impact of deforestation and drought is already visible. Carrying (productive) capacity of land seems to have declined. Soil erosion is evident in many areas. Crop loss, malnutrition, starvation and frequent migration have become a common scene today. In the last one decade as many as one thousand starvation deaths have occurred in the district... Ground water table has dropped below 400 feet at places". The *sal,* teak, *seasum,* rosewood trees, because of drought, are attacked by fungus (fomes and carryophylli insects) and suffer from brown heart rot.[10]

After analysing agriculture and forestry, let's now turn to industrial (manufacturing) sector. This sector is backward in two ways. Firstly, as compared to vast agricultural and forest resource potential both agro and forest industries are very few in number*. Secondly, if individual sectors are taken into

---

* According to the National Council of Applied Economic Research the known deposits of minerals of the district with the possible exception of bauxite cannot by themselves, sustain any heavy mineral based industry (survey of Backward Districts of Orissa).

consideration, industrial or manufacturing sector is the least developed one. These aspects have already been highlighted earlier in this chapter (% share of agriculture and industry in the data form given in the agriculture and forest section). Amongst the industries mention may be made of cottage industries such as lac processing, weaving of cotton, pottery, bamboo basket making, mat weaving and small scale industries like construction of plough and solid wheeled carts, brass ornament making, iron-smelting (especially in and around the Barang hills and the plateau areas). Apart from these many saw mills, rice mills, oil mills are found. Dozens of rice mills are located in the nodal town of Junagarh, and railway stations of Kesinga, Khariar road, and Rupra road. Few medium size industries and no large scale industry are there in the district. The industrial backwardness is also indicated by the percentage of the workers of the district engaged in manufacturing. It was 2.97 in 1971, only 2.55 in 1981 and 4.55 in 1991.[11]

The general causes which can be attributed for lack of any significant industrial progress are low availability of raw material (such as minerals), almost total absence of coal as an important source of power (though it has rich hydel power potential), insufficient rail lines and good quality road network, lack of skilled workers and entrepreneur and above all unutilised or misutilised capital. Before 1965 Panchayat Samiti Industries Scheme (which was based on local raw material), along with State Aid loan and loans from the Orissa Financial Corporation made a small beginning. Rural Industries Project came up in 1973 in the district. It was sponsored by the (Central) Planning Commission, for the development of small scale industries. The State Aid to Industries Act provides for concession in sales tax, purchase tax in raw materials and finished goods, exemption of *octroi* duty and establishment of 'Developed Areas'. However, none of these incentives could attract any entrepreneur into the district.

During the 1980s there was a steady rise of capital investment in industries and the number of factories have gone up from 27 in 1979-80 to 30 in 1993-94. But the number of persons employed in different years do not respond to the investment quantum, accordingly. It has dropped to 918 in 1993-94 from 2,147 in 1980-81. The unexpected fall in factory employment does not correspond to the rise and capital investment during 1982-83 and 1983-84. This shows the factories have made neither any definite progress nor any significant contribution towards job creation.

Table 3.2: Number of reporting factories, capital investments and total Persons Employed in Kalahandi.

Year	No. of factories	Total productive capital (in lakhs)	No. of Persons Employed
1980-81	31	227	2147
1981-82	31	241	927
1982-83	35	289	985
1983-84	32	291	694
1984-85	32	350	880
1993-94	30	385	918

Source : Directorate of Economics and Statistics, Orissa, Bhubaneswar.

Study of power situation of Kalahandi is of little use when whole Orissa is considered a power deficit state and depends heavily on the electricity which is purchased from neighbouring states. Yet, a brief analysis of such a condition could be meaningful at least to highlight the magnitude of under-development. For the first time in 1925 Bhawanipatna was electrified. Initially diesel power houses were installed in the district. Later these were replaced and the State Electricity Board started supplying power from the Hirakud Hydel Project.

Taking the recent electricity consumption data of the Board into account, one finds the district consumed only 15 million and 9 lakhs KWH power as compared to 3241 millions KWH power consumption of the State during 1983-84. Out of total 2,653 villages, the number of villages electrified in Kalahandi till 1984-85 was 870. Though bulk of the districts population (*i.e.* 93.99 %) lives in rural areas only 40 per cent of the villages were electrified by 1986-87. (Here electrification of villages not necessarily mean all the villagers are availing the facilities. In fact most do not and cannot get such benefit, because of poverty). Rest 59.82 (or almost 60) per cent villages go without light. On the other hand all the 5 urban centres of the district, containing just 6.01 per cent of the total population have been fully electrified. The urban areas and urban dwellers (comprising outside entrepreneurs, businessmen, officials, *marwadis, kumutis,* coastal Orissa traders, high class cultivators and a handful of resident population) consume almost the entire part of the electricity for commercial, industrial (30.3%) and street lighting (8.0%) purposes and large chunk of power used by them for domestic (32.5%) and agriculture (6.7%) purposes.

From the experience of Punjab and Haryana we learn, the impact of drought can be effectively mitigated if the vast underground water reservoir is fully exploited by installing required number of lift irrigation points and energizing them with sufficient quantum of assured power. But there are only 795* energized (Lift Irrigations Points) LIPs while the total NSA (Net Sown Area) of the Kalahandi is 589 thousand hectares (as per 1983-84 data). Frequent power cuts leave these LIPs idle and the district often starve for power.

We have already estimated that the district has huge running (surface) water potential. Equally high is the vast hydel potential of the rivers such as the Tel, the Indravati, the Jonk, the Sagada, the Hatti, the Udanti, the Sundar, the Uttei and number of tributaries. If utilised completely the power problem of not only the district but also the whole state can be relieved to a great extent.

Kalahandi unlike other districts of northern and western Orissa has small mineral reserves. And most of minerals are of low grade. Though bauxites, graphite, quartz, manganese, lithomargic clay, cobalt, galena are found here only except graphite, quartz and (mining of) some precious stones no other mineral has been exploited so far. About 1.8 million tonne bauxite deposit (of which 0.3 ml.t. are in Khariar highlands and 0.4 ml.t. in Karlapat plateau). Though of low grade, significant deposits of bauxite occur in Chandigarh-Karlapat belt. From the data of the Directorate of Mining and Geology, Orissa it can inferred that the mining work is not regular and the production and the value of the output vary highly from year to year.

Mining is not an assured source of income and work (see Table 3.2). The number of workers (all of them unskilled and mostly local) employed in mining operation of graphite were 99

---

* Data obtained from Tables 7.1 and 16.3 of *District Statistical Handbook*, Kalahandi, 1989-90.

in 1982, the number dropped to only 10 in 1985. Again there was a sudden rise to 50 next year and in 1987 it again decreased to 30.

Quartz is another major mineral of the district which accounted for 99.4 per cent of all mineral production during 1986. Lithomorphic stone are quarried near Sandale and Lukop. Although iron ore deposits of ten million tonnes are reported from Kalahandi, these are of lesser significance. The output of the mineral was 22814 million tonnes whose value was Rs.26.56 lakh in 1996-97. This is directly exported out of the district. The number of workers employed in mining during the same year was only 88 which is quite insignificant looking to the total workers (main and marginal) of 5.61 lakh in the district. (Also see Appendices to Chapter 3 p.343 & 347)

Thus mining except providing a handful of job, absolutely does nothing for the economic development of the district. Rather its utilisation accelerates the pace of underdevelopment of the district. History shows Kalahandi had trade links with outside kingdom ever since Mauryan and Kushan period. The items of trade were oil and rhinoceros hide. The river Tel played an important role in transportation. During the feudatory rule of the ex-state Kalahandi few rivers were used for carrying out trade. Only except that period, rivers had very little role to play. Even today they can hardly serve as reliable means of navigation and trade, because of their very non-perennial nature and winding course character. However, the higher volume of rainwater often facilitate teak log transportation (for example the Udanti and the Sundar, especially before the construction of Arang Khariar road and Vizagpatnam Raipur rail line were the only dependable means of wood transportation). In addition to that few good road network were existing there. Raipur-Visakhapatnam railway line was completed in 1932. This gave a boost to the Kalahandi trade later. Pre-independence period export items include rice, pulses, oilseeds, cotton and forest produce (such as lac and hide). Import items comprised salt, cotton clothes, brass, utensils, spices, petroleum and fancy articles. The volume of trade was low obviously due to limited local production and lack of water transportation network.

Post-independence period saw progress in transportation and

also in trade. There are now 8 railhead towns and total 70 km length of railway line in the district. Kesinga is the most important and busiest railway station. Kandel and Narla Road are the two other important railway stations which were opened in 1954 and 1960 for passenger traffic and goods traffic respectively.

During 1960s Orissa had strong links with both Bihar and Bengal in terms of trade. West Bengal, Bihar, Orissa having the important port Calcutta formed a single macro economic region. This is based on S.R. Hashim's study on Inland (Rail and river borne) Trade Accounts, 1965-66. By and large, Kalahandi was economically connected with this macro region.

The district headquarter is connected with different parts of the Kalahandi and with the Kesinga station. Construction of 261 km road in Khariar Division was undertaken in April, 1976. The State Highways No. 2 and No. 3 link this district with outside district roads and village roads of interior areas join the trunk roads. All these however do not mean that Kalahandi is developed from transport and communication point of view. Direct rail line between Kalahandi and the coastal Orissa is still lacking. Road network, though more extensive than rail lines, is no doubt inadequate and of inferior quality.

Gradually, afterwards major cities with which Kalahandi developed trade links are Raipur, Nagpur, Palas, Vizianagaram, Siliguri, Asansol, Kharagpur, Mumbai, Calicut, New Delhi etc. Even if the volume and items of export have increased overtime its composition has remained unchanged. In other words, Kalahandi's export is still based on primary products. That too it is mainly agro-based and forest based. Rice, rice bran, flattened rice *(chuda),* oilseeds, pulses, kendu leaves, mahua flower, timber, bamboo, myrobalan, hill brooms, charcoal, firewood, hides and skins, *siali* rope, cotton, tamarind and chilli etc. of rupees 3 crore worth are exported annually. But the value of annual import of sugar, wheat, kerosene, fertilizer, steel goods, aluminium utensils, oil, clothes, stationery goods, grocery items, agricultural implements, medicine and other processed products etc. hardly exceeds rupees 1 crore. Thus rupees 2 crore flows out of the district annually, which never return. Between 1973-74 and 1975-76 1,80,150 cubic feet of timber transported out (*District Gazetteer*, 1981, p. 173). The following table shows the inward and outward goods traffic in different years.

This is nothing but drain of resources which otherwise could have fetched a large number of jobs (works) with greater income for the poor people of Kalahandi, had those been processed locally before being exported.

Table 3.3 : Export and Import of goods, Kalahandi

Year	Outward flow (export)		Inward flow (Import)		Net outflow	
	quantity (in qtls.)	Value (in Rs.)	quantity (in qtls.)	Value (in Rs.)	quantity (in qtls.)	Value (in Rs.)
1951-52	1,83,547	6,70,951	1,44,159	1,64,730	39,388	5,06,221
1955-56	4,55,675	15,95,641	1,18,866	3,23,667	3,36,809	12,71,774
1961-62	9,43,063	23,44,558	1,64,179	3,93,165	7,78,884	19,51,393
1975-76	10,03,428	2,10,07,719	2,90,226	45,71,279	7,13,202	16,43,644

Source : Processed Data of District Gazetteer, 1981.

Widespread poverty, malnutrition, under-nutrition and starvation have led to diseases of various types and death.* The following figures, though under reported and not fully reliable it throws some light on the state of Kalahandi's underdevelopment. During the decade 1951-60 both birth and death rates in the district were more than the corresponding figures of the State.

Table 3.4: Birth and Death Rates in Kalahandi and Orissa (1951-60)

District/State	Kalahandi	Orissa
Birth Rate (1951-60)	30.2	25.8
Death Rate (1951-60)	19.6	16.2

*Source : District Gazetteer,*1981.

Similarly, during the same decade the percentage of mortality due to cholera, smallpox and fever (mainly malaria) in the district were 2.67, 5.89 and 78.70 respectively which is higher than those of the state.

Number of registered deaths and the number of registered births in 1997 were 14,154 and 40,910 respectively .The number of infant deaths recorded the same year was 2,445. (See also Appendix 3 p.345)

* Due to hot and moist climate the region is very much prone to malaria, black water fever and various intestinal diseases.

Table 3.5 : Death Rate due to different diseases in district Kalahandi and Orissa (1951-60)

Mortality due to	Kalahandi	Orissa
Cholera	2.67	1.51
Smallpox	5.89	2.76
Fever	78.70	57.70

Source : *District Gazetteer*, 1981.

After having a detailed account of natural and man-made processes and state of underdevelopment of the district as a whole let us now turn to the methodology adopted.

Methodology

To make this research comprehensive and exhaustive one an integrated study would be conducted in the following manner : .

1. District in the regional setting,
2. Ecological areas in the district,
3. Village studies from each ecological areas, and
4. Household level study.

At the village level (whose sociological form is 'community') division can be made on the basis of:

(a) high economic indicator villages.
(b) low economic indicator villages.

At the macro or meso level underdevelopment study is more relevant whereas poverty study would be more meaningful if it is conducted at (micro) lowest possible level. That is why household level study (including survey of households and family profiles) is to be taken finally.

Upto the village level, the researcher can rely upon the secondary sources of data. However, below that level, data has to be generated through primary survey. For this purpose, since it is not possible to survey all the households of the district 'Stratified Systematic Random Sampling Method' is to be adopted.

Secondary sources of data would include published books,

reports, monographs and articles such as District Census Handbook, Orissa District Gazetteers, Statistical Abstract of Orissa, Famine Code – Famine Commission Report, 1880, National Sample Survey Organisation, Report of Ministry of Tribal and Community Development, Government of Orissa, Season and Crop Report of Kalahandi, Agricultural Statistics, Orissa Relief Code, Settlement Reports and different guidelines and documents of the Planning Commission and Central and State Governments.

Composite Development Index and Delineation of Development (Sub-micro) Regions

Different studies by geographers as well as non-geographers show the striking disparities in the levels of development in India. Scholars like Schwartzberg (1902), Ashok Mitra (1961), Prakasha Rao, Sundaram *et al.* (1971), Biplab Dasgupta (1971), Marriss Jones (1975), Pal (1975), K.V. Sundaram (1978) and Amartya Sen (1998) have been worked in this area by taking different methods and indicators of their own choice.

Taking fourteen variables and data of seventies and with the help of Principal Component Analysis, Planning Commission delineated various regions (district being the unit of study) of different levels of development in 1978.

Mere Growth rates, Gross domestic production rates, Per capita income etc. are all gloss over inequality. Materials (*i.e.* material growth), no doubt, are important for enriching poor, but their effectiveness depends on group characteristics and different socio-economic circumstances, variations in which contribute to inequalities in poverty in a region. Aggregated values do not take into account the gap between developed or less developed and undeveloped regions and that of the rich and the poor people. So, the author devise an index which takes into account different variables such as population density, percentage of scheduled caste (SC) and scheduled tribe (ST) population, percentage of working population, cropping intensity, percentage of area under high yielding varieties (HYV) of seeds to net sown area (NSA), percentage of net irrigated area (NIA) to net sown area (NSA), population per medical centre, number of primary schools per thousand population, percentage of literacy, percentage of villages with *pucca* road, percentage of villages electrified, percentage of villages with drinking water facility and number of cooperative societies per lakh population, following Sen (1973), Kundu (1980) and Sen and Dreze (1998).*

The Composite Development Index (CDI) has been prepared using the formula $\Sigma \underline{x}_i / \overline{x}$

where $\underline{x}_i$ = Value of development variable
$\overline{x}$ = Mean value of a particular variable
Σ = Summation

(*Note*.: Where mean value $\overline{x}$ is much smaller than the corresponding $\underline{x}_i$ value then $\underline{x}_i / \overline{x}$ formula has been used instead of $\underline{x}_i / \overline{x}$)

The spatial significance of all the variables taken for the above purpose to measure the developmental level of Kalahandi has been detailed out in a separate section. Here we present justification for selected indices only, avoiding repetition. Care has been taken not to incorporate elements, without sufficient reason of inclusion in the construction of development index. Though the subjective elements which creep in while making choices, cannot be eliminated altogether.

Justification for choice of variable for Composite Development Index (Appendix to Chapter 4 p.352 to 355)

The biggest failure in India, according to Sen (1997), is social inequality. It takes its toll both directly in terms of the quality of life – and indirectly – in terms of reducing the economic opportunities that people have. I think it is illiteracy, the lack of health care, absence of land reforms, the difficulty in getting

---

* Prof. Amartya Sen put forward a measure of actual welfare of people and their status in 1973 in his work, 'On Economic Inequality'. He along with Jean Dreze coedited the book in 1998 on 'Indian Development : Selected Regional Perspective' to show regional disparities in development . Prof. Amitav Kundu (1980) of JNU has constructed Composite Indices in measurement of urban processes and regionalisation.

micro credit, that make the problem of inequality so large in India.[12] So our interest in development indicators lie not just in development as a phenomenon detached from poverty but in seeing development in the context of evaluating how specific items such as literacy, medical facilities, cooperative societies are doing in a region like Kalahandi.

Since independence in 1947 India has made considerable progress in higher education, but remarkably little in elementary schooling. In last census of 1981, only 41 per cent of adult population was found illiterate.... Elementary education has never received quite the importance that other social objectives have enjoyed in Indian public policy.... Indian illiterate is not acutely unhappy about being illiterate and seeking education is not one of the more intense desires of the deprived Indians...

But illiteracy is also unfreedom – not just lack of freedom to read, but also the curtailment of all the other freedom that are conditional on communication requiring reading and writing.[13]

These amply justify for the indices, 'number of primary schools for thousand population' and 'percentage of literacy', being taken for measuring development in Kalahandi.

Though the district is under-populated the micro regional distribution of population density reflects that higher densed areas have better resource endowment. It is a natural response of human concentration to natural distribution of resources. So, population density (average population of the district per population of an individual block in the district *i.e.* x_i / x_i) has been taken an indicator of measurement of levels of development (and so, indirectly that of poverty).

Percentage of scheduled caste (SC) and scheduled tribe (ST) population to the total population is a definite measure of underdevelopment. Larger the proportion of SC population to total population, greater is the development and lesser is the poverty in areas which witness seasonal or annual outmigration of SC labour. Because in Kalahandi it has been observed that barring few tribes like Gond and plain Konds, most tribes are inward oriented and stick to their own land even during drought periods. In other words, tribes are relatively less mobile outside their habitat. This type of group character often make a difference in the levels of development.

Working population signifies not just workers (in cultivation, industry, plantation, trade, commerce, transport, mining, construction, political, social and governmental works) in a region but also the potential number of working hands with purchasing power, in it. This is, therefore, an useful indicator of both poverty as well as development.

Kalahandi is commonly supposed to be a drought prone district which experiences low or insufficient rainfall. Paradoxically, if the total annual rainfall and existing water reserve is taken into consideration the district comes under rather one of the water surplus belt of India. Obviously, lack of equitable and timely water supply (or water management planning) is the whole problem. (see irrigation section of the 'Area of Study'). We have taken 'percentage of net irrigated area to net sown area' as an indicator to highlight this problem along with levels of development (including development in agriculture) in Kalahandi.

Though for majority of poor of Kalahandi 'high yielding varieties of seeds to net sown area' is a mockery of development in India, quite a substantial proportion of rich and powerful land holders use HYV seeds to raise their production manifold with the help of their own irrigation facilities fertilizer and the landless labourers of the local area. The group (class) contrast between high or low land holding farmers and that of between landlords and labourers are reflected in space variation in development and poverty.

Cropping intensity is a major index of agricultural development. Kalahandi is primarily an agricultural economy which produces exportable surplus. Again this very area suffer starvation (food scarcity). Although these seem to contradictory, they are in fact, facts based on available data (see Appendix to Chapter 4). The reason is because certain pockets of the district, which are in possession and direct control of big landlords and outsiders are well flourished showing higher intensity in cropping due to better irrigation facilities. Large areas have lower intensity in cropping and still larger areas are left uncultivated (uncropped). So, cropping intensity has bearing on development and to measure the later we have to pick the former also.

Underdevelopment parts are usually marked by diseases and higher (infant) mortality rates. Kalahandi is no exception to this (see Area of Study section in this chapter) Poverty breeds ill health. By opening hospitals and dispensaries towns are better placed to combat the poverty through the indirect process of good health, curtailing death rates and reducing the cases of diseases. However, in the rural areas of district many people still believe in and depend upon traditional methods of treatment and village quacks. Medical facilities has been taken as a proxy variable of development and poverty.

Transportation lines are regarded as life lines (arteries) of development. The age old inaccessibility (posed by rugged terrain, steep slopes, dense forests, plain lands criss crossed by rivers, streams and rivulets) prevent smooth inflow of developmental inputs of the government and easy outflow of local products to the outside markets. Our experience shows in both ways local people suffer though they get outside fund and materials for their own progress. No doubt, outside interaction is a must for peoples progress, since local rich exploit the poor taking advantage of their geographic isolation but in most cases it has been found that outside traders (moneylenders, *dalals* and contractors) more vigourously carry out their suction process once the area is opened to outside world through transportation. Thus, accessibility (laying down of transportation network) with its intended objective of economic growth brings development along with expanding the sphere of underdevelopment. In either case, 'percentage of villages with *pucca* road' is a crucial component for measurement of development and hence poverty:

Looking to mass poverty and outmigration on the one hand, and tremendous resource potentiality on the other, (see area of study) it is often proposed to open more avenues of employment by setting up mills, factories etc. for the local populace. Some favour small and medium scale industries while others contend that large industries are the only solution for the unemployment problem in the district. Whether it is small scale or large scale industries, electrification (power supply) is an essential prerequisite for industrialisation of Kalahandi. The areas having more electrified villages have not only better potential for industrialisation, irrigation etc. but also better placed in development scale. So, electrification in itself is considered a major developmental index.

Due to lack of safe drinking water people suffer from many water borne diseases. During summer season as the rivers become dry (since most of the rivers, streams are non-perennial today) womenfolk walk miles down the valleys to scoop water making water holes on the dry river bed. While naturally Thuamul Rampur side of Dharamgarh forested plateau has larger number of perennial river, Madanpur, Rampur and eastern side of Nawapada plateau suffer acute shortage of water and the plains of intervening belt have fairly better supply of drinking water, that too in its towns only. Thus, both the importance of drinking water in the district as a whole and its spatial variation make the 'percentage of villages with drinking water facilities' imperative to incorporate in the composite development index.

The basic raw data has been collected from *District Statistical Handbook*, Kalahandi, 1989-90. The calculated Composite Development Index (CDI) has been tabulated in appendix to Chapter 3, for different blocks of Kalahandi. Then after, the aggregated value of CDI of different blocks have been suitably divided into four hierarchical divisions. The district, thus has been categorised into four different levels of development, *viz.*

(a) Developed Area (CDI >16.50)
(b) Moderately Developed Area (CDI 14.50-16.50)
(c) Less Developed Area (CDI 12.50-14.50)
(d) Depressed Area (CDI < 12.50)

Delineation of Ecological Sub-micro Regions for Sample Survey and Poverty Study

By super imposing 'Natural Regions' (Physio-Cultural Regions, which were taken from Cartographic Regionalisation of India, Census of India, 1981 upon the Development Regions (prepared through CDI given above) nine different Ecological Sub-micro Regions have been delineated. From each of these ecological regions a pair of villages (one from high economic indicator villages and the other from amongst low economic indicator villages) were selected randomly for sample survey. (See also Appendix – 3 in page 350)

Criteria Adopted for Choosing Sample Village

Kalahandi district has 2840 villages with 13,39,192 population spread over 11,772 sq. km. geographic area (till 1991 census). First, all the villages were listed out against their triple criteria, *viz.*,

(a) percentage of non-workers to total working population of the village.
(b) percentage of marginal farmers (having less than one hectare of land) to total farmers of the village.
(c) percentage of irrigated area per farmer* of the village, and fed in a computer.

Next, the values of each criteria were divided by two to determine high percentage category and low percentage category. The average values of each category were then found out. Computer print out of all the villages having 'low economic indicators' and 'high economic indicators' were taken out separately for all the three criteria. For example, to find out sample village of high economic indicator villages, the villages having low percentage of non-working population, low percentage of marginal workers and high percentage of per farmer irrigated area were taken into consideration. Equal number of villages (by gradually extending the number range say 10, 20, 30 etc.) from above and below of each average value of the three criteria of high economic indicator villages were marked till a common village was obtained. That common village was taken

---

* Per farmer irrigated area has been taken instead of irrigation per cultivated area, because of three reasons : (i) In the drought prone district wherever irrigation is available, it is in the form of tank, *nallah*, *bandha*, *chuha* (dugwell), *kata* (stream diversion) etc. In other words informal sources of irrigation is predominant. (ii) Irrigation facility is limited to a village or few households on a community basis, with one big and / few small land owners and rest dependent labourers (*sukhbasis*, *halia* etc.). (iii) Authentic data on cultivated area is not available. Areal data is rather misleading. Since formal (Govt. provided sources) of irrigation is very limited.

as sample village for 'high economic indicator village' category. The ecological sub-micro region (as delineated already) to which that sample village belongs was noted against the village location. In the same way sample villages for high economic indicator villages of rest of the ecological micro regions were marked out.

The process was repeated to find out the sample villages of low economic indicator villages for all the corresponding ecological micro regions of the district. (The location of the sample villages has been given in a separate map in Chapter 5 on poverty. The list of high and low economic indicator villages of varied micro regions has been presented along with their percentages of non-working population, marginal farmer population and irrigated area in the Appendix-3 page 332).

A self-prepared questionnaire (as given in the Appendix 3 p.319), based on pilot survey was utilised to carry out the survey for collecting poverty related data. Basing on the village poverty level which is representative of the regional poverty two areal maps (for low economic index villages and other for high economic index villages) were prepared to study deprivation.

The raw data were fed in computer to find different variables in tabulated form with their association and correlation.

Analysis

Both inter areal and intra areal comparisons can be made to find out the geographic structure of poverty and underdevelopment of the district. In non-food areas production of commercial and cash crops might be generating cash but since the people there have to buy food from outside, probably they would not be getting good quality nutritious food of adequate amount. So, the poverty would be more severe there.

Coming to village level, since organised community with its bargaining power can develop more infrastructure, the level of underdevelopment and poverty would be less there. In other words, within each area (region) we can have organised and unorganised communities and perhaps on that basis there would be variation in resource utilisation and hence poverty differentiation. Household level data can be categorised under the following groups:

(a) Size (Big, medium, small)
(b) Income (High, medium, low)
(c) Landholding (Large, medium, small)
(d) Education or literacy
(e) Caste.

Few households can be chosen for making family profile. Similar category families can be taken from different ecological areas for poverty comparison and to present possible geographic explanation. While interpreting poverty most emphasis was laid on 'land' and 'soil'. Because these in fact are the controlling factors of poverty.

Other controlling factors being 'labour' [including wage labour, area, number or percentage of workers of a household and effective labour (which looks at not only number or percentage of labourers but also their productivity along with percentage of dependent persons of the family)].

For correlating land and soil with poverty the researcher depended on two kinds of processed data. (i) Primary (Survey or Fieldwork) data, where weighted score of land and soil of each village was looked into, in order to assess and on that basis explain spatial variation in poverty. (ii) Secondary data where village level economic indicators through percentage of marginal farmers to total farmers have been shown.

Availability of work, within the village or outside, emerged another influencing factor of poverty. This may depend to large extent on the demand for agricultural or non-agricultural activities within the region. Since people are not capable or have capacity to undertake job in the urban settings, their economic depedence is largely on the local conditions. Therefore, incidence of poverty is heavily influenced by local employment, largely in agricultural operations.

Though 'Labour' itself is an economic entity, its availability, rent, labour productivity, nature and kind of labour migration all are essentially geographic in character. For measuring the impact of labour on poverty, *i.e.* correlating poverty with labour the author depended on secondary sources of data as well as primary fieldwork data. For example, secondary data (village level economic indicator indirectly takes into account the labour factor through the percentage of non-workers to workers of a village) and primary data gives us the village level household to household labour income and labour area apart from dependency, especially per capita labour income per labour and dependency ratio.

Since irrigation, not rainfall has decisive control over agricultural production and poverty that part of effort in correlating rainfall variation with poverty as a crude method of geographic study has been deliberately omitted.

So far as access to water or irrigation is concerned, not only the district has less irrigation facilities but data on irrigated area is scarce. So the only available secondary data (for example percentage of irrigated area per farmer in case of measuring high or low village level economic indicator) has been relied upon.

Data through primary survey on irrigation is meagre not because the surveyor did not enquired about artificial water supply but because whatever traditional sources of irrigation is available is very less than the requirement.

As far as forest is concerned we have only primary sources of data which indicates the annual income of a family from collection and sale of forest products. From this income the minor or major forest produces which helps in construction of house or household materials and for fire wood consumption have been excluded from total forest income of a family. On this basis one can also correlate spatial poverty with forest. Of course, income generated from forestry or forest related activities merely minimises the impact of poverty rather than it significantly controls poverty.

Villages having similar socio-economic indicators have been taken from different sub-micro regions and cross-comparison has been made in order to find if there is variation in poverty levels among or between them and the poverty variation have been explained on the basis of possible geographic factors which amply justifies 'Poverty is a function of regional characteristics'.

A question may arise while analysing poverty and its economic correlates, 'If economic factors are not sufficient to explain poverty can we say rest other factors are geographic and they are enough to explain poverty?

(i) Among the economic and social criteria 'land' and 'labour' seem to be the most important ones, but they are not enough to explain poverty. Therefore, geographic criteria have been taken into account. When one takes the whole district into consideration and correlation and chi square values of poverty and its correlates one finds 'land' and 'labour' have strong positive correlation with poverty in the context of Kalahandi and they are the major determinants of poverty.

Since it is a common observation that water scarcity too has a role in crop failure and hence overall poverty, we have chosen percentage of marginal farmers to total farmers, percentage of working members to non-working members and per household irrigation facilities as the major economic and household determinants of poverty. But, when we look the three variables across and between the regional poverty, they do not sufficiently explain spatial variation in poverty. But that does not imply they become less important in explaining poverty in general.

(ii) All the non-economic factors taken to be geographic because they have a dimension/coordinate element of space with them. The non-economic factors have an interplay and interaction among themselves *vis-à-vis* man in a given ecological set-up (region). That is why they are called geographic factors.

Otherwise there is no absolute parameter which is geographic. For example, soil is a pedological and water is a hydrological indicator and could be termed geographic if they vary (naturally) across distance with a definite corresponding impact on soil fertility, production and hence poverty, the interest of our investigation.

So, when the author holds all the non-economic factors are geographic it quite implies that they have got their designation and meaning changed since they operate interrelatedly and interdependently with different other elements in a given micro ecological set-up.

Our geography is as distinct as the regional delineation of characterised space. The fact that we have initiated our study within scientifically delineated micro regions, whatever factors do explain poverty in that very region are themselves geographic and those factors which do not, are non-geographic.

So with this very concept of geography the author argues that poverty is a function of geographic characteristics, apart from other characteristics.

Whatever true for the whole district is also true for each and every micro regions inside the district, but the impact of economic factors is overshadowed (not reduced in intensity) by the emerging geographic factors under analysis.

Constants to Study Regional Variation

There is positive correlation between poverty and its correlates which has been displayed in chapter 5. The regional variation in poverty is not adequately explained by its corresponding variation in economic and household indicators is what has been shown in the chapter 6. So the regional variation explained partly by regional factors. Let's now see what has been kept constant to study regional variation.

The delineation of the micro regions has been made scientific by superimposing development regions upon natural regions, the formation of which were based on wide range of criteria. Zero or negligible economic variation should produce zero or negligible economic impact regionally, which must be reflected in poverty. But this is not the case, it means the variation in poverty is contributed by other 'region specific' factors which are non-economic. When in a controlled regional set up we keep economic variables constant, we render them with an effect which is neutral. Consequently, its impact on poverty should be negligible which would have a correlation impact otherwise. Now, whatever change is marked in the level of poverty is due to other factors limited to hidden in the regional unit.

Like laboratory test on chemical reactions in which given temperature and pressure conditions point at a valid chemical law or reaction, regional unit is the laboratory and poverty is the result here. Under given household and economic conditions (which are constant), possible elements involved in the process have been taken to be geographic, showing the impact of geographic unit. Keeping aside constants, poverty variation over a statistical frame which the economists mostly adopt to examine economic laws, is statistics of different variables; but poverty variation over a geographic frame is geography of different variation.

The nature of attributing factors depends on the nature or type of frame or situation or circumstances. For example, the attributing factors would be political if the frame upon which the test is conducted is political. The impact of a particular industry on the economy of a democratic, socialistic or capitalistic country can be tested in a frame based on the political ideologies or the government of the country.

Similarly, the attributing factors would be geographic if the frame or division upon which the experiment conducted is geographic. To what extend the attributing factors are political or geographic depends on to what extent one's frame is scientific.

The total division of Kalahandi into nine regions would make it too complicated and too confusing an analysis. So for convenience we have condensed the divisions into three distinct regions to study poverty after development and production relation. In the similar triple division frame we would analyse government programmes evaluation. The compressed categories are: hilly-forested region, plain region and mixed region.

The impact of environment is a truth based on experience (observation). The author advances double ways of establishing the truth,

(i) by delineating the region scientifically, and
(ii) observing or measuring facts within the region to term the causes geographic which, of course, includes strictly different non-geographic reasons.

Geographic effect implies the sum total effect of an environment (of interacting and interrelated elements). Since the effect of economy is virtually zero or negligible or invariable, *i.e.* constant, the effect of a region could be 'regional', the reasons or factors of which are intertwined in a meaningful geographic unit.

When the author holds that poverty is geographic, it does not mean other non-geographic factors are unimportant or less important, rather they are more important but geographically. In other words, only within a delineated region, they (especially entitlement, deprivation, political economy) in addition to pure physical factors have a meaningful or logical explanation.

Reconciling Contradictory Conclusions

On the one hand, the author finds that 'land and labour' to be the most important correlates of poverty, in the next chapter he begins with the analysis showing that the economic indicators (land, irrigation and labour) are not explaining poverty.

The contradiction is obvious. In chapter 6 the influence of economic factors are determined taking poverty as an universal condition of the people of the district as a whole (*i.e.* without drawing any controlled line of geographic delimitation within it).

In chapter 7 we test the association between the basic economic criteria and poverty in a conditional situation, *i.e.* within delineated regions. And given the variations in topography, soil, water resources, vegetation etc. we uncover that there is responding differentiation in corresponding poverty. Without going into the traditional method of cross-comparison of poverty with the individual attributes of geography, the author compares poverty on the one side, with the rest of the geographic (regional) factors taken together, on the other. The conclusion of this chapter adds to that of the former, finally, to hold that poverty is not merely a function of community and household (*i.e* socio-economic) characteristics but also that of regional (geographic) characteristics.

Thus, instead of showing how poverty is separately related to individual geographic elements, we have tried to show how poverty is an amalgamated outcome of the combined impact of geographic circumstances. More effort is being given not to elaborate geographic components themselves, but to the exploration and establishment of linkages between local poverty and micro geography.

Organisation of the Study

The thesis constitutes nine chapters starting from 'Introduction' to 'Summary and Conclusion'. The introduction highlights Kalahandi as a problematic area in western Orissa which is one of the least developed regions of India. It outlines the objectives of the scheme and formulates hypotheses.

The second chapter on 'Conceptualisation' deals with the meaning, approaches (to measurement) and literature review of poverty and underdevelopment. The third chapter on 'Area of Study and Methodology' provides a detailed description of physical conditions, resource potentiality and their utilisation and the challenges faced by the people of Kalahandi. It also contains data base, sampling frame, justification for choice of development indicators, delineation of micro regions, chapterisation etc., apart from the techniques adopted for calculating and analysing poverty and underdevelopment.

The fourth chapter examines the spatial patterns of development and presents their analytical underpinnings.

The next chapter on 'Production Relation in Rural Kalahandi' looks into certain structural questions relating to class configuration, ownership of means of production, varied access to resources, constraints on the choice of the people, in-migration and out-migration, export, import and above all, the political economy which largely explains poverty and underdevelopment in a geographic framework.

Determining a poverty line on the basis of the study of Jain and Tendulkar, the subsequent chapter is devoted to empirical analysis. It has been divided into two sections. The initial section finds the correlation between dependent variable (poverty) with those of independent variables (social groups, land, labour and expenditure). The later section works out the values of correlation mainly between 'land' and 'soil', 'literacy' and 'social groups', after presenting justification for why 'land' is a proxy variable of poverty.

The chapter entitled 'Spatial Incidence of Poverty and its Economic Correlates' accounts for the variation in standard of living in the administrative unit. It shows the limitation of socio-economic factors and emerging influence of regional variables in explaining poverty.

The eighth chapter intends to analyse the efficacy of the governmental programmes in relieving poverty in various ecological micro regions. The governmental effort though gigantic in terms of resource allocation has, however, failed to mark a dent in the condition of the poor. The question remains if the existing institutions are unfavourable for the common people, major resources are inaccessible and the degraded environment irreparable, then how the people have been adapted to the changing circumstances ? The chapter 'Survival Strategy' perhaps answers this. It depicts three separate strategies of survival in the district, namely,

(i) Survival Strategies in forested hilly areas,
(ii) Survival Strategies in plain land, and
(iii) Survival Strategies in the region of mixed physical character.

The closing chapter summarises the thesis before making up a prescription for the economic recovery of Kalahandi. It offers a package to tackle the peculiar spatial problems, advising appropriate policy option to reduce regional disparities. And finally, it presents an alternative model for the development of the region.

One obvious question may arise as to why the chapter on development comes prior to that of poverty though the title of the thesis is "Poverty and Underdevelopment in Kalahandi : A Geographical Analysis". Firstly, underdevelopment economy is an economy of stagnation. Secondly, the study of development geography of the area Kalahandi reveals not only how backward the region is, but also how stark is its intra regional variation.

The presentation of developmental background smooth the analysis of spatial poverty which is the core theme of the dissertation, by logically laying a base for main theoretical construct. So, the primary topic on poverty is mid-placed after the topic on development thereby arranging the chapters, poverty and underdevelopment in a reverse manner of the expected order.

NOTES

1. Directorate of Agriculture and Food Production, Orissa, Bhubaneswar, 1986-87.
2. *District Gazetteer of Kalahandi*, 1981, p. 126.
3. Sen, A., *Poverty and Famines – An Essay on Entitlement and Deprivation*,

Clarendon Press, England, 1982.

4. Satpathy, R., "Kalahandi and Politics make volatile mix", *Times of India*, 14-8-1991, p.1.
5. *Gazetteer*,1981, *op.cit.* p. 138.
6. Satapathy, R., "Kalahandi and Politics make volatile mix", *op.cit.*
7. Pattanayak, P., "How green was your forest", *The Indian Express*, 30-6-91.
8. Fernandes, W. *et al.*, *Forests, Environment and Tribal Economy: Deforestation, Impoverishment and Marginalisation in Orissa*, Indian Social Institute, New Delhi, 1991, p.67.
9. A report published in *Times of India*, August 24th, 1991, P. Business Times and District Gazetteer, *op. cit.*, p.123.
10. Pattanayak, P., *How green was your forest*, *op. cit.*
11. Census of India, 1971, 1981 and 1991.
12. Sen, A., "India's Achievements over 50 years of independence," *Frontline*, August 22,1997.
13. Sen, A., "Individual Freedom : Basis for a social commitment", *The Times of India*, October 12,1998.

4

LEVELS OF DEVELOPMENT IN KALAHANDI

As discussed in the previous chapter, Kalahandi District is one of the least developed districts of India. In this chapter, it is proposed to examine the spatial patterns and underpinnings of development within the district.

On the basis of Composite indices[1] (the detailed calculation of which is already mentioned in the methodology section) the district has been divided into four development zones. The zones along with their respective composite indices are:

1. Depressed Area (score : less than 12.50)
2. Less Developed Area (score:12.50 to 14.50)
3. Moderately Developed Area (score:14.50 to 16.50)
4. Developed Area (score: more than 16.50)

(These terms are used to indicate only relative position. They are not absolute conditions.)

Each of the zones have been defined in terms of physical, socio-economic and demographic characteristics in the ensuing sub-sections, the exercise which ultimately reveals linkages between indicators of human environment and levels of development.

Depressed Area

Madanpur Rampur, Lanjigarh, Thuamul Rampur and Komna blocks fall under the Depressed Area category, which has Composite Development Index lower than 12.50. The Composite

Development Index of the individual blocks is 11.94, 10.73, 11.46 and 12.34 respectively.

Physical Characteristics

Madanpur Rampur area is dotted with low hills, with an average height of above 600 m. A number of small and medium rivers, streams, originating in the upland flow northeast following the general slope. The Utei and the Raul are the two right bank tributaries of the Tel which drain off this block. That the region was once quite precipitous, is reflected in the remnant of dense mixed jungles of Sal and Bamboo.

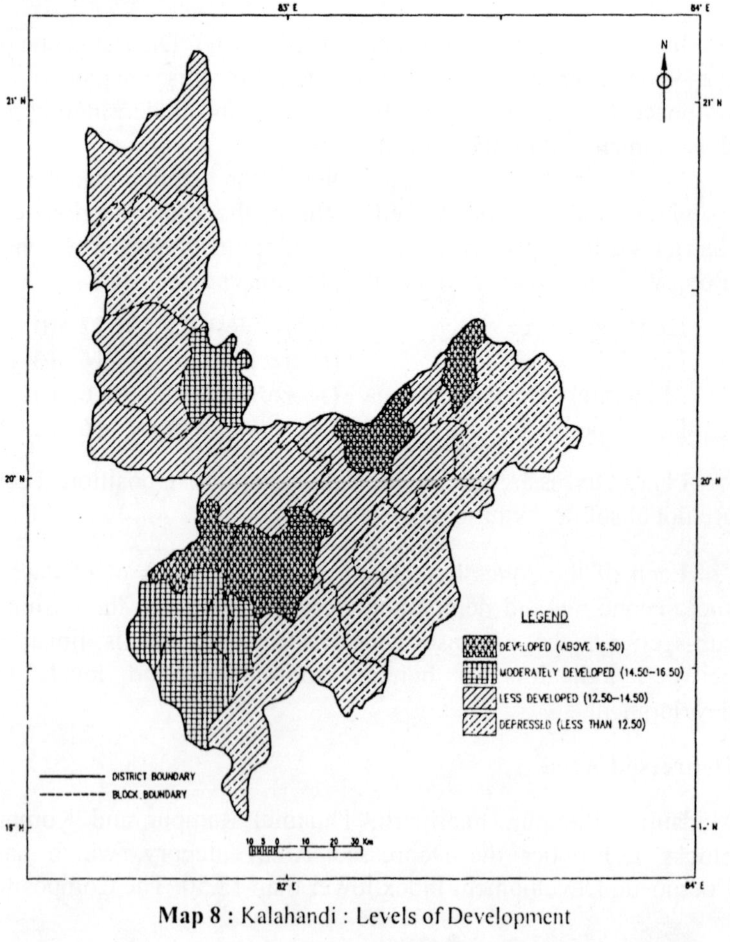

Map 8 : Kalahandi : Levels of Development

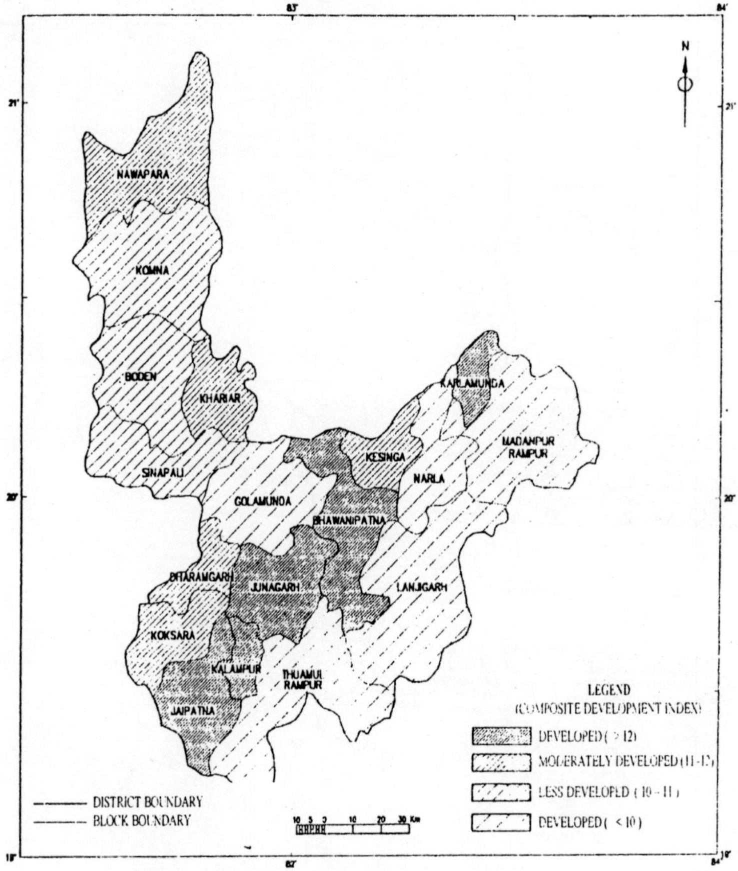

Map 9 : Kalahandi : Levels of Development (1997)

Komna block physiographically has two divisions : Hilly forested west and the Sunder valley of the east. Rough terrain, waterfalls dense mixed forests pose a major hurdle against the opening up of this area to development.

The average height of the twin blocks of Lanjigarh and Thuamul Rampur which constitute major part of Dharamgarh plateau is above 1000 metres. The sub-micro region is a combination of high hills which align from north to south, intervened by innumerable rivers and streams (such as the Indravati and the Ret). Many rivers originate in the plateau of the area itself. Some of them are south flowing, others north flowing.

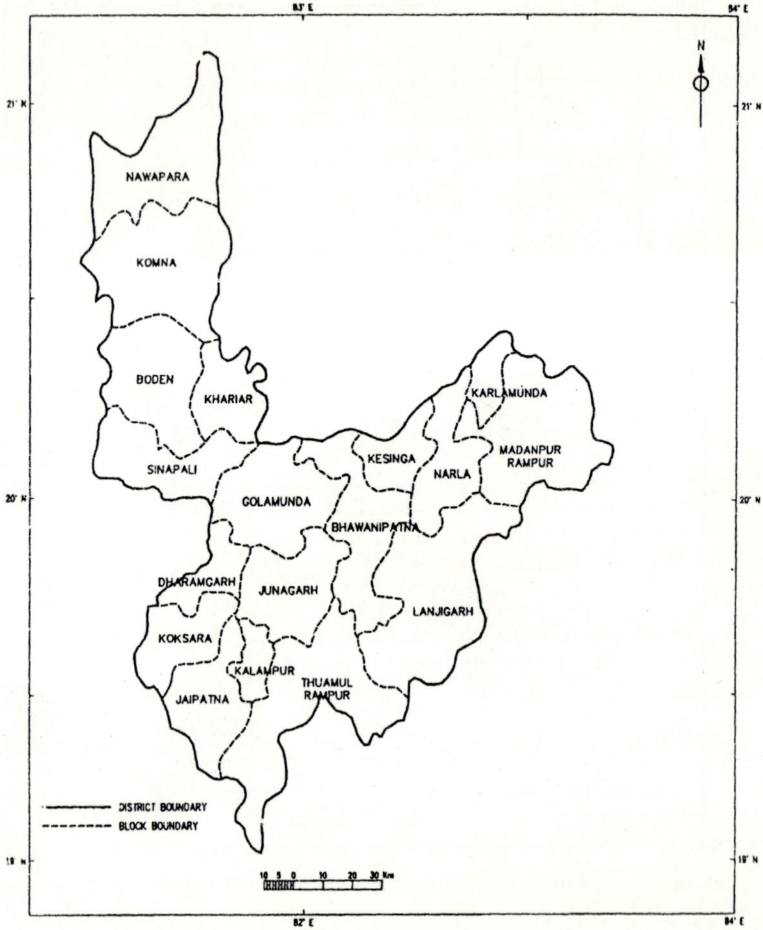

Map 10 : Kalahandi Blocks

Deep gullies, gorges, rugged terrain apart from dense forest cover hinders human movement and have left the region one of the most backward patch of Kalahandi. (See map on Natural Division of the district).

Economic (Agricultural) Characteristics

In terms of percentage of area under HYV crops to total cropped area Komna stands at 10.2, Lanjigarh at 6.1 only. Percentage of net irrigated area to net sown area is also low. This is 7.7 for Madanpur. Rampur, 10.2 for Komna and only 6.1 for Lanjigarh. The developmental index of irrigated area is low for Lanjigarh (0.5) and medium (0.84) for Komna. The index of proportional area under high yielding seeds is low for both Madanpur-Rampur (0.91) and Komna (0.80).

Madanpur Rampur is a drought prone block. It receives (limited) little water from Utei Irrigation Project. Orissa Lift Irrigation Survey Report considered more than 2.5 thousand dug wells feasible in this block. The soil here is alluvial, sandy and sandy loam. Fragmented occurrence of red colour laterite layer are found in hilly uplands. Silica is leached from the soil and so it is less fertile. On the narrow valleys usual plough cultivation and on the hill slopes occasional *Jhum* and Terrace cultivation are in practice. Local and long duration paddy are grown apart from maize, ragi, millets, *bajra* and pulses. Lately, High Yielding Varieties of wheat, groundnut and potato have been taken up in irrigated areas. Though the area has excellent potential for horticulture no systematic effort is being made in this direction. Rice, maize, bajra are the staple food of the people of Madanpur-Rampur forested upland. Scope for mechanization of farmers is rather limited except in case of Saidalanga Gram Panchayat where Utei Medium Irrigation Project supplies water for cultivation.

The hilly block of Komna is also drought prone. The alluvial soil and black cotton soil are most widespread. Black cotton soil of broken country is deeper and richer in iron, lime, magnesium, aluminium and potash. It is highly retentive of moisture. But the soil is poor in phosphorous. Laterite and red soil are noticed in the slopes and ridges.

Agriculture is the only subsistence economy of the people. The tribes such as the Bhunjias are in the habit of carrying on shifting cultivation which they call *Bewar*. Besides shifting cultivation wet cultivation in the plains is still in practice. Paddy is grown in the plains. It is sown broadcast in the lands which are situated at the higher level where there is no source of water for irrigation. In the lands of the valley transplantation are done after ploughing, puddling and levelling. Local varieties of paddy such as *Sankari, Banskanthia, Dubraj, Jalli, Setka, Kuli, Bairiguntha* are commonly used. HYV seed use is still limited to specific non-tribal plain groups. Almost all the lands are rain fed. Maize and pulses are produced substantially. Bhunjias cultivate upland *artijami* and prepare kitchen garden *(barijami).* Few households are lucky enough to have dug wells allotted by government. They produce cash crops like sugarcane. Vegetables like banana, brinjal, tomato, cabbage and chilly in seated kitchen gardens. But in most cases either the wells have not been dug or they have been left unused. Fishing, hunting and root collection are common practices of the people of the area.

Like other two blocks Thuamul Rampur and Lanjigarh are also drought prone, though the former receives maximum amount of rainfall in the whole district. Sandy loam soil occurs in Lanjigarh and to some extent in Thuamul Rampur. This soil is suitable for oilseeds and root crops. According to Orissa Irrigation Project Survey more than 3.5 thousand dug wells are feasible in both the blocks which fall in the natural division of Dharamgarh plateau. In sharp contrast with neighbouring Tel Hatti basin which is more prosperous agriculturally, cultivation here is outmoded (*i.e. Jhum* practised). Maize is irregularly grown on the hill slopes. Jowar, *arhar,* blackgram, niger, mustard, castor, ginger, turmeric and minor millets are often raised in a mixed pattern. Acute soil erosion takes place after the loss of forest cover due to *podu.*

Lanjigarh is a hilly-cum-plains block with its 75 percentage of geographical area being covered by hills and forests. More than 80 percentage of its workers are engaged in agriculture which is the primary occupation of the people of the region. Crops grown in the area includes paddy, ragi, millets, maize pulses and oilseeds in addition to high yielding paddy (in small patches in Lanjigarh Gram Panchayat where cross bunds have been constructed across the perennial hill streams to provide irrigation.) (See Appendix – 4, p.349)

Thuamul Rampur is rather an isolated block. 92 per cent of its physiographic area is covered with hills and forests. Here, agriculture is also primary occupation of the people. Local variety of paddy, ragi, minor millets, pulses, oilseeds are produced domestically. HYV paddy is also grown but in small patches around perennial hill streams and *nallahs.* The monsoon potato is grown in Karlapat Gram Panchayat. Excepting few hill streams and tanks, there is no irrigation of any significance.

Climate and topography of Lanjigarh and Thuamul Rampur are quite favourable for the production of beverages, mango, banana, pineapple, papaya, orange, guava and jackfruits. Potential for developing horticulture is tremendous. But no planned initiative has ever been made in this direction. In absence of marketing facilities major part of the local products are collected by the middle men at very low prices and are exported outside in huge quantities. This is one of the reasons of backwardness of the twin blocks of southern Kalahandi.

Social Characteristics

In terms of social variables (except medical facilities) this economic division is also most underdeveloped. The index of hospital facilities for Rampur and Lanjigarh is low, 0.71 and 0.22 respectively. It is medium for Komna (0.83). Population per medical institution in Madanpur Rampur, Lanjigarh, Thuamul Rampur and Komna are 28.4 thousands, 21.6 thousands, 22.1 thousands, 28.9 thousands respectively. Compared to most other blocks these blocks are better placed only in terms of medical facilities. The percentage figure of literacy for corresponding blocks are 16.9, 10.4, 5.4, and 15.8 only. Looking to the percentage of villages electrified Thuamul Rampur has not even a single such village. The value is only 2.3 for Lanjigarh, 7.7 for Madanpur Rampur, and 14.1 for Komna. Except Komna (which has medium index) all the other three blocks have low indices in electrified villages. Villages having drinking water facilities are 19.5 per cent, 25.3 per cent, 13.7 per cent and 36.2 per cent in Madanpur Rampur, Lanjigarh, Thuamul Rampur and Komna respectively. Barring Lanjigarh rest of the blocks exhibit poor index of drinking water supply. One of the main reasons for such low social variables could be availability of few *pucca* road facilities, which is 7.0 per cent in Madanpur Rampur, 5.5 in Lanjigarh, 14.1 in Komna and almost nil in Thuamul Rampur. The index with respect to the *pucca* road linked villages happened to be the lowest in Lanjigarh and Thuamul Rampur in the whole district.

Low density of road network, less number of electrified

villages and poor literacy justify why the four blocks are highly backward. Madanpur Rampur blocks lack transport facilities in almost 2/3rd of its area. There is no organized storing and marketing facilities, Service Cooperative Societies to supply seeds, fertilizers, pesticides, etc.

Madanpur Rampur is a hilly-cum-plain and forested area about 65 per cent of its geographical area is covered with forests. Rampur, the block headquarter is connected with Bhawanipatna by an all weather motorable road. Except Rampur Madanpur and Saidalanga other towns are inaccessible during monsoon. State Highway No. 1 crosses this block in north-south direction. Another metalled road passes in east west direction. Apart from these, footpaths and cart-tracks are the only means of communication in forested hilly lands. Thus from transport and communication point of view the block is very underdeveloped.

Because of physical inaccessibility large part of western Komna is devoid of any kind of metalled road. On the valley of Sundar, State Highway No. 3 runs parallel to the river in north-south direction.

Equally worse is the condition of twin blocks of Dharamgarh Plateau, (*i.e.* Lanjigarh and Thuamul Rampur). State Highways No. 2 and No. 6 cross the region. Only after 1982-83 the block headquarter Thuamul Rampur became connected with Bhawani-patana by a metalled road. Otherwise footpaths and carttracks have been the main means of communication until recently.

Demographic Characteristics

Percentage of SC population and working population are high and density of population is low. These further indicates very low degree of development of the area. For example, the percentage of scheduled caste population in Lanjigarh, Thuamul Rampur, Komna and Madanpur Rampur are 53.8, 53.4, 46.8 and 37.3 respectively. Percentage of working population barring Madanpur Rampur is high if not very high in Lanjigarh (36.3), Thuamul Rampur (36.8) and Komna (33.9). The ST population index is low for Lanjigarh (0.67) and Komna (0.76).

Thus because of physiographic hindrances, insufficiently exploited and primitive nature of farming system, predominance of middle men in absence of any organised storing and marketing facilities, large illiteracy, low electricity and drinking water facilities and very poor road linkages, this geo-economic division is most Underdeveloped or Depressed Section in the underdeveloped district of Kalahandi. Turning from region of lowest level development, depiction of the features of region of highest development is to be made to mark a line of sharp distinction between them. Later, regions of moderate development values have been picked up to draw overall conclusions.

Developed Area

This group of blocks having Composite Development Index (CDI) more than 16.50 show least underdevelopment. The blocks (with their individual CDI are Kesinga (16.53), Junagarh (16.67), Karlamunda (18.81), Dharamgarh (18.86). The group, in sharp contrast with the previous one, is most developed among all the developmental regions of Kalahandi.

Physical Characteristics

Dharamgarh and Junagarh are bounded by hills on the western and eastern side. The northern side is opened towards Udanti Basin and the southern side towards the wider Tel Hatti Basin of Kalampur, Jaipatna and Koksara. The blocks are devoid of any kind of forests. The undulating plains of Kesinga and Karlamunda are located to the south of river Tel in northeastern Kalahandi. They are separated by intervening Narla block.

Demographic Characteristics

High population density of this division (*i.e.* Dharamgargh 233 persons/sq. km. and Kesinga 194 persons/sq.km.) reflects its better economic condition. Large chunk of the population belongs to general caste, most of whom have external origin. This means they are not the native or original inhabitants of Kalahandi. Share of tribal population is not that high. The percentages of SC is highest in Kesinga (74.7). In rest of the blocks the percentages are very low, giving further indication of better economic situation of the region. Given below are the two tables of agricultural development.

Economic (Agricultural) Characteristics

Kesinga and Karlamunda have high developmental index in cropping intensity. Dharamgarh and Junagarh have moderate and high development indices respectively in area under HYV crops. As far as percentage of Net Irrigated Area to Area Sown is concerned, Junagarh has developmental index and rest three blocks have medium developmental indices. Comparing Table 4.1 with Table 4.6 we find this developmental division under consideration is moderately developed in agriculture in the whole district.

Table 4.1: Agricultural Indicators of developed area, Kalahandi

Blocks	Cropping Intensity	%age of area under HYV Crops to total cropped area	%age of Net Irrigated Area to area sown
Kesinga	140	9.5	15.2
Karlamunda	146	11	45.6
Dharamgarh	161	10.9	5.1
Junagarh	179	14	14.8

Source : *District Statistical Handbook*, Kalahandi, 1989-90.

Dharamgarh and Junagarh are located in Tel-Hatti basin which is known as the "Rice Bowl" of Kalahandi. The basin is termed so because it produces surplus rice under favourable monsoon condition. Though flood prone this physical part has best quality arable lands, inhabited by a number of progressive (Kulta and other) farmers. Of course, irrigation in general is lacking. Still then provision of artificial water supply, use of chemical fertilizer and modern implements are not uncommon. There are a number of tanks of different sizes in these two blocks. These tanks apart from providing facilities for irrigation, serve the purpose of drinking, bathing and pisciculture. A number of wells are also used for similar purposes.

River Tel offers the scope of lift irrigation. The ground water potential is already exploited in some villages. The seed multiplication plant of Kesinga supplies high yielding varieties of seeds not only to that block but also to Dharamgarh and Junagarh. High yielding varieties of crops and paddy are grown in *Rabi* season in areas of assured irrigation. *Bajra*, and pulses are produced substantially. Even if allied agricultural activities on a commercial scale is not yet developed, cattle rearing, goat rearing and poultry keeping are noticed to be popular subsidiary occupations. The villagers sell milk in towns. There is, however, no organized marketing or purchasing facility.

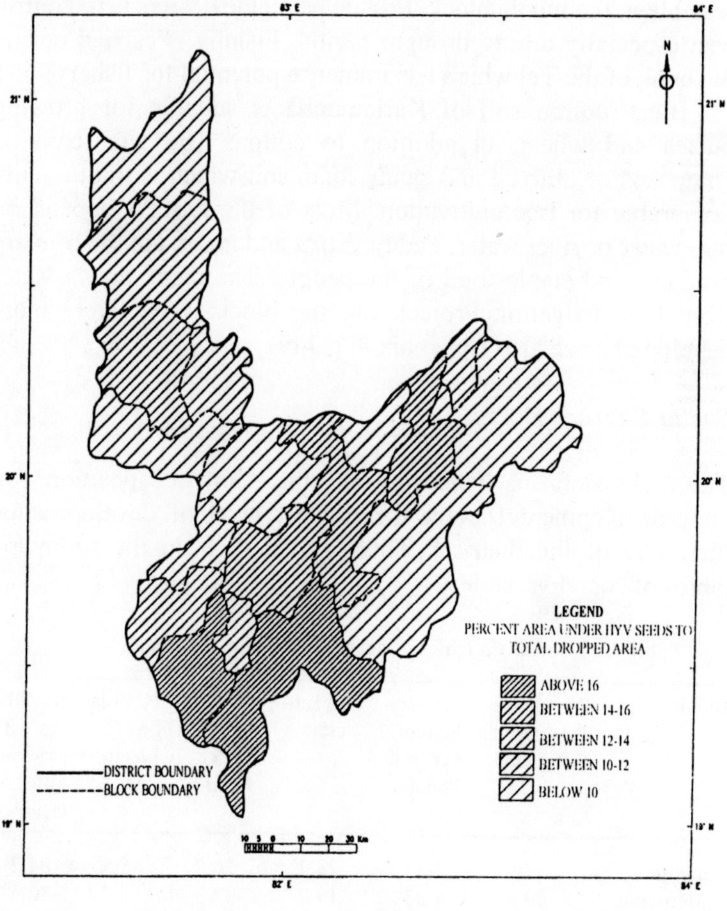

Map 11 : Kalahandi : Area Under High Yielding Varieties of Seeds

In Kesinga soil is red and yellow (which are of medium quality). About half of the cultivated land is under double cropping and a significant portion of land is under HYV. Sixty per cent land under cereals raise paddy only (Pattnaik Manjurani study). Income of the people is supplemented by pulses, oilseeds and cash crops which are grown more extensively. In not more than one-fourth of the total area irrigation facilities are available. A large (surface underground) water potential is yet to be utilised. More than one thousand dug wells are considered feasible in the whole block. Private pesticide dealers help control pest especially during drought period. Fishing is carried out on the bank of the Tel which has immense potential for fishery.

Black cotton soil of Karlamunda is suitable for growing pulses and wheat, in addition to cotton. The Utai bank is composed of alluvial and sandy loam soil which is traditionally favourable for rice cultivation. Most of the farmers depend on rain water or river water. Paddy, *bajra* and maize are the primary products and staple food of the people. The block draws water from Utai Irrigation Project. So, the block is relatively more developed. (See also Appendix 4, p.349)

Social Characteristics

This division is placed at the lowest position of underdevelopment (*i.e.* in the highest level of developmental hierarchy of the district). This is evident from the following tables of social variables.

Table 4.2 : Social Variables of developed region, Kalahandi

Block	Population Per Medical Institution	Primary School per '000 Population	% Literate	% Villages with Pucca Road	% Villages Electrified	% Villages with Drinking water facility
Kesinga	37.5	1.33	23.2	26.7	45.5	84.2
Karlamunda	20.8	1.33	19.0	32.3	7.7	82.3
Dharamgarh	42.0	1.06	19.6	26.1	89.9	79.7
Junagarh	53.6	1.29	19.7	18.3	60.4	23.4

Source : *Statistical Handbook*, 1989-90.

Except "number of primary schools per thousand population" and "population per medical institution" the blocks are quite developed in all other criteria. Amongst all the above blocks Dharamgarh has very high medical facilities. Karlamunda is the lone block that shows high schooling facilities. [Refer the Development Index Table].

Table 4.3: Social Variables for the Kalahandi district

Blocks	Population per Medical Centre	Primary School per '000 Population	%of Literates	% of villages with Pucca Road	% of Villages Electrified	% of Villages With Drinking water
Bh. patna	11.6	1.70	18.9	14.8	28.4	25.3
Kesinga	37.5	1.33	23.2	26.7	45.5	84.2
Narla	43.1	1.90	24.2	16.5	8.2	67.0
M.Rampur	28.4	1.46	15.9	7.0	7.7	19.5
Karlamunda	20.8	1.33	19.0	32.3	7.7	82.2
Lanjigarh	21.6	1.72	10.4	5.5	21.3	25.0
Th. Rampur	22.1	1.50	5.4	0	0	13.4
Dharamgarh	42.0	1.06	19.6	16 .1	89.9	79.7
Junagarh	53.6	1.29	19.7	18.3	60.4	23.4
Jaipatna	46.8	1.20	16.3	12.0	6.5	77.2
Koksara	18.1	1.17	9.8	13.9	21.5	27.7
Kalampur	39.1	1.64	35.2	16.7	14.8	35.2
Golamunada	18.9	2.16	16.8	7.8	10.6	49.7
Nawapara	22.1	1.82	14.5	8.4	19.8	35.9
Komna	28.9	1.59	15.8	14.1	12.8	36.2
Khariar	34.4	1.57	12.1	21.4	33.0	27.7
Sinapali	32.0	1.50	17.4	8.5	7.6	84.8
Boden	58.6	1.45	14.4	7.3	6.3	76.0

Source : *District Statistical Handbook* , Kalahandi, 1989-90.

Economic (Industrial) Characteristics

Kesinga town has a few small scale industries such as rice mills and oil mills and a seed multiplication plant. Being one of the two important railway towns, it handles heavy goods and passenger traffic and performs the role of a relatively advanced centre (node) for trade and commerce in the backward district. This town joins Rupra road, a small railway station south of it. For want of bridges over the river Tel some of the existing roads continue to be fair weather roads, impeding the traffic flow and marketing of agricultural produce.

Because of recurring droughts, low agricultural yields and poor infrastructural facilities economic climate is not that conducive for the growth of small and medium industries in Dahramgarh and Junagarh. However, a few industries like rice mills, rice hullers, household industries such as weaving, carpentry, pottery and rope making are found over the area in scattered pockets. Junagarh town itself is the centre of industries and trade. It is a well developed commercial node. Most of the existing small scale industries (such as rice and oil mills) are of conventional type.

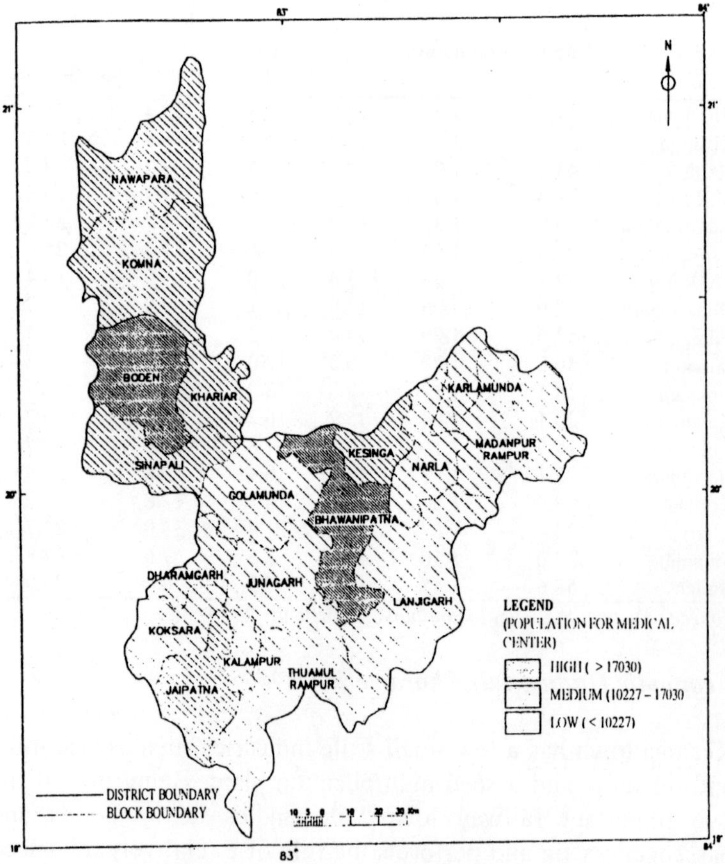

Map 12 : Kalahandi : Medical Centre (1997)

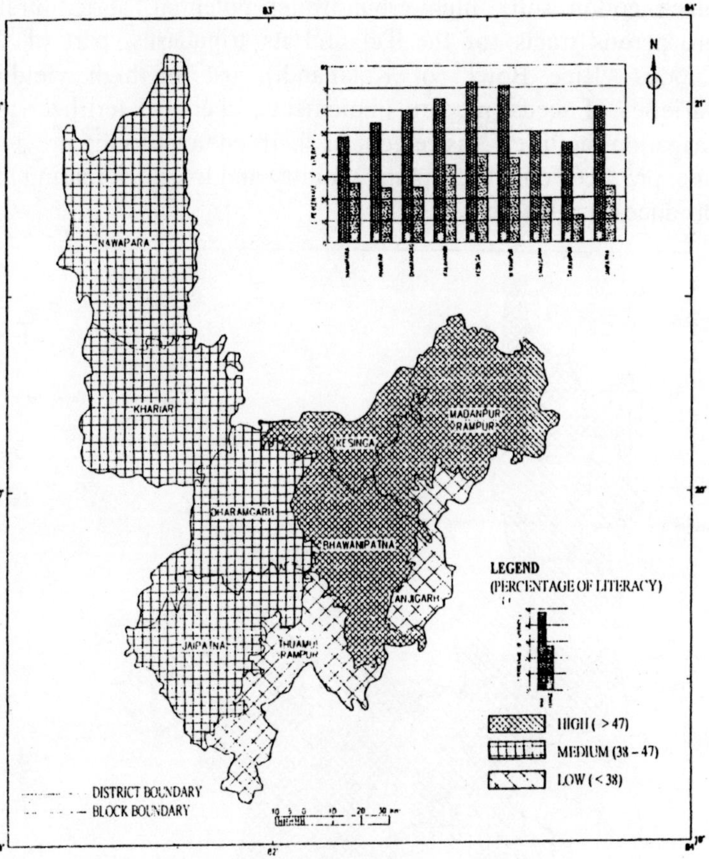

Map 13 : Kalahandi : Literacy (2001)

Dharamgarh is a small scale trading and commercial centre. Flow of traffic and agricultural produce into the town is disrupted during rainy season due to the absence of any bridge over the river Tel. This town is connected with Bhawanipatna, the district headquarter by an all weather road. The road density is maximum in Kesinga, Karlamunda, Dharamgarh and Junagarh, indicating high level of areal development.

To sum up, the minimum degree of backwardness of this part of the district is reflected by the (micro regions) high population density, large exotic (general class) population and inhabitation of progressive "Kulta" farmers. Because of the undulating flood plains, fertile lands (of alluvial, sandy loam and black cotton soil), high groundwater potential, agriculturally prosperous tracts (of the Tel and its tributaries, part of the famous "Rice Bowl" of Kalahandi), use of high yielding varieties of seeds, modern implements, chemical fertilizer and irrigation facilities, this region, in sharp contrast to the previous one, practices double cropping, poultry and livestock rearing and produces surplus rice.

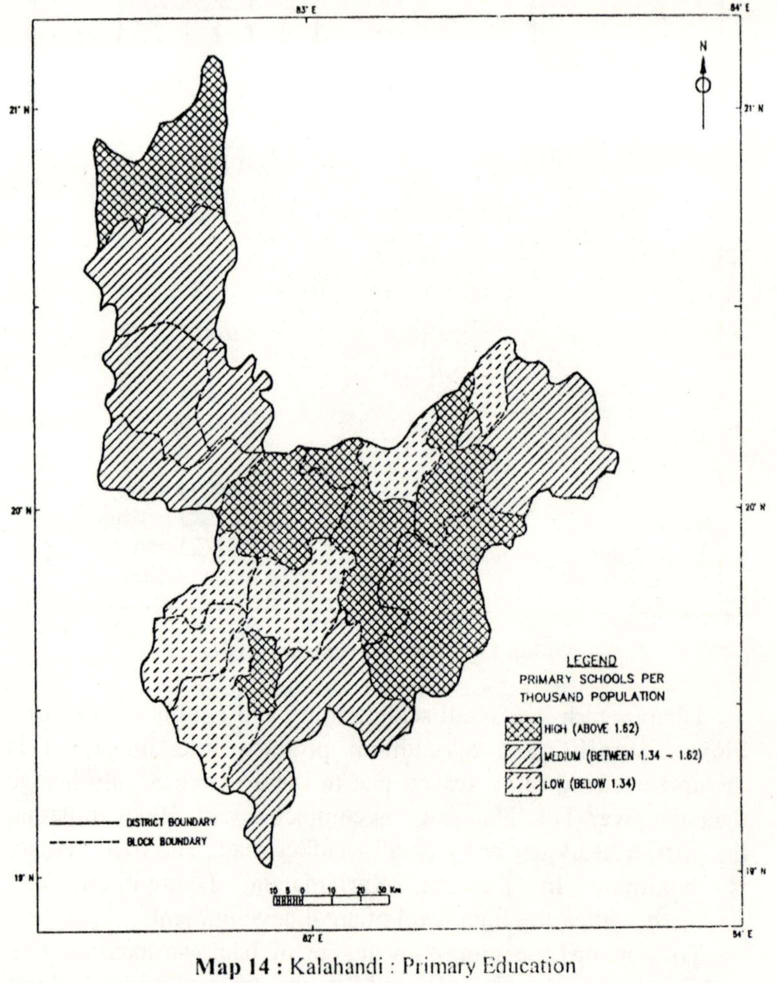

Map 14 : Kalahandi : Primary Education

The ecological area has easy accessibility with far better infrastructure for electricity and drinking water. It has a number of small scale industries and trading centres.

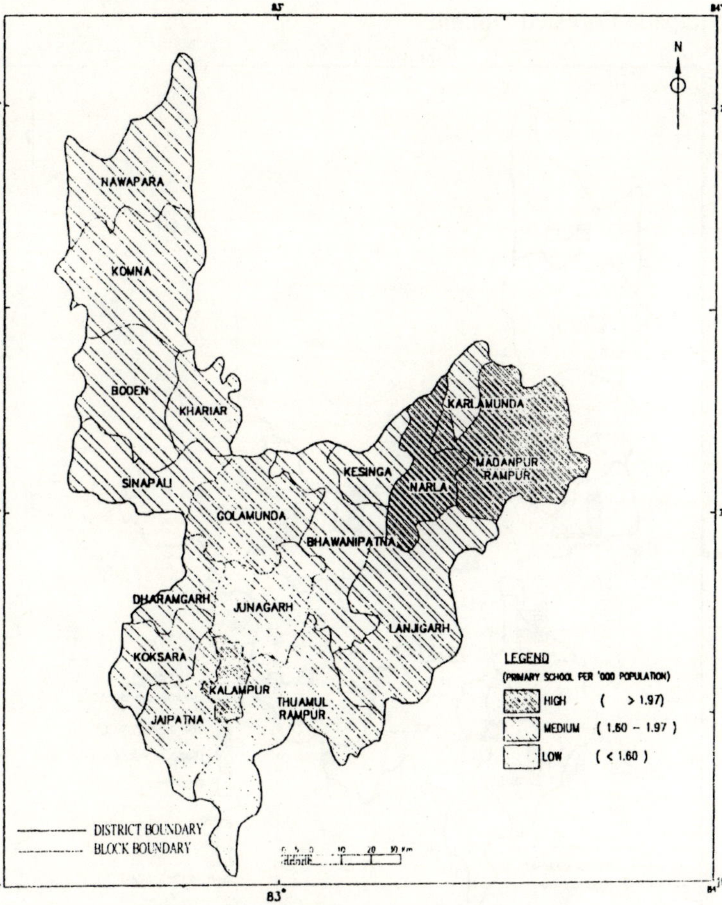

Map 15 : Kalahandi : Primary Schools (1997)

Moderately Developed Area

Jaipatna, Koksar, Kalampur and Khariar blocks fall under "Moderately Developed Area" whose developmental index ranges between 14.50 and 16.50. The group (of blocks) occupies second position in the developmental hierarchy. The first three blocks, i.e. Jaipatna, Koksara and Kalampur are located together in the southern part of Tel-Hatti basin. Only very small part of Jaipatna and Koksara are situated in the Dharamgarh plateau which is most underdeveloped. Khariar block (CDI 15.53) is a segregated (and distant) portion of this main area. Part of Khariar lies in the Tel valley and the south western part is covered by Nuapada Forested Upland.

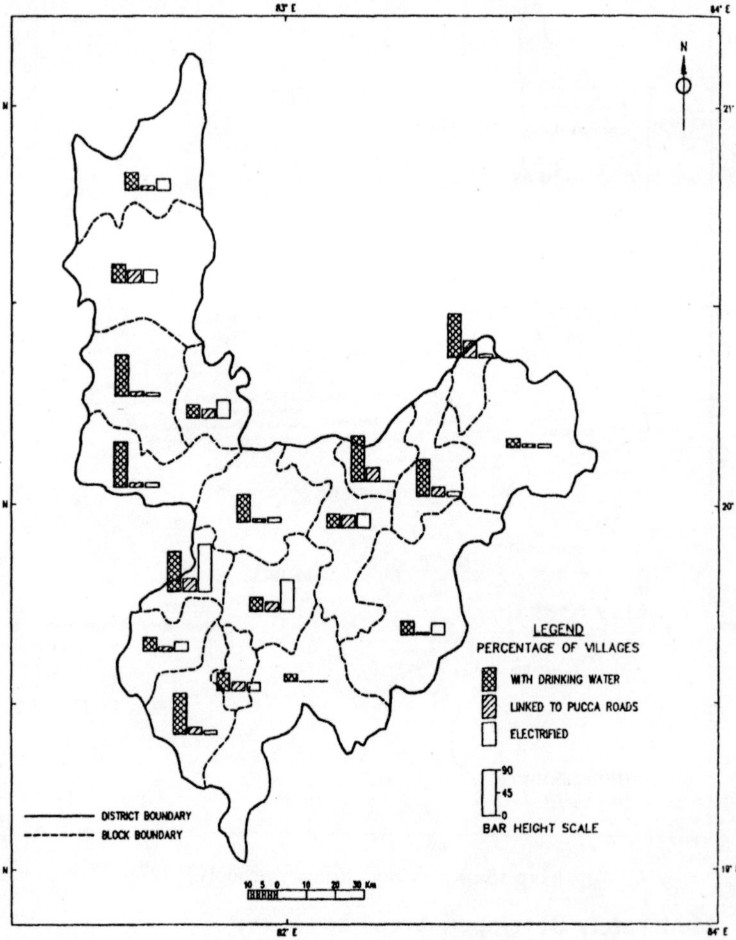

Map 16 : Kalahandi : Infrastructure

Physical Characteristics

The principal area of this developmental division lies in the Hatti-Behera depositional basin, surrounded by high hills in all sides except north. The Nawarangpur plateau (610 m.) is in the west. The basin is not uniform physiographically. Scattered hills and intervening valleys break the monotony of the plain which is one of the most fertile tract of Kalahandi. A small patch of south-eastern side has a series of longitudinal hills. Koksar-Ampani plain, Dharamgarh plains and Sahajkhol hilly areas which are drained by the Behera and the Motter rivers form integral part of this sub-micro region.

Western Khariar is composed of small denuded hillocks, forests and the eastern Khariar is a plain carved out by the Sundar. The block tilts gradually towards southeast. Mixed dense jungles and open forests cover the hilly areas. Small water falls often act as source of water.

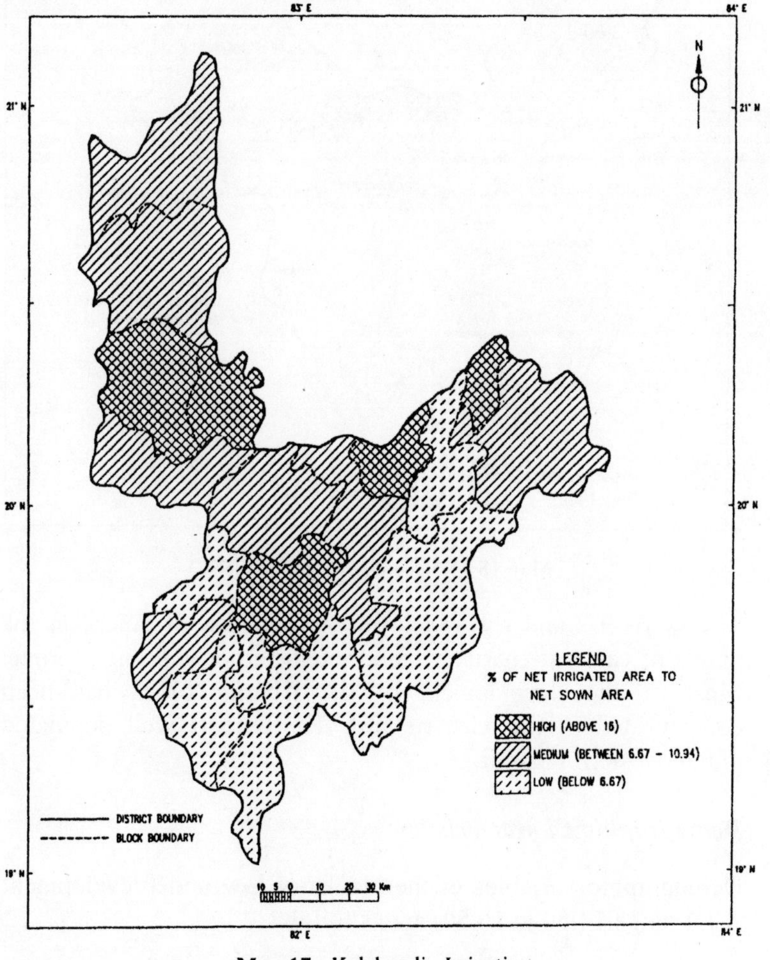

Map 17 : Kalahandi : Irrigation

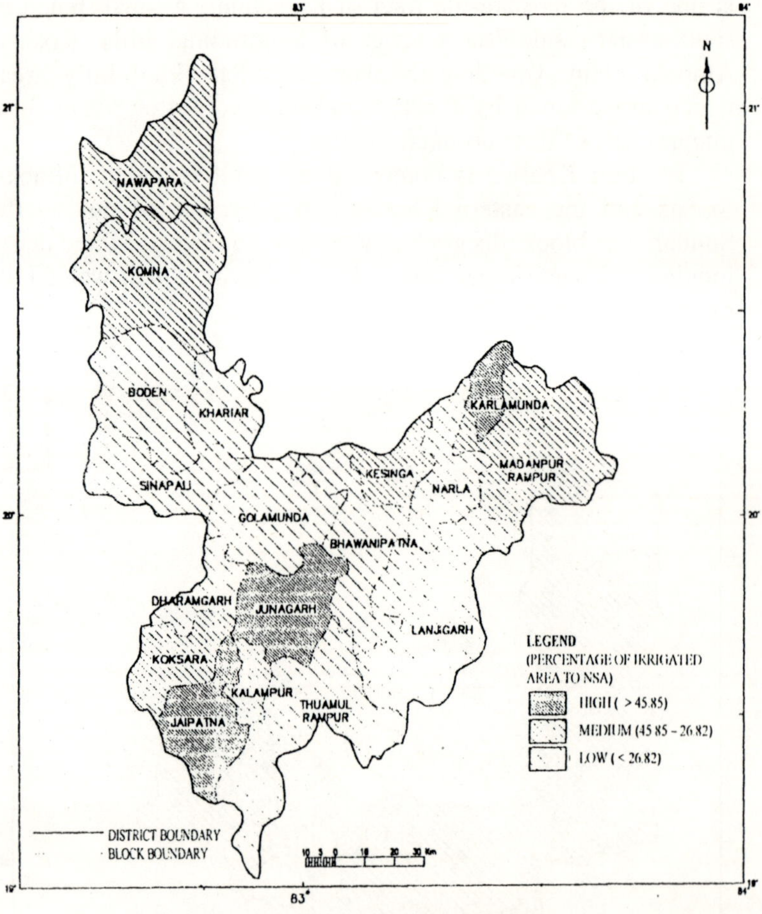

Map 18 : Kalahandi : Irrigation (1997)

As river Sundar flows towards southeast, it enters in the plains of eastern Khariar which though fertile is drought prone. Most of the development of the Khariar block has been concentrated in this eastern part. The area is well populated unlike western Khariar.

Demographic Characteristics

Demographic variables of the blocks of low underdevelopment (CDI range 14.50 to 16.50) are as follows:

Table 4.4: Demographic Variables, Division of Moderately Developed Area, Kalahandi

Blocks	Population Density	%age of ST Population	%age of SC Population	% of working Population
Koksar	212	14.0	20.1	38.2
Kalampur	253	15.4	25.8	38.8
Jaipatna	237	10.7	23.5	31.0
Khariar	218	15.2	29.3	34.0

Source: *District Census Handbook*, 1989-90.

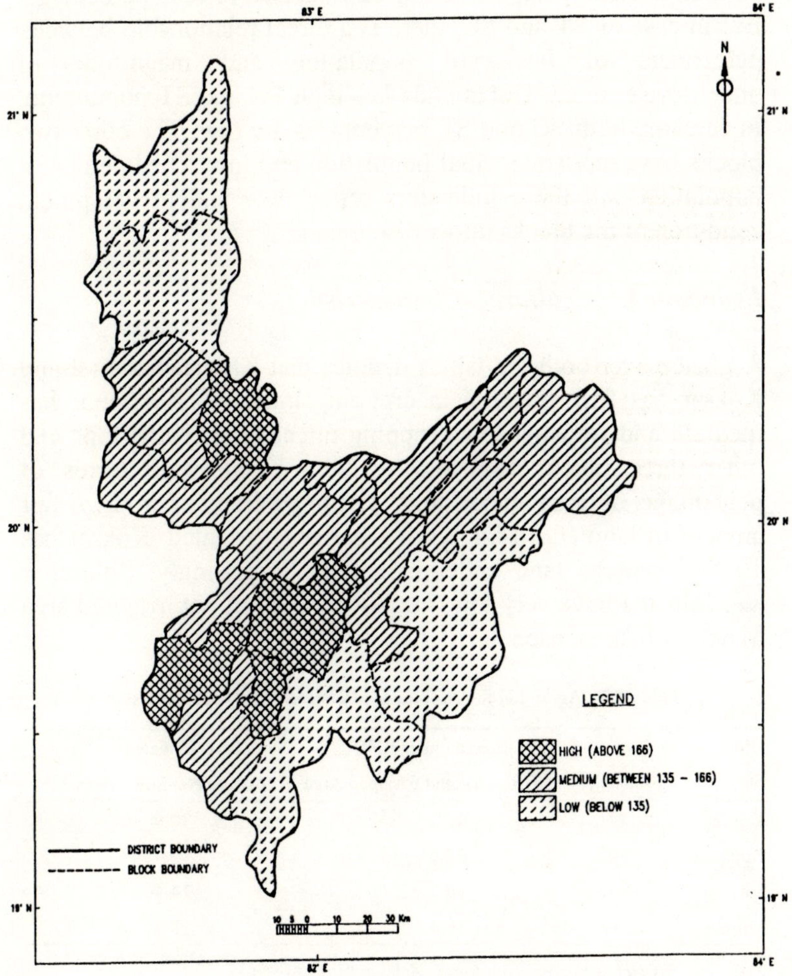

Map 19 : Kalahandi : Cropping Intensity

Amongst all the blocks Kalampur tops, while Jaipatna ranks second position, Khariar fourth position and Koksar fifth position in population density. Higher the (population) density lower is the degree of underdevelopment. This seems to be true for the backward district Kalahandi. This inverse relation could also be true for working population. Golamunda has highest working population (*i.e.* 60.9 in the whole district). Koksar and Kalampur have second and third highest percentage of working population. Jaipatna, however, has second lowest percentage. But in case of ST and SC, there is a direct relationship between percentage of backward population and magnitude of underdevelopment. Golamunda has high SC and ST population. In Jaipatna both SC and ST percentages are low. The other two blocks have moderate tribal population and low scheduled caste population. All these indicators reflect low underdevelopment condition of the blocks under discussion.

Economic (Agricultural) Characteristics

A glance over both the tables denotes that Khariar has first and Koksar has fifth position in cropping intensity. Kalampur has medium and Jaipatna low cropping intensity. Jaipatna tops and other three blocks fall into medium category in terms of percentage of area under high yielding variety of crops. A fair amount of land (*i.e.* 14.4 %) of Khariar is irrigated. Koksar has 10.9 percentage land under irrigation. Surprisingly, Kalampur and Jaipatna have very low, *i.e.* 2.4 per cent of net irrigated area to net sown area, each.

Table 4.5 : Agricultural Variables of Moderately Developed Division

Block	Cropping Intensity	% of area under HYV Crops to total Cropped Area	% Net Irrigated Area to Net Sown Area
Koksar	171	13.5	10.9
Kalampur	167	12.6	2.4
Khariar	196	10.1	14.4
Jaipatna	143	19.3	2.4

Source: *District Statistical Handbook*, Kalahandi, 1989-90.

Table 4.6 : Agricultural Variables of all the Blocks of the District

Blocks	Cropping Intensity	% of Area Under HYV Crops to Total Cropped Area	% of Net irrigated Area to Net Area Sown
Bh.patna	164	15.5	8.0
Junagarh	179	14.0	14.8
Jaipatna	143	19.3	2.4
Koksara	171	13.5	10.9
Kalampur	167	12.6	2.4
Golamunada	152	8.5	8.0
Nawapara	125	7.6	10.4
Komna	127	10.2	9.1
Khariar	196	10.1	14.4
Sinapali	146	4.2	8.9
Boden	157	12.8	12.1

Source: *District Statistical Handbook*, Kalahandi, 1989-90.

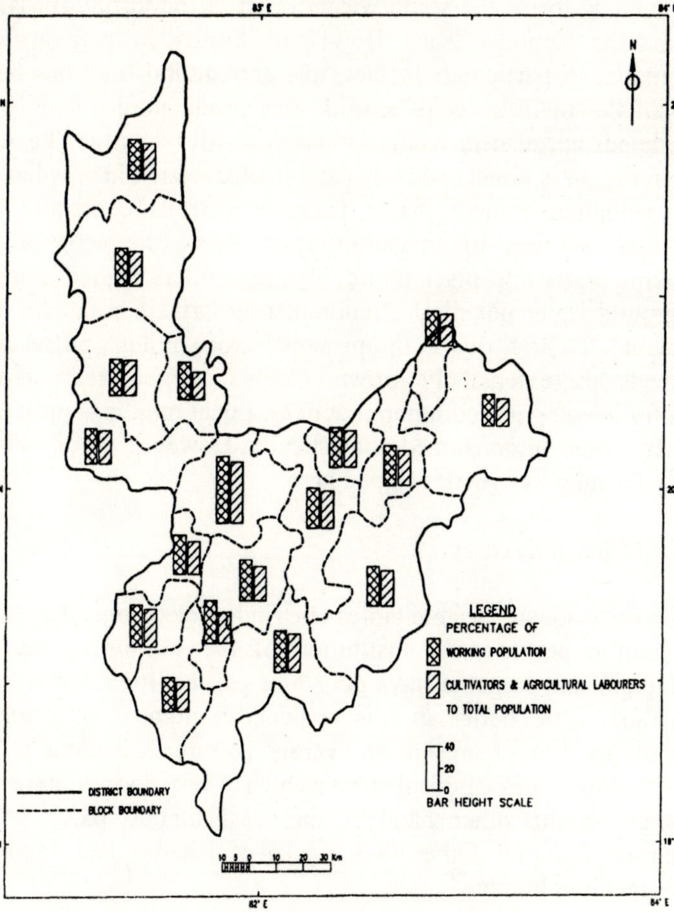

Map 20 : Kalahandi : Agricultural Population

Agriculture is the primary occupation of Khariar. Tanks, rivers and rivulets are utilised to supply water to cultivating fields. Rice, maize, *bajra* and variety of vegetables are main agricultural products. Khariar Seed Multiplication Plant produces HYV seeds for local farmers. (See Appendix 4 p.349) On the black soils of the plain lands cotton and wheat area grown. Maize and pulses are grown in the hilly part of western Khariar. Frequent drought in the second year has severely affected the crops in the area. Otherwise, the block is one of the most productive patch of Kalahandi.

The combined (joint) area of Koksar, Kalampur and Golamunda forms the south western part of the fertile Tel-Hatti basin, the famous "Rice Bowl" of Orissa in general and Kalahandi in particular. In fact, this agricultural tract has been one of the main areas of surplus rice production, not only in Kalahandi but also in whole Orissa state till recently. The sub-micro region is almost entirely rural in character. There is hardly any irrigation project, here. Tanks and wells constitute the principal sources of irrigation apart from (the sources of) drinking water and pisciculture. The region has a good amount of ground water potential. Predominating farmers are small and marginal. Though rice is the principal crop, millets, pulses and oilseeds are extensively grown. Cattle and goat rearing and poultry keeping are common practices. Local milk is supplied to nearby towns or consumed domestically. However, no organised dairy farming has yet developed here.

Social Characteristics

Looking to social variable tables one finds Koksar tops the list of population per medical institution of the sub micro region. Kalampur and Jaipatna have poor medical facilities. Khariar, is somehow little better in this respect. In number of primary schools the blocks present an average picture. Kalampur is the most literate block of this district (which is very poor in literacy). Koksar on the other hand is the least literate block, after Thuamul Rampur. Other two blocks of Khariar and Jaipatna have medium literacy.

Economic (Industrial) Characteristics

Khariar and Kalampur have a good percentage of villages linked with *pucca* road. Footpaths and unmetalled roads are the only means of communication in rural areas. The geographical inaccessibility of south-western and western part of Koksar, Kalampur and Jaiptana section hinders free movement. Only the State Highway No. 2 passes over it. In terms of percentage of villages electrified and villages having drinking water facilities these blocks have neither very high nor very low position.

Despite low level of underdevelopment these blocks (except Khariar) are too weak infrastructurally to support independent industries. However, certain household industries such as carpentry, pottery, rope making and tiny industries like rice mills are not rare to see in this some micro region. Khariar is a well developed urban centre having educational and commercial facilities. A large number of rice mills and oil mills are concentrated, here. Handloom weaving is a common occupation of the people of some villages. Khariar is connected with Khariar Road Town and Titlagarh by State Highway No. 3. This block is one of the most developed one in the entire district in terms of transport communication and urbanisation.

Table 4.7: Social Variables, Region of Moderate Development

Blocks	Population per Medical Institution ('000)	No. of Primary Schools per '000 Population	%age of Literacy	%age of Villages Linked with Pucca Road	%age of Villages Electrified	%age of Villages Having Drinking Facilities
Koksar	18.1	1.17	9.8	13.9	21.5	27.7
Kalampur	39.1	1.64	35.2	16.7	14.8	35.2
Khariar	34.4	1.57	17.1	21.4	33.0	27.7
Jaipatna	46.8	1.20	16.3	12.0	6.5	77 2

Source: *District Statistical Handbook*, Kalahandi, 1989-90.

Thus, the sub-micro region represents a peculiar case of mixed character. Though large part of it falls under a basin and valley, part of it is hilly and forested plateau. The low level of its underdevelopment are owing to high to medium intensity of cropping, moderate use of high yielding variety of seeds, fertile drought prone Khariar valley, surplus rice production of Tel-Hatti basin during year of favourable monsoon, average social indicators and the Khariar urban centre (with few industries).

Less Developed Area

Finally, in between Developed and Moderately Developed Areas fall the category of "Less Developed Area" (of CDI 12.50-14.50) which includes Bhawanipatna, Narla, Golamunda, Nawapada, Sinapali and Boden. Economically, this category is better than the region of Depressed Area, less developed than the region of Moderately Developed Area and lesser developed than the region of Developed Area. In other words, with respect to rank, this sub-micro region of Less Development occupies third position in the hierarchy of four level economic divisions. It has largest area spread, containing six blocks within it. The continuity is broken by highly underdeveloped Komna block. Individual CDI of the blocks of Bhawanipatna, Narla, Golamunda, Nawapada, Sinapali and Boden are 12.85, 14.34, 13.34, 13.31, 13.14 and 13.31 respectively.

Physical Characteristics

Nawapada and part of Boden fall under the ecological zone of the Nuapada Forested Upland. Western part of Nawapada block is hilly and eastern side is a plain area. The river Jonk of Kuramupri and the Sundar drains off the northern and eastern part of Nawapada. Because of its poor quality soil, Jonk valley is less productive than the Sundar Udanti valley or Tel-Hatti basin. (A narrow hill range (water divide) disconnects this valley from the valley of Sundar-Udanti). The valley is covered with intervening black cotton soil and a tract of teak forest. The Masakund river also flows in the Nawapada plain. Barring few pockets surrounding Saipala, Lakhna and Nawapada Road railway station area, the entire Jonk-Masunda valley is almost deforested, for acquiring land for cultivation. The northern plains of Nuapada sub-division is disconnected from the southern plains of the sub-division by a narrow passage, lying between the elongated hill ranges in the west and the Komna range in the east. The western parts of Nawapada and Boden contain a broad plateau of 610 to 915 metres high. The plateau which is cut off from the plains below by a range of precipitous hills is known as Sonabeda plateau. The area was a stronghold of Bhunjias and was once well cultivated. Today, it is a site of old and abandoned villages with few dispersed settlements, indicating that the area is no more that productive. The climate is cooler and drier in the plateau than the adjoining plains.

Dry mixed forests with Teak, *Asan, Dhaura, Piasal, Bandhan, Sisoo, Karla, Sidha, Maikasi, Kender, Salia,* Bamboo are common in Boden. Valuable trees and forest products are exported outside. Local people use forests only for domestic purposes, in a very limited way. Contractors and middle men earn lot of money at the cost of local forest and local people. As a result the area remains underdeveloped and poor.

Boden as well as Nuapada, because of continuous deforestation, experience frequent drought. Low lying areas of Nawapada is however, flood prone.

Demographic Characteristics

The region is thinly populated. As mentioned earlier the broad hilly parts have scanty habitation. Nuapada block is one of the least densed blocks of Kalahandi. Its population density is nearly 98 persons per sq. km. (1981) Boden, having 169 persons per sq. km. is moderately populated. Percentages of SC population are 11.8 and 13.2 and those of ST population is 32.8 and 41.3 in Nawapada and Boden respectively. This shows that the blocks are more tribal in character. More than one-third population are workers in both the blocks. These reflects somehow, less acute degree of under development.

Sinapali, western Golamunda and southern Boden of this economic division comprise the Udanti basin. Certain characteristics of this micro natural region shows neither very low nor so high magnitude of underdevelopment. The basin is created by the Udanti river and its tributaries at the upper catchment area. A number of reserved forests are found on the hills and uplands within the shallow plain. The region is bounded by hills and plateaus (for instance by the Sonabeda plateau in the north and the Dharamgarh plateau in the southeast, and hills and plateaus of M.P. in the west and south) all along its sides except northeast where the Udanti drains out through a narrow gap. Both Sinapali and Golamunda are drought prone blocks. Famine is so acute in this area that there were reports of starvation deaths from this poverty stricken part in the recent past. This however, does not mean that the basin is infertile and barren. In fact, this is part of a black cotton tract and rich teak forest belt. Until recently the region was abundantly covered by valuable teak trees.

After opening of transport lines and the grant of rights to standing trees on private lands to villagers (1948) large scale deforestation and export of wood logs took place, ultimately leaving this area degraded. Today, only *bija* and minar forest produce such as *kendu* leaves and bamboo bound the basin. Very few patches of good quality teak exist in the northwest of the Udanti valley.

The area has good ground water potential. A geo-hydrological survey by Orissa Lift Irrigation Corporation Limited considered around two thousand tube wells feasible in the two blocks.

Northern Bhawanipatna falls in the Tel valley. A smaller part of Southern Bhawanipatna and Narla (except small patches of Narla in the north and west) fall in Dharmagarh plateau and Madanpur Rampur Forested Upland. Again Southern Golamunda lies in the Tel-Hatti basin. Thus this micro economic division has mixed physiographic properties.

Demographic Characteristics

The population density of Golamunda, Narla and Sinapali (171/114 sq. km) is moderate and that of Bhawanipatna is low. Bhawanipatna (20.6 %) Narla (17 %) and Golamunda (30.2 %) have high percentage of SC population. In Sinapali (12.4 %) SC percentage is low. The percentage of tribal people is high (if not very high) in all the blocks, ranging from 29.6 in Narla to 41.7 in Golamunda.

Economic (Agricultural) Characteristics

Here is the agricultural data for all the blocks of this hierarchical section.

Except Nuapada and Sinapali where the cropping intensity is less than the districts average, all other blocks have medium cropping intensity. Sinapali shows lowest area under high yielding variety of seeds, in the district. Barring Bhawanipatna and Narla rest of the blocks have medium to high percentages of area under HYV.

Table 4.8 : Agricultural Variables, Division of Less Development, Kalahandi

Blocks	Cropping Intensity	%age of Area under HYV to Total Cropped Area	%age of Net Irrigated Area to NSA
Bhawanipatna	164	15.5	8.0
Narla	154	14.8	5.5
Golamunda	152	8.5	8.0
Nawapada	125	7.6	10.4
Sinapali	146	4.2	8.9
Boden	157	12.8	12.1

Source : District Statistical Handbook, Kalahandi, 1989-90.

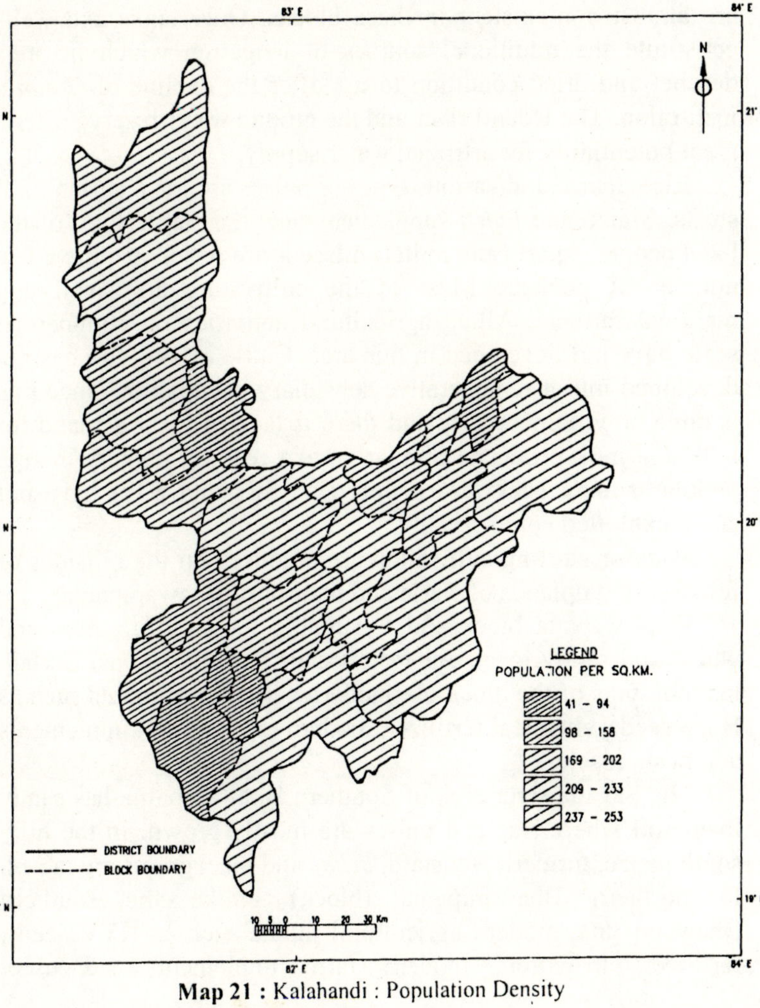

Map 21 : Kalahandi : Population Density

Amongst the blocks of this division Boden has highest proportion of area irrigated. The block, however, comes under just "High" irrigated category (not very high category) when seen against all the blocks of the district. Other five blocks have medium percentages of irrigated area.

The principal economic activities of the inhabitants of Boden, Sinapali, Golamunda is agriculture. Though official data shows a small portion of the agricultural land is under irrigation, looking to the magnitude of demand of water in these drought prone blocks it is not wrong to mention that irrigation facilities are almost non-existent in these blocks. Only tanks and wells constitute the traditional sources of irrigation which lie in a derelict and dried condition today, after the decline of *Gauntia* institution. The Udanti river and the ground water reserve offer a great potentiality for artificial water supply.

Rice, maize and various types of pulses are main agricultural stuffs. Maize and *bajra* supplement rice, the staple food of the local people. Apart from millets oilseeds are raised in quite a few number of pockets. Most of the cultivators are small and marginal farmers. Allied agricultural activities on commercial scale have not developed in this area. Cattle rearing too has not developed into a remunerative subsidiary occupation, since this is done only domestically and there is lack of local demand for milk and milk products. Similarly, goat rearing, piggery though popular among backward people (*i.e.* SCs and STs) have not being exploited commercially.

Podu or shifting cultivation are practised on the hillsides of few forested uplands of Narla and plateau of Bhawanipatna.

In Nawapada block soil is suitable for cotton, pulses and wheat and sandy loam soil for oilseeds and root crops. Certain landholdings of the block use modern agricultural inputs such as HYV seeds, chemical fertilizer, modern (agricultural implements and pesticides).

The Sagada river area of Southern Bhawanipatna has sandy loam soil where rice and pulses are mostly grown. In the hilly south maize, turmeric, mustard, *arhar* and blackgrams are raised. In northern Bhawanipatna (block) unlike the southern Bhawanipatna, modern agricultural inputs such as HYV seeds, fertilizer, irrigation, modern farm implements are used.

Pesticides stocked by private dealers, district headquarters, block headquarters ensure timely assistant to farmers. Bhawanipatna also has a government dairy farm along with few small dairy units and a government poultry farm which cater the needs of the local people. Fishery on the river Tel is not yet developed, though its potential is immense.

Tanks of the blocks are renovated for pisciculture. Purusottam, Suratrangini, Ramsagar etc. are important tanks in this town of Bhawanipatna.

In northern Narla rice is produced in the alluvial and sandy loam soil whereas in the southern Narla, groundnut and potatoes are raised in the sandy loam soil. Milk produced in southern Narla is consumed domestically. Dairy farming is not popular here. Ragi, millets and pulses are grown basically for subsistence purposes. (See also Appendix - 4 p.349)

Social Characteristics

The table of Social variables of the blocks justify later's common status of "Less Development" in a clearer way. (Cross compare the following table and the common table of the district given previously.)

Table 4.9 : Social Variables of Less Developed Area, Kalahandi

Blocks	Population per Medical Centre	Primary School per '000 Population	% of Literacy	% of Village with Pucca Road	% of Village Electrified	% of Village with drinking water facilities
Bhawani patna	11.6	1.70	18.9	14.8	28.6	25.3
Narla	43.1	1.90	24.2	16.5	8.2	67.0
Golamunda	18.9	2.16	16.8	7.8	10.6	49.7
Nawapara	22.1	1.32	14.5	8.4	19.3	35.9
Sinapali	32.0	1.50	17.4	8.5	7.6	84.8
Boden	58.6	1.45	14.4	7.3	6.3	76.0

Source: *District Statistical Handbook*, Kalahandi, 1989-90.

The more the 'population per medical institution' the less is the development in an area. In this respect, Boden, Narla and Sinapali are among the most backward blocks, Bhawanipatna is the most developed block and Golamunda and Nawapada have average figures.

Number of primary schools per thousand population is highest in Golamunda. This figure of Golamunda is highest not only for the division but also for the whole district. Rest of the blocks show much lower figures within the range of 1.45 to 1.90.

Among the six blocks Narla is the most literate one. Rest of the blocks have moderate to low literacy. In terms of percentages of villages linked with *pucca* road the whole division, by and large is very backward. Barring Bhawanipatna and Nawapada other four blocks have very limited number of villages electrified.

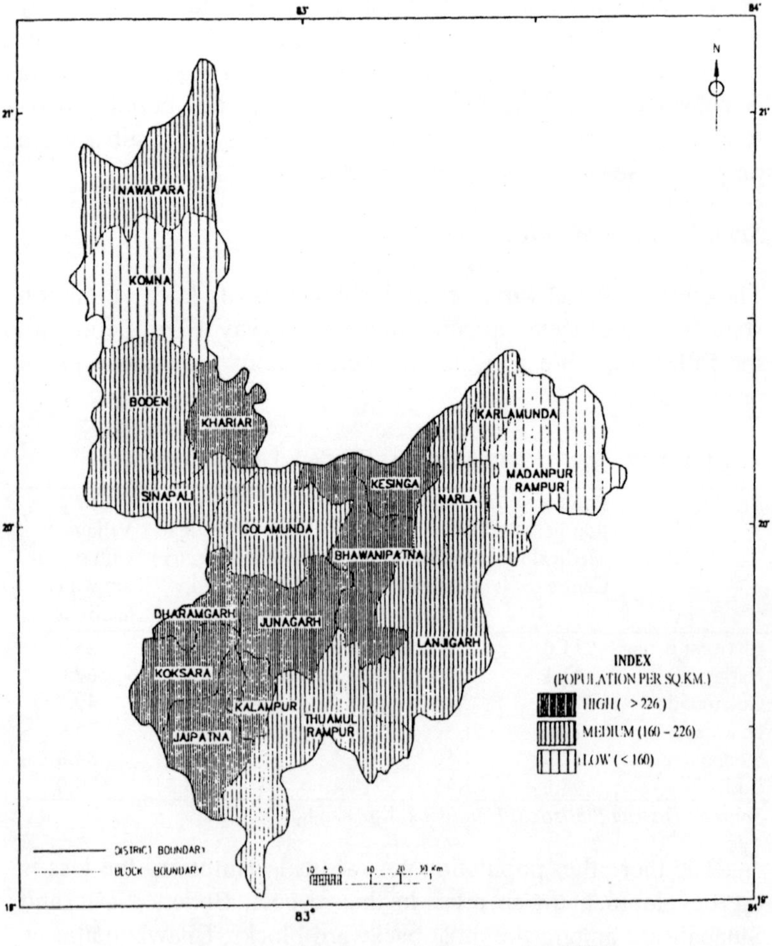

Map 22 : Kalahandi : Population Density (1991)

More than three-fourth villages in Boden and Sinapali, more than half villages in Narla and Golamunda, one-third villages in Nawapada and surprisingly just one-fourth villages in Bhawanipatna have drinking water facilities. These figures correspond to the figures of other blocks of high, medium and low percentages of villages having drinking water facilities.

Bhawanipatna is one of the most developed blocks in surface communication. State Highways No.1, 2 and 6 criss cross this block forming a node. Country boats help local inhabitants cross the river Tel during rainy season.

Bhawanipatna is not only a block or sub-divisional headquarter but also the district headquarter. It is an administrative and commercial centre. Many well to do families reside here. Outside businessmen dominate it. Prosperous Kulta agriculturalists have settled in the Tel valley. They use modern agricultural implements. Several pump set dealers of Bhawanipatana help them flourish in agriculture. Farmers take benefit of the District Tractorisation Unit, seated in this town. There is also state governments zonal service centre here.

Golamunda block is best served by roads and it remains inaccessible during rainy season. That is why hardly any industry is established here.

The Udanti river which flows in Sinapali and Golmunda had been used for teak log transportation till recently. The construction of Arang-Khariar road and Vizagpatnam-Raipur railway line instead of serving the purpose of local development has led to large scale deforestation of this once teak rich area. Hardly any all weather road links southern Boden, Sinapali, Golamunda area with Bhawaniptana, the district headquarters. Except block headquarters of Sinapali the entire Udanti basin in which southern Boden, Sinapali and western Golamunda are situated is rural in character. In other words, it is backward in terms of urban development.

Economic (Industrial) Development

Due to poor infrastructural facilities very low agricultural yield and frequent droughts the division is not (suitable) for industrial growth.

No industrial infrastructure and urbanisation is developed in the whole Narla block, excluding Narla town.

South western Boden has absolutely no transportation facility. Due to this dairy farming is not developed here. Northeastern part of Nawapada has a short rail route passing from Khariar road (which is second most important railway station of Kalahandi to Lakhna Railway Station. State Highway No. 3 is constructed through this block. The winding course of the Jonk River, the Sonabeda Plateau, Godhan waterfall, Katinpani *Nala* etc. hinders free surface transportation. Because of seasonal variation in the volume of water flow non-perennial nature of river and undulating character of its course neither navigation nor regular irrigation is possible in the Jonk Valley of Nuapada. The western plateau

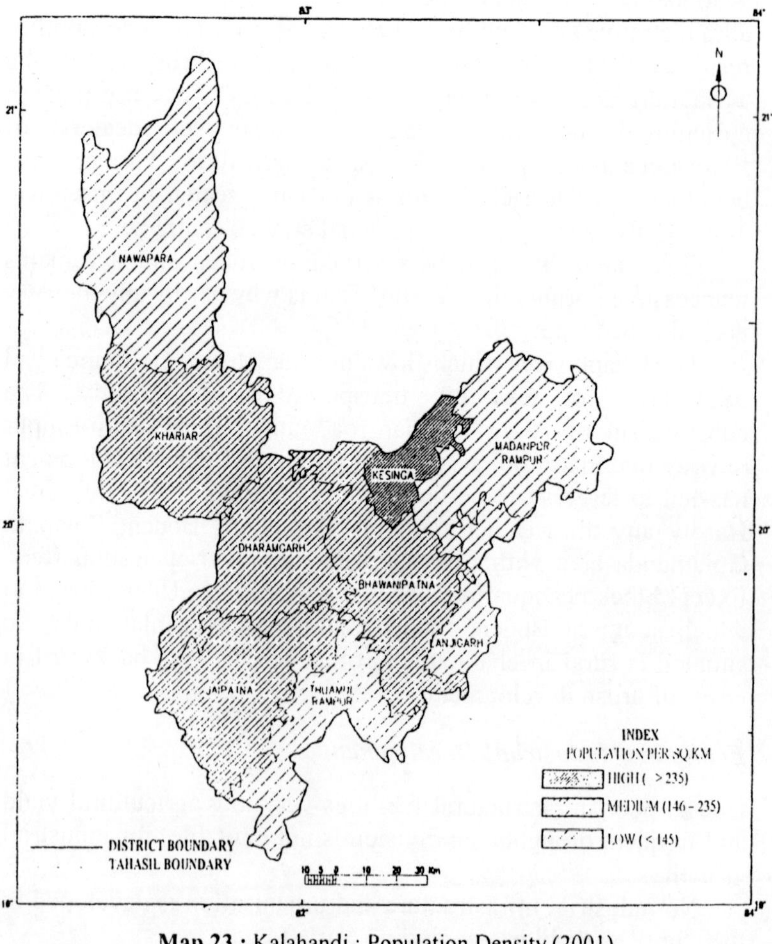

Map 23 : Kalahandi : Population Density (2001)

hardly has any communicational facility. Certain difficult passes such as Gaighat and Mahan Chuan are perhaps the only link between eastern plains and western plateaus.

Kharia Road town of Nuapada block has a number of rice mills and oil mills which export the local products in a processed form to nearby cities in Madhya Pradesh and other parts of India. So, this trading centre is a cause of more underdevelopment rather than development of the area. No medium or large scale industry is found in this division.

Table 4.10 : Demographic Variables of all the blocks of Kalahandi

Blocks	Density of PPN	%of SC	% of ST	%of Working PPN
Bhawanipatan	94	20.6	35.6	36.7
Kesinga	194	16.8	74.7	36.6
M. Rampur	63	11.5	37.3	29.0
Narla	158	17.0	29.6	35.7
Karlamunda	209	12.5	16.6	31.1
Lanjigarh	43	20.7	53.8	36.3
Th. Rampur	41	22.6	58.4	36.8
Dharamgarh	233	16.8	18.5	35.8
Junagarh	202	16.3	20.2	37.1
Jaipatna	237	10.7	23.5	31.0
Koksara	212	14.0	20.1	38.2
Kalampur	253	15.4	25.8	38.8
Golamunda	114	30.2	41.7	60.2
Nawapara	98	11.8	42.8	36.3
Komna	103	14.4	56.8	33.9
Khariar	218	15.2	29.3	34.4
Sinapali	171	12.9	32.9	32.4
Boden	169	13.2	41.3	35.1

Source : District Statistical Handbook, Kalahandi, 1989-90

In this way, this largest areal segment is a region of mixed physiographic properties, comprising plateaus, basins and river valleys. The placement of the region in the lower section of development (*i.e.* third quarter of underdevelopment) is justified in view of its. "Moderate to Low" indices of cropping intensity, area under high yielding variety of seeds, medical facilities, electricity and drinking water facilities. Remaining in the higher and lower edges of the scale, few indices of extreme values balance each other so as to exert negligible influence on the overall value of low development. The development of net irrigated area shows, three blocks (Bhawanipatna, Narla and Boden) have high indices and the remaining three have low indices. In schooling facilities, barring

Golamunda which has larger number of schools, all other blocks have smaller number of primary schools per thousand population. While Boden and Sinapali blocks have high proportion (3/4 th) of villages with drinking water facilities, in terms (percentage) of villages linked with *pucca* road the whole region is very backward. Though the sub-micro region proudly possesses the largest urban centre (*i.e.* Bhawanipatna, the district headquarter) almost its entire area, by and large, is rural in character.

Conclusion

Before closing this chapter the chief points of analysis may be summarized in the following manner. Firstly, despite large and qualitative potentiality of soil, water and forest resources, Kalahandi remains backward in the backward state of Orissa. This is partly because of large scale deforestation and irregularities in rainfall and mainly because of exploitation by elements which include businessmen, traders, middlemen, dominant groups, contractors, government officials and politicians. The process of underdevelopment seems to have outpaced the rate of development. In terms of important demographic, agricultural and social development criteria, Kalahandi has four distinct developmental sub-micro regions. The depressed area lies in the southeastern Kalahandi, which is thickly forested and mountainous. This part is with high tribal concentration. The most developed or least underdeveloped section, on the other hand is a fertile and well cultivated tract, being occupied by prosperous cultivators, businessmen and traders. The sub-micro regions which lie in-between the depressed and the developed area, have medium developmental indices, conforming to their mixed natural character (*i.e.* partly hilly, partly forested and partly plain). These transitional sub-micro regions are also the regions of caste-class interaction. (See Appendix 4 p.356)

These aspects establish the fact that there is a definite link between natural-cum-socio-economic conditions and degree of development.

NOTE

1. Kundu, A., *Construction of Composite Indices in Measurement of Urban Processes : A study in Regionalisation*, Popular Prakashan Pvt. Ltd., Mumbai, pp. 87-118, 1980. (See also Appendix-4 for Composite Development Indices.)

5

PRODUCTION RELATIONS IN RURAL KALAHANDI

To discuss starvation in Kalahandi is to discuss a peculiar paradox as this region is endowed with rich natural resources nevertheless it is here that poverty is acute. How come the land that is physically so fertile is witness to hunger? How come the area where access to rich mineral deposits is possible while people's access to food virtually is impossible? What explains Kalahandi's predicament? Why is it that a well flourished civilisation should at all suffer such inhuman indignation ? (Nanda, 1991)

This chapter, therefore, looks into certain structural questions relating to class configuration, ownership of means of production, varied access to resources, in migration and out migration, export, import and above all political economy which can largely explain poverty and underdevelopment. But these issues in themselves are not enough. Everything has a geographic dimension too. Pure structural analysis often exaggerate or oversimplify certain aspects of relative deprivation. Poverty must be seen in its cultural and ecological frame specific to spatial units.

In the previous chapter we have concluded that accessibility to resources and place of work are major determinants of regional poverty. It is ecological set-up and stage of underdevelopment that makes a cultivating and labour class of population vulnerable to the crises of basic human needs (food etc.) before the fundamental economic factors give rise to the structural framework of poverty. Contradicting the neoclassical economists who hold that with greater prosperity there can be greater welfare, the author contends that the distribution of the prosperity (resources and growth) is as important or even more important than the prosperity itself. Again the distributive justice would be less flawless if we understand 'the production relation against local resource base', better.

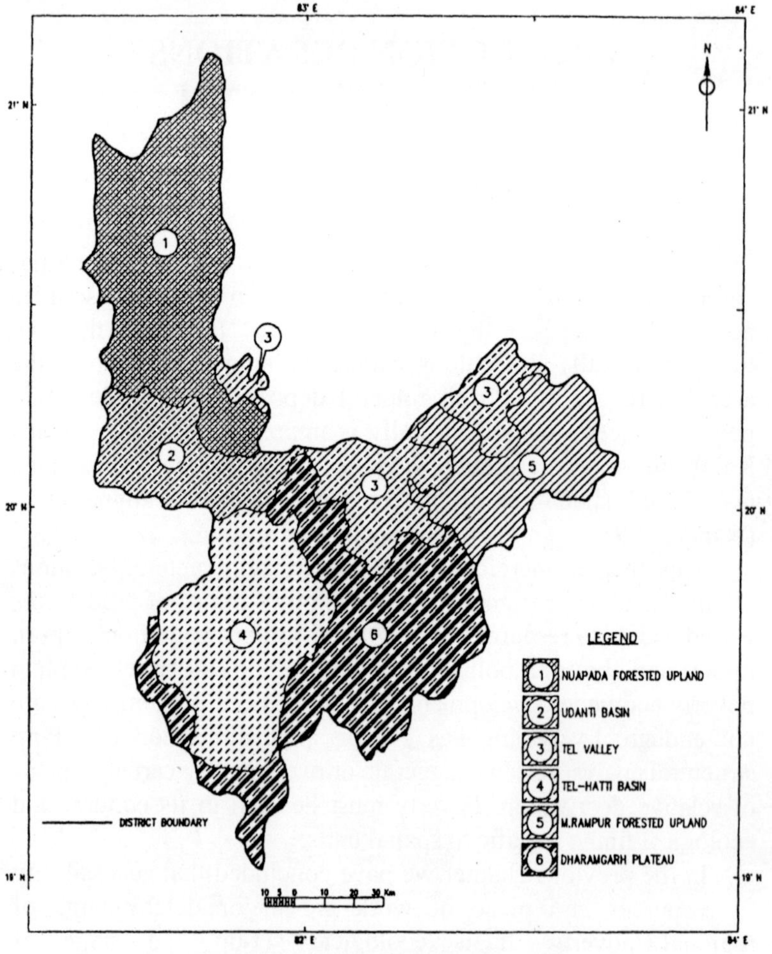

Map 24 : Kalahandi : Natural Divisions

We examine man-resource interaction with the presumption that the intensity and nature of poverty changes according to man-man interaction and kind of natural resources produced by an ecological setting. Assuming that poverty never occurs in isolation and the very presence of rich among poor is a sign of wealth accumulation (in the hands of a few), this chapter investigates certain pertinent questions. Who produces wealth ? Who distributes it ? And who consumes it? Again, when, where, how and why wealth is produced, distributed and consumed ? The answer to these questions have been sought from geographical angle in an attempt to explore or enquire the distortions over space, the dynamic process of mal distribution and underpinning or fundamental causes of poverty (rather than visible or triggering factors of it). Instead of going into the study of each and every sub-micro regions we have aggregated them up into three major groups of broad resource region .The regions are:

1. Predominantly hilly-cum-forest region.
2. Predominantly cultivable plain land region.
3. Region of mixed resource base (partly hilly forest and partly plain land). (See Appendix 5, p.356)

Sub-micro region falling in the first category of resource region are Dharamgarh plateau of low development and Dharamgarh plateau of high development. They show high poverty in general. Sub-micro regions belong to the second category of resource regions are:

1. Tel Valley of Low development.
2. Tel Valley of High development.

These sub-micro regions exhibit low poverty in general.

Region of mixed resource base which has varied intensities of poverty (ranging from 'low' to 'moderate' to 'high' poverty) includes the following sub-micro regions:

- Udanti basin of Low development,
- Madanpur Rampur Forested upland of Low development,
- Nuapada Forested Upland of High and Low development, and
- Tel-Hatti basin of Low development.

Under the heading of each resource region both general as well as particular cases of institutional production relation has been analysed hereafter.

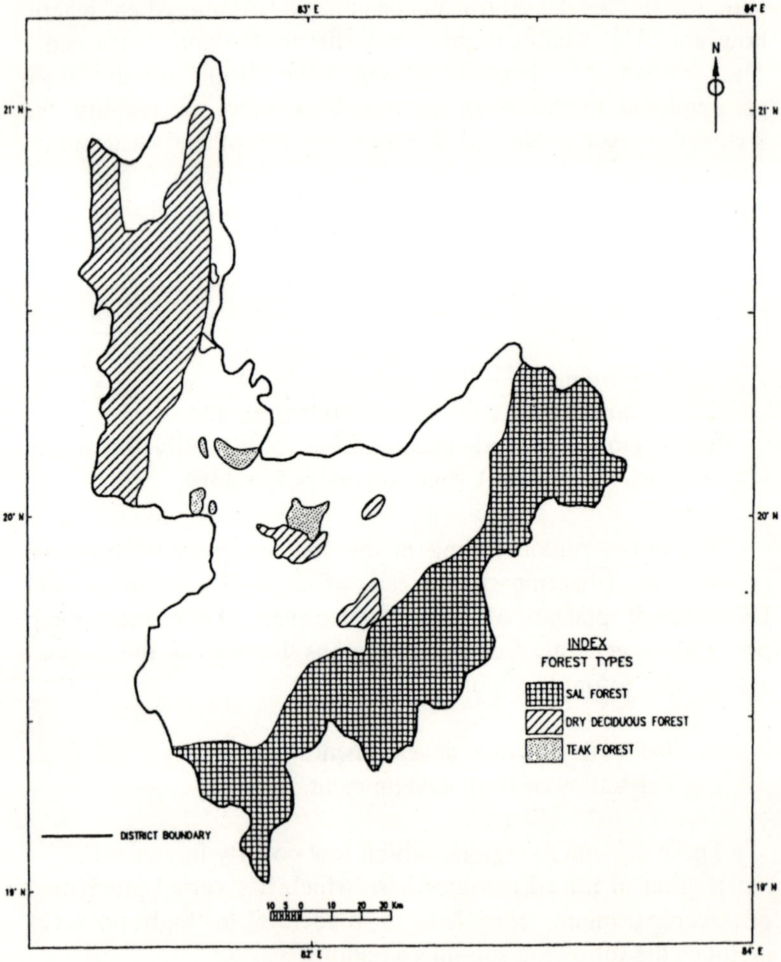

Map 25 : Kalahandi : Forest

Hilly-Forest Resource Region

The resource types of the region can be divided into two major categories, viz. (a) forest, (b) *dongar.* The interacting groups include mainly, tribals and non-tribals (SCs, General Castes). The intensity of exploitation in all the accessible pockets of the region is of highest order as compared to other two regions, because of the very nature of products and sharp disparity in consciousness between tribals and non-tribals. In the following paragraphs contextual approach to varied issues have been taken into consideration to draw some specific summarised conclusions.

This resource region like all other resource regions of underdeveloped world is under serious threat. The district of Kalahandi was known as Mahakantara (*i.e.* great forest) in the history of ancient India, now is no more than a wasteland. Once the people of this land were self-sufficient and contented with abundant forest product and ample harvest, are now looking the firewood and facing food problem.[1] Besides the local population pressure industries involved in massive tree cutting to meet their demand of raw materials, clandestine export of wood and logs by corrupt contractors, businessmen, governmental encouragement of tree felling for revenue requirements, agricultural and developmental processes, have been the major institutional causes of forest resource depletion and degradation. Certain ethically, socially and environmentally unacceptable methods, are resorted to for satisfying sheer political and commercial interest. The answer to why forest dwellers cause "deforestation" lies in their social realities, changed outlook and economic compulsions. Before going into details, first the forest related governmental plans and programmes are to be analysed.

Forest Policies

The first forest legislation in the form of memorandum was issued by the colonial government. Local inhabitants depend on forest products and forest related activities in innumerable ways encompassing food, fodder, clothing, shelter, medicines and various socio-cultural practices. There was various financial constraints faced by the government in 1955. Since it was difficult to extract taxes from land owning classes who were politically more powerful, the forest resources of tribals and landless people who had hardly any bargaining power became the easy source of revenue for the British government. So, the first Act of 1978 subdivided forest into Revenue, Protected and Village Forest and put a curb on the movements of local inhabitants within it.

National Forest Policy of 1952 though pious in its pronouncements, did the same in practice by further restricting peoples' right overforest resources. The study of Indian Social Institute, New Delhi found the protected forests over which the people have rights are preserved much more than the reserve forests which are clear felled for industrial purposes. In Kalahandi too protected forests were clear felled after they were categorised as reserved. Many forest blocks are surrounded by thickly populated villages with practically no village forest (not even village pastures), as a result of which the forests are subjected to heavy hacking and grazing much above their carrying capacity. Hence, many forest blocks like Daka, Ghatul, Guja, Limi, Adabari, Paniagaon, Pariagarh, Khandul, Garjan, Singari, Udaygiri, Talchirka, Minagtada, Dulkibandh, Raktaboden, Sinang, Bhalu, Dhanupanc, Dhangda, Dhangidi Nangal, Karla, Kamei Lumersingha Truchi, Lange parts of Sahjkhol Chura 'b' Kumkot Ghana have been depleted considerably. The other day Nageswar Reserve forest coupes which contains natural teak were fetching very high price.[2]

The Forest of Kalahandi division was first brought under systematic management in 1934-35. The present plan (1983-84) mentions that there has been significant shift in the system of management adopted earlier (Revised Working Plan *op.cit.* p.37). This is an indirect confession by the Forest Department officials that the methods adopted earlier was grossly inadequate to serve the very purpose of conservation. The document talks of the interest of the industries, first, which is apparent form the introductory statement. 'A soft wood working circle and a pulp wood working circle have been constituted in the new plan to meet the raw material requirement of the paper mills and other wood based industries.' The next sentence is like this, 'considerable stress has been laid for rehabilitation of the degraded forests and accelerated plantation programme to enrich the forests.' This further indirectly points out that there was a considerable loss in forest wealth over the past decades, despite the direct intervention, involvement and concerted and extensive conservational efforts of the Forest Department. The failure if not entirely but can mostly be attributed to the Government Forest Department.

Encroachment into Reserved Forest blocks, in course of last twenty years, has increased manifold besides a few blocks mentioned in the last plan. At present much larger areas in some more blocks are under active *podu* was prevalent in Pahadpadar, Benbhate, Jalkride, Nchela, Jerka and in narrow strips in Nageswar. But now it has spread to Daka, Sahajkhol, Singari, Udaygiri, Jugasapatna, Narla, Jerka, Madanpur Rampur Range also.

One of the major reasons for destruction of tribal habitat is the practice of shifting cultivation by tribals themselves, it is commonly hold. To quote the Working Plan of Kalahandi Forest Division. "It is by far the worst form of encroachment into the Government Forest. It is a wasteful and harmful method of land utilisation".[3] This is how the plan perceives the age old practice instead of going into the question of ecological suitability of *podu*. Probably, it is the belief of Government officials that if force is used tribals would quit *podu*.*

Though *podu* outwardly seems to be an environmentally unsound method, and less productive, it is essential for tribal survival and its multiple pattern of crops has an in built insurance against vagaries of nature. The integration of tribals and other non-tribal poor with market economy and outside traders, scarcity of plain lands due to outsiders' occupation of limited forest plain lands, apart from general infertility of the soil, resistances of forest ecology rather compel the tribals to stick to this primitive practice.

Encroachment into the demarcated forest blocks and the inaccessible areas is due to the exploitation of tribals by the non-tribals who have snatched away good plain cultivable lands. Since the tribals have no asset (except their labour) they have found inaccessible remote forest areas as haven for their activities. To add to it, utter callousness of staff people have found it safe to make encroachment on the plea of *'Kudki' patta*.[4] Thus the problems of *podu* and deforestation should not be seen in isolation, thereby holding tribals entirely responsible

---

* Kalahandi district has an area of 1,323. 50 sq.km. under shifting cultivation (*podu*) a sort of crude/primitive practice of farming, which is carried out by about 33000 Kond tribes (*Source* : Govt. of Orissa 1983 : 166-68).

for them. The maximum damage incurred to forest is due to outsiders usurpation of forest plain land, callousness of forest staff, regulation of tribals free movement for the fulfilment of various economic pursuits and consequent tribal frustration. The customary rights of common ownership of clan land and tracts of forests has more or the less disappeared. So has the social mechanism of management of such communal land and legitimate use of such common resources. The department of forests which claims state ownership fails to evoke collective responsibilities and guardianship over resources.[5]

Very few would look at shifting cultivation as an exclusively economic proposition. The author views it from its historical and socio-political context as a product of hierarchical feudal societies which pushed the defenceless tribals to the marginal hills and forest areas and made them refugees in their own habitat. As such it is linked not merely to the environmental problems but also to the distribution of power. Our data confirm that *podu* cultivation is closely linked to the distribution of power not merely between forest dwellers and outsiders but among the tribals themselves.[6]

In this district upper classes practise '*podu*' not as a means of survival but something for generating higher profits. This very motivation, of commercial benefits increase their land under *podu*. They simply manage the business by employing more labourers which is cheaply available. This is a very peculiar case as against the popular belief that only poor and landless tribals practised *podu*. Upper class peoples' involvement obviously often displace the poor tribals from dongar, who are reduced to labourers in absence of suitable *podu* plots. (Based on field observation.)

Not the basic needs of the poor but profit (greeds) of the better off farmers guide which type of crops should be grown in what proportion. The increased production of pulses over and above cereals is a clear-cut indication of the fact that pulses are grown for cash by the rich. The outside money lenders first enter the forest resources – region for lending money to the poor tribals. Soon they turn into cultivators by appropriating large dongar lands and gradually extend their control over the resources and produces of the area. During the early stage of immigration few new settlers were traders who later bought land and consequently gained the stamp of civilisation. The rich occupy not only bigger plots but also better quality plots with higher yielding capacity. The study of Indian Social Institution confirms this.

The proccss of the outsiders encroachment gives rise to a general model of forest land use. Population of the Kalahandi forest division (which includes the Sadar and Dharamgarh sub-division only) is about 9,38,986 spread over 8197.35 square kilometres (1981 census). So, the density calculated about 114.55 persons/sq.km. According to 1961 census it was 104.55. Thus, there has been a rise of 10.55 persons per sq. km. over two decades.

The following Table 5.1 shows recent data on population of the district:

Table 5.1: Orissa comparative population size of the districts

(2001 Census Provisional Figures)

State/ District	Decennial Growth Rate (%)			Population Density		
	1971-81	1981-91	1991-2001	1981	1991	2001
Orissa	20.17	19.50	15.94	168	202	236
Kalahandi	15.06	18.88	15.50	113	135	153
Cuttack (Undivided)	20.93	18.89	14.37	–	494	570
Phulbani	16.38	19.70	18.02	–	77	101

Source : Directorate of Economics and Statistics, Orissa, 2002.

The bulk of the population, however, is concentrated in plain tract. *Dongerla* hilly area is thinly populated. Tribal population of the division is 2,77,665 which accounts for 29.57% of the total population. Tribals mostly inhabit the hilly tract along with a very small percentage of non-tribals. Any change in population structure of the plain tract affect that of the *dongerla* thereby affecting the production distribution balance of caste and class groups. Earliest major in migration was made by Kultas into the Tel valley after 1867 from Sambalpur. Many businessmen from north and western India entered the district to inhabit the Tel-Hatti basin especially after 1965. Costal Orissa Inmigrants settled in the area mostly during the same period.[7]

Due to outsiders influx and population pressure reservation of large tracts of protected forests and consequent closure of *podu* cultivation plots, massive deforestation (especially during last three decades) increasing the distance between forests and settlements, reduction of forest areas near villages, relative scarcity of minor forest produce and food, indebtedness, land alienation and absence of work, large number forest dwellers have resorted to *podu* cultivation today than the number engaged twenty years ago. For instance many scheduled castes who are not traditional shifting cultivators, today do the same *podu* which has become their main source of food for survival. As a result the dependence on forest land has increased, within the hilly-forest resource region.

People compete for limited cultivable land or *dongar*. The rich people and outsider money lenders are best able to buy what they desire whereas poor tribals who have less bargaining power have little or no choice. Several money lenders who have appropriated tribals lands have settled down in forest villages and have taken to shifting cultivation for growing commercial crops by exercising their financial power. They appropriated maximum and best quality *podu* plots. Competition increases for the remaining areas. The lowest class belonging to marginal farmers and few landless families has little option but are left with worst type of *podu* lands to raise food for their survival.

The result of this competition is the creation of typical *podu* land zones by different class and/or caste groups in the ecological belt. Those who are thrown out of the process and displaced, turn into permanent labourers and join the rank of labour classes. Thus, the principle of survival of the fittest operate in the region within the framework of unequal distribution of power not merely between tribals and outsiders but between the forest dwellers themselves.

It can be looked in a different way. Primarily, it seems to be a symbiotic relation where the caste groups over living space reflect their respective occupation and social status. Competition not at the production level but at the distribution level is apparent.

Non-tribals of *dongerla* plain (*i.e.* plain on higher plateaus) are ecologically, economically and structurally mid-placed between tribals of hill slopes or foot hills and stream and (*nala* beds) and non-tribals of *pahilpar* (*i.e.* plain tract of river basins and valley). They grow autumn paddy. Tribals of the *dongerla* areas raise Ragi, Maize, Mustard, *Kandu, Kating* and Millet *(janah)* on the hill slope using flow irrigation and hill paddy *(Amdhan)* along the *nala* beds

Unlike the western concept of competition and subsequent segregation over space as we find in (Darwin's survival of the fittest), sectoral model of Burgess or Von-Thunens agricultural models, here we find no competition of that nature for limited available space. Rather it could be a symbiotic relation where each inhabiting social group is satisfied with their respective eco-section/niche and thinks to have secured the best for its need. This static picture, however, does not reflect the nature of interaction and subsequent exploitation.

The dynamics of space reveal different interactions. Competition is apparent not at production level but at distribution level. This indirect control of rich over production of tribals takes place through moneylending. As soon as the crop is harvested the *mahajan* realise it for his loan and huge interest advanced during 'push *punei'* festival. This would be discussed in more detailed form later. Tribals go for exchange for satisfying the basic needs, non-tribals interest is mainly to fulfil their larger needs (or greed). This results in the exploitation of former by the later and birth of poor by rich. Helpless poor with his lone asset labour try to put more pressure on existing land and forest by reducing *podu* cycle and acquiring more and more lands. Rich acquires more and more *podu* lands and employ poor tribals for indirectly carrying out shifting cultivation gradually slowly squeeze them out. So poor is subjected to gradual loss of entitlement over forests and is squeezed out.

Before independence, the *podu* was confined to the lower two-third of hills, upper one-third was left untouched. But after independence (when forest department took up the forest management in a regular manner and especially after 1960s (when traders inflow into the district was conspicuous) there was growing demand on *podu* products like *Alsi, Kating, Kandul* etc. along with sal logs and minor forest products. The traders in connivance with the forest officials and contractors, therefore, expanded the area of deforestation and *podu* cultivation clean felling rest part (upper one-third) of the hill. Besides there was pressure on the existing *podu* lands on the lower two-third of foot hills.[8]

The reserve forests, are not much affected by the problems of encroachment except in the *dongerla* area where the aboriginal tribes practise *podu* cultivation. The unreserves are not practically free form this menace. Thus goes the observation of the working plan of Kalahandi Forest Division. Many traders settled in Bhawanipatna. They, by and large, constitute upper classes who started illegally practising *podu*, being guided by profit consideration, despite the official ban on shifting cultivation in Bhawanipatna. Due to stronger economic and political powers, the rich cultivators perhaps in connivance with forest officials availed more and more virgin/new plots even in reserved forest. Some traders instead of taking possession of land and the botheration of cultivation extended their indirect control over the products of forests for getting quick money and easy gain. The example of Singhjhar (in Udanti basin) can be cited in this context. So, any effort to break the traditional Gauntia (landlord) system without doing away with the new trader forest official nexux would solve little purpose. Except Boden block the poor traditional cultivators who has less bargaining power were squeezed by the displacing force of new better off cultivators on one side and the prohibitory order of forest officials into the reserve forests, on the other. They had little alternative but to withdraw themselves from their rights over their own soil to find themselves labourers. In more inaccessible *dongerla*[*] area, however, ignoring the ban on entry into the reserve forests many tribals practise *podu* clandestinely. Fragile *dongerla* ecology has very limited population holding capacity since the availability of plain area itself is very limited.

Both, due to population rise (not through natural growth but through immigration) and greater demand on forests and *podu* produces by outsiders (especially profiteering businessmen),

---

* The portion of Eastern Ghats on the east of southeast Kalahandi, including Madanpur Rampur, Lanjigarh and Thumamul Rampur mainly.

increasing land conflicts (for example usurpation of *adivasi* lands by local *Harijans (doms)* themselves), *podu* cultivation has increased so much that even *nalas* and streambeds are hardly spared. To quote District Working Plan, "*podu* cultivation which is practised extensively in and through out *dongerla*, the *nala* stream beds on higher reaches are being widened gradually to grow paddy...". Though marginally, the number of *podu* practitioners has increased over the years. Both the per capita (1.23 ha) land cultivated and the per capita pulses (325.1 kgs.) and cereals (363.3 kgs.) grown are higher in Kalahandi than Phulbani (0.53 hectares) 135 kg. cereals and 191 kgs. pulses[9] another most backward district of Orissa.

With the rich class (outsiders) encroachment the pressure on the forest resource region in general and dongar (*podu* lands) in particular was intense, is evident from the following analysis. During *Durbar* administration a few people were granted *Kudki patta.* No occupancy right has been granted for *podu* cultivation, apparently under *Kudki patta* as indicated by latest Land Revenue settlement report. On a flat rate of 8 *annas* was fixed rent per *Kudki* (since it was the intention of the government to discourage poor). In all 7,485 numbers of *Kudki pattas* were given. It has been estimated that per *Kudki* 5 acres of area are cultivated. Thus 37,475 hectare of land on hill slope was estimated to be under *podu* cultivation. At present area under *podu* will be much more than this.[10] Again there was clear felling of even few reserve forests after the lifting of *Kudki patta*. (after a discussion of the researcher with Mr. Nilakantha Mohanty, a forest official, Bhawanipatna.) If we see the decade-wise natural population growth of the district and especially the growth of Kond tribes (which rather show a decline in population) we find no reason explaining deforestation and expansion of *podu*.

Population growth rate of Orissa as a whole was 19.7 per cent, while in Kalahandi district it was as low as 14.26 per cent during 1971-81.[11] Though the district is drought prone and underdeveloped its overall population has shown an increase during the past few decades. This could mainly be due to the differential growth rates of non-tribal population. The case of certain tribes, however, presents a different picture. There has been an abnormal decrease in the population of Kond, the second largest and most widespread tribe who are mainly the traditional shifting cultivators of Kalahandi. During the period of 1961-71 and 1961-81 the decline were 21.77 per cent and 11.77 per cent respectively. Although the population has increased from 11,644 to 12,96,749 during the decade 1971-81, the growth (13.81 per cent) of this period was much lower than the fall (21.77 per cent) in the population of decade 1961-71.

It is not the growth of tribal population itself but probably the growing demand of *podu* products and land by greedy businessmen and rich farmers is responsible for extension in *podu* areas. Due to the occupation of larger lands of dongar by better off cultivators poor tribal *podu* practitioners were forced to withdraw themselves into the less accessible areas of safety.* As a consequence of this process we find more accessible Bhawanipatna area is relatively exposed to intensive shifting cultivation and in someway, deforestation, vertically over hill slopes, whereas interior areas of Thuamul Rampur and Lanjigarh is subjected to lesser intensive practice and more horizontal deforestation following the practice of tribals and other *podu* cultivators.

The impact of outsiders encroachment into the district occurs in a peculiar way. From *podu*, production is just enough for household consumption (in other words *podu* is a sort of subsistence economy). This does not generate surplus to meet commercial needs in any sense. Unfortunately, *dongar* products has been linked with the commercial needs of the traders. It is for this reason there is greater pressure on dongar patches. Of course, tribals need to sell part of the harvest especially *Alsi*, Castor, Till, Mustard etc. to get cash for buying certain essential items. There is nothing but a kind of exploitative relation which develop between the traders and the tribals once the later approach the former. Because of all the encroachment tribals are pushed into interior areas in two different ways :

---

* This withdrawal is more conspicuous on the Nawapada Forested Upland as pointed out in the study of Fanimdam Deo, Khariar.

(a) Horizontal spread in lesser density areas, *i.e.* in Thuamul Rampur, Lanjigarh, where deforestation has taken place horizontally and also in the lower one-third portion of the hills *i.e.* foothills and hitherto untouched areas. Dependence of tribals on the *podu* increase because of their integration with market economy.

(b) Vertical spread in relatively higher densed tribal areas where population density is more and tribes have lesser lands to spread horizontally (so they have spread upward in the sense, the upper two-third portion of the hills is subjected to deforestation and *podu* to meet the growing demand of timber, minor forest produce and *podu* products of traders). Gradual loss of entitlements (of forest products such as *Kendu* and *Mahul*) make tribals more compelling to migrate into interior areas.

What is to be marked here is that lesser densed tribal areas have larger land for horizontal spread. Moreover, the hills are taller than the hills of less densed areas for lesser vertical spread.

A similar pattern of outsiders encroachment, vertical deforestation in accessible areas and horizontal deforestation in the interior, withdrawal of weak or poor (especially tribal) *podu* practitioners into the interior is observed in the Nawapada Forested Upland. However, the only difference in the human interaction is that the encroachment in this case is not just for shifting cultivation but for plough cultivation, timber (especially teak) collection and establishment of settlements or new villages. In this case Western Khariar, Nawapada and Sinapali town-part are the geographic counterpart of Bhawanipatna. Moreover, there is variation in physical resource and demographic bases of the two regions in that the later has lower altitude (smaller hills) and lesser density and growth of forest as well as inmigrant population. The impact of encroachment in the form of deforestation and spread of settlements is visible more because of which both drought and poverty is more in this part of Kalahandi, though not that high as in that of south and south-east Kalahandi. Within the exploited and deprived class of indigenous population (especially scheduled castes and scheduled tribes) a new order of interaction is noticed.

ISI study found that over last two decades few tribals and scheduled castes of the area have become rich by lending money and/or selling goods to their fellow tribals or caste people like the outsiders of the past. After becoming rich and being allured by trade in *podu* products tribals and some outsiders continue to involve in shifting cultivation whereas scheduled castes whose traditional occupation is not *podu* and who took to slash and burn cultivation as a means of survival in the years of crop failure and food scarcity quit the practice (*podu*) once they become rich. Though the majority of the tribes are poor the rich minority among them tilt the balance in favour of tribals showing higher per capita land as well as production than the SCs, much higher proportion of whom belongs to the lower class as compared to the tribals.

Exploitative Interaction in Firewood and Minor Forest Produce (MFP)

Lower classes depend on sale of firewood for survival. However, they have lesser access to it as compared to upper classes. According to the fieldwork data the collection, consumption and sale of firewood by poorer section is 66.08, 59.16 and 22 respectively whereas for rich section of population these are 95.68, 86.82 and 47.33 respectively.

But in recent years due to wide deforestation of village forests consumption of firewood has declined. Since longer distances are to be covered by wood collectors than the distances covered in the past. Moreover, closer village forests are mostly occupied by well off families. Even in distant forests, poor villagers are often harassed and exploited by forest guards.

'Need' is an economic question but the means of satisfaction of the need and accessibility are social and geographic questions. The ironical contrast or paradox one comes across is that those who are hardly in need of resources, own and command it. And, those who are real needy of minor forest resources have little capacity to procure it. Thus, we find in many sample villages of the district richer people are less dependent on minor forest produce (like mango, *mahua, kendu, sal* seeds) than the poorer sections. But most produces are accessible to the former than the latter. Another important field observation is that the rich people to prepare liquor and earn large amount of money collect *Mahua* more whereas the lower class whose traditional source of nutrition during the lean seasons is *Mahua* flower can hardly find it. Similarly, more nutritious seeds or fruits like *sal* seeds and mangoes etc. fall in the hands of better off families either due to their ownership of forest land or due to higher purchasing power and better bargaining capacity.

Social distance or stratification has a bearing on geographic distance and/or stratifiction. Consequently, this leads to a typical forest resource use pattern around the villages. Rich people live closer to the forest resources they own, and the poor live farther from the resources.

Reduction of forest cover and diminishing supply of minor forest produce has led to a kind of competition outside and also within the village by different caste class groups of external as well as internal origin. Commercial agents and businessmen reap the maximum benefit by selling out forest products. According to an ISI estimate rich people on an average get Rs. 675 while the poor MFP collectors get only Rs. 100 a year from the sale of forest products. It is ironical to note that the moneylenders demand the repayment of loan from the poor borrower just after or during their hard collection of minor forest products, badly needed for their subsistence. As a result the weaker sections are compelled to sell out their products at much low price against their will to save the products necessary for their survival.

The social organisation basis variation is also interesting. Tribes being the son of the forests depend more on forest products than any other community.

Certain concessions have been allowed to the local people for the collection and removal of roots and fruits, honey, flowers and creepers free of any payment by the Forest Department. If bamboos are not available in a forest block local villagers are permitted to take their *bona fide* personal requirements of bamboos from outside blocks* on payment of royalty at full rate.

---

* According to the Working Plan of Forest Division, Kalahandi, there are total 96 forest blocks in Kalahandi.

It means that even if local forests are destroyed and timber smuggled out by outside contractors or forest officials and in the process there is local shortage of wood (timber), bamboos and other minor forest products, people have to bear the burden of royalty for getting the same from outside block. It is pity to see that poor who is never directly involved or responsible for the plunder pays the cost of scarcity of forest products.

The working plan under 'rights and concessions' section further mentions that 28 *praja* coupes were opened from where they take the materials on payments of royalty at the tenants rate plus supervision charges. In case of teaks only poles below 20 cms were allowed. Further the tenants enjoying these concessions are required to assist when called upon to do so in clearing the boundary line on payment of wages or on contract rates and to render assistance in extinguishing forest fires. Failure to fulfil these obligations may involve cancellation of above concessions for specified period.

But the problem is that the poor has little money even to pay for the royalty essential for the procurement of the minimum requirements. Moreover, the provision that the failure to fulfil the above obligations would lead to cancellation of above concessions creates a psychological alienation between forest officials and people and replaces mutual trust and 'we feeling' with threat and compulsion.

As we have mentioned before the purpose and nature of exploitation of forest resources of the poor (especially tribes, scheduled caste people and other low caste local people) are different from that of rich (contractors, other middlemen, businessmen and industrialists). The former try to satisfy his immediate economic need whereas the later remain busy for satisfying his immediate commercial greed. Though natural regeneration of vegetation is possible, it takes a long time. Artificial afforestation has its own limitation both over space and time. Remaining at a structurally advantageous position rich unlike the poor can command large resources. However, he feels the scarcity more since his perceived need (i.e. greed) itself is more, Forest (officials) Department in the hope of getting increased revenues, royalty and other (open or secret) benefits pretend to be the sole protector of forests. Apart, they try to curb poor men's practices (like collection or gathering of minor forest produce, hunting, age old shifting cultivation etc.) indirectly favouring the elite interest. Ultimately greedy rich survives at the cost of the needy poor.

The Culprit in Bamboo Forest Loss

It is a well known fact that large scale auction and supply of bamboo to different paper mills of Orissa is the biggest cause of bamboo forest loss. Because of this perhaps who were formerly dependent on bamboo are unable to get a regular supply.

Unfortunately, the Forest Department holds the contrary view by accusing the poor for the fall in bamboo cover. To quote the plan collection of tender bamboo shoots (*kardi* as it is called locally) for food during the rains is a menace. Damage to the crops on account of this is quite considerable. Two things has to be borne in mind. First, because of very scarcity of food in the hilly deforested areas during pre-harvest period and non-availability of wage labour due to temporal disruption of road communication by the torrential monsoonal rain the poor finds no alternative but falls back upon *kardi.* Secondly, poor cultivators and their *podu chas* which is often discouraged strongly by the government and others rather contribute to bamboo growth. The plan itself admits, "On account of *podu* on the hill slopes the tree species have given ground to more hardy species so that bamboo could come up. On account of repeated *podu* with impoverishment of soil bamboo has come up with exclusion of tree species from the area". However, regeneration and establishment of bamboo is satisfactory. The fact that industrial demand is considered only a secondary cause of deforestation by the Forest Department is deplorable.

Traditionally, the middlemen initiate and link exploitation. Many of them act as moneylenders as well. They cheat the poor, less conscious, illiterate labourers or collectors of MFP (Minor Forest Produces) who have very weak bargaining power. They buy the forest produce cheap from the forest developers and sell them to merchants at higher prices, thereby getting large profits*. Forest *podu* produce like cereals, mustard and niger are said to be brought from them on a system of mortgage in advance.[12] Since the role of moneylending and act of an agent often combines, sometimes a shopkeeper plays the triple role of money lending, goods or articles selling and dealership (*dalali*). Advancement of loan during lean season enable them to collect minor forest produce or agricultural produce at very low prices just after the harvest is over. The powerless harvesting tribals are forced to sell basic nutritional items needed for their very survival. Tribals are less familiar with money economy and modern numerical measurements and so interact through exchange method (for example one kg. *Mahua* for one kg. Salt) Poor people are always exploited by large margins. But they remain. However, it is not that the forest dwellers are unaware of the gross unfair dealings of the *dalals* (middlemen). But they remain mute witness of the circumstances of their own helplessness before the shrewd traders and merchants. Since any protest would spell starvation, they prefer tolerance and silence.

Role of Government Institution vis-a-vis *Minor Forest Produce*

Except leaves and seeds the collection and sale of which is under the exclusive control of Orissa Forest Development Corporation (OFDC) in all other forest produces private agents operate. For example, while in the exploitation of timber and bamboo contractors and industrialists are engaged, in collection of firewood, flowers and fruits businessmen remain busy.

To prevent rampant exploitation of tribal resources and tribal labour by private traders the Government has set-up different public sector organisations, such as LAMPS (Large Multi-purpose Societies) MPCS (Multipurpose Cooperative Societies) to procure minor forest produce from the tribals and sell them to businessmen and industrialists. The pronounced objective of the institution are

---

* *Mahua* flowers procured for fifty to ninety paise/kg. are sold at Rs. 1.50. Similarly, mangoes are sold by the people to businessmen at Rs. 0.50/kg. and their price in cities where the same businessman sells out them rises to Rs. 3 to Rs. 5/kg. (*Source* : Fieldwork)

to purchase forest produces from the collectors at reasonable prices and the distribution of essential commodities (like rice, salts, kerosene, clothes etc.) at a fair price to the tribals so that they have not to go to private traders and middlemen for their requirements. In practice, however, they have failed to eliminate middlemen except, few cases. For example, in Boden block of Nuapada Forested Upland of high underdevelopment villagers are well organised, politically conscious, legally aware and sell forest produces to Tribal Development Cooperative Corporation (TDCC) by passing middlemen, (ISI Study). Consequently they receive higher money than the villagers of many other parts of Kalahandi where the noble institutions of LAMPS and TDCC have slipped into the grips of private businessmen and their dealers.

Other cases show inadequate funds and staff besides lack of initiation on the part of the staff has defeated the objectives of Tribal Development Cooperative Corporation (TDCC) in saving the tribals from unscrupulous traders and middlemen. What is more, the corporation helps traders procuring the produces at prices relatively lower than the ones at which they buy from the tribals.[13]

The profit attitude of businessmen is a known fact. But what is surprising and unfortunate is that the so called sacred protectors of the tribals interests, *i.e.* the LAMPS, TDCC in course of time have turned into profit-making state sponsored institutions. Now, they rather look after the state interests to satisfy their unintended objectives. This is amply substantiated by Walter Fernandes *et al.* (1991) in their study on Forest, Environment and Tribal ecology (pp.41-142). The government marketing organisations has its own limitations. To quote the news item of the *Indian Express* 'With only six fieldworkers LAMPS units engaged in the procurement of forest produce. Besides funds short allocation last year was just Rs. 27 lakhs as against a requirement of Rs. 43 lakhs. Only 232 quintals of niger, oilseed, and 33 quintals of mustard two major products could be bought. And procurement of maize and millets was almost nil, it is gathered'.

Procurement touched a new low this year. Against a minimum requirement of Rs. 35 lakhs towards the purchases of niger, mustard and horse gram *(kuthi)* and other produce, a niggardly Rs. 4 lakhs was allotted to the TDCC. The purchase naturally figured at 200 quintals of niger oilseeds, 30 quintals of *kulthi* and 100 quintals of *kating.*[14]

Middlemen collected *kendu* leaves through local people on behalf of Orissa Forest Corporation. The wages are much less than the declared wage rate of the state government. The OFC collects huge amount revenue by selling *kendu* leaves to *Bidi* companies. For example, *Kendu* Leaf Organization (KLO) purchases *kendu* leaves from collectors at a rate of 10 paise per twenty leaves which comes to Rs. 100 to 120 per quintal selling price is Rs. 3,500 to 7,000. The profit gained by the government Forest Department is very high. The plucker gets not more than Rs. 30 to 50 per day. Taking 8-10 days term per month the total wage a labourer receives during plucking season *i.e.* April to May is about Rs. 400 to Rs. 500.

The whole district has been divided into 7 ranges. Around 3,000 pluckers are engaged in each range for *kendu* leave collection.* Thus, the total pluckers and their collection wage comes around 21,000 and Rs. 20 crores respectively. The *kendu* Leaf Organization (KLO) after selling leaves earn Rs. 10 to Rs. 12 crores each year.[15]

In fact, *kendu* leaves and *sal* seeds constitute the single largest revenue earner for the state exchequer. Forest Department in the Working Plan document of Kalahandi admits, "To add to it is the craze for revenue out of forests. Being a source of non-tax revenue it contributes to over- exploitation of forests."

Similarly, in case of bamboo, *sal* seeds and other minor forest produces, if we calculate the wage rate offered to the labourer and collection, distribution and sale prices, we would find that the state government especially Forest Department and middlemen are the main gainer and local people with their resource reserve are the biggest loser.

The commercialisation of forest products at the cost of the rights of son of the soil by the so called protectors of vegetative

---

* *Kendu* leave collection from *dongerla* area is less. Dharamgarh sub-division and its fertile soils is good for *kendu* leave production.

wealth under the pretext of integrating tribals into the national mainstream is perhaps the greatest irony of institutionalised capitalism.

In the mad race of accumulation of quick and easy wealth, outsiders, traders, contractors, middlemen government and Forest Department not only directly exploit the poor by employing them for very low wages and forcing them to sell local products cheap but also indirectly exploit them by misutilising or plundering various minor forest products and continuously degrading the natural resource base which the poor fall back upon during the periods of scarcity. (Also see Appendix 5 p.362)

The Problem Resulting from Economic Interaction

Deforestation is a combined human assault on silent nature. The market demand and consequent road and rail construction have led illicit smuggling which take place in a big way. *Sisoo* woods are being transported in large quantities almost daily through trains to Vizagpatnam (Andhra Pradesh) which are used in cart making particularly. The forested blocks of Madanpur Rampur, Lanjigarh and Bhawanipatna and Thuamul Rampur Ranges are subjected to over-exploitation wrongly interpreting the provisions of marketing rules. The steep and precipitous slopes which should be excluded from exploitation are also not being spared. Network of extraction paths and dragging lanes are being laid out through the forest as a result of which forests are getting opened out.

Again large scale collection of *sal* seeds is posing a serious problem for natural regeneration. The collection season starts from 15th May and ends in 15th June. During the period maximum seed fall takes place. *Sal* seed has a peculiar character that it loses viability within 15 days. Failure of pre-monsoon shower creates problem for seedling regeneration. To and to it, almost 95 per cent of the seeds falling on the ground is being collected by outsiders. This is certainly a big blow to natural regeneration of *sal*.[16]

When ground grasses is dry and leaf fall is maximum. This is basically human activity the deeper analysis of which points out certain institutional shortcomings and structural distortions caused by the unholy alliance of Forest Department and traders.

Fires are caused for collection of *mahua* flower, to obtain ash manure by burning the shrub of forest floor, spreading of fire from adjoining areas where *podu* cultivation is done, spreading of fire from near by village lands out of carelessness or for collection of other minor forest produces like honey.

Today lack of care for forests means loss of sense of belonging among the people. Poverty, partly explains such state of affairs which can be fully and properly understood if we examine situation within the structure and institution.

Condemning *podu* bluntly as a cause of fire is to overlook many inner reasons of human interactions and compulsions. It is not that traditional tribal system of *podu* lacks knowledge on safety measures for ecological balance. Rather the practice follows certain methods which are ecologically ethical. In *podu* site selection, tribes give enough attention taking sunlight wind direction etc. into consideration. The direction of wind is important because only in that way fire spreading can be prevented. In fact the tribals were developing enough attention to avoid any such mishap. Similarly, in the collection of *mahua* flower, local folks were used to wait till they naturally fall on the ground.

Today, the situation is different. With the commercialisation of *podu* and minor forest products including *mahua,* contractors and traders who are interested in quick and large scale collection of forest resources rather indirectly or directly compel the starving poor (labourers or cultivators) to use fire as a crude tool for production and collection of larger resources/products in shorter time duration. Needless to mention that *mahua* flower trade is one of the most flourishing business in Kalahandi these days. It is one of the largest revenue earner for the State Government. Poor can no longer remain that holy/disciplined nor can he sincerely follow the sound environmental practices/ethics because of his desperate search for work, wage and food (coupled with added pressure from above of traders and contractors). Similarly, in case of *kendu* also we find it is not local poor but traders and State Government are directly responsible for forest fire. Since the time this trade was in the hands of outside traders it has been a practice to set fire to forest as a result of which *kendu* bushes are charred and fresh flush of leaves appear. Coppicing the *kendu* bushes, in the forest is quite expensive. So this method which is cheapest is adopted and called as double coppicing. Even now after the *kendu* leaf nationalisation (Nationalisation of trade). Since 1973 the practice continues and probably in more extensive manner.

The paragraph 2.48, section two of District Working Plan mentions that massive drive should also be made to educate the people about the evil effects of forest fire. This seems to be rhetoric. On the one hand, state has created an economic structure living in which poor is compelled to habitually set fire in the forest and on the other it talks of education and awareness among them to protect forests from fire.

Role of Exploiters

We find that very exploitative mechanism has remained unchanged over the years but what have been currently changed are:

(a) The number and hierarchy of exploiters (in which State has the dominant dictating role).
(b) The size of exploited class (since population, impoverishment and poverty has increased over the decades).
(c) The rate and intensity of exploitation by the exploiters of the past (which includes businessmen, contractors, middlemen) as well as those of the present state institution like OFC, TDCC, LAMPS, AMCS, etc.

The ultimate victim is the poor, *i.e.* the already victimised group. The ultimate sufferer is the nature, whose precious and non-replenishable resources have been plundered throughout. These simply have raised the poverty of the people along with the areal underdevelopment.

The idea of integrating tribals with the market economy does not seem to be a sound argument. The aforesaid arguments, institutional experiences and experiments of the past stand in favour of the statement. Those who man government machinery in development effort often possess little knowledge about tribal sentiment, culture and they show little concern for their struggled life.

The Government (on its part) in order to feed its ever starving exchequer tries to collect as much revenue as possible. The twin options opened before it is either to raise the selling price of MFP or reduce the collecting expenditure. When act under the structured groups of varied bargaining power, the state adopts the later means rather than the former throwing the state burden of economic need or compulsion on to the backs of the poor (labourer-cum-producers), the powerless flock.

Distribution of Processing Units and Exporting Centres

Kalahandi forests were brought into the commercial network, like other forest areas, by the turn of this century. Earlier leases were given to BTT company and BN Dutta and Company. In the past 1947 period the Orient Paper Mills got a long lease for the bamboo from Kalahandi forest area.[17] Though the major centre to which region supplies bamboo is M/s. Straw Products Ltd. the paper mills at Jankaypur (near Raygada), small forest based industries have also been clustered at Narla, Kesinga, Ambadola of the District Tetlagarh, of Bolangir, Muniguda, Raygada of Koraput (which lie in the vicinity of this resource region). Certain industries are located in a linear manner along the railway lines resembling colonial pattern. For example, a number of saw mills are located all along the rail line connecting Kesinga Rupra Road, Narla Road, Ambadola, Lanjigarh Road, Muniguda and Rayagada from where the forest resource region supplies timber for building railway sleepers, beams, planks etc. Minor, forest produces like barks of *Asan* and *Ariun* are sent out of Titlagarh which are used for tanning purposes. Similarly, other cottage industries (making agricultural tools, furnitures etc.) depend on the available minor forest produces of the area. For instance, hill broom making unit of Kesinga and carpentry units of Titlagarh. Country liquor distillers and rice mills (which consume a sizeable quantity of firewood) spread over the entire resource region. Small manufacturing units like graphite processing factory, *ayurvedic* medicines, agro-chemical industries, agricultural implements, factories, biscuit factories etc. are also found in the district.

One important aspect to be emphasised here is that most of the products which are produced by the above industries using the regional resource and regional labour hardly consumed or utilised by the local poor. Rather these are exported outside, the process from which city dwellers with requisite purchasing power are amply benefited. Traders and private manufacturer or producers reap the maximum profit and poor labourers are only marginally benefited.

Due to virtual absence of local markets, the local products by and large, are exported out through the same production business centres like Kesinga, Narla Road, Lanjigarh Road, Rupra Road which in fact functions as suction points representing a typical pattern of neo-colonisation. Kesinga and Narla Road station which are situated on Raipur-Vizianagaram Railway line handles larger percentage of the products. DBK Railway Project connecting Titlagarh with Sambalpur indirectly despatches goods to North India from Kalahandi. Rohtak, Delhi, Ranchi, Calcutta and Raipur import most of the timbers from the district. The commercial timbers in great demand include *Sal, Bija, Sisoo, Haldu, Asan, Dhaura, Kasi, Bandhan, Tangan Mundi, Kendu Jamu* etc. Teak and *Champa* are in short supply, *Sal* poles are exported to the Chhotanagpur mining belt.

Firewood is mainly exported to Calcultta, Bobilli and Vishakhapattanam, Bhubaneswar, Cuttack and Chennai. These are collected from Coupes. However, for meeting the local demands, forests in the close vicinity of villages are hacked.

Forest Department collects and processes *kendu* leaves before these are marketed by Orissa Forest Development Corporation Limited. Almost the entire portion of the produce is auctioned publicly and later sent to *bidi* factories of Calcutta, Chennai, Cochin and Ahmedabad. Sometimes the produce is send even to countries like Sri Lanka and Bangladesh.

Bamboo is consumed both locally and by the paper industries outside. Forest dwellers and other villagers in adjoining plains use it for house construction, fencing and ware making. Substantial portion of it, however, goes for pulp and paper mills at Jaykaypur near Rayagada, whom the forest produce is leased out on a long-term basis. Green debarked firewood too are consumed by the paper industries.

Minor forest products of the district are sent to consumption centres of north and south India, by Tribal Development Cooperative Corporation Ltd., the collecting and marketing agent. The minor forest produce includes *Mahua* flower and *Mahua* seeds, hill brooms, *Ban tulsi, Siali* leaves, *Siali* fibre, Jungle Jute, Myrobalans, *Genduli* Gums and other Gums, *Char* seeds, *Lac, Sal* seeds. After the nationalisation these are collected and sold out by Orissa Forest Development Corporation Limited to the industries of the state and outside the state.

Utilisation of Forest Produce

The expansion of *pucca* roads and entry of trucks into the area have made the bulk transport easier and faster for carrying timber and other products from the interior areas to the depots. This accelerated the rate of exploitation. Barring the *praja coupes* all the coupes are being worked by the Orissa Forest Development Corporation Limited whose policy is to eliminate middlemen. Prior to 1982-83 coupes were publicly auctioned to contractors. The working season for timber coupes as well as bamboos is from 1st October to 30th June. The *praja coupes* are left open to the public also during the same period after which contractor enters the forest to work the balance materials.

Sal seeds which are collected by the M/s O.F.D.C. Ltd. were nationalised in the year 1983. The charge of *kendu* leaves collection and distribution took up by the same agency in 1973. Previously, the twin products were in the direct control of businessmen. *Sal* seed collection takes place between 15th May up to 15th June.

Irrespective of who utilises the forest, there has been continual degradation of the resource of the region. Sahajkhol block is completely devastated. Udaygiri block is now subject to heavy hacking and *podu.*[18]

In the previous chapter, it has been established that, regional forests contribute to the household income of the poor only marginally. In other words, forest has a resource base does not add significantly to family income. It merely changes the nature of poverty (by relieving its intensity and breaking its perpetuity).

Local people are benefited from forests in three different ways. First, by directly procuring forest produce for consumption, they partially satisfy their basic needs such as food, fuel and house construction and fencing etc. Second, by selling the fuelwood, fodder and or other minor forest produce or their processed form they earn for the requirement of family need for a couple of days. Third, by engaging themselves in various seasonal operations of forestry, they get daily wages for stipulated time period. Though none of these ways provide them adequate earning even for the marginal expenses of the poor, some how it provides little relief to them.

The forest and tribal communities depend on the forests for firewood, timber, house building, roof thatching, food and medicines. Commercial exploitation of forests through large scale export of forest products and restrictions on the use of forest products have considerably affected the lifestyle of the tribals and other poorer sections of this district. The forest communities have also misused the forest because of ignorance.[19]

By denying the customary rights to common land and depriving local communities of their ancestral resources the government agencies have often encouraged unscrupulous contractors and *sahukars* to appropriate local support for subsistence.[20]

Unemployed youths often act like middlemen or contractors and are involved in sale (business) of *sal*, *sisoo*, or even firewood, with the cooperation of forest staff. Wide deforestation took place when village forests were allocated to the landless people. Moreover, contractors were given the task of cutting the mature trees, dying or diseased defective trees of thicker growth or vegetation. This right was, however, misused by them. In reality they started felling more trees than they are entitled to. Curiously, local tribals are perceived as the villains responsible for the deforestation and degradation of their own ecology, many a times they themselves carry such self-perceptions as they find themselves compelled to exploit forest resources.[21]

According to a rough estimation*, around 1600 to 1700 hanging bundles of wood are carried by the shoulders of males and about 1000 to 1200 head loads of wood are brought into the town by females to meet daily fuel wood demand of Bhawanipatna alone. Around 100 persons bring wood charcoal. The local price for hanging bundles is Rs. 25 that of a head load bundle of wood is Rs.15 and that of a charcoal bag is Rs 40.

Bhawanipatna has a nodal location. The converging routes through which fuel wood and charcoal sellers enter the town are – Thuamul Road, Jeypore Road, Lanjigarh (Vishwanathpur Road) Bhawanipatna Ambadoli Road, Bhawanipatna-Khariar Road. No doubt, poor is benefited. But non-poor grab the larger share. Forest is the ultimate loser.

For all kinds of forestry operations like marking, cleaning, thinning, road repair and construction, collection of *kendu* leaves and *sal* seeds forests department employs local labour which are unskilled and cheap. Moreover, except the sowing and harvesting period the labourers readily offer their work throughout the year. Large section of the regional labourers are absorbed in the collection of minor forest produce. Given below is a table of wage rates for three base years.

Table 5.2: Wage Rates (Rs./day) for 1963,1983 and 1993

Year	Male	Female
1963	1.35	1.05
1983	5.00	5.00
1993	30.00	30.00

Source : District Labour Office, Kalahandi.

Note : 1993 data was collected from fieldwork. The wage has been made uniform for both male and female in 1983 and 1993. This non-discrimination is justified on the ground that both sexes are capable of doing equal amount of work except timber collection.

Drain of Resources

Following is a table showing Revenue Expenditure list of Forest Department, Kalahandi Division.

* Calculated after a long discussion with Nilakantha Mahapatra, ex-forest ranger.

Table 5.3: Net Earning from Forest (in Rs.)

Year	Revenue	Expenditure	Net earning consumption
1960-61	1014277	424196	590081
1965-66	1894744	530624	1364121
1970-71	3384784	895210	2489575
1975-76	4671350	2347209	2324141
1980-81	18549620	2208386	16341232
1981-82	28426040	2515558	25910481

Note : Revenue figures of 1975-76, 1980-81 and 1981-82. excludes the *kendu* leave revenue which contributes the largest share to the total figures.

Source : District Working Plan.

The high expenditure of the Forest Department seems a colossal waste. Because the institutional intervention management, plantation working, collection, transportation etc. has hardly produced any results in forestry. This is evident from the field observation.

The forest cover of Kalahandi has substantially reduced and degraded. The southern part of the district was covered by moist deciduous forest having commercially valuable *sal.** The northern part especially, Khariar side was rather covered by dry deciduous forest having valuable trees of excellent quality (B.K. Deo, the Ex-MLA and Prince who resides in Bhawanipatna). In the Buckingham palace the Kalahandi teak was praised to be the best of its kind in the world.

The working plan mentioned about the scientific management and cutting of woods from specific demarcated segments rotationwise. But in practice trees were felled simultaneously from patches of various demarcated segments**. Earlier, in the initial section it has already been discussed how the top 1/3rd of hill forest cover which was left untouched during pre-independence period, was destroyed as soon as the traders

* The girth of *sal* trees were about 18 feet on an average. The logs were solid trees. The inner portion was fully covered without any hole or break. According to Moonis, the author of the working plan *sal* of Kalahandi is the best in Asia.

** The random, haphazard and ruthless practice caused irreparable damage to the precious wealth of Kalahandi.

and contractors with the direct support of forest officials entered into *podu* cultivation and timber collection.

Mostly after independence in the region of Mixed Resource base we shall see how wide-spread teak felling was carried out in the Khariar *Zamindari* after the private ownership of forest land was allowed to the local cultivators. The devastation of *sal* and teak is phenomenal.[22]

Seventy per cent of geographical area was filled with Tropical Dry Deciduous forest. Official data puts the present cover at 46.38 per cent, *i.e.* 8300 square kilometre of the total area of the district. Satellite imagery shows that not more than 10 per cent of forest cover is left to day. Moreover, almost all the pious prescription of the working plan had never been implemented seriously.

The State Government under the apparent (plea of) pretext of safeguarding national interest appropriate the huge surplus generated from the regional forest which is supposedly meant for regional and local inhabitants.

The principal revenue contributors are timber, firewood, bamboo and *kendu* leaves. They account for more than 90 per cent of revenue the government collects form forest produce which revenue added up to about one crore in the year 1976-77. The forest revenue increased from twenty-five lakhs in 1964-65 to about 128 lakhs in 1977-78. Individual itemwise, the timber revenue was about 7 lakhs in 1959-60, which rose to 32 lakhs in 1977-78; Firewood revenue was about 2 lakhs rising to 11 lakhs in 1977-78; Bamboo revenue which was 0.85 lakhs in 1959-60, rose to 11 lakhs, *kendu* leaves raised its revenues from 13 lakhs to about 60 lakhs by 1976-77.

Given total population of about 13 lakhs (1981 Census) the revenue collection of 127 lakhs makes a ten rupee contribution per capita. All this with the official reporting of the sales of by the contractors and traders, the real revenue contributed by the tribals and other poorer section of the district will one presume, comes to a staggering figure.[23]

This reflects that the district is not at all poor in forest resources. The poverty of the people is, therefore, could be due to the drain of resources without any compensation mechanism of investment and proper circulation of capital which flows into the district in terms of grants, loans etc.

Given below is the production of timber, *mahua* seeds, and *sal* seeds of the Bhawanipatna Forest Division.

Table 5.4 : Stock flow of Round timber at forest (Bhawanipatna (T) Divisions)

Items	(Production in tones.)			
	1986-87	1987-88	1988-89	1991-92
Round timber	5322	4255	1133	–
Unsawn F W	7359	3263	2197	–
Sawn F W	182	–	–	–
Sawn I	159	114 Cum.	20 Cum.	–
S.Saw	242	24	–	
Mahua	–	–	–	8865
Sal Seed	–	–	–	4000

Note :. The *Mahua* seed selling rate is Rs. 42,000 per tonne (1991-92). It was Rs. 1900 per tonne the previous year. Timber cutting was banned after 1989.

Source: Office of the CFC (Chief Conservator of Forest), Orissa.

All these shows the forest resource of the region has been siphoned off to the common detriment of the poor. The satisfaction of diversifying needs of the poor that can raise the family income substantially is hardly possible.

Local Barter (Exchange) System

In the following paragraphs tries to exhibit how the crude exchange system is exploitative in nature.

During 1960s many outside traders settled flow in the district. Few traders (of North India or Coastal Orissa) are solely dependent on peddling goods either directly or through local SCs and middlemen (locally called *dalals).* They bring from plains various goods including coastal products like salt, spices, dried fish, which are exchanged or bartered with forest or *podu* products such as pulses, large amount of millets, oil seeds etc. and even gold.

We are already aware of inaccessibility in interior Orissa from the study of Nayak and Sinha poor condition of roads, in fact, is the cause of growth of a number of mobile *haats* by coastal traders in the district, where the exchange of products between the primary producers of the forested upland and *'dalals'* take place.[24]

The middlemen bargain well and barter profitably with the tribals by selling (out) items like brass and aluminium utensils cooking and storing pots, clothes, blankets, sweaters etc. They have thus introduced the market economy in the relatively simple, self-sufficient tribal economy. With the entry of non-tribal products, the self-sufficiency of comparatively less exploitative barter system of tribal producers declined. In the year of crop loss and food scarcity the grain prices are normally high and tribals face hardships in satisfying their requirements of subsistence. This results in widespread tribal indebtedness. The traders exploit this situation to acquire more wealth in the form of exorbitant interest, harvest produces and land.

The middlemen set out to offer loan to villagers on the eve of *'Nuakhai'* and *'Push punei'*, the popular pre-harvest festivals when the tribals spend lavishly. The middlemen can be from scheduled caste or from among the village touts.

As soon as the harvest (which is done just after few weeks of private loan disbursement) is over the traders go on recovering the loan along with high interest. Repayment is usually made in the form of agriculture produce which is collected at fixed depots, set up for every cluster of two to three villages. In some cases the borrowers (villagers) directly submit the loan or agricultural produce. This trade was monopolised by North Indian traders. Before 1970 brass men, a business community of Ganjam and Cuttack district were quite active in their trade.

Mobile Haat and Space in Suction Mechanism

For profit motivated sellers and businessmen location choice plays an important role. It is evident in the following section.

There are about 7 big *haats* and few smaller *haats,* each attracting tribal customers from villages located within eight kms. radius. Selling vendors or mobile sellers move from *haat to haat* rotation wise in different days of the week. A seller on an average sells goods of about 20-25 thousands in a single *haat.* Barring Bhawanipatna (which is a permanent market place)

Madanpur, Dharamgarh, Khariar, Nuapada in the plain lands and northern forested up lands serves temporary market place or *haats* where permanent fixed shops and weekly shops are set.* (Also see Appendix 5 p.358)

The extent of exploitation by middlemen can be gauged from the following table. The distance between Thuamul Rampur and Bhawanipatna is not more than sixty kilometres.

Table 5.5 : Comparative Price Index between Bhawanipatna and Thuamul Rampur

Items	Place of Purchase	Place of Sale	Unit	Purchasing Price	Selling Price
Banana	Th. Rampur	Bh. Patna	100 pcs.	Rs.20	Rs.70
Mango	Th. Rampur	Bh. Patna	1 kg.	Rs.2	Rs.6
Guava	Th. Rampur	Bh. Patna	One	Rs.0.50	Re l.
Papaya	Th. Rampur	Bh. Patna	1 Kg.	Rs.0.50	Rs.3.
Maize	Th. Rampur	Bh. Patna	1 pc.	Rs.0.15	Rs.0.50

Source : Primary Survey, 1991.

The brass men buy the old utensils (brass and aluminium) at Rs. 50 to 90 and after polishing and anodising sell out the same utensil at Rs. 100 to Rs. 120.

The hindrances in smooth transportation is somehow a blessing in disguise for small traders who take little strain to sustain their business in remote areas.

The big businessmen find themselves comfortably settled in Bhawanipatna. The minor business often settle down in interior village of larger size, thereby avoiding the cut throat competition from big traders one is likely to face at the block and district headquarters (from big traders). Few *dalals* use public transport in carrying the goods to and from the sellers and traders.

Limitation of Voluntary Efforts in Production Plantation or Regeneration

The natural wealth once destroyed can never be replaced by any artificial means. Moreover, plantation involves many people and takes a long period. But destruction can be done within a short

* Interview with K.K. Parida, a school teacher in Bhawanipatna.

time duration. The example of Kelia Reserve Forest can be cited in this context. The forest has an area of about 500 acres. This had rich cover in 1970s and gradually due to over population and greater requirement of people the forest was depleted and it was prescribed in the working circle. The plantation was taken up and there was a pole crop in this 500 acres of Reserve Forest. But during the year 1984 when Assembly and Parliamentary election were held, all the forest staff were deputed for election duty. Through some political speeches, the people were instigated to cut the forest and take it as it belonged to them.

The people cut out those 500 acres of forest within a couple of days. Later on, with the help of Madhusudan Sanskrutik Anusthan, Masigaon under the leadership of Shri Kesav Nayak, a youth organisation was formed and they had composed songs to influence the protection of trees and planting up of trees in their local languages and they had made *padayatras* in Masigaon and surrounding villages for three days and they have also organised awareness camps with the help of collectors and other officers of the District. This created such a great impact that in next three years *i.e.* during 1986-89, the total area of 500 acres was again full of lush green trees. But it has come to the authors notice that again the forest was chopped off hardly within two days recently.[25]

It is not important to start a scheme. From the past experience of plantation of Forest Department and the following reasons, the success of social forestry is in doubt. First, the wage of the watchman is lower than what ought to be. In such a condition the guard will remain prone to corruption and bribery in future which will possibly be a danger for forest protection.

Second, the valuable plants planted like teak *sisoo,* and commercial species like bamboo is probably going to serve the interest of middlemen and rich people (*i.e.* of contractors, smugglers and other unscrupulous officials or guards etc.) in the long run.

Moreover, general fuel scarcity due to loss of earlier forest cover nearby will allure people to cut the trees for their domestic needs, before these become fully matured (in fact this is what the researcher noticed during the field survey while travelling from Dharamgarh to Kulihariguda.)

Voluntary bodies like Gram Vikas, Thuamul Rampur Administration block which set up development society to insure standard support price for produce and FAAR, Lanjigarh transact the deals of forest produce and save the tribals form the grip of the middlemen.

Assisted by village committee and its staff the society has made inroads into the inaccessible rural pockets covering as of now about 100 hamlets. Tribal farmers were being paid an advance of Rs. 500 to Rs. 600 on a quintal of the produce apart from being assured of a bonus of approximately Rs. 50 to 100 after the sale was made.

Society rules stipulate that the profit accrued was to be spent on the welfare of the tribals and community development. Freedom from rampart oppression of the middlemen and barter system of the produce were the two benefits of the society system.

The experiment has proved a success but beset by the backlash of musclemen, political touts, police and traders who detained the trucks transporting the stock are the clouds in the sky.[26]

Politicians who were most vocal about Kalahandi are often lukewarm in their sincerity. They take the poverty and hunger of Kalahandi people as a "trump-card" to create a political base for themselves and do not look for a permanent solution to the problem.[27]

The service spirit of voluntary organisation not always revolve around the axis of sacrifice. Many subconscious personal or group motives often override the communal welfare activities. During the fieldwork, the research thus observes.

The very preponderance of multiple growth of NGO and their restricted activities and other marginal intervention point out the fact that unemployed youths go for social service because of their economic needs to earn a stable or precarious living in a district of poverty, job scarcity and low education. They satisfy their basic economic necessities as the district gets (lump sum) time to time grants, aids and assistance from various national and international institutions.

Secondly, some NGOs after becoming familiar among the local people try to build a political base for themselves. Making people politically aware has been mistaken as imparting real consciousness. Belief and value system of most of the people are such exploitation becomes a natural result. However, few voluntary organisations have shown their true voluntary spirit in taking up few welfare activities.

Conclusion

Thus, in this part of the region with forest resource base we find the son of the soil is treated as a secondary citizen in his very forest habitation. Elitist approach rather blames him for deforestation. Whether it is governmental or non-governmental institution the protectors have always been open exploiters. Natural vegetation belong to the local inhabitants, first. But their natural as well as statutory rights have been snatched away by various institutional elements in production relation. The traders, contractors, forest department remain at the root of this system siphoning off the forest products through various mechanisms and processes. These amply explain the critical poverty and underdevelopment of Kalahandi.

Cultivable Plain Region

The region encompasses the Tel valley (of Kesinga, Narla, Karlamunda and Eastern Khariar, Northern Bhawanipatna and part of Golamunda); the Tel-Hatti basin (of Dharamgarh, Junagarh, Kalampur, Jaypatna and Koksara).

Dharamgarh and Junagarh are bounded by hills on the western and eastern side. The northern side is opened towards Udanti basin and the southern side towards the wider Tel-Hatti basin of Kalampur, Jaipatna and Koksara. The blocks are devoid of any kind of forests.

The undulating plains of Kesinga and Karlamunda are located to the south of river Tel in northeastern Kalahandi. They are separated by intervening Narla block. The region pedologically is the most fertile part of Kalahandi. It possesses water surplus stretches of the drought prone Kalahandi.

Existing historical facts and figures suggest that Kalahandi was not niggardly but bountiful in forest as well as plain land resources. Merchants used to sail in the Telavaha river with their merchandise *(Jataka).* Taitilaka Janapada, which was situated in the west of Kalinga was famous for trade in rhinoceros hides. (Taitilaka Janapada). Towards land rent or *takoli* Kalahandi was paying about Rs. 5330 per year to the Bhonsla of Nagpur during the later end of eighteenth century. Forests, minerals and some non-conventional produces are major sources of state revenue to day. Of the total geographical area (in '000 hectares) of 1177.2 in 1981 of the district, net cultivated land constitute 509, *i.e.* 43.2 per cent. The region registered 35.59 per cent of the main workers as agricultural labourers compared to 27.76 per cent for the state. Among the operational holding 63.75 per cent belong to medium and small farmer category occupying 28.75 per cent of total operated area in the district in contrast to 77.89 per cent and 41 per cent in case of the state. So, the proportion of landless agricultural labourer is high. The poor landless agricultural labourers have no access to any material resources. They mostly rely on large farmers, land owners or businessmen and remain at the mercy of the forest officials. The nature of bondage is different. Despite the effort of voluntary organisation (like OXFAM) this problem still persists with vested interests holding sway.

The prevailing system of production relation includes several kinds of economic interaction that leads to exploitation. These are *'sukhabas'?* (wage labour), *'bahabandha'* (advance taken towards tying arms *i.e.* labour), *chidol* (instalment adjustment for leased land). In case of *goti* one receives his payment in kind (*i.e.* about one *puti i.e.* 75 kgs of paddy per month and an annual payment of 4 *putis).* The poor people find the existing system quite secured in absence of regular and alternative sources of work. Many immigrants acquired large tracts of land and other natural resources during pre-British period displacing original inhabitants. Though there is marginal development in the district 'new settlers' of colonial period continue to benefit out of the socio-economic backwardness of the larger populaces and the implementation of developmental schemes of the government. They have fully established themselves as *zamindars, gauntias* or owner of *Brahmottar Rom Devottar* grants or as occupancy tenants. The royal family along with the newcomers and traders now constitute the handful section of rich people in the district, who appropriate the large share of agricultural production using their economic and political power. During the pre-British period (of Monarchy) Marwaris, the first trading community entered inside the district followed by Sindhis, Sikhs and others in fifties and sixties.

In the previous chapter it has been mentioned that how underdevelopment (especially underdevelopment in road and communication) is a major cause of poverty of the people of Kalahandi. But looking in a different perspective this under-development is rather a blessing in disguise since it accentuated free trade in agro produces in late nineteenth and early twentieth century.

In recent years, this area has witnessed a spurt in agricultural production by introducing non-conventional technology, HYV of seeds and irrigation facilities. The rise is in production of crops such as oilseeds, sugar, non-food or cash crops such as sugarcane, spices etc. and food crops such as paddy and other food grains and pulses. Due to integration of Kalahandi with outside market there has been growing demand on cash crops. The cropping intensity and total integrated area to total cropped area were 125 per cent and 4 per cent respectively for mainly the land resource region (in 1975-76) and 156 per cent and 11 per cent (in 1984-85) respectively for mainly the land resource region. However, this has hardly benefited the poor as the outside market force eke out the major share of the production from land like the previous forest resource region diversion of land here in this case is towards cash crops. The net area under ragi, jowar and small millets and other cereals of poor men have decreased. According to an estimation percentage change of proportion of total cropped area in case of wheat is 54.2, ragi is 14.4, jowar is 18.5, small millets is 36.8, during the period of 1977-78 and 1984-85. However, the plain land resource region contributes more to national economy than it receives back from it in the form of loan, subsidy, aid or grants. As emphasised once and again this is a major causative factor behind the underdevelopment of the region.

Change in Ownership of Means of Production and Kond Rebellion

Here, is a case from history. The "Kond Rebellion" explains how the historic incident acted as a force of reorganisation of local communities over space and the consequent change in production-relation following allocation of cultivating lands. During British period however, excess and systematic demand on land revenue led to impoverishment of the local peasantry. Feudalistic rulers and village *Gauntias* were tuned to the British system of ever growing revenue collection. Udip Pratap Deo (1853-1881), the then ruling prince took a historic step enhancing the land revenue. He encouraged the *kulta* cultivators of Sambalpur to migrate into the fertile Tel valley. The Kultas in turn displaced the indigenous kond from their own land and started to exploit them.*

Kultas through money lending and liquor trading, alienated Konds from Konds who were relatively simple-minded and faithful. Being landless the Konds were forced to work outside as labourers. In most cases they had to serve as bonded labourers in the houses and cultivating fields of the very Gauntias whom they lost their lands. This kind of exploitation through gradual displacement and total loss of status along with the very means of livelihood were severely resented by the Konds as they become more and more aware of the changing situation. Their sheer frustration (deprivation) soon turned into an organised rebellion in 1882. The terrified Kultas in order to save life from the advancing militant Konds left to areas of safety. For instance, Kultas of Mahichala (Junagarh) left and settled in Borda (Khariar border, Dharamgarh sub-division). Similarly, Kultas of Narla withdrew themselves to MP border closer to Khariar Zamindari after resigning from *Gauntiaship*. After the rebellion was over, calmness prevailed. Local Branamins started buying selected lands with lower rates and soon turned into Gauntias in place of the Kultas. However, the *durbar* government banned land transfer in 1932 from backward castes thereby providing protection to *adivasis* and

---

* This culminated in the terrifying Kondh rebellion (1882) under the heroic guidance of Chakra Bisoyee. Being horrified Kultas ran towards plains in the forested and hilly south. They left towards west and north away from the Kondh habitation of south. Again during the same period the abolition of various kinds of levies on trade attracted outside businessmen and merchants further into the resourceful district.

harijans (J.C. Singh Deo, a descendant of past ruling family of Madanpur Rampur).

Gauntia, the Prime Landholding Class

Gauntias were from various communities and settled in different areas of the district. Among them mention may be made of.

(a) *Kultas,* the agriculturalists of Sambalpur who settled in the Tel valley, being invited by the king (Udip Pratap Deo).

(b) *Brahamins* of Sambalpur and coastal Orissa were initially given land grants along with the performance of *Puja* (temple worship). They were gradually absorbed in Dharamgarh, Jaypatna and Junagarh areas (Land were allocated through *Brahmottor Devottar.)*

(c) Few of the Muslims who initially came as horse traders, started residing in the Khariar area of Kalahandi. They became *Gauntias* later on.

Barring these groups some tribals such as *Konds, Gonds* function as *Gauntias* in many villages in different parts of the district. Gonds of Kulihariguda, *Majhis* or *Konds* of *Matia,* Brahamins of Mankadashola though belong to different castes or tribes, are also *Gauntias. Kultas, Gauds (milkmen), Mali* (General caste people) are also found to be traditional *Gauntias* in different villages. So, *Gauntias* are not from a particular caste group but they themselves constitute a class group.

Qualities of Cultivated Lands

The land qualities of the Plain Land Resource Region were classified into four principal categories. Grade wise, these are:

(i) *Bahal*	(ii) *Berna*
(iii) *Mal or Bhata*	(iv) *Bhata* or *Att (Rom).*

Other categories of land included *barchha* (Sugarcane plots) and *bari* (homestead land). The soil is mainly sandy loam, northern fringe is black and southern fringe, laterite. The plain country was mostly inhabited by Kultas, the agriculturist population. (See Appendix 5 p.349)

Landless Labourers

Labourers comprised

(i) *Baha bandha,*
(ii) *Barsikia,* and
(iii) *Bhutias.*

Non-SCs and STs are mainly landed groups. Most *Gauntias* belong to them. On the other hand, few Harijans possess cultivating lands. Though implementation of ceiling system has led to distribution of surplus land among many landless SCs. They hardly have actual control over the lands. In some cases, size and quality of distributed land are such these are often uneconomic to cultivate. So, the general landlessness, apart from non-availability of other viable alternatives, is a basic cause explaining why the tendency among SCs for outmigration is more.

Wages available outside are constant, regular, fixed and sufficient to meet day-to-day family expenses. They remain alluring for SC migrants who make rational decision, sometimes by mortgaging their land. SCs outmigrate in search of *Kuli* (labour), percentage share of agricultural labour and cultivators among main workers were 37 and 86 respectively in 1971 and were 41 and 86 respectively in 1981. Fieldwork data (1992) shows 35.2 percentage of households were landless labourers.

Thus, these show there is even greater proportion of workers entering into agricultural activities. The small and marginal farmers' proportion has increased over a period of time. In 1992 48.3 percentage households belonged to small and marginal farmers. The presence of the farmers on the one hand and traders on the other, has contributed to the growth of three or four trade centres in the district which draw the agricultural produce from the surrounding villages and extend a market for the various industrial goods.

Development planning has released quite a few economic agents and generally the area they enter in are the trade, transport, contract work and the latest are the gems. The State sponsored bank loan dependent scheme did generate some of the new economic agents who are also part of the beneficiary group but most often they are drawn out of the traditional beneficiary group. However, one may not miss to observe few 'rags' to 'riches' phenomena. The process of expansion of new economic phenomena though attempts to develop infrastructure (physical as well as social), has thus mostly benefited the new agents who also share with the traditional owners and the major losers are again people, mostly dependent on labour or on forests.

In the previous section we have already discussed about the proportion of cultivators and labourers across various caste groups. 1981 census shows that there are 50.74 per cent of cultivators to total worker and 35 per cent agrarian labourers in the district. Caste-wise distribution is:

Table 5.6: Caste-wise Labourers Index, Kalahandi

Caste/Tribe	Percentage of Cultivators to total Labourers	Percentage of Labourers
SCs	39.57	45.84
STs	54.63	38.66
Others	51.75	30.16

Source : Census, 1981.

Percentage of workers is more among SCs than STs. In other words, the proportion of workers among SCs is more than among STs, even if STs are more laborious. As discussed already STs in Kalahandi have considerable dependence on forest products for extra food and cash requirement beyond agricultural practice.

Land Allocation to the Labour Class

Subsequent Chapter 6 analyses that tribes are the poorest group; SCs are the least poor group; and general caste people fall in middle. However, the inter-group variation is very low. The inequalities among the above groups has probably reduced because of the implementation of ceiling laws (Laws protecting land alienation of SCs and STs from general caste people). In fact, Ceiling Act has been implemented to the advantage of SCs and STs. SCs are the main gainer since higher proportion of SCs were, landless earlier.*

Land allocation itself has however, not brought real change in poverty. The casual food scarcity and insecurity among the poor is largely due to bad quality of land allotted, low work availability, low purchasing power and sending of surplus food by the traders.

Development of Underdevelopment

It is interesting to observe a typical colonial pattern of development in which suction points grow in a linear manner along the lines of communication. Sindhis, Marwadis, Vaisyas (the trading communities from Haryana and Gujarat) have settled in the tiny but strategically located urban centres lying in between Khariar Road, Titlagarh, Kantabanji (Blolangir district), Kesinga, Narla and Bhawanipatna. A number of rice hullers or mills along with collection depots of *mahul, kendu* and other minor forest produce have been mushrooming in these towns which lying in the margins of the hinterland processes iocal raw material and send them out to Raipur, Vizianagaram and far beyond.

The landed gentry (from among the trading communities) exploit the local people and area and control local politics. They too control market economy. They have secured their entry deep into the interior villages from where they acquire various agricultural and forest produces (rice, pulses, cotton and oilseeds). In fact, this is an important reason which explain the poor men's entitlement.

---

* In some peculiar cases relatively more exposed SCs prove their intelligence and greater conciousness. The ceiling rule provides for, 'without the prior permission of Block Development Officer or Tehsildar the land of a cultivator (owner belonging to lower caste (*i.e.* SCs or STs) cannot be transferred or sold out. 'Taking advantage of this provision lower caste people borrow money against land mortgaged. The lender (usually belonging to higher class or caste group) because of less awareness later realises this mistake, when the low caste-class borrower with the help of revenue authorities (*viz.* B.D.O., Tehsildar or collector) recovers his mortgaged land without repaying the debt. The author noted few such cases in Basantpada, Jaypatna and Podapadar. It is rather the institution which helps the suppressed people to often play tricks against their age old exploiters.

Because of traders' exploitation, today, Kalahandi has turned to be a typical hinterland which provides resources, labour and raw materials (agricultural as well as forest products) to cities and areas of rich consumers which are again linked with national and international markets.

Basic Process of Suction Mechanism

Local inhabitants resort to borrowing under various circumstances. Liquor drinking is customary and rooted in the socio-cultural life of the people of Kalahandi. As we know on the occasions such as birth, death, marriage, festivals (like *toki parab, Nua Khai, pus punei*) settling village or group dispute, penalty payment, community or village party, recovery from illness or ghost effect, election etc. they engage in drinking, meat eating (after animal sacrifice) apart from other ways of spending. Obviously they run to *Mahajan* to borrow money. For meeting various household (domestic) and agricultural expenses they also frequently approach the moneylender who promptly respond to their need.

The moneylenders are usually from higher classes (*Mahajan* or *sahukars*) who often combines or associates himself with the activities of cultivation and trading and may be with liquor selling. The *sahukars* make the borrower obliged by meeting his occasion's urgent need. It is one of the reasons why private money lending has better and easier acceptance than bank loaning. In turn the borrower promises to repay the loan in kind (*i.e.* grains) at half the market price during harvest. The *Sahukar* keeps the grains stocked only to release them in the months of scarcity (*i.e.* lean season like rainy seasons) and demands one and half times more than the original purchasing price from the buyers who incidentally happen to be his earlier borrowers and sellers of agricultural products. This type of manipulation of time enable the shrewd traders-cum-money lenders to draw out high profit often amounting to two and half times the original investment (in terms of lending). (As high as two and half times more than the original money lent). This kind of money circulation which produces easy and magically swelling wealth is due to the initial cash the moneylender holds. Even this little investment capital they often receive from governmental sources.

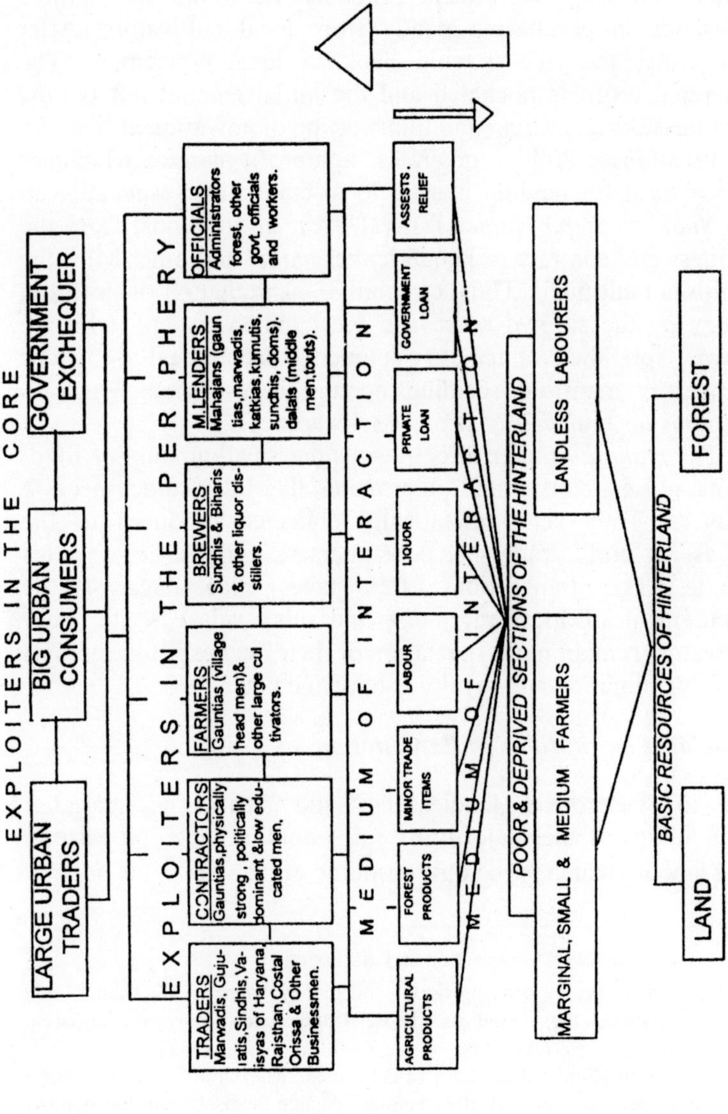

Fig. 5.1 : Suction Mechanism

For instance for the rice mills (the geographical location of which have already been discussed), rice traders, say, receive five thousand rupees in advance for processing a fixed amount of paddy from the government. Probably, he would spend three thousands in purchasing paddy from local cultivators. After processing, the rice is sold back to local consumers. The generated profit is pocketed and the initial amount left is now used for storing, milling and transporting of government rice.

Private rice hullers thus raise high profit margins which are further used for lending loan to local cultivators (especially on the *Nuakhai* or *pus punei* festival eve). In additions, from the business and contract of kendu leaves *mahul* and other MFP the wealth is multiplied. Thus, circulative manipulation of time and money by the shrewd north and west Indian traders (who are known for their business acumen) economically benefit themselves manifold residing on the very region which is infamous for hunger and strong backwardness.*

The *mahajan* trader directly sells out small amount of food-grains, pulses, clothes and other materials of day-to-day need to villagers. They send out locally collected produces to the processing units, traders or consumers residing in larger cities outside. The transaction often takes place against the procurement of local ragi, *alsi* and other oilseeds etc. Poor cultivators remain mute spectators of their own exploitation. His primary obligation and loyalty is bargained out.

Associated Institutions in Exploitation

Due to widespread landlessness and small and marginal landholdings of the majority of cultivators, reliance on earning from labour (which is the only resource of many poor) is heavy**

---

* Based on fieldwork observation and discussion.

** Kulta *Gauntias* by offering liquor and money secured land from Konds and rendered them landless. Those Konds later turned to labourers especially bonded labourers.

Apart from Kond tribes *Doms* (a scheduled caste) and *Gauds* (a general caste) who are poor and often landless engage themselves in the bonded labour group and many of them work in the houses of *Gauntias* even today (*Source*: Mr. J.C. Singh Deo, M. Rampur, ex-ruling prince). The system of bonded labour is still prevalent in Kalahandi though loosely. Prime cause of this is poverty. In Boden block the farmers are used to pay

(*Continued next page*)

Various forms of labour includes *Bethi, Begari, Bahabandha, Halia, Kuli* etc.[28] From among these feudal institutions *Bethi* and *Begari* were abolished in early twentieth century. The released labour force was absorbed in railway construction work going on during that period. Afterwards, there was again a situation of labour surplus. Though many people (especially scheduled castes) temporarily outmigrate the district.

The labour supply within the district exceeds the required demand. Small farmers, marginal farmers and workers who fail to get any work resort to borrowing. The incapacity of repayment of which lead to indebtedness.* The fieldwork data analysis will discuss the sources of moneylending, efficacy of banking system and success or failure in loan disbursement under various poverty alleviation schemes in the forthcoming chapter. What is worth mentioning here is that despite expansion in the banking system and huge governmental effort in providing highly concessionary loans# in recent years most poor depend on the private moneylenders as the later are easily approachable and help the needy at the time of their need. *Mahajans* are faithful and they generate sense of security and obligation among the borrowers by advancing loans on the eve of *Pus Punei* or *Nuakhai*## So, they are

---

their servant *Halia* 5 to 8 *puties* (3 to 5 bags) of paddy per annum besides cloth and some feeding. 16 to 20 *puties* (11 to 14 bags) paddy in total is paid to the '*Halias*' of Khariar block. The labourers take some amount of money called 'Bahabandha' and unless they refund it back they cannot be liberated. The labourers lead a miserable life. But barring a few the condition of the farmers is not well. Their produce from land is insufficient for a year.

* Usually, borrowing accompanies liquor drinking. Following is the list of various occasions when people often borrow cash for drinking, new cloth-wearing or meat-eating. These are : (a) Birth, (b) Death (for carrying corpse neighbourers demand liquor), (c) Marriage, (d) Festivals (like Toki parab, Dhangada dhangadi, *Nuakhai, pus punei*, Dashhara), (e) Penalty payment after compromise of a conflict, (f) Election eve. (g) Magician for ousting a ghost.

\# Highly concessionary as compared to huge interests demanded by private moneylenders of the local area.

\## *Nuakhai* is a Great Traditional Festival of the tribals of Kalahandi which they observe with much zeal, enthusiasm and intoxication. Marginal, small and medium farmers usually go for borrowing in advance in the month of September when '*Nuakahi* and *pus punei*' the two popular folk festivals of Kalahandi are celebrated. On the first day which marks Great Tradition the

(*Continued next page*)

more reliable and dependable source of loans than bank officials. Usually, the conditions *Sahukars* (moneylenders) impose on the poor cultivators are grossly unfair and literally blood sucking: As soon as the standing crops are ready for harvest in the month of December they come to purchase the produce at half the rate of the normal price of the post-harvest period (*i.e.* January and February) following immediately after. The borrower becomes debt free once at the above rate the price of the produce sold equals to the advanced loan borrowed. Thus, one can imagine the huge margin of interest in terms of profit the *mahajan* accumulates within a period of just two months. What is more ironical is that often the same *mahajan* sell the same produce to almost the same cultivator-borrower with a much higher rate during the season of scarcity (especially pre-harvest season/rainy season). Manipulation of time and money multiply money for *mahajan* only to render the cultivator ever poor.

Multiple exploiters

The economic history of the district provides us enough evidences that the district like other rural areas of India had a 'self-sufficient Subsistent Economy'. Today we find it has turned into a 'Dependent Subsistent Economy'. The compound effect of different exploiters is responsible for such state of affairs where rich exists on the very natural resources and production force of the poor.

Means of exploitation

The effective means or tools through which exploitative system continues are the following.

Initial capital and manipulative skills

The traders, brewers, contractors, moneylenders and middlemen *(dalal)* enter into the district's resource field with little material wealth and shrewd business motive of fast accumulation of wealth.

---

people worship mother Earth first, wear new clothes, use new utensils, prepare various cakes. This is a day of integration. The second day is the day of disintegration marked by perversion. People eat meat, drink liquor and fight among themselves. It may be referred as little tradition.

Exchange (or trading) Items

The vast cultivating labour class purchases salt, clothes, brass or aluminium utensils and daily consumable items in turn of *mahul,* paddy, rice, *tola, alsi, mung* etc. The primary products are assigned lower values and the very method of bartering proves unfair.

The Measuring Units

The conversion of traditional measuring units such as *tola, bada, gida, mana, puti* into kg, gram, litre etc. is beyond comprehension for many people. Most of them are easily deceived both due to their ignorance as well as poor bargaining power and faith in traditional traders and moneylenders. Barter or conventional exchange system still prevails in many areas. For example, *dalals* collect one bag *mahul* for one bag of salt. Looking to the price and quality value salt stands no where before *mahul.*

Time Tactics

Purchasing condition and price are fixed by the moneylender-cum-trader in an arbitrary manner. This is done before the harvest season when the poor cultivators badly need cash for celebrating the popular festivals like '*Nuakhai*' and *'push punei'*. After the harvest, especially during the periods of scarcity the traders open the accumulated agricultural products to the *haats* (periodical local markets) and sell them at a price several times higher than the rate at which products originally bought. Most ironical fact is that the daily purchasers of ration who buy directly or indirectly from the traders are none but the seller-cultivators who sold out their agricultural products to pay back the loan earlier.

Why producers sold out their produces to middlemen?

Throughout the year the hard working poor cultivators-cum-gatherers remain busy in their fields or forest produce collection. Naturally, they need relaxation and temporary relief from the strains and year long burden of physical labour. Festivals, provide them the necessary outlets. Secondly, instead of selling out produces gradually, going again and again to local *haat* and waiting for buyers, some want to sell them out at a time and get ready cashes. Thirdly, middlemen approach the producers at their very doorstep. They offer the daily necessities (like salt, clothes, blanket etc.). This often allures the producers and food gatherers.

In Kalahandi's context let us look at the labour exploitation in a different perspective. Landless poor is always deprived of his physical entitlement. Beyond this stage hardly any physical tools are left with him which can be exploited. Again in an area of low job availability getting a work is rather a sign of good fortune for the *Sukhbasis* irrespective of the fact that how much wage one receives for what kind (duration) of labour which in fact becomes secondary.

Just like underdevelopment is not a stage which falls within the development scale, a landless *Sukhbasi* in a state of unemployment cannot be included in 'exploitation scale'.

Labour of landless is thus not exploited, but the land, forest and water surrounding them is exploited.* Before terming a condition as exploitation we must see whether exploited object has at all any potentiality to become exploited.** If such potentiality is very low or negligible, and further exploitation must be termed as contributing utilisation of object (for example here the Labour or *Sukhbasi*). The landless labourer neither have the cultivating lands against which to request the *mahajan* for an advanced loan nor do they have the capacity to repay the loan in above terms. What do they do then ? They are equally poor and needy. During summer the *Sukhbasis* manage to get advanced loan only with a pre-condition that they would work for the landlord and moneylender at half the wage rate. He goes on working for the *mahajan* till all the loans are paid back in that very wage term. The exploitation of labour takes place in this manner.

Adivasis out of desperation go to the *mahajans* for loans and in exchange they keep their lands in mortgage. Being illiterate

---

* Based on Chandipur, Jaypatna experience.

** Out of 30 days of month people get 3-10 days of work in Chandipur. So, it is illogical to hold that they are exploited? Rather those who provide them with work for those few days contribute for their food and drink during period of scarcity and want.

they fail to realise the terms and conditions put forth by the *mahajans* and despite repayment of loans including interest are never able to free their lands from the clutches of the *mahajans*[29] who often instigate government officials to harass the poor (*Sun Times*, 17 October, 1988). Field experience shows that the villagers still hold the ex-*Gauntias*, the traditional administrative head of villagers, in high esteem. They were *de jure* owner of the agricultural lands. Once all the lands (or *pattas*) were in the name of the *Gauntias*. Rest of the villagers were mere tenants. After the implementation of Ceiling (Orissa Land Reform) Act, *Gauntia* institution has declined. As the kings, patronising the *Gauntias* possessed no power any longer, the later had become powerless much earlier. Even if land has been allotted to the landless labourers, *Gauntias* still retain their traditional authority directly or indirectly. The former still fear or respect later.* The age old system still remain in the mind. It is ingrained in their social life.

Cases of rural poor losing the lands to moneylenders have been reported by Janakalyan Anusthan, a voluntary Organisation at Pandigaon of Kalampur block. Money lending and land alienation if not that frequent (like the Dharamgarh plateau) region and like that of the past, it is still not rare in the land resource region. Poor are aware of IRDP loans disbursed under banks. Despite that, villagers approach traditional money lenders because banks have not been able to take people into confidence and they feel disgusted over the formalities, unnecessary delaying procedures, compound interest and the coercive paths

---

* In Kulihariguda survey village of Golamunda block (Junagarh police station) the Gond *Gauntia* family has 60 acres of land with more than 15 family members. Earlier it has 90 acres of land in the village from where it migrated. The family produces large quantities of rice, *tola* etc. partly for domestic consumption and partly for sale. Around 1.5 quintal of *tola* oil it crushes out every year. Besides, the family members get mahul collected from their own field which they sale to middlemen *(dalals)* of traders who pass by with their carts. The *gauntia* family head is now elected as "Samiti member". His son is trying to take contract of construction of different government projects for which he already possesses a licence. True, *Gauntia* as an institution has declined but its new role in the changed situation by and large enabled it a to maintain its economic-political status at the grass root level.

the institutions adopts in loan recovery. Out of those who have taken IRDP loans, many are unable to repay. (As evident from the Reports of the 'Janakalyan Anusthans').

Realising the incapacity of the poor to repay bank loans provided under various Anti Poverty Schemes, government allowed certain relief measures (concessions), even loan waiving* (up to rupees ten thousands), works are provided under various development projects. In the last decade huge funds have been spent under Areas Development Programme for Poverty Termination (ADAPT). In addition to that Water Harvest Structure (by soil conservation department), Indira Awas Housing colonies have been executed. Still these were not enough to overcome the strong impacts of poverty and drought. Instead, improper planning and hurried execution of various programmes have led to wastage, misuse of funds, mismanagement and maldistribution.** These aspects have been discussed in greater detail in the chapter on "Evaluation of Programme Implementation".

Gauntia Institution in Transition

Ceiling Regulations were effectively and more widely implemented in early 1980s in Kalahandi. These have mixed results ranging from failure to success, somewhere they have produced only partial success. Here are few examples collected from the field.

Mohanty (DU, 1991) writes that, the *Gauntias* have been holding the means of production (i.e. land) and so power in the rural economy. This is not always true. Author's field experience shows that the activities of the so called *gauntias*, by and large, have declined and in some places they have reduced to destitution. For example, in case of Basantpada and Matia villages, strict but blind enforcement of the Ceiling Act has taken

---

* In the more exposed areas surrounding block headquarters like Khariar block and Kesinga block people are more conscious and shrewd in their dealings with officials and financing institutions. They take undesirable advantage of loan waiving.

** According to the evaluation report of IRDP, ERRP, Department of planning and coordination.

away hundreds of acres of land from the *gauntias* leaving behind only twenty to thirty acres of land for very large families (having several house wives, young men and many children). However, in many cases *Gauntias* by dint of their name, status and large family size still retain direct control over production forces.

Land usurpation or forcible occupation still takes place secretly because of two reasons. First, the deprived classes because of their poverty, illiteracy, dependence and inferior complexion have little courage to complain against a *gauntia*, the village headman and *mahajan*. Secondly, rich *gauntias* or money-lenders usually maintain good relationship with governmental officials, who are in charge of implementation of Ceiling Act. The officials in turn ignore (if at all there is any) complain of land usurpation. *Gauntias* save their lands from the application of ceiling surplus rules by showing them falsely in the name of their servants or debtors (According to *Lok Drusti,* Voluntary Organisation, Khariar).

In Matia (Kesinga block) the Majhi *Gauntia* because of his simplicity could not establish manipulative relationship with *Tehsildar*. Initially he had about 200 acres of land leaving only 65 acres, rest amount of land was distributed among 50-60 households. He gets only bad quality of land, which were grossly insufficient for a family of ten brothers. He has thus reduced to a pauper.

Singhjhar village (Sinapali) has different picture. Even if surplus land has been redistributed among the landless *sukhbasis*, the *Gauntias* holds indirect control over it. Land remains in the name of the beneficiaries only. The *Gauntia* with its traditional dominance used muscle power to get the ceiling surplus (redistributed) lands cultivated through middle class cultivators who pay half of the total produce to the former. The *sukhbasis* do not venture return to their lands. *Gauntias* are, however, not always merciless. They have distributed few acres of lands among the landless, although lands are of very poor quality in most cases. With the active cooperation of *Tehsildars* *Gauntias* have saved themselves from the impact of ceiling laws (based on fieldwork observation).

In Dharamgarh land resource region many *gauntias,* who are educated and conscious (especially Brahamin *Gauntias)* have escaped from ceiling trap. They have distributed the lands in the name of their own family members and relations elsewhere (including own *halias).* However, in scme cases the descendants of these *halias* have become independent by separately cultivating these very pieces of land. Apart from developing cordial relations with revenue officials, they have released only *Bhatta* and poor quality lands as ceiling surplus.

However, unlike the past there is hardly any *gauntia* having thousands of acres of land today. This is partly due to strict ceiling law implementation and partly due to land fragmentation and redistribution among the members of ever growing *gauntia* families (Fieldwork observation).

The Orissa Land Reforms Act protects the interests of STs declaring null and void any transfer in favour of any person not belonging to the tribe and empowers the revenue officers to take immediate action to restore the land to the tribals (P.H.). Few NGO's like AWARE and AGRAGAMEE took lead in bringing various kinds of exploitation into limelight. The bureaucracy who remained insensitive and apathetic to people's agony was forced to act actively and promptly under the influence of the voluntary organisations. Lands were restored to the tribals who were earlier deprived of them. Surprisingly, the groups which deprived the people of their lands were none but the scheduled castes (locally called *doms),* a slightly economically better class than of tribals.

Statutory provisions are also there which protect the interests of the SCs, in case they are victims of such kind of exploitation.

Traders and *Gauntias* do not always play the role of an exploiter only. In some ways they also contribute to the village economy and livelihood for the village inhabitants. They remain exploiter when we see they accept more than they return to the people, nature and the system. But they contribute to the economy in the following ways. They send *dalals* to collect raw materials or agricultural products at the doorsteps of the villagers, who face the real problem of selling their products and earning some cash. They provide the poor with loan when the later badly needs them for festivals, marriages and other urgent occasions. They at least provide them foodgrains exactly when the poor starts starving.

Traders have indirect control over cultivating lands, trees (such as *Kendu*, *Mahul,* and *Kusum* etc.) standing on those lands and the forests. So, if the *gauntias* and *Harijans (Doms)* and few rich tribals have direct control over land (physical entitlement), Marwadis and middlemen exercise indirect control over them Landless '*sukhbasi's* take up *dongar chas* or depend on collection of roots from the forests, few other supplement their income from meagre cultivating land. Though not regular, their casual income earned by selling of forest products is enough for buying liquor. It would be wrong to express that the landless people's labour is always exploited. Rather by providing them with work (irrespective of amount of wage) relatively rich households someway contribute for their day's earning of food and liquor.

Who is the Real Exploiter?

Because of preponderance of economic interactive groups or agents one is confused as to who is the real exploiter.

History depicts the Kond rebellion was against the more prosperous immigrant cultivators, *i.e. Kultas* of Sambalpur. Recently, there is a strong anti-regional feeling against the coastal Orissan people known as *Katkis.* There is less truth about the fact that *Katkis* are the only dominant exploiter group. It is rather a political-regional term used by the urban oriented (more conscious) western people including old (or initial) settlers or immigrants of coastal Orissa itself to create a east-west divide for political gain.

Identifying the Exploiters

We find numbers of non-governmental organisations are locally based. Few local persons have become privileged enough to establish direct connections with the central ministers to get fund or has become ministers themselves at the central and state level. Keeping aside their limitation one often is surprised to see that the district has still remained neglected and there is no well prepared exhaustive plan and course of action for the uplift of the poor. The outside traders and distillers are the regaining masters. The system has not merely thrust from outside. It has been well accepted by few dominant groups, local people themselves (for example SCs), some semi-educated unemployed youths.

It is true that coastal Orissa officials and settlers have been cunning, often ruthless in their dealing with the common people. But the political wave of consciousness is so hot and deep penetrating in the district today that their influence is often nullified. *Katkis* are neither the only such groups nor are they most powerful groups. Rather association of the local inhabitants with their own bigger exploiters is stronger than their dissociation with smaller exploiters.

Impact of Resource Draining

Thus, within the micro region, we find a sort of colonial model of production relation where the hinterland has export far larger than imports. The top heavy and bottom weak pyramidal structure of metropolitan (national) economy would collapse one day with its own weight. Modern government may delay this process by taking palliative measures and mask the propaganda but it cannot evade nor can it totally eliminate the eventuality.

The structural advantage enjoyed by small section of urban population and almost perpetual dependency of major sections of the population of the periphery on the 'Cores' has a strong counter force in neutralising any effort in development and eroding the existing levels of development. Government in order to cover up these structural contradictions and the inherent exploitative mechanism of the current economic system has introduced various welfare programmes.

The huge and successive pumping of state funds into the district in the recent past has hardly been able to alleviate the poverty to any significant level. Instead Kalahandi has been witnessing thousands of cases of morbidity, malnourishment, starvation and some cases of even starvation deaths itself. This is the ultimate consequence of long and systematic process of "man's exploitation by man". The annihilation of the district's age old man-nature economy seems complete now.

The initial effect of unrestricted outflow is observed. The outflow of foodgrains etc. is a major cause of underdevelopment and hence poverty*, which is understood from the following table of per capita nutrient consumption. Low per capita food consumption is obviously due to the unhindered export of rice, pulses, oil seeds, fruits etc. out of the district (See Appendices 4, 5 p.357 and p.363). In the Region of mixed resource base this occurs but with lower intensity.

Table 5.7: Per capita Consumption of different Foodstuffs, Kalahandi

Food Stuff	Consumed in grams	Recommended requirement in grams
Cereals	334	400
Pulses	16.7	85
Leafy Vegetables	24	!14
Roots	30.5	170
Fruits		85

Source: District Gazetteer, Kalahandi, 1980.

Conclusion

A particular caste-class group has never retained plain land, the basic resource. What invariably has occurred in the resource region is that there is no change in the status of the 'deprived' sections (scheduled tribes and weaker scheduled castes')** who suffer persistent hunger. Though through institutional interventions attempts have been made to improve the economic

* The export of cheap raw material and labour and foodgrains from an underdeveloped region (like that of Kalahandi) in the initial stage is justified on the ground that the fiscal resources would flow into it and its overall economic condition may improve.
But this does not mean that in the very stage this larger export (over import) process would gain all the people of the region. Only a small section or minority would be benefited from this by accumulating more and more resources.
And rich minority with their wealth power would later gain better control over production relation and would multiply their riches.

** Migrant SCs have raised their economic conditions by becoming conscious and earning money outside where assured and regular wage labour is available. So, they have better standard of living than the non-migrant 'rest' who are termed weaker SCs here.

conditions of the district and the poor, the efforts have only altered the agents of exploitation without changing the very process of exploitation. Thus, we find in the early period Konds were replaced by *Kultas* who became the traditional *Gauntias* after Gonds and Majhis. Other subsequent castes and religious groups (such as *Brahmins,* Muslims, local *Gauds* and *Malis)* enjoyed the privilege of being *Gauntias*. The historic events like *Kulta* inmigration, Land Ceiling Act of the government did not bring radical change but merely changed the ownership without providing the poorer section their legitimate powers. The whole process also gave birth to not only marginal and small farmers but also landless labourers and created vulnerable situation for new landholders of SCs and STs. The outlet for some poor and SCs was outmigration. But for the rest of the low landed and landless group it remains a sad tale of continuing deprivation.

Region of Mixed Resource Base

The region is comprised of Nawapada Forested Upland and Madanpur Rampur Forested Upland (including Nawapada, Komna, Boden and Madanpur Rampur blocks). Being a vegetative plateau both plain land and forest resources exist in equal proportion. But a marked difference in the two plateau lands is that Nawapada area, remaining in the rain shadow Sunabeda is less moist than the relatively more watered part of Madanpur Rampur. Earlier ruling classes, *zamindars*, outside higher caste people (*brahamins*, traders) are the exploiters in Madanpur Rampur block, while *Gauntias* and royal families are the traditional exploiters in Sunabeda and the adjoining Sunder valley.

Khariar road, Madanpur Rampur road are the gateways in the above two uplands respectively. The entry of North and Central Indians through the former route and the entry of migrants from both inside and outside the state through the later have given rise to two different sub-sets of production relation.

In general, the poverty level in the region is less as compared to Dharamgarh plateau (forested hills) though the drought impact is more in this part. The double resource bases help natives overcome the food problems more easily than those of the plain lands with single resource base (land) (where there is crop failure).

Again within the division, Madanpur side is less prone to drought and associated problems as compared to Nawapada, which has recorded few of the hard hit famines in recent period. Because of higher intensity of drought food scarcity is not uncommon here.

People are used to visit local *'haats'* instead of going to distant towns which involves more time and money. The sheer geographic distance, incapability to pay for bus fare daily (in case of distant market places), loss of day's work and wage prevent the local cultivator to go for direct selling of their products. So, they prefer to rely on middlemen even if the later literally deceive the former in several ways. The case of *Kuchian* coming to the Khariar market can be cited here.

As mentioned already, in absence of any regulated market, proper communication and processing industries private purchasers or local *dalals* go on buying produces from interior villages and collect them at Block headquarters and or village *panchayats* after last week of November as harvesting starts. Though the government declared the support price for paddy, cultivators sell out it with much lower prices. (For example, in Madanpur Rampur area the selling price of paddy was only Rs. 180 to Rs. 200 while the declared price of government was Rs. 230 to Rs. 240 per quintal). The rice traders purchases bulk paddy, ragi, *alsi, dal,* vegetables during harvest. Naturally, they collect the products at much cheaper rates than the poor cultivators, labourers who mostly go to buy them during pre-harvest period of scarcity.

Changes in the Transitional Belt

Human interaction and forest resource presents almost similar picture like that of the predominantly hilly-forest region. Forest restrictions, especially on "*podu*" cultivation and the commercial exploitation of forest disturbed the tribals traditional way of life. The *zamindars* also encouraged the felling of forest to increase the area for cultivation. The loss of forest upset the ecology of the area. Specially in the plain areas the tribals lost their subsistent economy due to this disruption. Food gatherers and hunters either withdrew to the interior where still sufficient forest was left for their need or stayed on and became labourers for their livelihood.[30]

In the Nawapada forested upland *Khariar Zamindari* had proprietary rights over the forest and by 1909 not even single big timber was left uncut in these forests *(Raipur District Gazetteer*, 1909). During the post-Second World War period extensive land reclamation led to reckless tree felling.

Land (Soil) Quality

In the forested upland, mixed soil (black, sandy loam and laterite) are found extensively. But the local land categories included Bahal (low land), Berna (medium land) and *Att* or Mal (high upland) each category may also be sub-divided into *Khari, Mamuli* and *Pani* or *Unhari* sub-categories. (The land classification is made on the basis of water retaining capacity of land.)

Bahalpani is considered to be the best quality of land which with even scanty rainfall is able to produce sufficient paddy crops. Berna needs adequate water supply whereas for *Bahal Mamuli* and *Bahal Khari* medium quantity of rainfall is required. *Att Unhari* and *Att Khari* cannot grow rice under any water temperature condition. In other words, these are rather unfit for the purpose. *Att Mamuli,* however, is useful for raising paddy crops, if rainfall or artificial water supply is high and in the high upland of *Att Unhari* and *Att Khari* which are generally owned by poorer classes, crops requiring less moisture like *Kodo* and *Mandia* can be raised (It may be noted here that from *Bahalpani* to *Att Mamuli)* lower the quality of land, greater is the need of water rainfall or irrigation for paddy cultivation. Under normal conditions the maximum productivity (for paddy) of the three major land types are:

(i) *Bahal*, 10 to 15 quintals/acre
(ii) *Berna* is 10 quintals/acre
(iii) *Att* is < 5 quintals/acre

Since the land quality of *Att* is the poorest, water required by it is highest. It is prone to maximum crop loss especially when drought is continuous and hence it demands largest investment which poor can ill afford. So in most cases *Att* lands are left unutilised. Rich is rich because he faces least obstacles by nature, being in possession of better or best quality of land which are most favourable for rice cultivation.

Role of Inmigrants

Behind the coming of outsiders, drought and certain human factors play an important role. Kalahandi has a long history of drought. Interestingly and surprisingly, streams of inmigration follow each drought year in the district. One of the earliest inmigrations is reported to be made by the 'Sundhis' the traditional liquor distillers, brewers of Ganjam district of Orissa after 1866 drought.*

This was due to attractive force of Kalahandi which was less affected by the then, "Great Famine" as compared to the coastal Orissa and other part witnessing unprecedented crop failure. Drought and food scarcity continued up to 1868. During 1867 many *Brahmins* came from Sambalpur. Although involuntary in nature, the immigration of *Kultas* took place during the same period. The post-drought years of 1921 saw similar waves of migration into the district...[31] *Marwadis* (a trading community) started arriving in the plains of the Tel valley and Tel basin and the Tel valley soon after the long dry spells of 1965.

The coincidence of occurrence of drought and mobility of the people into that very drought affected area, as evident from the above events, shows very peculiar case of human migration. Following causes are advanced to explain the counter migratory behaviour in the period of crop failure and food scarcity.

---

* Tribals were initially used to brew their own liquor. 'Sundhis' were the first distillers who started selling liquor after 1866. After independence, Bihari distillers monopolized liquor business with whom local distillers (Sundhis) could not compete. Bihari brewers have successfully managed to establish their *bhattis* in many villages by bribing police officials and even local politicians. Liquor plays an important role in land alienation.

1. Local people outmigrate once they lose all hope of survival. They start selling out their land, household belongings and other transferable properties. Outsiders (newcomers) take full advantage of this situation of distress sale.
2. The outsiders entry into the system of regional production relation becomes easier once they go on buying land and other means of production.
3. After establishing in the area (as soon as the drought impact was over), (many of) the exotic population engaged themselves in business relating to agriculture and/or forest products and later acquired dominant group position in the economic and socio-political structure of Kalahandi.
4. Land is cheap and plenty in Kalahandi as compared to Sambalpur irrigated area and coastal Orissa. The district has rich land and forest resources.

Banjara tribals started trade in salt. They brought salt from coastal Kalinga (Past Orissa) and exchanged it with local forest produces. This initially brought local people in contact of outsiders economically, (Anthropological Society of India). About two main trade routes of Kalahandi has already been discussed (Nayak, P.K.). Eliot Report (1853) confirms barter system. In 1960, tax system was introduced.

Spread of Jagannath Cult and Entry of Brahmins

With the temple (especially Jagannath temple) construction, many *Brahmins* from Sambalpur and other parts of Orissa were invited by the kings.* Reports of land grant (amounting from few acres to hundreds of acres) are available from the old

---

* Jharua *Brahmins* were invited from Sambalpur. Aranyak *Brahmins* came subsequently after 1855 and in 1859 some "Oriya Brahmins", i.e. Brahmins of Puri and Ganjam coastal districts of Orissa who are experts in 'TANTRA SHASTRA' settled in Brahmin Sasan, *i.e.* Jagannathpur Gopinathpur. They had the duty of worshipping in temples of Manikeswar, Lankeswar in Bhawanipatna and Junagarh respectively. Ganjam Brahmins were came to worship in temples of Manikpur. Reclaimed forest land of 5.20 acres were allotted to each Brahmin family (who never acted like exploiters).

temples of Dharamgarh, Jaypatna, Bhawanipatna and Kalampur and from the new temples of Karlaket, Junagarh, Mukhiguda, Bijamara and Ladugaon (near Jaypatna) and Thuamul Rampur. The priests of Srikrishna temple, Kanakpur, Jaypatna, were allotted 60 acres of land. This information was collected from the priest of Mahulpatna, where a new Jagannath temple has been erected recently. All these temples, including the famous Manikeswari temple of Bhawanipatna are located in plain land resource region and associated with the cultivating communities mainly.

During *Durbar* administration of Kalahandi, the Brahmins were the exploiters and therefore, lot of gold-bricks and innumerable wealth are found hidden among the Brahmins of Dharamgarh and Junagarh area.*

Thus, it can be inferred that the Brahmins, social status and dominance were derived from royal patronage. Huge land grant made by the kings provided them vast means of production and hence economic control over the cultivating masses. Many turned to be *Gauntias* of different villages of the fertile plains land of the Tel-Hatti basin and the Tel valley.

This enabled the priest community to amass lot of wealth and emerge as a distinct caste class group to play an important role in the political economy of Kalahandi.

'Literacy' and 'Awareness' among SCs and STs

These aspects have a bearing on the production relation, political economy and overall poverty of the region. Raja Brijmohan Deo was against providing education to SCs. Raja P.K. Deo was liberal. He introduced a system known as *Gaer Hajir* (according to which any SC student if remains absent in a school, his parents were required to provide free service as a form of punishment, in the king's palace).

---

* Excerpts from the personal letter of J.N. Singh Deo, Prince, Khariar, Kalahandi, written to the researcher dated 20-7-1992.

After 1947, STs were given permission to take formal education.

Of course, the general level of education is very low in Kalahandi, but within the district if we compare SCs with STs the former are more literate or educated and conscious than the latter. The causes are the following :

1. SCs became conscious (aware) not only before the STs become so but also prior to the spread of literacy and education among themselves.
2. Drinking is more widespread among STs than among SCs. Former spend more on liquor, while the later spend more on clothes.

A New Class of Emerging Rich

In this backward area of poverty middle and higher class cultivators, petty traders, industrial and tertiary sector officials and workers constitute a relatively dynamic class in progress. Their socio-cultural status (including economic and educational positions) is higher than the vast majority group of poor but lower than the top class traders and a handful population of relative affluence.

Today, a phase has come when a *khadi* clad village tout (mostly and originally from coastal Orissa, Sambalpur side or from local *Dom* or SCs not from traditional *Gauntias*) have acquired deeper control over local politics. *Gauntias* as a high land owning class is in decline (after land distribution and ceiling law implementation). In their place the new *gauntia* elites today are none but the costal inmigrants. They have acquired many acres of land after taking up petty governmental or teaching job or by opening up tiny shops through which they first get control over the village economy and gradually extend their hands into village politics. Better education, consciousness and often shrewd dealings of theirs help them to gain dominance over the local inhabitants while interacting with outside agencies including police, new traders and sellers.*

Land Tenure System

Regha : In this case land is rented out for a fixed period especially one year against cash or kind equivalent to the average or potential production. Risk of losing land is minimum here. Barring this common practice of the Plain land Region other practices are:

Adhia (Share cropping): Given for not more than one year. The *Mahajan* (landowner) is entitled to receive half of the produce raised by the share cropper at the end of every cultivation year. Risk of losing land is involved here.

Bandhak (*Land mortgage*): Land in this case is mortgaged against a certain amount of loan advanced. Conditions of returning the land is fulfilled once the principal along with the interest is paid off by the borrower.** The risk involved in this case is maximum. In the resource region, therefore, most people go for, *Regha* and *Adhia.* Sometimes, however, because of acute poverty few become constrained to accept *Bandhak* or land mortgage.

In recent years hardly any person shows interest in advancing land ceiling implementation. Officials of the district have become active and strict in restoring the land to the owner thereby giving legal protection to (specifically) SCs and STs. Who should approach whom for the above types of land transactions depends on the economic status, bargaining capacity and need of the 'interested person' and 'land owner'. In *Regha* the interested person comes to the landowner, whereas reverse is the case in *Adhia* and *Bandhak.*

---

* *Source*: Formulated after discussion with an Additional Superintendent of Police on the way back to Jaypatna from Jariguma.

** During fieldwork the researcher came across a poor Brahmin family in Barbandha village (Madanpur Rampur), who in order to earn for his daily living without letting erode his family status preferred to *Regha* instead of entering into land tenure system of other contracts.

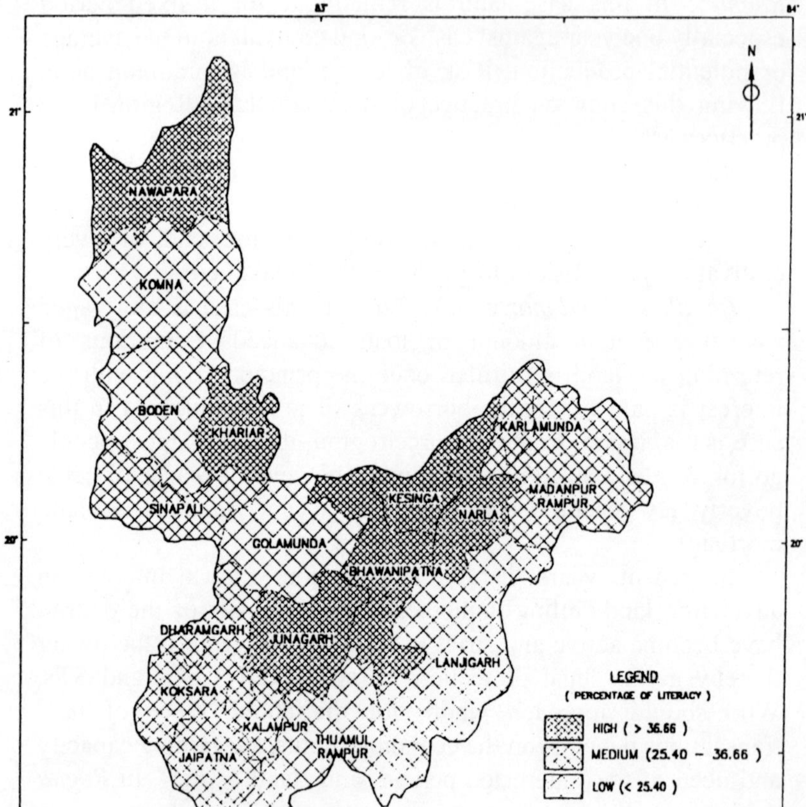

Map 26 : Kalahandi : Literacy, 1997

Class Adaptation

According to a study conducted by Anthropology Department of Utkal University, 1988-89, most poor farmers belonging to small and medium categories, cultivated *Kodo, Guruji, Rasi,* Jute etc. in order to escape the impact of drought. Poor investment has reduced the production and productivity to a great extent even among rich farmers. Many were forced to stop cultivating *Att* and Berna lands due to acute scarcity of water. In the village case study majority of farmers because of prolonged drought could not cultivate their land. Among the rest, almost half households have given their lands on *Regha* to others while the other half decided to outmigrate and engage in wage earning through manual labour. From a status of self-sufficiency many farmers have become paupers due to indebtedness, mortgage, distress sale of belongings and even own children. (According to a village level worker of Madanpur Rampur). Because of better quality and larger amount of land the higher class farmers with their better resilience capacity overcome the impact of drought more easily than the poor. However in exceptional cases of prolonged and continuous droughts rich and poor are equally affected in terms of total crop failure and scarcity of foodgrains.

If there is severe crop loss, big farmers are often compelled to curtail the number of labourers in their cultivating field. Leaving aside *halias* who provide lifelong service to his master (*mahajan* or landlord), small and marginal farmers or agricultural labourers who depend on works available within their own or neighbouring villages are forced to migrate to areas lying outside district or even state. Temporary migration for non-agricultural work are mostly found among general caste people or SCs, *i.e.* non-tribals. Volume-wise outmigrating groups are (i) *Harijans,* (ii) Tribals, and (iii) others. Among non-tribals, marginal and small farmers are the most mobile. Apart from them it has been seen that during the period of scarcity few families either borrow foodgrains, money etc. from their relatives living outside the drought prone area or find job there till the next cultivating season. These aspects have been highlighted in greater detail in the following chapter on survival strategy.

Mixed Production Relation of Varied Groups

Tejipada (Madanpur Rampur), the sample village, reflects the general socio-economic condition of this "Mixed Resource Region". The village has various sections of population *viz.* Brahmins, Oilmen, Potter, SCs and STs (especially Konds). There are three different *padas* (strips) or sections in a village having different communities belonging to three different income categories. The first *pada* belong to scheduled castes who have medium income, the middle one belongs to Brahmins who have high income. The last *pada* has only ST population. They are with very low family income. Most people are migrants as evident from their fluency not in dialect of Kalahandi but in Oriya language and drinking habit. SCs and few general caste people are landless labourers who lead a life on daily "earn and consume" basis. They receive hardly Rs 10 per day whenever work is available. Unlike the other surveyed village of this area Barabandha, this village has slender forest base as very good forest is hardly found nearby. Still then villagers fetch "*Mahua*" and firewood from the surrounding vegetative area. The villagers have relatively better economic condition and do not suffer hunger like other parts of Kalahandi.

Tejipada is the study village in the block of Mandanpur Rampur. Most of the households are landless labourers. Private employers pay less than Rs. 10 (ten) per day. Forests are located away from the village. Except *mahul*, firewood local people are not benefited much by the forest which provides only narrow base for peoples living. However, the very appearance of the people and interview with them shows that they don't suffer frequent starvation like the poor of other parts of Kalahandi.

Apart from land, local labourers are engaged in labour of various kinds and terms

(i) *Kuli bhuti* (Casual labour)
(ii) *Halia* (Yearly house labourer/servant)
(iii) *Goti* (Halia for continuously several years)

Bamboo cutting is a popular occupation of the people of the area. Since SCs are not accustomed to this job, tribals are mostly engaged in it. Forest Corporation provides handsome wage (*i.e.* Rs. 25 to Rs. 50) to the bamboo cutters.

Desia Kond of plains are intelligent like other plain inhabitants. *Kutia* Konds live on the hill. They visit plain occasionally to exchange or sell ragi, sugar, beet, turmeric etc. in exchange of rice and salt. They are faithful and simple. But once cheated they don't allow the enemy to remain alive.

People depend both on cultivation and collection of wood, food etc. During pre-British (transitional) period villages were self-sufficient. The ecological condition was better. Water availability for cultivation was plenty since tank irrigation facility was there in almost every village. Forest was abundant to meet the food, fuel and fodder needs of the people. In the British period contractors were given auction of forest area employing local people in wood and bamboo cutting during off seasons of the year. Land was probably better managed. In recent period, forest has declined. Forest Corporations bamboo cutting is limited to specific areas and specific seasons of the year. So, wage earners go without work for a considerable period of time.

The researcher has a discussion with Mr. Mahakhud, village level worker of Madanpur Rampur. Basing on the discussion, it was found that the natural and institutional roots of the poverty of the cultivators of Madanpur Rampur are the following:

> When there is partial or total crop failure due to drought, farmers resort to immediate borrowing from village '*sahukar*' (local moneylender) who usually demands high interest in return of his "timely loan". By the end of the next harvest season, the principal loan with interest together becomes three times that of the original amount initially borrowed by the farmer. Such a huge amount the cultivator is able to repay provided the crop harvested is 100 per cent. If the weather is fully favourable and there is absolutely no loss of crop in the following year the cultivator can be able to repay the amount. Very little crop is left with him. In some cases the whole harvest goes towards loan repayment, despite favourable monsoon after the drought year. It necessitates the borrower to go for loan once again. Gradually, he enters in a debt trap, which render him

landless. Many *Sukhbasis* have their origin in this process who often take shelter in forest depending on its food and fuel. Thus, the basic cause of poverty is natural but its continuance is man-made.

Conclusion

In conclusion, this transitional area of mixed geographic properties possesses varied population groups. The typical land tenure system assumed importance because of constant influx of population both from within and without. Rich class has better adaptation in the event of a drought and crop failure since they possess better quality and big holdings. The poorer class become the worse sufferer as they face the problem of both crop failure (sometimes even land loss) and reduced work availability. Areas with its double resource base (land and forest) and varying population types exhibit multiple production relation and so less intense poverty.

Thus, in all the three resource regions, it may be noted that the son of the soil is treated as a secondary citizen in his very habitation. Elitist approach rather blames the natives for deforestations as well as for their own poverty.

The author finds that 'deprivation' is a meaningful concept to understand the institutional blockade of resource distribution causing poverty. It would be appropriate to express that local inhabitants were deprived of their primary rights over soil, water and forests. The statutory rights have been withdrawn by various institutional mechanisms in production relation. Whether it is governmental or non-governmental organisation the so called protectors have turned into exploiters. Government employees (especially those of Forest Department) often function in tune with the exploitative process.

The traders, administrators, public workers, traditional village men, petty politicians, contractors, literate mass, low educated unemployed youth, vested associations or organisations and shrewd scheduled caste people join hands to exploit the poorest of the poor and their rich natural resources. All of them remain at the root of the system siphoning off the agricultural and forest produces through a typical suction mechanism. These amply explain critical poverty and underdevelopment in Kalahandi.

Except few welfare works, voluntary organisations have not been able to impart real consciousness of development among the poor. The belief and the value system of the people are needed to be reoriented and fashioned along a non-exploitative line.

NOTES

1. Mishra, M.K. (1990) : *Drought pictures in the Folklore and Folk life of Kalahandi*, Friends Publishers, Cuttack, p. 1.
2. Pattanaik, D.S. (1993), *Revised Working Plan of Kalahandi Division* for the period from 1983-84 to 1992-93, Koraput,Working Plan Circle, Orissa, p. 62.
3. *Ibid*, p. 37.
4. *Ibid*, p. 63.
5. Nanda, B.K. (1991) : *How to survive starvation and struggle for the dignity of life in Kalahandi* ? Paper presented in district level workshop, Bhawanipatna, Kalahandi, 31st December, 1991.
6. Fernandes, W. *et al.* 1991, *Forests, Environment and Tribal Economy : Deforestation, Impoverishment and Marginalisation in Orissa*, Indian Social Institute, New Delhi, p. 67.
7. Senapati, S.N., *District Gazeteer*, Kalahandi, 1981.
8. Emerged from the discussion of the reasearcher with Mr. B.K. Deo, the then M.L.A. of Bhawanipatna, who belongs to a royal family which ruled Khariar.
9. Data collected from Indian Social Science Institute, New Delhi (Fernandes *et al., op.cit.* p. 75).
10. Pattanaik, D.S. 1993, *op. cit.* p. 39.
11. 1971-81 Census Commissioner, 1981a : 30.
12. "Tribal exploitation in Kalahandi District" 1990, a report in the *Indian Express,* 5th February, 1990.
13. *Ibid.*
14. *Ibid.*
15. Discussion with Mr. N. K. Mohapatra, Ex-Ranger, Bhawanipatna.
16. Pattanaik, D.S., 1993, *op.cit.* p. 62.
17. "Drought syndrome : A report on Kalahandi District" by research scholars of Sambalpur University, *Economic and Political Weekly*, November 3, 1985.
18. *Revised working plan of Kalahandi Division, op.cit.* pp.46-47.
19. Panda, A.C., (1991) : "Peoples participation in management of forests in Kalahandi" paper presented in the workshop on *Hunger and Underdevelopment : Is there a way out for Kalahandi* ? Bhawanipatna, Orissa, December 28-29, 1991.
20. Nanda, B.K., (1991) : "How to survive starvation and struggle for the dignity of life in Kalahandi", *op. cit.* p. 4.

21. *Ibid.*
22. Panda, A.C., *People's participation in the management of forests of Kalahandi, op.cit.*
23. *Drought syndrome – A report on Kalahandi District, op.cit.*, p. 8.
24. Nayak, K.C. and Sinha S.N. (1985) : *Transactions*, Bhubaneswar, Vol. 14, January, 1985.
25. Gaurinath, M. and Acharya, P.C. (1991) : 'Participation in afforestation activities in Kalahandi District during the year 1985-90', paper presented in District level workshop on *Hunger and Underdevelopment: Is there a way out in Kalahandi* ? Orissa, December 28-29, 1991.
26. Tribal exploitation in Kalahandi District, a report in *Indian Express*, 5th February, 1990.
27. Mishra, D. and Rao, R.S. (1992) : 'Hunger in Kalahandi : Bickered Understanding,' *Economic and Political Weekly*, June 15-20, p.1245.
28. Mishra, M.K. (1989) : *Folk Songs of Kalahandi,* Mayur Publication, Bhubaneswar.
29. Few Mahajans are none but ex-gauntias who have turned into moneylenders. Gauntias take advantage of *adivasis* (the deprivation and helplessness of the *adivasis*). They lend loans or materials and get the lands of *adivasis* mortgaged. Even if large money, several times more than the original loan amount is returned to the gauntia-cum-moneylenders the mortgaged lands have not been restored to the poor *adivasis* in most cases. In few cases, the moneylenders have forced the borrowers serve them as bonded labourers indefinitely. The Gauntia of Bhawanipatna, Jagsaipatna, Kerpai, Dumerpadar in addition to Thuamul Rampurand Lanjigarh are reported to be in possession of hundreds of acres of lands. (*Source :* "Will the tribals be freed from there exploitation of the Gaunitas of Kalahandi," port in *The Samaj,* 14 November 1988.)
30. Deo, F., "Differential response of Tribal Groups of Nawapada sub-division to external pressure", Paper presented to Orissa History Congress, proceeding of the XV Annual Session, venue – Rajdhani College, Bhubaneswar, 4th to 5th November 1989, pp.94-95.
31. Roy, S. (1990), *Political Economy of Food Crisis, op.cit.*, p.57.

6

INCIDENCE OF POVERTY AND ITS SOCIAL CORRELATES

Unlike the previous chapter this chapter on 'Incidence of Poverty and its Social Correlates' is exclusively devoted to empirical analysis. At the outset poverty line for Kalahandi (Orissa) has been calculated at current prices. The topic is divided into two sections. The first section finds the correlation between dependent variable (poverty) with those of independent variables (social groups, land, labour and expenditure). The second section works out the values of correlation mainly between 'land' and 'soil', 'literacy' and 'social groups', after presenting justification for why 'land' is a proxy variable of poverty.

The poverty line is Rs. 2001.43 per capita per annum at current prices for Kalahandi (Orissa), with the help of the work of Jain and Tendulkar* and consumer price index of Reserve Bank of India.

Of 309 sample households surveyed** from the entire district of Kalahandi, 144 households lie below the poverty line. In other words, 46.50 per cent of the families of the district are poor.

---

* According to the calculation of Jain and Tendulkar, average per capita total expenditure is 34.13 during 1970-71. Consumer price index for agricultural labourers for the same year is 212. Basing on this the APCTE for the year 1991-92 is 166.786 (since the CPI for 1991-1992 is 1036). So the poverty line for 1991-92 is 166.786 × 12 = 2001.43 per capita per annum.

** The fieldwork was undertaken in May-June, 1992.

Table 6.1 : Consumer Price Index, Average Per Capita Total Expenditure (APCTE) and poverty line (in rupees) during 1971, 1983, 1991 and 1992 for Orissa (including Kalahandi)

Month Year	CPI numbers for agricultural labourers	APCTE and poverty Lines (in brackets)
1970-71	212	34.13*
1983	–	103.53
1990-91	830	133.62
1991-92	1036	166.786 (2001.432 per annum)
May 1992	1029	165.659 (1987.908 per annum)
June 1992	1045	168.235

Source : CPI (Consumer Price Index) numbers for agricultural labourers from Reserve Bank of India (RBI) Bulletin, February, 1993 (at July, 1960-June,1961=100).

Social Groups

Kalahandi has multiple social groups of varied caste and communities due to influx of outsiders with the native population at different points of demographic history. The population migration like other parts of the underdeveloped world, has been guided by geographical and economic factors throughout. Today, dominant groups command more resources than the other weaker ones leaving majority below the starvation level. Table 6.2 presents the percentages of households falling below and above the poverty line by social groups [which includes scheduled castes (SCs), scheduled tribes (STs), and other castes (general castes)]. All other Hindu or non-Hindu groups are clubbed together under 'other castes' category since the sample size of any individual group is not sufficiently large. Of the total households 26.2 per cent are SCs, 35.3 per cent are STs and 38.5 per cent are of other castes.

Table 6.2 : Variation in Poverty by Social Groups (in percentage)

	SC	ST	Other Castes
Below Poverty Line	31	36	33
Above Poverty Line	22	35	43

Source: Primary survey.

One notices from the table, households belonging to ST category are the poorest among all social groups of the district and there is greater poverty among general caste people (other castes) than among SCs. In the sample the difference between the poorest group and least poor group is, however, 5 per cent only. Inter-group variation in poverty is very low. Other caste people are worse off than even scheduled castes in terms of poverty though the difference between them is only 2 per cent. This is because OBC is as backward and poor as SCs and STs.

The proportion of better off families is maximum among general caste and minimum among scheduled castes. The scheduled tribes come in between. Here we find there is perceptible difference (of 10 %) between SC and ST households.

So far as the overall economic condition of the three groups are concerned, scheduled tribes are relatively better off than scheduled castes and worse off than other (general) castes. The mobility of SCs is more than that of STs who are emotionally attached to the soil[2] and to earn money they (SCs) remain prepared to do any work outside where as the general caste people have some social inhibition to take up such manual works. This partly explains lesser poverty among SCs than the other two groups.

Land Size Classes

Land is a precious and most fundamental resource of means of production. Other important resources like soil, water and forests are contained by it. Agriculture, the basic economic pursuit is practised over it to produce food and materials necessary for other activities of man.

The quantity of land owned is considered to be a proxy variable of poverty. No doubt, the quality (including the soil productivity and water retaining capacity) of land is an equally important factor. But, in Kalahandi it is a common phenomenon that big land owners have better quality of lands in their possession. Determining 'classes' on the basis of land size group is, therefore, quite logical. Often higher class people are none but persons from higher caste category. In other words, lower classes usually coincide with lower castes that occupy not only smaller amount of land but also lands of inferior quality.

The households of the district have been classified into five categories by different size class of land possessed. Out of the total 309 households 35.2 per cent belong to the landless, 26.9 per cent to marginal farmers, 21.4 per cent to small farmers, 10.4 per cent to medium farmers and 6.1 per cent to big farmers.

Table 6.3 shows the percentage of households falling below and above poverty line across various land size groups :

Table 6.3: Variation in Poverty by Land Ownership in Kalahandi

Land size class (in acres)	Land-less (0)	Marginal farmers (0-2)	Small farmers (2-7)	Medium farmers (7-12)	Big farmers (>12)	Row Total (%)
Below Poverty Line	42.4	25.7	18.1	9.7	4.2	100
Above Poverty Line	29.1	27.9	24	10.9	7.9	100

Source : Fieldwork.

Houses without any landed property (*i.e.* with zero acre of land) are "Landless". Households possessing 2 acres of land are regarded marginal farmers, 2.1 to 7 acres of land are small farmers, 7.1 to 12 acres of land are medium farmers and >12 acres of land are large farmers.

As expected, the landless class turn out to be the poorest group having 42.4 per cent families lying below poverty line. The percentage of poor families declines sharply with each higher land size group. It naturally indicates that there is an inverse correlation between land size and poverty. Perhaps, the poverty of the medium size farmers (9.7 %) and large farmers (4.2 %) is either due to the poor quality of soil (land) or due to lack of sufficient and timely water supply to their agricultural fields. There are several instances showing the out migration of even these higher class families in search of job during the periods of prolonged drought.[3]

Previously, we have seen STs are the poorest social group. Again here we find landless and marginal farmers are predominantly poor. So we may logically conclude that scheduled tribes are mostly the landless and marginal farmers. This, however, can be confirmed afterwards when we shall analyse the cross table and correlation of 'Caste' and 'Land Ownership'.

Poverty and Income from Land

Mere ownership of land does not guarantee production. As mentioned already soil quality water availability apart from certain human factors determine the real income from land, which in turn has a bearing on poverty. Income from land (agriculture) could also be taken a proxy variable of poverty.

In Table 6.3 we saw 35.2 per cent of the total households are landless. Here we find 24.3 per cent households have 'zero' income (absolutely no income) from land. It implies that 10.9 per cent families, though landless, have some earning from land. How is it so? In fact, they practise either *podu* on communally owned or public (hill slope side) land, *i.e.*, *dongar* or on leased out land or on other farmers land on a sharing basis. 234 households have land as a source of earning. 59.8 per cent or almost 60 per cent (*i.e.* 3/5th of the poor households) have an annual land income less than Rs. 2000. (Majority of the tribals who are poor fall in this group.) 75.5 per cent or 3/4th of the total have "Land -earning" not exceeding Rs. 4000. (See Table 6.4a)

Table 6.4a : Relation between Poverty and 'Annual Income from Land' (in %)

	Annual Income from Land				
	Rs.2000 (Low)	Rs. 2001-4000 (Low Medium)	Rs. 4001-6000 (Medium-High)	Rs. 6000 & above	Row Total (%)
Below Poverty Line	59.8	15.7	12.7	11.8	100
Above Poverty Line	42.4	28.0	12.9	16.7	100

Source: Fieldwork.

The decrease in percentage of poor households with the increase in size-class of "Land Income" confirms that there is a direct correlation between annual income from land and per capita consumption expenditure (*i.e.* poverty) of a family.

Families above poverty line show similar trend except the slight increase in rich class families in high income group.

Barring 24.3 per cent families with zero income, 37.9 per cent have low income (Rs. 2000), 17.2 per cent have low to medium income (Rs. 2001-4000), 9.7 per cent have medium to high income (Rs. 4001-6000) and only 11 per cent of the families have high (Rs. 6001) income from land.

Table 6.4b shows of income from land and income from sale of products show those who have low income from land depend on the meagre earning of sale of crudely processed products.

Table 6.4b: Cross Table of Land Income and Income from Sale of Products (Raw Data)

Income from Land (Rs.)	Income from the sale of products (Rs.)				
	0	500	501-1000	1000	Total
< 2000	90	14	5	8	117
2001-4000	47	4	2	0	53
4001-6000	29	0	1	0	30
> 6000	32	0	1	1	34

Source : Fieldwork.

Usually, households which have at least three members having less than Rs. 4000 income from land and some supplementary income from sale of products are poor. So, the poor households having income both from land and selling of processed products constitute about one-fourth of the population below Rs. 4000 land income.*

Therefore, lower the income from land lower is the per capita expenditure. A quarter of the relatively poor (having low to medium land income) population supplement their land income by selling home processed products.

Poverty and Place of Work

When income from immediate sources is inadequate people look for work. Again, if the work within agricultural fields is not enough, villagers do not hesitate to outmigrate. As evident from

* (14+4+5+2+8) = 33.0 or 33×100/144 = 22.9 per cent of the total poor have below Rs.4000 land income.

Table 6.5, 15.2 per cent of households have some other means of earning. Obviously, incidence of wage earner is as high as 84.8 per cent. One-fourth of the poor households (*i.e.* households below poverty line) go to work at multiple places. This proportion is much less, *i.e.* only one-sixth to one-seventh for relatively better off households.* If a household worked outside village first, inclination to work at village later, if it works in more than one place is very low** (As marked during fieldwork, this is a typical behaviour of SCs).

Table 6.5: Poverty and Labour Areas

House holds	0.0	Within Village	Outside village Within District	Outside District	Row Total
0.0	1	1			[2]
Below poverty line	21	110 [14]	6 [18]	5 [19]	144 [31]
Above poverty line	25	124 [1]	9 [11]	7 [8]	165 [20]
Column Total (%)	47 15.2	235 [5] 76.1	15 [29] 4.9	12 [17] 3.9	309 [51] 100

Note : [ ] No. of Households working at more than one place/multiple places.
Source : Computerised cross tab of Fieldwork.

Since five households (9.8%) work in the village at the second instance, these households must have worked at a place outside village at the first instance.

Thus, out of these 10.3 per cent who worked outside village at the first instance but worked at a different place as well, only

* Total households below poverty line who worked at some place is 121. Out of them 26+15 =31 households work at more than one place, *i.e.* 20/140 × 100 = 25.62 per cent.
Number of households above poverty line who worked at some place is 140 out of them 10+10 = 20 households work at more than one place, *i.e.* 20/140 × 100= 14.29 households work at more than one place.

** Number of households who work in the village first time = 235, *i.e.* 235/262 × 100 = 89.69 per cent (262=309 – 47) and 15/262 × 100 = 5.73 per cent worked at district level (within district but outside village) and 12/262 × 100 = 4.58 per cent worked outside district, *i.e.* a total of 10.3 per cent (5.73 % + 4.58 %), worked outside village at the first instance.

9.8 per cent preferred to work in the village.

It can be logically concluded that if a person worked outside village at more than one location, his inclination to work at village later is very low.

Only a marginal influence of economic status *vis-a-vis* poverty line is there on the choice of place of work. Households which are below poverty line and worked at some place is 121. Out of these 121, 110 worked in the village. It means 90.91 per cent of poor households below poverty line preferred to work in the village. The corresponding figures for poor households above poverty line who preferred to work in the village is 88.5 per cent. There is only a marginal influence of economic status *vis-a-vis* poverty on the choice of place of work.

Thus majority depend on wage earning and a quarter of the poor make a living by working hard at multiple places. Let us find the link between the working members of the household and workplace and also poverty and income from labour.

Working Members and Workplace

Table 6.5a : Variation in Work Place by Percentage of Working Members of households

Working members of a Household		Own Village or neighbouring Village	Within District	Outside District	Row Total
0	26[47]	21			47[47]
1-25	4[41]	40	2[6]	2[1]	48[7]
26-50	9[86]	80[3]	10[10]	7[7]	106[20]
51-75	3[46]	49[1]	1[5]	3(41	56[10]
76-100	5[38]	45[1]	2(8]	[5]	52[14]
Column Total	47[258]	235[5]	12[17]	12[17]	309[51]
Col.Total (%)	15.2	76.1	4.9	3.9	100

Note : [ ] shows number of persons who work at more than one place.
Source : Fieldwork.

The above cross-tabulation along with the very strong positive correlation coefficient value (see Appendix VI) and high association value (shown by chi square test) reveal that with increase in proportion of working members of the households there is general increase in percentage of households who work at multiple places.

From Table 6.5 we see that the percentage of households which go to work at multiple places is more in case of poor than in case of better off. Thus, we can derive from these two statements that poor peoples' households have higher proportion of working members, who go to work at more than one place, *i.e.* multiple places.

Poverty and Income from Labour

Like the previous table, here also out of total 309 households, only 15.2 per cent are non-workers. From the rest 262 households, 45 per cent of all the households have less than (or equal to) Rs. 1000 per labourer income from labour, 23 per cent of the households have Rs. 1001-2000 per labourer annual income from labour and only 16.8 households have more than Rs. 2000 labour income. 17.6 per cent of households below poverty line earn more than Rs. 2000 per worker per annum, who could have been working in more than one place (multiple places) to earn the highest amount. Table 6.5 shows 25.6 per cent poor households work at multiple places. The rest 8 per cent of the multiple place working households might be earning the medium amount, *i.e.* Rs. 1000-2000 per labour per annum perhaps due to low wage rate of labour areas lying within state but outside village.

Poverty and Dependent Persons

There is a high negative correlation or inverse relation between per capita total annual consumption expenditure and percentage of dependent persons of a household (see Appendix VI). In other words, higher the percentage of dependent members of a family lower is its per capita total annual consumption expenditure. It implies that, as expected, higher dependency also increases poverty. 23.9 per cent, *i.e.* 74 households have no dependent person, two households completely depend on their relatives and begging (see Table 6.7).

Table 6.6: Relation between Poverty and Labour Income

Poverty	Per capita labourer income from labour]			
	< Rs. 1000	Rs. 1001-2000	> Rs. 2000	Row Total
Below Poverty line	65 (52)	39 (31.2)	21 (16.8)	125
Above Poverty line	74 (57)	32 (23)	30 (25)	136
Column Total	139	71	52	262

Table 6.7: Percentage of Depĕndent Persons Across Poverty Line

Households	% of dependent persons				
	25	26-50	51-75	76-100	Row Total
Below Poverty line	10.4	40.9	36.5	12.2	100
Above Poverty line	13.6	44.9	32.2	9.3	100

Note : Values in parenthesis are the percentage values of the individual slab/ block to total. There is however, negative or weak correlation between the two variables.

Source: Field work.

Per Capita Annual Food Expenditure

The consumption expenditures of food, clothing and shelter are added together before determining the poverty line. Conversely, poverty decides how much is to be spent on those basic needs. Amongst all the items, food has a major share in net expenditure in so far as deprivation is concerned. Usually, poor spend largest proportion of his income for satisfying hunger, the most urgent primary necessity. Items of food includes not only the natural produces suitably grown in specific regional climate but also certain outside products which are of cultural likings (tastes of the people) of a particular caste or class group. There is, however, a general pattern of food habit in each region.

Table 6.8 presents percentages of poor and better off households across three different category-sizes of per capita annual food expenditure. About 60 per cent of the total sample data consume medium amount, 20 per cent households low amount and only 17.8 per cent spend highest amount on food. Normally, people eat coarse rice and *kanduli dal*. Poor take various roots, *saag (bhaji)*, bamboo shoots and fruits in the months of food scarcity.

The inter-group (those households below poverty line and those above poverty line) variation in food consumption is striking while 44 per cent of the poor households spend the lowest amount on food only 2 per cent of the well off families spend the same amount. Again when 34 per cent of better off families spend highest amount not even a single household of poor families is there who can afford such a high amount. However, the difference between the worse off and better off families is not large (8%) in the medium amount (Rs. 1201-2400) category size.

Among the poor we find though maximum percentage (*i.e.* 56%) of households consume moderately on food item nonetheless a substantial proportion of the families, *i.e.* 44 per cent spend minimum amounts (*i.e.* Rs. 1200) on edible items.

Looking to the original raw data table, one observes that 17 (6%) of the households (H.H.) even if spend their entire family expenditure could hardly be able to touch the upper margin of the lowest food expense class (*i.e.* Rs. 1200). In fact, annual expenditure on food alone might be much less than Rs. 1001 since the per capita total annual consumption expenditure which includes food, intoxicants and clothing together is Rs. 1001. These 6 per cent could have been critically poor, exhibiting severe malnourishment and undernourishment. Time to time occurrences of starvation deaths might have been reported from among this group. To quote a newspaper report "... the condition of her three children, all malnourished, the youngest one severely so. Both Phanas and Banita were earning Rs. 100 a month in their job till a shortwhile ago.[4] Now they earn Rs. 210 a month about a third of what they could get if they were..."

Table 6.8 : Per cent variation in Poverty by size of per capita food expenditure.

Poverty category	Per capita amount food-expenditure (in Rs.)			Row Total
	1200 (low)	1201-2400 (medium)	2401 (high)	
HHs below poverty line	44	56	0	100
HHs above poverty line	2	64	34	100

Source: Fieldwork.

Though the district in general suffers from starvation, Dharamgarh plateau (Lanjigarh and Thuamul Rampur), part of Udanti basin and certain pockets of Nawapada are infamous for starvation deaths.

Annual Intoxicant Expenditure of Family

After food intoxicants can be categorised as the second most important item of expenditure. In Kalahandi people often spend lavishly on liquor even if their income is meagre. The coefficient of correlation value (see Appendix VI) shows that there is a strong positive correlation between poverty (based on per capita consumption expenditure) and annual intoxicant expenditure of a family. It means higher class people spend higher amount in intoxicants.

Majority (almost 70%) of the poor families annually spend Rs. 500 on intoxicants. Field observation shows this small amount spending could have been made on less expensive tobacco (country *cheroot*) *bidi, gudakhu, gundi*. These families which spend Rs. 500 on intoxicants usually consume country made liquor. Liquor consumption is rampant in Kalahandi among various groups irrespective of their economic condition. However, rich spend more than poor.

Table 6.9 : Per cent Variation in Poverty by Annual Intoxicant Expenditure Size of Family.

	Annual Intoxicant Expenditure					Row Total
	0	<500	501-1000	1001-1500	>1500	
HHs below Poverty line	19.4	69	18	5	8	100
HHs above Poverty line	12	45	22	14	19	100
Column total	15.5	47.2	17.2	8.4	11.7	100

Source : Fieldwork.

Table 6.10 precisely shows that relatively higher standard of living enables to spend higher amount on intoxicants. As it is observed from fieldwork, poor spend less on intoxicants obviously due to their lower capacity to buy intoxicants especially liquor.

Table 6.10 : Aggregated form of the previous table

Intoxicant Expenditure	< Rs. 1000	> Rs. 1000	Row Total
HHs below Poverty Line	87	13	100
HHs above Poverty Line	68	32	100

Source: Field work

Among SCs who mostly work outside there is rather better consciousness. The female members and housewives* who often work as labourers outside are rather more careful in maintaining households expenditure.

Food Expenditure and Intoxicant Expenditure

The positive correlation between food and intoxicant expenditure (as evident from Table 6.11) indicates that higher spending on food is possible if family's income is higher and higher income would also enable higher spending on intoxicants (confirmed by Table 6.10). That way families who spend more on food are also families who spend more on intoxicants.

Table 6.11: Total intoxicant expenditure of family across various per capita food expenditure

Per capita food Expenditure (Rs)		Total Intoxicant Expenditure of a family		
		Low <1000	High >1000	Row Total
Low	1200	84	16	100
Medium	1200-2400	75	25	100
High	>2400	71	29	100

Source: Fieldwork.

As observed from Table 6.11 and the fieldwork, poor households who have lower income and less spending on food also consume less intoxicants.

Out of 44 per cent of the poor who consume lower amount (< Rs. 1200) on per capita food expenditure about 84 per cent of families have low intoxicant expenditure (*i.e* < Rs. 1200) and

* In Kalahandi because of high sex ratio and economic necessity a single male often marries more than one female who act as labourers (asset) and thus possesses several co-wives at a time.

about 16 per cent have high (>Rs. 1000) intoxicant expenditure.

Again drinking country-made liquor is a custom and practice among people of Kalahandi at different occasions like birth, death (funeral ceremony), marriage, guest visit, festivals, cure from diseases or freeing evil spiritis. In the past when liquor brewing was allowed to only licence holders, many land transfers took place through the process of liquor sale and indebtedness. At present, the field experience says that people (especially scheduled castes) are more conscious and poverty conditions hardly allow poor to go to '*bhattis*' except occasionally and when easy loan money or government assistance is available.

The cross table of the percentage of dependent persons per household and per capita food expenditure per annum shows an inverse correlation between the two. Correlation of cross table of per capita food expenditure per annum and percentage of working members reveals positive correlation between the two variables.

So higher dependency compels more family members to go for labour work and then the initial per capita food consumption is increased. Kalahandi district has high sex ratio. So more and more females join the wage labour as the dependent children of the family increases. Consequently, with the increase in income, more is spent in liquor. Therefore, these three variables–dependent persons, working persons and spending on intoxicants keep the per capita food expenditure at a stable or optimum level. For poor labourers it becomes lower and for better off labourers it (per capita food expenditure) becomes higher than the average (stable level).

Clothing Expenditure

Out of the three basic needs clothing assumed more significance after the civilised world exposed gradually to the modern urban culture. Migrant labourers (especially SCs) earn more and obviously spend more on clothing after fulfilling their requirements of food and liquor. There is a direct strong association (as marked by chi square test) between per capita household consumption expenditure and clothing expenditure.

Almost one-third of the total households fall in each of the low (Rs. 800), medium (Rs. 800-1000) and high (Rs. 1600) annual clothing expenditure category.

Clothing Expenditure and Land Income Size

There is a very strong correlation (*i.e.* 4061 at .001 level) and high degrees of association between land income size and clothing expenditure.

Table 6.12 : Per cent Variation of Clothing Expenditure by Total Annual Land Income Size

Total Annual Income from land (in Rs.)	Annual clothing expenditure (Rs.)	
	< 600 Low	> 600 High
< 2000	74.99	25.01
2001-4000	62.25	37.75
4001-6000	51.73	48.27
> 6000	21.21	78.79

Source: Based on fieldwork data.

With the increasing income from land the proportion of families falling in high annual clothing expenditure column is also rising. This points at the direct/positive correlation between income from land and clothing expenditure. Disaggregated percentage figures, however, gives an unsymmetrical picture. Putting it in other way, lower the income from land higher is the proportion of families falling in lower annual clothing expenditure column. Naturally, poor people spend less on clothing. This is further confirmed by high expenditure and correlation value of the table of poverty and annual household expenditure and clothing.

Land Owning Classes and its Correlates

As mentioned already 'land ownership' is the proxy variable of poverty. Again not just the anomalies in land distribution but land quality highlight inequality and gross disparity. Quite a number of families in Kalahandi do rely on labour to supplement their marginal production from land. Literacy, no doubt make people aware of their liberty but it hardly enables them to fight out the injustice in order to release themselves from the bondage of poverty.

Land Income

The percentage of households of landless, marginal farmers, small farmers, medium farmers and large farmers are 35.2, 26.9, 21.4 and 6.1 respectively.

Out of total 309 households of the district 109 HHs are landless. Households of marginal farmers and two medium farmers due to some reason or the other, don't cultivate their land and so they have zero income from land. Rest 193 farming HHs of different land size classes have various amount of earning from land.

Forty-one of the landless families, however, earn some income from land. How is it so? Many tribes are landless in conventional sense since they hardly possess private land or plots like plough cultivators but they raise crops on *dongar* and so have income from land. Some landless labourers through share cropping or lease etc. earn for themselves from land also.

In Table 6.13, we observe many medium and large farmers also have very low (< Rs. 2000) annual income from land. This could be due to misinformation provided by the respondent or due to bad quality soil or due to portion of cultivating land being left fallow (uncultivated). Similarly few marginal and small farmers have high (Rs. 6000) annual income from land. This may

Table 6.13: Percentage variation in land owning classes by land income categories

Farmers of different land size (acres) groups	Land Incomes (in Rs.)				Row Total %
	1-2000	2000-4000	4000-6000	6000 & above	
Marginal farmers < 2.0	67	24	6	3	100
Small farmers (2.0-7.0)	35	33	15	17	100
Medium farmers (7.0-12.0)	27	6	37	30	100
Large farmers > 12.0	21	21	—	57	100

Source: Fieldwork.

be due to wrong information provided. Better soil quality and availability of irrigation facilities apart from use of modern agricultural inputs could have been the causes for high production even by small and marginal farmers.

The percentage of HHs of the former case is more than those of the later case. This shows the vulnerability of large chunk of not only marginal (67%) and small farmers (35%) but also medium (27%) and large farmers (21%) who because of their low production from land even during normal years are compelled to outmigrate in search of labour, leaving behind or selling out land once there is severe crop failure due to drought.

Land Owning Classes and Working Members of Family

The correlation coefficient value shows that there is an inverse relationship between percentage of working members and land size of a family. This is evident from Table 6.14.

Table 6.14 : Percentage of Working Members of Household by Land Size Classes

% of working members	Marginal farmers	Small farmers	Medium farmers	Large farmers	Row Total	% of Total HH
Low	50	31	19	0	100	19
Low to Medium	49	30	12	9	100	41
Medium to high	46	38	8	8	100	22
High	31	42	7	10	100	18

Source: Fieldwork.

Again Table 6.2 shows that there is an inverse correlation between land size and poverty. It mean there is direct correlation between poverty and percentage of working members of the family.

Thus, lower the land size lower is the income from land and higher is the poverty [Table 6.4(a)] and so it necessitates greater proportion of family members' involvement in labour and in labour earning works (cross table of percentage of working members and annual income from land-correlation coefficient).

The same Table 6.4a shows that 62.5 per cent HHs have earning both from land and labour. It means their land size is not sufficient to subsist upon. Hence, they supplement their land income with that of labour.

Table 6.15: Percentage of working members to total members of a family and annual income from land

% of working members	Land Income (in Rs.) /Annum				
	1-2000	2001-4000	4001-6000	6000 above	Row etc. %
1-25	46	31	20	20	100
26-50	58	22	7	13	100
51-75	58	24	13	5	100
75-100	50	17	20	13	100

Source : Fieldwork.

The previous two variables show very high association through chi-square test and very strong correlation of – 0.2247 at +0.001 level (calculated through computer).

Table 6.16: Per labourer annual income of a family and percentage of literacy

Income size in Rs.	Percentage of literacy				
	0	1-25	26-50	51-75	76-100
1-1000	56	23	14	8	1
1001-2000	48	8	11	1	3
2001 & above	25	16	5	6	–

Source: Fieldwork.

225 (72.8%) households are regular labour (wage) earners, though the total wage earners are as high as 84.8 percentage (according to Table 6.5).

Along each labour income category we find there is a general decrease in number of families across different literacy categories. With increasing per labourer income there is decrease in number of illiterate families in each subsequent slabs.

As evident from negative correlation and strong association values, families having higher percentage of literacy have lesser per capita labour income. The reason is obvious. More literate families have less preference for manual work of wage labour.

Combining this above correlation with the previous statement, we see the lower the land size and lower the income from land higher is the poverty (Tables 6.3 and 6.4a); so it necessitates greater proportion of family members involvement in labour to earn more; lower the income from land higher is the per labourer income from labour (See Table 6.16).

This very diversion towards earning through wage labour keep the family members off from formal schooling as a result of which higher labour earning households have lower proportion of literacy.

Table 6.17 : Per labourer annual income of a family and annual income from land of the family

Per labourer	Land Income (in Rs)/Annum				
Annual Income (in Rs.)	2000	2001-4000	4001-6000	6000	Row total
1000	75.9	27.9	20.7	10.3	100
1001-2000	61.0	31.5	1.9	5.6	100
2001	57.7	23.1	15.4	3.8	100

Source: Fieldwork.

From the very high association (chi-square value) and very strong negative correlation value (*i.e.* – 0.3864 at +0.001 level) between the two variables it is evident that lower the income from land higher is the per labourer income from labour. Similarly, strong correlation (+0.1573 at +.01 level) and very high association (chi-square value) between per labourer annual income of a family and percentage of dependent persons in household suggest that families going for more labour productive (labour income per labourer) works have higher dependency ratio. Thus, poor families have more dependent persons.

Thirty-eight households or 16.9 per cent labourer families have not even a single dependent person. It means, their all the family members are working members who have definite earning from labour.

In Table 6.3, we earlier saw how medium and big farmers who are poor probably outmigrate during prolonged drought. Their poverty could be due to low earning from both land and labour or from land alone. Very strong positive correlation and very high association values between classes owning different sizes of land and their land income are obvious. From this, if we modify the previous correlation statement we find.

Table 6.18 : Per labourer annual income of a family and per cent of dependent persons in a household

Per labourer annual income	% of dependent persons				
	<25	26-50	51-75	76-100	Row Total %
1000	15.9	48.9	29.5	5.7	100
1001-2000	10.2	37.2	39	13.6	100
2001	7.5	50	25	17.5	100

Source: Fieldwork.

Lower the land size lower is the income from land (Table 6.13 correlation), higher is the poverty (Tables 6.3 and 6.4a), so these necessitate greater proportion of family members involvement in labour (Table 6.5a) and/or correlation and chi-square value (of Table 6.14) and/or in more labour productive (*i.e.* greater labour income per labourer) works (correlation of Table 6.15). Again families participating in more labour productive works have generally higher dependency ratio. (Table 6.18 correlation, association). Earlier in poverty section we have noted that higher dependency increases poverty (Table 6.7). Thus it becomes a vicious circle. Poverty leads to poverty.

Land Holding Classes and Soil Quality

Just like land ownership is a proxy of poverty, soil quality could be taken as a proxy variable of land. In other words, to cross compare land holding classes and soil quality is to analyse the relationship between poverty and land ownership. However land quality (which depends on water retaining capacity, slope, terrain condition etc.) is not the same as soil quality. High association (chi-square value) and very significant correlation establishes that higher landholding families have better quality soil and *vice versa*. This is reflected in *Bahal* and *Bhatta* category of soil respectively. *Bahal* soil in fact, reflects best the positive correlation. Here, the proportion of households of each size class families increase significantly than its previous class size.

Table 6.19: Percentage variation in land owning classes by soil quality

Farmers	*Bahal*	*Berna*	*Att*	*Bhatta*	Row Total
Marginal	34.7	13.3	22.7	29.3	75
Small	47.6	4.76	30.2	17.5	63
Medium	63.3	10	10	13.3	30
Big	76	5.9	5.9	11.8	17

Source: Fieldwork.

The proportion of families falling in higher land size class first decrease very steeply and then increases marginally pointing out the fact that lesser proportion of higher land owning classes have worse quality soil. Relating this with the previous findings we have lower the land size, worse is the soil quality, lower is the income from land and higher is the poverty (correlation of Tables 6.18 and Table 6.3). Small lands coupled with their poor qualities of soil aggravate poverty of marginal and small farmers.

Land Holding Classes and Literacy

It is a common observation that people owing higher acres of land are better off economically and so can afford for their children's education. Poor people with marginal or no agricultural land can ill afford primary or elementary education. Because by sending their children to school they loose working hands (daily wage earners). Our data analysis presents a different picture.

Out of 109 (or 35 % of the total HHs) of landless families 63.3 per cent have not even a single member is literate. Illiteracy and poor literacy is mostly found among the landless. These decline among big farmers, marginal, small and medium households as one proceeds. In 'low to medium' literacy, 'medium to high' literacy and high literacy categories the predominating classes are landless, marginal farmers and small farmers respectively. The very strong correlation (.2256 at .001 level) value indicates that, there is a direct relationship between land ownership and literacy.

From the raw data table it may be made clear that in medium to high literacy only 29 households and in high literacy merely 9 households fall. Again in medium to high literacy of the landless families only 4 households fall. Similarly, just a single household of marginal farmer under high literacy category, 6 households of small farmers in medium-high and high literacy category are there. So, looking to the percentage figure one should not be surprised.

The potential diversion towards earning through wage labour or cultivation, apart from other causes, keep the family members off from formal schooling. As a result higher labour earning households have lower proportion of literacy (Table 6.20).

Table 6.20 : Variation in per cent of literacy by land size classes

Literacy	% of Land Owning Classes					
	Landless Farmers	Marginal Farmers	Small Farmers	Medium Farmers	Big Farmers	Row Total %
0	41.3	28.1	21.6	5.4	3.6	100
< 25 low	34.5	22.4	20.7	15.5	6.9	100
25-50 Low-Med	34.8	21.7	26.1	6.5	10.9	100
50-75 Med-High	6.9	41.4	10.3	31.0	10.3	100
> 75 High	22.2	11.1	33.3	22.2	11.1	100

Source: Field work.

Land Holding Classes and Social Groups

Though land is not the sole determinant of standard of living, poverty analysis becomes more striking when cross comparison is made between land ownership and social groups. The general observation is that the higher caste people are in occupation of larger tracts of land and *vice versa*. Table 6.21 shows how various proportion of the three social groups (SC, ST and others) distributed under different land size or landless class sizes. More than half (56.79%) of the landless families are from scheduled caste group. While general caste people predominate among marginal and medium farmers, scheduled tribe households are in majority in small and large farmers.

The calculated weighted scores for SCs, STs and other general castes are 30, 80 and 80.5 (see Table 6.22). Thus in general, higher caste households belong to better land owning classes. And there is not much difference between ST and general caste households, so far as land ownership is concerned.

Earlier in Table 6.1 we observed that the poverty among SCs is least. Contrary to it, here in the two succeeding tables we find landlessness (56.79%) is maximum among SCs. Again the share of SCs is minimum among other social groups as far as various land size classes are concerned. This points out the fact that land ownership in this very case is not a cause of poverty and engagement in higher wage works outside the district are perhaps responsible for their lower poverty.

Thus, lower poverty of SCs is not due to their position in land ownership but because of their greater involvement in more productive works outside.

Table 6.21 : Percentage variation of land owning sizes by different social groups

Group	Landless Farmers	Marginal Farmers	Small Farmers	Medium Farmers	Large Farmers	Row Total %
SC	56.79	22.2	8.6	7.4	4.9	100
ST	28.4	22.9	30.3	8.3	8.3	100
Others	26.9	33.6	21.8	5	5	100

Source: Fieldwork.

Table 6.22: Percentage distribution of landed households (200 only)

Social Groups	Marginal Farmers	Small Farmers	Medium Farmers	Large Farmers	Total weighted Score
	(Farmers of different Land size group)				
SC	9	3.5	3	2	30
ST	12.5	16.5	5.5	4.5	80
Others	20	13	7.5	3	80.5

Note: Table 6.22 is prepared using weighted score method. The corresponding units are Marginal farmers – 1, Medium farmers – 3, Small farmers – 2, Large Farmers – 4.

Source: Fieldwork.

However, in case of STs and general caste land ownership are definitely a factor for their better overall economic condition. (Looking to the households below poverty line and above poverty line together and especially those HHs falling above poverty line. See Tables 6.1, 6.21 and 6.22).

Therefore, not simply land but also labour is an equally important factor in poverty.

A transitional phase is visible is Kalahandi. SCs were

initially powerless in their home. But their gradual exposure to the outside world and rising wage earning have enabled them to involve in moneylending, land purchasing or middlemanship. In the chapter on Production Relation in Rural Kalahandi we shall see how they play an important exploitative link in the district between rich businessmen, moneylenders on the one side and tribals and other poor people on the other. Perhaps this very role of theirs is slowly raising the percentage of poverty among STs.

About half of the high earning workers, one-fifth of the medium low earners and just about one-eighth of low earning labourers go to work at multiple places. Therefore, families especially, SCs who have generally higher dependency ratio participate in more labour productive works outside or work at more than one place.

Therefore, families (especially those of scheduled castes) who have generally higher dependency ratio participate in more labour productive works outside or work at more than one place (Table 6.23).

Table 6.23 : Per Labourer annual income of a family (in Rs.) and main labour area

Per labourer Annual Income (Rs.)	Labour Area			
	Own village	Within district	Outside district	Row Total
<1000	92 [12]	5 [3]	3 [9]	100 [14]
1001-2000	64 [1]	1 [9]	3 [3]	66 [13]
2001 &Above	32	7 [17]	7 [4]	46 [21]

Note : [ ] HHs work any at more than one place.
Source: Fieldwork.

Conclusion

Therefore, lower the land size, worse is the soil quality (correlation of cross Table 6.19), lower is the income from the land (correlation of cross Table 6.13), higher is the poverty (Tables 6.3 and 6.4a). In other words, land size, soil quality and income from the land are significantly correlated with poverty. This is especially true for scheduled tribes as evident from Table 6.2. Households having lower income from land marginally supplement their earning through the sale of small amount of manually processed agricultural products (Table 6.4b) and insignificant income from sale of forest products. This necessitates involvement of greater proportion of family members in labour (Table 6.14 and or correlation and chi-square value of Table 6.15) and or in more labour productive (*i.e.* labour income per labourer) works (correlation of Table 6.17). This reduces poverty especially for SCs as reflected in Table 6.2. Families (especially SCs) who have generally higher dependency ratio participate in more labour productive works outside or work at more than one place (multiple places, Table 6.23). Earlier, in the poverty section we have noted that higher dependency increases poverty (Table 6.7). Thus for some poor families it becomes a vicious circle, poverty leading to poverty. In the later part we found that higher dependency compels more family members to go for labour and thus the initial low per capita food consumption is increased. In Kalahandi sex ratio is high. So, more and more females join the wage labour as the dependent children of a family increases (field observation).[5]

With increasing income, mores ending is made on liquor and other intoxicants. Thus, these three variables, *viz.* dependent persons, working members and intoxicant expenditure keep the per capita food expenditure at a stable level. For poor labourers per capita food expenditure becomes lower and for better off labourers it becomes higher than the average (stable) level.

Finally, our finding on intoxicant and clothing expenditure is that poorer households spend lesser on these items. As the income or standard of living increases, more and more expenses are made on intoxicants and clothing.

Land and labour seems to be the most important influencing variables of poverty in the study area.

NOTES

1. Jain, L. R. and Tendulkar, S.D. (1990), "Role of Growth and Distribution in the observed change in Head Count Ratio Measure of Poverty : A Decomposition Exercise for India," *Indian Economic Review*, Vol. XXV, No. 2, p. 192.
2. "The situation of Scheduled Tribes appears to be unique, as they do not seem to resort to migration to alleviate their miseries, and continue to stick to their traditional micro ecological niche eking out their living by time

tested traditional cultural practices" a fact corroborated by micro level study of Jagannath Dash in Nayak, P.K. Mahajan, A. (1991), *Human Encounter with drought*, Reliance Publishing House, New Delhi, pp. 26-27.

3. Choudhry, K. (1991) : "Stricken Kalahandi : Commission confirms deaths." *Frontline* Sep.28-Oct. 11.
4. "Nine Years later Kalahandi remains the same" by P. Sainath in Faces of Poverty report series, *Times of India*, New Delhi, 22-3-1994, p. 22.
5. In addition, relatively higher participation of Kalahandi females as 'marginal workers' as compared to Orissa and India is indicative of higher aggregate economic stress and a larger proportion of poorer sections of population in Kalahandi as compared to Orissa and India is a demographic indicator of relative underdevelopment of Kalahandi [Nayak, and P.K. Mahajan, A. (1991) : *Human Encounter with Drought*, Reliance Publishing House, New Delhi, p. 28].

7

SPATIAL INCIDENCE OF POVERTY AND ITS ECONOMIC CORRELATES

This chapter on 'Spatial Incidence of Poverty' is devoted to the analysis of how and why the levels of development varies from region to region even within a small administrative unit and to what extent economic variables explain poverty.

Towards this end, Kalahandi district has been divided into micro-regions by superimposing development regions upon natural regions*. These micro regions are:

1. Nuapada Forested Upland (Low and high levels of development)
2. Udanti Basin (Low development)
3. Tel Valley (Low development)
4. Tel Valley (High development)
5. Madanpur-Rampur Forested Upland (Low development)
6. Dharamgarh Plateau (Low development)
7. Daramgarh Plateau (High development)
8. Tel-Hatti Basin (Low development)
9. Tel-Hatti Basin (High development)

Pairs of villages having high economic indicator (H) [*i.e.* low percentage of non-working population to working population, low percentage of marginal farmers to total farmers

* The "natural regions" were taken from cartographic regionalisation of India, Census of India. (For details see the section on 'Methodology and Data Base'). The Underdevelopment regions were prepared by the researcher himself by using "Composite Development Index" (For details see Chapter 4).

and high percentage of irrigated area per farmer] and low economic indicator (L) [i.e. high percentage of non-working

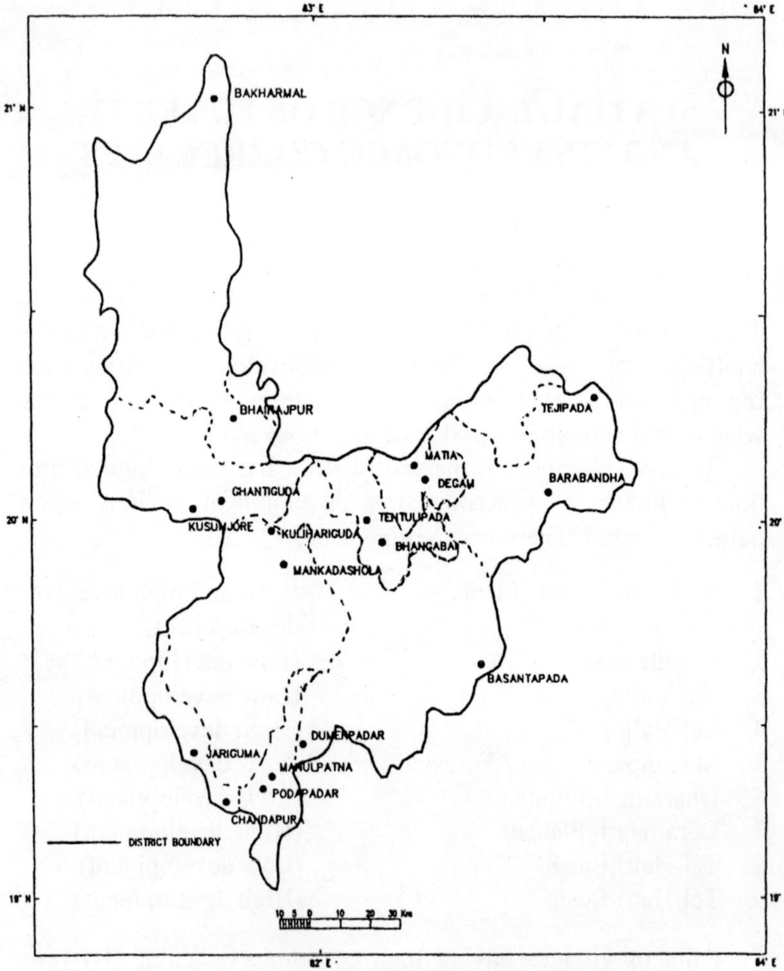

Map. 27 : Kalahandi : Sample Villages

population to working population, high percentage of marginal farmers to total farmers and low percentage of irrigated area per farmer] were taken from each of the sample regions. The sample village pairs for the respective sample regions are :

	Selected Villages	*Natural Regions*
1.	Bakharmal (H) and Bhairajpur (H)	Nawapada Forested Upland
2.	Ghantiguda (L) and Kusumjore (H)	Udanti Basin (Low Development)
3.	Tentulipada (L) and Bhangabari (H)	Tel Valley (Low Development)
4.	Matia (H) and Degam (H)	Tel Valley (High Development)
5.	Tejipada (L) and Barabandha (H)	M. Rampur F. Upland (Low Development)
6.	Basantpada (L) and Dumerpadar (H)	Dharamgarh Plateau (Low Development)
7.	Jariguma (L) and Chandpura (H)	Dharamgarh Plateau (High Development)
8.	Padepadar (L) and Mahulpatna (H)	Tel-Hatti Basin (Low Development)
9.	Mankadashola (L) and Kulihariguda (H)	Tel-Hatti Basin (High Development)

(See also Appendix 7, p.356 and p.351).

Significance of the Indicators

As we observed from the table of social correlates of poverty in Chapter 6, the inter-group variation in poverty is very low (5%). So, the dropping of caste/tribe as a controlling factor of poverty is justified. As against this, the two variables of land and labour are considered significant to influence poverty in the study area. This was noted during preliminary fieldwork and was later confirmed by the correlation analysis. Kalahandi being a drought prone district, it was thought that much of its variation in land production and hence levels of poverty could have been due to varied degrees of irrigation (water) availability.

The percentage of marginal farmers to total farmers, of non-workers to total workers, and of irrigated area per farmer were therefore considered important factors in selecting sample villages. (The method for selection of villages and households are already given in Chapter 3.)

Few Modifications in the Frame

From the Tel valley of low underdevelopment region, *i.e.* Kesinga two villages of similar economic indicators has been selected for sample survey. This is done to test whether the two villages, despite all similarities in geographic (regional) and village level economic characteristics have at all any variation in level of poverty. If so, why?

Jubarajpur, the sample village of high economic indicator in Dharmagarh plateau (low development) was dropped for fieldwork, as the researcher found that the process of displacement of the villagers has already started due to the fear of its submergence after the inception or initiation of the nearby Indravati Project. Later another village named 'Dumerpadar' was chosen in its place for poverty study on the basis of secondary data only.

From Nuapada Forested Upland two villages of high economic indicator (instead of one high and one low economic indicator) were taken for sample survey from extreme parts having varied local geographic conditions. This is to verify intra-regional variation in poverty rather than inter-regional variation (as has been done in most other cases). Since one forested upland (Madanpur Rampur) already provides two villages for sample survey the researcher felt hardly any justification of the repetition of the same procedure here in this forested upland.

The village level poverty which represent the regional poverty for villages of low economic indicator or high economic indicator has been analysed on the basis of local and regional factors. The intra-regional and inter-regional variation have been accounted for.

Out of 309 households surveyed, 140 households, *i.e.* 43.4 per cent of the total families of the district fall below poverty line. Table 7.1 includes the list of villages along with their percentage of households below poverty line (or respective poverty-values).

Table 7.1 : Percentage of households below poverty line in different village-pairs

	Pairs of Village Names	Total HH Surveyed	No. of HH below poverty line	% of HHs below poverty line
1.	Bakharmal (H)	20	8	40
	Bhairajpur (H)	18	5	50
2.	Ghantiguda (L)	18	12	27.77
	Kusumjore (H)	18	9	66.66
3.	Tentulipada (L)	18	9	50
	Bhangabari (H)	19	5	26.31
4.	Matia (H)	18	7	38.88
	Degam (H)	20	8	40
5.	Tejipada (L)	15	7	46.66
	Barabandha (H)	17	4	23.52
6.	Basantpada (L)	19	13	68.42
	Dumerpada* (H)	108	48	44.44
7.	Jariguma (L)	19	10	52.63
	Chandpura (H)	18	7	38.88
8.	Padepadar (L)	18	10	55.55
	Mahulpatna (H)	17	11	64.70
9.	Mankadasola (L)	19	4	21.05
	Kulihariguda (H)	18	7	38.88

* Based on ORSAC (Orissa Remote Sensing Agency), Bhubaneswar data of 1989-90.

Source : Fieldwork.

Analysis of Spatial Poverty

(Based on the study of Sample Villages of High Economic Indicators)

Bakharmal and Bhairajpur, though situated in two different economic regions (low development and high development parts respectively) of the same natural region (Nawapada Forested Upland), have lower (40%) and higher (50%) poverty respectively. Perhaps, their local geographic factors rather than broad economic indicators (low and high) have a bearing on their poverty. Again, if we look at the micro economic conditions, Bakharmal has more irrigated land than Bhairajpur.

The high poverty of both the villages is justified since they are located in rain deficient or drought prone region of

Kalahandi. Thus, in general, we can say that ecological or geographic conditions are the basic cause of poverty, specific economic conditions of the two villages explain the real reason of poverty. The collected fieldwork data in the tabulated form have been analysed later.

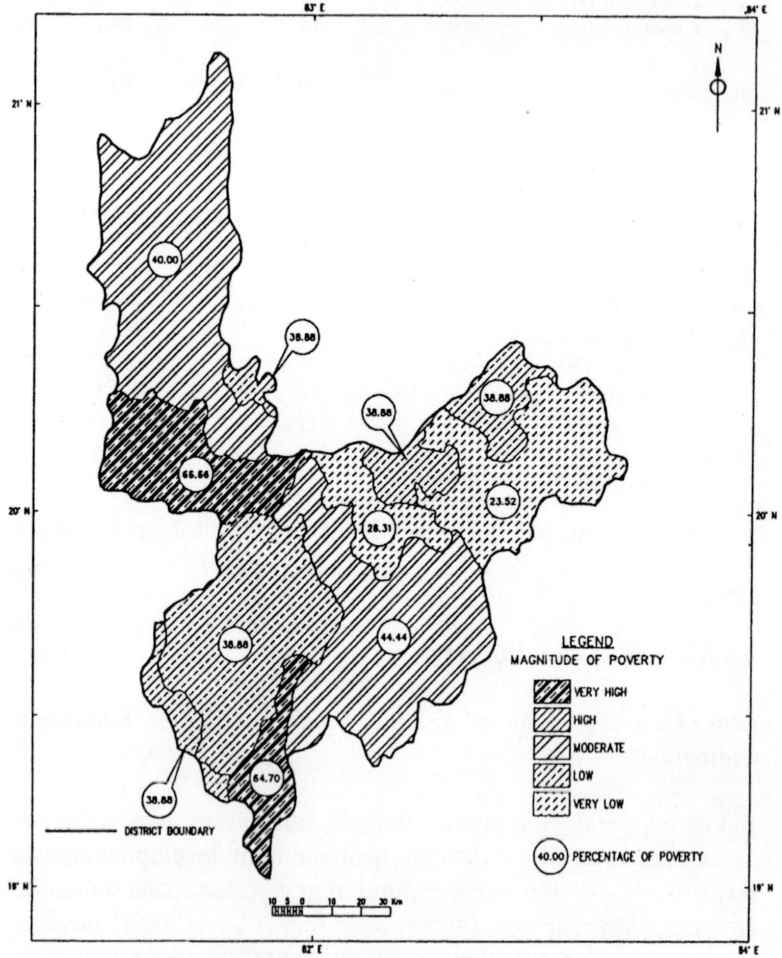

Map 28 : Kalahandi : Poverty in Different Sub-Micro Regions (for High Economic Indicator Villages)

Bakharmal and Degam have equal but moderate percentages (*i.e.* 40% each) poverty. There seems to be no common reason behind it. Bakharmal is situated in low developed part of Nawapada Forested Upland. Moreover, the entire part receives very little rain, being in the rain shadow zone of Sunabeda plateau. Looking to the weighted score of land and soil we find the sample villages have some local causes for its poverty. About 20 per cent households (HHs) are landless. Another 25 per cent have low scoring and 40 per cent HHs have moderate scoring. (see the "Weighed Score" table in Appendix 7, p. 370 - 371). 35 per cent of the families work outside to supplement their meagre income from land (as in case of landless).

However, Degam is a peculiar case. Even if it is located in the Tel Valley (of high development) and it has high village level economic indicator (as evident from census data), it exhibits moderate level of poverty. The local geographic reason, may be attributed to this. The weighted scores of land and soil of the village are poor. 8 HHs out of twenty HHs have scoring values of 3-4. Six households are absolutely landless. Rest six households have higher scores out of which 3 households have scoring value 5 only. Poor scoring is not simply due to landlessness but due to poor sandy soil of the village agricultural fields, located on the bank of the river Ret. Some households, however, go for outside labour in absence of land. But hardly their income compensate poverty.

Matia, Chandpur and Kulihariguda each have 38.88 per cent of poverty score. This low poverty is due to favourable physical factors, *i.e.* fertile and well watered lands of Kulihariguda (Tel-Hatti Basin) and Matia (Tel Valley) and high development as in case of Chandpura and Matia. While Chandpura and Kulihariguda's lone advantage is upgraded by their better economic characteristics (*i.e.* higher percentage of irrigation, lower percentage of non-working population and marginal farmers having 1 ha. of land) the double advantage of Matia is balanced down by low economic characteristics of the village, *i.e.* lower percentage of irrigated area, higher percentage of non-working population and marginal farmers). As a result, all the villages exhibit same level of poverty.

We now compare "Kusumjore" with "Barabandha". First of all, the two villages are perfectly comparable, since they not only belong to "high economic indicator village" category but they have very close values with respect to percentage of non-working to working population (98.6 and 94.9 % respectively), percentage of marginal farmers to total farmers (57.4 and 64.4 % respectively) and percentage of irrigated area per farmer (11.5 and 7.64 % respectively). When we look these two villages against their poverty level it is highly surprising to find that Kusumjore has very high, *i.e.* 66.66 per cent of poverty while Barbandha has mere 23.52 percentage of very low poverty.

Landlessness in the two villages (5.5 and 47 % respectively) obviously do not account for such variation. Labour and wage rate too do not explain it, since in both the villages people work within the village and wage rate differs in accordance with their respective local price of grains and other edible or consumable items. Therefore, their variation in poverty condition could be due to certain geographic factors. In Kusumjore 27.7 per cent households have low landholding of poor soil quality (land and soil weighted score is 2 to 4) whereas in Barabandha 23.5 percentage households have same cases. Again in the score column of 5 the former has 22.2 per cent families and the later has only (17.6% families) (See Appendix 7, p.370).

The relative geo-economic advantage of Barabandha over Kusumjore, as I observed during fieldwork are the following :

(i) Apart from average of 128 days work availability within agricultural season in both the villages, additional working days in Barabandha include erection of fences, thatching, earth carrying and wood cutting and especially bamboo collection. Madanpur Rampur Forests are famous for their bamboo supply. Wage earned from bamboo cutting is more than the *Mahul* picking for which the Udanti Basin is better known.

(ii) The Udanti Basin in which Kusumjore is situated is now left largely deforested (except *Kendu, Bija, Mahul,* Bamboo patches) after the massive felling of teak woods (1948) whereas Madanpur Rampur Upland (>1000 metres) (in which Barabandha is situated) is still rich in forest (*i.e.* > 65 percentage of the area is forested) the forest products [like, *mahul, kendu, tentuli,* sal leaves and sal seeds, mango, varied edible leaves *(sag), Kusum* seeds, roots *(kanda),* tender bamboo shots *(kardi), Kulathi* (horse gram), millets like *Jhudang, Kang, Kodo, Guruji*] are raised more in the plateau, gullies and rugged terrain which are the origin place of many river.*

(iii) Udanti Basin is relatively more flood prone. It is created by the Udanti river and its tributaries at the upper catchment area. Food scarcity is common in both the regions during pre-harvest seasons. Udanti Basin is, however, infamous for starvation deaths.

(iv) In Barabandha villagers have enough exposure to the outside world. Some of them have outside origin. They have more political, educational and administrative access as compared to the people of Kusumjore.

(v) Barabandha has *Gram Panchayat,* Post Office, dispensary and school (up to class seven) and a college (in the nearby Rampur with which the village is well connected by a fair weather forest road).

On the other hand Kusumjore is relatively less accessible. It is at the remote corner of western Kalahandi, bordering Orissa and Madhya Pradesh. It has no hospital and school facilities. It is connected by *Kuccha* earth road with the village, Singhjhar (which is again joined through a fair weather road with Sinapali, the district headquarter).

(vi) The Composite Development Index shows the Forested Uplands [Madanpur Rampur (1.48) area and Narla (1.22)] is more irrigated and hence agriculturally more developed than Sinapali (0.35) and Golamunda (0.70), *i.e.* most part of the Udanti Basin, even if the later has larger potential of ground water reserve than the former. Area under HYV seeds is the lowest in Sinapali.

---

* The soil of Madanpur Rampur region is sandy, alluvial and sandy loam with fragments of laterite layers of hilly uplands. Local and long duration paddy apart from maize, ragi, millets, bajra, pulses are grown. Later, the cultivation of High Yielding Varieties of wheat, groundnut and potato are taken up in irrigated areas. Udanti Basin on the other hand is a part of black cotton soil tract. Its agricultural products are less diverse. These include rice, maize, bajra and somewhere oilseeds.

So far as percentage of working population is concerned Madanpur Rampur (0.79%) shows low index, Udanti Basin [Sinapali (0.89%), Boden (0.96%) moderate and Golamunda (1.67%) high index] show moderate to high index.

Thus, the above geographic causes (some are regional and others local) perhaps explain sufficiently the regional variation (since the two sample villages are taken to be the perfect representative of their respective sub-micro regions) as well as local variations in poverty.

[Village Bhairajpur also belongs to "high economic indicator" category which, like the two previous villages has almost similar percentage of non-working population (130.7), marginal farmers (51.4) and irrigated area (5.2). Its poverty level, however, is 50 per cent, which is 16.66 per cent more than Kusumjore and 26.48 per cent more than Barabandha. Through possible geographic (causes)/factors if we can explain the differences between Bhairajpur and Kusumjore, the explanation can automatically differentiate Bhairajpur from Barabandha].

Matia of Tel Valley also belongs to high economic indicator group having 38.88 percentage of poverty. Economic similarity of the triple villages (Matia, Bhairajpur and Kusumjore), nevertheless show disparity in poverty. Here, the possible causes would again be geographic.

First glance over the map of development creates the impression that with increase in backwardness of the blocks there is increase in the level of poverty in the three corresponding villages. Matia (38.88 % poverty) is situated in the block of very low underdevelopment (composite development index 10.50%) Bhairajpur (poverty 50%) is in Khariar block of low underdevelopment (C.I. 14.50 to 16.50%) and Kusumjore (poverty 66.66%) is in Sinapali block of medium underdevelopment (C.I. value 12.50 to 14.50%).

Again, physiographic location of Matia (which lies in the Tel Valley) rightly lowers down its poverty from that of Bhairajpur (which is in Nuapada Forested Upland) and Kusumjore (which lies in the Udanti Basin). However, it does not explain why an agricultural village of forested Upland should have lower poverty from that of a basin. Before going into details of physical characteristics, let us consider how the relative inaccessibility of the three villages more accurately determines their poverty. Matia (which has lowest poverty among the three) is hardly 4 km, away from Utkela, the small town on the State Highway linking Bhawanipatna-Kesinga, *i.e.* the district headquarter with the block headquarter, though a small intervening river Ret disconnect the village from the town during rainy months. Bhairajpur is about 8 km away from Khariar, the block headquarter and the State Highway connecting Nawapada-Khariar-Titlagarh. River Sundar temporarily disrupts the poor *kuccha* road communication between the village and Khariar (which passes *via* Duajhar) during rainy season. Kusumjore (with highest poverty among the three) is in fact, located in remote and most inaccessible part of the Udanti Basin. It is more than 30 kms. farther form Khariar on the above mentioned State Highway and one has to walk or paddle down 8 km only to reach a fair weather *kuccha* road at Sinapali, the block headquarter. The author remembers how during his last day of fieldwork he was advised to leave even Sinapali because of an imminent danger of road dislocation due to flash flood in the river Udanti, after a heavy afternoon shower.

Coming to physical-economic condition the sub-micro region (as mentioned elsewhere), in which Matia is situated, because of its undulating open flood plains, fertile lands of alluvial and sandy loam soil, high ground water potential, agriculturally prosperous tracts of the Tel and its tributaries, use of high yielding variety of seeds, modern implements, chemical fertilizer and irrigation facilities, practises double cropping, poultry farming and livestock rearing and produces surplus rice.

Bhairajpur falls in the South Western part of Khariar, which is a part of Nuapada Forested Upland. The sub-micro region is composed of denuded hillocks, patches of forests. The general slope of it is towards south-east into the Tel valley. Mixed dense jungles and open forests cover the hilly area. Small waterfalls often act as source of water for drinking and cultivating purposes. River Sundar passes through it before entering into plains of eastern Khariar lying below.

Khariar block in which the village is located has highest cropping intensity. Rivers and rivulets are utilised to supply water to the cultivating fields of the upland villages. Maize and pulses are grown in the hilly western Khariar. It is basically a drought prone area because of its rain shadow location. Only 14.4 per cent of lands of the block is irrigated. However, most of the development, specifically agricultural development is concentrated in eastern Khariar by which the village is indirectly benefited.

Previously, we have already mentioned about the Kusumjore which is located in Sinapali block of Udanti Basin. A number of reserved forests are found on the scattered hills and uplands within the shallow plain. Famine is acute in this area. Continuous plundering and clandestine felling of trees has left the once teak rich basin drought prone, moderately underdeveloped. Though the area has a good tract of black cotton soil, sand cast due to floods, occasional aridity coupled with least exploited ground water potential, lowest area under HYV of seeds, large chunk of small and marginal farmers, poor agricultural production are some of the regional causes attributing high percentage of poverty in Kusumjore.

The relative weighted scores (land and soil) of the villages are as follows :

Matia has not a single landless family but 5.55 per cent families fall in score '2' group. Just reverse is the case of Bhairajpur and Kusumjore (*i.e.* 5.55 per cent are landless and zero families fall in score '2'). In succeeding score groups both Matia and Bhairajpur possess 11 per cent and 17 per cent households. In the weighted score column of '5' Matia has 28 per cent, Bahirajpur 33 per cent and Kusumjore 22 per cent households only. These values somehow throws light on their differential poverty. (See Appendix 7 p.370-371).

The physiographic division of Matia is absolutely devoid of any forest. Villagers burn cow dung for cooking. Few for satisfying their fuel, wood and bamboo needs go even upto Lanjigarh.

On the contrary, both the physical divisions surrounding Bhairajpur and Kusumjore are forested, the former with a greater areal coverage than the later. Though forest does not significantly contribute to the rural peoples income, at least it serves as an assured source of earning especially during days of food scarcity. Either through wood selling, *kendu* leave, *tola* or '*mahul*' collection or sell of minor forest products people manage to gather a days earning for daily expenditure. It does not reduce poverty but it relieves long strain of starvation by temporarily offering various fruits and wild roots for *Adivasis* and *Harijans* alike. Fieldwork data reveals while each and every household of Bhairajpur for one purpose or the other depend on forest to marginally mitigate their wants, only 67 per cent Kusumjore families turn to their sparse woodland for poorly supplementing their meagre income.

Another couple of villages of high economic indicator, *viz.* Mahulpatna in the Tel-Hatti Basin of low development and Bhangabari in Tel Valley of low development depict very steep variation in poverty. The proportion of poor population in the former village is 64.70 per cent and that in the later is 26.31 per cent. Because of their similarity in basic micro level economic characteristics, theoretically, they should exhibit some degree of parity in their condition of deprivation. Instead there is a big gap (38.39%) between them. This sharp inequality seems to be due to certain factors which are essentially geographic.

The first glance over the patterns of levels of development makes it visibly clear that the block in which Mahulpatna is situated is a block of low development having a Composite Development Index (CDI) 10.50 to 12.50 whereas Bhawanipatna in which Bhangabari is situated is a block of medium underdevelopment with CDI 12.50 to 14.50 per cent.

The Tel-Hatti Basin Low developed region is a transitional zone between the Tel-Hatti Basin High development and Dharamgarh Plateau of Low development. The intermediate region in which Mahulapatna* is situated possesses many natural properties of the former and development characters of the later. In fact, its exact location is on the margin of Dahramgarh Plateau, due to which a large number of families are landless here. The fieldwork data shows only 17.6 per cent of total families possess some land, probably not on the land scarce plateau but down the valley elsewhere. The landless people (locally known as *sukhbasis* work for land owners *sahukars* or in the houses of outside traders or in the governmental projects involving manual labour.

---

* The micro economic region of Mahulpatna is in fact a transitional strip of mixed character.

Due to want of ploughing lands 55.7 per cent of the *sukhbasis* practise shifting cultivation. Again from amongst the *podu* practitioners 16.67 per cent are of general caster (Gaud and Sundhi). This is an indication of the fact that the typical geographical (topographical) condition along with economic compulsion force even non-tribes to practise *podu.* Although income from *podu,* in purely monetary term, is very less as compared to the production from plain lands, the multiple cropping of the primitive practice not only serves as an instrument against vagaries of nature but also satisfies domestic consumption needs and cash requirements (for buying clothes and salt etc.) of the poor.

The Dharmgarh Plateau is above 1000 metres. The sub-micro region is a combination of high hills which align from north to south and innumerable rivers and streams which originate in the Plateau. Deep gullies, gorges, rugged terrain apart from thick forest cover hinders extensive plough cultivation as well as human movement in search of (or other) economic pursuits. It equally poses barrier to developers, officials and others in delivering development inputs that is why the region is left as one of the most backward patch of Kalahandi.

The area receives maximum amount of rainfall. Flash floods often sand cast the cultivation fields lying down the edge of the hills. Acute soil erosion takes place in deforested parts (of *podu).* Drought is, however, not a rare phenomena. Untimely and unreliable nature of monsoon often damage the rice production..

Podu or *jhum* cultivation is still in vogue. Maize is irregularly grown on hill slopes. Jowar, *Arhar,* black gram, niger, mustard, castor, ginger, turmeric and minor millets are often raised in a mixed pattern. High yielding varieties of paddy is also grown but in small patches around perennial hill streams and *nallahs.* Excepting hill stream and few tanks there is no irrigation facilities of any significance.

Cool, moist climate and sloppy, rugged topography are quite conducive for the production of beverages, mango, banana, pineapple, papaya, orange, guava and jackfruits. Natives in their private orchards or backyards raise these fruits since there is no planned initiative in horticulture yet. Moreover, in absence of marketing and smooth transport facilities major part of the local products find their way to the *bazaars* of Bhawanipatna and elsewhere within and outside the state through middlemen who buy them cheap from the local growers and sell them dear making big profit margin. This is one of the reasons of poverty and backwardness of this isolated plateau.

Forests of the area has a insignificant economic contribution. Nevertheless, it plays a special role in the life of the native people. People sell firewood and on an average a family earns Rs. 480 per annum from the selling. Apart from this, forest provides a plenty of various kinds of edible roots like *Pita Kanda, Bhat Kanda, Cherenga Kanda* and various edible leaves like *Kochli Sag, Pipar Sag, Sit Kirei,* and seeds like sal seeds etc. Natives also get earnings from temporary works provided by forest department for *Mahul* and *Kendu* leave collection.

Difficult terrain coupled with very poor road linkages, low electricity and drinking water facilities have left this strip most underdeveloped which ultimately renders large percentage of people worse off.

Bhangabari falls in a sub-micro region of undulating flood plains and plains drained by the river Tel and its tributaries. It is devoid of any kind of forest. The underground water table is higher than the plateau region. The groundwater potential is already exploited in few village. High yielding varieties of crops paddy are grown not only in Kharif season but also in Rabi season in areas of assured irrigation. Soil is very fertile. It is alluvial and sandy loam. Since within this area the district headquarter Bhawanipatna is located supply of fertilizers, modern agricultural implements, insecticides and pesticides during drought period to farmers is easier and relatively more. The region is inhabited by progressive '*Kulta*' farmers. *Bajra,* maize, pulses, oilseeds and certain cash crops are grown substantially. Allied agricultural activities include cattle and goat rearing and poultry keeping.

The region is moderately populated. From transportation* communication and urbanisation point of view it is one of the most developed section.

---

* State Highway Nos. 1, 2 and 6 criss the region. Metalled and unmetalled roads provide good transportation facilities. Country boats on the river Tel assist local traffic during rainy season.

In terms of overall development it is only moderately developed.

Low poverty of Bhangabari is perhaps best explained in terms of its proximity* to Bhawanipatna, the administrative, educational and commercial centre besides its location on the major district road connecting Bhawanipatna with Khariar. The village is primarily agricultural in nature where cultivator to labourer class ratio is 2.2:1. Field survey data points out that 56.25 per cent and workers families come to the nearby city and return in the evening with handsome amount of earnings. Some do governmental jobs, others carpentry, tailoring or still others who engage themselves in minor trading, roadside selling, or working as vendors etc. Per worker per day wage rates are Rs. 25 (governmental) and Rs. 15 (private). Income from extra landed work compensate more than economic deprivation arising due to landlessness of 31.57 per cent families and due to low land ownership of 24.68 per cent families.

On the other hand, Mahulpatna is not only situated in an area of difficult terrain but also it is badly served by transport links. It can be approached either from Jayapatna (Tel-Hatti Basin) side through a circuitous road or through a meandering road of forested plateau from Thuamul Rampur side. In neither case Mahulpatna is easily approachable. This inaccessibility has a definite bearing on labour mobility.

A couple of families in the village are land owners and rest are the landless workers** of which most work in the village in the farmers houses or agricultural fields. However, since the labour earning from within the village is insufficient they collect firewood from the forest for selling or look for work outside the village for additional wage. Recently, few labourers work at the Indravati Project adjacent to the village. Still then the average annual per capita income from labour figures up Rs. 4452.37

---

* The village is bare by 6 kms away from the district headquarters over the major metalled road.

** Out of total 17 surveyed households, as many as 14 households are without any cutivating land at all. Weighted scores (land and soil) of 4.5 and 9 have a single household each. So unlike Bhangabari, Mahulpatna is basically a labourers village where the primary occupation of most of the family members is manual work.

which comes only about half of* that of Bahngabari (Rs.8605.84).

All these clearly show how because of the very locational advantage Bhangabari has an edge over Mahulpatna in standard of living.

Analysis of Spatial Poverty

(Based on the study of Sample Villages of Low Economic Indicator)

'Padepadar' and 'Basantpada' are such type of villages which have high percentage of non-working population (157.1 and 248.41 per cent respectively), high percentage of marginal farmers (75.2 and 81.1 per cent respectively) and low percentage of irrigated area (5.3 and 18.8 per cent respectively). They, thus belong to low economic indicator category and logically, supposed to show least variation in their poverty indicators. But their actual differentiations in their poverty condition is 12.87 per cent.

The Tel-Hatti Basin (High Underdevelopment) containing Padepadar and the Dharamgarh Plateau of High Under-development containing Basantpada have many commonality in the level of their development (*i.e.* low or high under-development) but many dissimilarity in their natural conditions. These perhaps justify their high but unequal poverty (with 12.87% gap).

The Tel-Hatti Basin is a depositional basin of physiographic non-uniformity. Scattered hills and intervening valleys break the monotony of the plain, which constitute one of the most fertile tract of Kalahandi. The soil ranges from alluvium, sandy loam to slightly red. A small patch of south eastern side has a series of longitudinal forested hills. Being a transitional zone the sub-micro

---

* The calculation is based on the fieldwork data, which includes the recent rise in wage availability of Rs. 25 at the Indravati Project. Before the inception or incoming of Indravati Project the wage rate per day per worker in Mahulpatna was much lower Rs. 3 or 2 kg. of unhusked rice at the *sahukar's* place. Average annual earning from wood selling per family is Rs. 480.

region (Basin of high underdevelopment) is neither as low as the northern part of the Basin (200 m.) nor as high as the Dharmgarh Plateau (950 m) lying southeast. The area is partly forested and partly plain. It has low cropping intensity (0.97), some lands under high yielding variety of seeds, very low percentage of net irrigated area to net sown area. Tanks, wells, streams and rivers are the main source of irrigation as well as drinking water and pisciculture in this topographical area of mixed nature. The region has fair amount of ground water potential, as discussed earlier. Though rice is the principal crop millets, bajra, pulses, maize and oilseeds are also grown. Livestock rearing and poultry keeping are practised. However, since the area is tiger infested; it remains unsafe for livestock farming especially goat rearing. These partly account for high poverty marked by moderate to low population density of the area.

Contrarily, the area of Basantpada, *i.e.* Dharmagarh Plateau of high underdevelopment is a combination of knot of hills with a general alignment from north to south, higher forest cover, table lands of about 1000 metres high, numerous valleys of northward southward flowing rivers, stream and catchment area gullies. Seventy-five percentage area is covered by hills and forests. Settlement in this region is scanty. Most of the settlements are found in the small plain lands along the hills or along the communication lines. This reflected the high backwardness of the region.

Though the region receives maximum precipitation in Kalahandi drought is not entirely unknown here.

Agriculture is practised in the small plains in the north and practically absent on the hills. Outmoded cultivation, *i.e. Jhum* and terrace cultivation are practised irregularly on the hill slopes. The sandy loam soil of the area is favourable for oilseeds and soils of lateritic origin is infertile. Maize, *jowar, arhar*, black gram, niger, mustard, castor, turmeric and minor millets are raised in a mixed pattern. Tribes being the common inhabitants of the region fishing, hunting and root collecting form part of their economic pursuits. Though agriculture is underdeveloped, more than eighty percentage of workers are engaged in this activity which is the primary occupation of the people. This very regional character speaks well about the widespread poverty of the area.

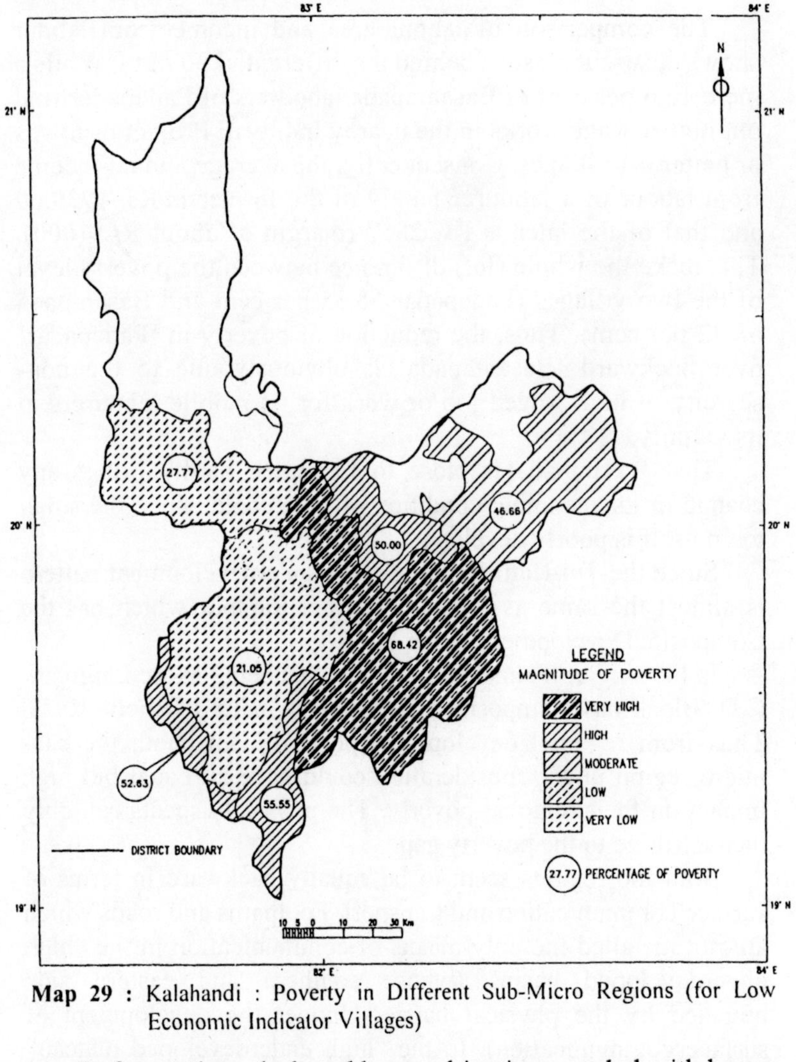

Map 29 : Kalahandi : Poverty in Different Sub-Micro Regions (for Low Economic Indicator Villages)

Deforestation, slash and burn cultivation coupled with heavy currents of monsoonal rainwater cause not only land slides but also heavy soil erosion.

Like Mahulpatna area, the climate and topography here too is suitable for production of various fruits. But again no planned collection and marketing facilities provided by the government yet. Middlemen take advantage of the situation. All these cause very high regional poverty in the most backward Dharamgarh Plateau.

The comparison of labour area and income from labour shows clear-cut reasons behind the differential poverty. While a mere 16.6 per cent of Basantapada labourers of Padepader find out higher wage works in the nearby Indravati Project or towns or better off villages. Consequently, the average annual income from labour of a labourer family of the former is Rs. 1939.60 and that of the later is Rs. 2857 (margin of about Rs. 1000). This make the whole (lot) difference between the poverty level of the two villages (Padepadar 55.55 per cent and Basantpada 68.42 per cent). Thus, the reduction of poverty in 'Padepadar' over backward 'Basantapada' is obviously due to the non-scarcity of high waged job or work for its mobile labourers in its vicinity.

That Basantpada is close to Lanjigarh hardly brings any change in its economic condition of the people, since the small town itself is poorly developed.

Since the Tel-Hatti Basin of high underdevelopment pattern is almost the same as that of Thuamul Rampur which has the Composite Development Index 11.46.

In the similar manner Basantpada area being in the Lanjigarh C.D. Block has Composite Development Index of about 10.73. Thus from regional development point of view both the sub-micro region under consideration could have an equal but high impact on their regional poverty. The physical aspects can only then attribute to the poverty gap.

Both the regions seem to be equally backward in terms of surface communication and transport. Footpaths and roads which are not metalled the only means of communication in the "high underdeveloped basin" (whose southern and eastern side bounded by the physical barriers hinder the development of surface communication). In the "high underdeveloped plateau" without metalled roads especially footpaths and cart-tracks are the main means of communication.

The high poverty of both the villages is also because of the exploitation of STs and landless labourer classes by local dominant persons' group such as SCs and outsider inmigrants (general caste people). Liquor and moneylending or borrowing has definite role. These aspects would be discussed extensively in the chapter on "Institutions and Production Relation" later.

But few important points the researcher feels are worth mentioning here.

There are about 31.5 per cent households who are absolutely landless and 36.8 percentage are virtually landless (having very small pathches of ceiling land which are often of inferior quality and go uncultivated or disputed) in Basantpada. The corresponding figures for Padepadar are 38.8 per cent and 27.7 per cent respectively. The only economic outlet (option) before these deprived sections is forest and *podu.* 46.2 per cent of deprived families of Basantpada and 41.6 per cent of those of Padepadar depend on the sale of forest products. 53.8 per cent and 66.6 per cent of families of those sections are directly involved in *podu* to earn for themselves in the respective village. But it is interesting to note that all the higher landowning families (including non-tribals) too practise *podu* either because of their economic necessity or for surplus generation and trading (in *podu* products), depending upon their family size.

This leads to the exploitation of tribals and/or poor landless labourers in varied ways (such by employing the tribal labourers, taking away tribals traditional rights over *dongar* and *podu* products thereby marginalising them etc.). Looking it in other way this trend of higher class families shifting themselves to *podu* seems to be a recent one. Perhaps, this is a response of theirs (higher landowning families) to state of loss of theirs lands due to implementation of Land Ceiling Act. Anyway, the already deprived landless section especially tribals are always the worst sufferers and greatest losers. Much of the relative poverty of the two villages under consideration is the result of all these factors.

Last but not the least couple of villages chosen for exploring geographic/regional dimensions of poverty are Basantpada and Mankadasola. Since we have already discussed thoroughly about Basantpada, only the main contrasting features of the village shall be outlined in the following analysis.

Mankadasola which is located in the Tel-Hatti Basin of low underdevelopment has very close percentage values of non-workers, marginal farmers and irrigated area with Basantpada. (The value are 216.2 and 18.8 per cent respectively). The low overall economic indicators of the two villages and low percentage gap in-between them no way correspond to their level of poverty which is as low as 21.05 per cent (in fact lowest) in the whole district in case of Mankadasola and as high as 68.42 per cent (in fact highest in the whole district) in case of Basantpada. The reasons are purely spatial.

The maximum poverty gap between the two villages is well understood from their ecological identification, *i.e.* their respective location in a river basin of low underdevelopment and forested plateau of high underdevelopment. The cross-regional comparison of the Mankadasola village *vis-a-vis* the Tel-Hatti Basin of Low Underdevelopment and the Basantpada village *vis-a-vis* the Dharamgarh Plateau of High Underdevelopment can be made in the following ways which amply justify why there is such a big differentiation, between the two villages, at all?

Firstly, the Tel-Hatti Basin is a drainage basin of subtle denudation. It is bounded by hills on the west, south and east. It merges with the Udanti Basin on the north through an open narrow flood plain (150 metres high) (in which Mankadasola is situated). The region thus slopes gradually towards north-southern part being an area of higher altitude (900 metres). The early habitation or settlement of the region by plough cultivators is evident from its appearance of very sparse vegetation and fertile soil cover, which is alluvial, sandy and sandy loam. The basin has, earned the fame of 'Rice Bowl' of Kalahandi as it produces marketable rice over and above its domestic needs during the years of favourable weather. However, except tanks and wells there is hardly any irrigational facilities available in the area, though it has good reserve of untapped underground water. *Kulta* and general caste farmers often use chemical fertilizers and modern implements. Though rice is the principal crop, millets, pulses and oilseeds are extensively grown too. Livestock rearing and poultry keeping are somehow popular practices.

As against the physical agricultural advantages of the basin, the plateau has severe limitations (physical constraints). It is a table land (1000 metres high) of ununiform character, with high hill chains, luxuriant vegetation cover, several catchment areas, valleys and deeply carved gullies of streams and rivers. This poses obstacles in the growth of human settlements and agriculture which are found to be sparse and restricted to the scarce plain lands of stream sides and river beds and those along communication lines. Patches of sandy loam soil are found over the general lateritic spread. Such being the ecological set-up, tribals practise fishing, hunting and root collecting, apart from their age old slash and burn cultivation and occasional terrace farming. Although both production and productivity* of the area are meager, the crops grown in combination are many, which include paddy, maize, jowar, *arhar*, black gram, oilseeds like niger, mustard and castor, turmeric, minor millets and root crops of various kinds. Excepting paddy almost all other crops, however, are grown on *dongar.* The labour intensive nature of cultivation and very high (80%) workers participation in such primitive and poorly productive economic pursuits, or indicate not only high backwardness of the area but also abject poverty of the masses.

Favourable agro physical conditions (in conjunction with) better developmental pattern (low to very low level of under-development) of the Mankadasola sub-micro region (*i.e.* the Tel-Hatti Basin of Low underdevelopment) naturally offers higher earning** to labourers. This is an important reason which brings a perceptible variation poverty in the two spatial units. In Mankadasola area or Tel-Hatti Basin a cultivator of 10 acres of land on an average employs 250 to 300 labourers (including both males and females). The high wage rate and plenty of work enables labourer families to generate surplus. According to an estimate if five members of a family go for labour two members income is enough to meet the expenses of all five thereby

---

* In terms of money value, the total land production and productivity (Rs./acre) of Basantpada is only Rs. 44,950 (including income from *podu*) and Rs. 690.50 respectively. Whereas these values for agriculturally prosperous village of Mankadasola is Rs. 82,852 and Rs. 1,441 respectively. Thus the average low economic indicator village of Tel-Hatti Basin has a production and productivity which is double that of a similar village of Dharmgarh plateau. (Calculation based on fieldwork data).

** Per labourer annual earning from labour is Rs. 1,193.20 for Mankadasola and Rs. 895.20 for Basantpada.

producing a net saving equivalent to the earning of three. Given below a table of relative wage chart (based on information collected during field survey).

Chart of Relative Wage

Nature of work		*(Wage in terms of weighted paddy)* Male	Female
Cultivation	Transplantation	5 *sola* 3 *ada*	5 *sola*
	Ploughing	3 *ada*	×
	Reaping	1 *mana*	3 *ada*
Bamboo cutting		5 *ada*	×
Wood Cutting		1 *mana*	×

Note : - 1 *sola* = 1/4 *ada* = (approximately 250 grams)
1 *ada* = standard unit = (approximately 1000 grams)
1 *mana* = 4 *ada* = (approximately 4000 grams)
(3 *ada* paddy is equivalent to Rs. 7)

Daily average wage rates in term of money value are Rs. 10 (for a male labourer) and Rs. 8 for a female labourer.

Few points of contrast which bring sharp distinction between the two poverty regions are as follows :

As observed already the Basantpada is full of forests, and free of *dongar* (hill side sloppy land suitable for *podu*/shifting cultivation), and marginal ploughing plain lands.

On the other hand, the Mankadasola region is a basin of double resource base such as, plenty of fertile flood plains (favourable for agriculture) and less dense and less diverse forest base.

Depending upon these regional resource base different caste or class groups have adopted different styles of living (occupation and trade), often symbiotically. For example, in Basantpada the general cast people like other plain land dwellers elsewhere, stick to plough cultivation on the fertile basin. Scheduled caste people in addition to cultivation, mostly go for labour as their prime source of earning. The remaining tribals, by and large, are left with hunting and collection of forest products. As against this triple caste-cum-occupational groups, there are mainly two class groups (*i.e.* cultivators and labourers which constitute a typical agrarian relation) in Mankadasola. In the later village, labour is a more productive means of livelihood (the reasons of which are mentioned already). Whereas in Basantpada work availability is rather inadequate and so also the income from labour for the toiling wage earners.

So far as the trade is concerned, bartering is carried out mostly in *podu* products and forest products in Basantpada, while the non-conventional sale and purchase takes place primarily in agricultural produces in Mankadasola.

It is paradoxical to note that Basantpada village which is rich in varied forest resources has lower percentage (31.5) of people engaged in forest related trade whereas Mankadasola which is rather poor and less diverse in its forest wealth (having mainly fuel wood and bamboo bushes) has a larger percentage (45) of families (found to be) involved in the forest trade. What explains this is a question of neither the availability of saleable materials, nor the sellers, not even the potential buyers alone. The geographic distance between the concerned village and the area of better off consumers (*i.e.* moneyed people who are in need of forest woods, bamboo etc.) assumes significance here. In this respect, Basantpada has its own limitation while Manakadasola has a favourable location.*

How outside middlemen and businessmen take advantage of this situation is part of the subject matter of the already depicted in previous chapter.

Conclusion

It is a well embedded notion among many developers that gross economic controllers, *viz*. 'Land ownership', 'Water supply' and 'Labour' are central to the studies of poverty and as such poverty is a purely economic phenomenon. True, that the basic facts or figures used to measure poverty and its fundamental correlates such as nonworking population, proportion of marginal farmers and irrigation facilities (as used for this very study on Kalahandi)

* The location of Mankadasola is favourable because the market area (of potential purchasers) is within the easy reach of the poor wood-cutters and sellers of the village.

are organically economic. But these factors in themselves do not adequately and exhaustively explain 'serious deprivations' if one looks at their unequal regional effects.

The researcher observes here in this chapter, that certain geographic determinants directly or indirectly impinge upon poverty affecting regional or local economics. It is neither numerical size of land nor the percentage of marginal farmers alone, but the location, terrain (or topographic condition), sites, slope etc. besides water availability and soil quality (of landholding of different households) more accurately determine the areal production and productivity and hence regional poverty.

Again, it is neither non-working population, nor labourer to dependent population ratio of pure economic arithmetic but accessibility of the area to the place of work, migrating distance *vis-a-vis* labour area, relative wage rate (depending upon locational work availability), level of development, soil production and productivity and manual earning from labour are dominant factors of poverty.

Not so much governmental provided irrigation facilities but local level topographic drainage conditions, underground water availability and their exploitation through traditional and informal methods of irrigation, *i.e.* tanks, ponds, *chuha,* wells, *nalas,* streams, springs, *bandhas, katas* have a real significance for a backward and drought prone district like Kalahandi, so far as its crop production and standard of living is concerned.

Moreover, forests which are region and location specific, if not considerably alter the annual income of a household, definitely act as an contributory factor. They change the nature of poverty by relieving its intensity and breaking its perpetuity.

Combining the previous findings, it can now be argued that the correlates of land, labour etc. (of pure economic analysis) are important to understand poverty but their effectiveness depends on sum total of geographic circumstances, the variations in which contribute to disparity in the district.

Thus, it is geographic and local ecological set-up which makes a cultivating and labourer class of population vulnerable to the crisis of basic human needs (food, clothing and shelter) before the basic economic aspects determine the structural framework of (hunger, starvation or poverty).

As the purchasing power (labour wage and income from land) of one household depends on its position in the ecological structure (set-up) and the mode of production in the economy, one has to take into account the spatial economics of production, distribution and consumption for exploring the different dimensions of areal deprivation.

8

GOVERNMENTAL PROGRAMME EVALUATION

This Chapter intends to analyses the efficacy of governmental programmes in relieving the poverty in the district as well as in various ecological micro region. In combating chronic hunger, public action (*e.g.* institution building, legal reforms, assets redistribution or provisioning in kind) play an important role (Dreze and Sen 1989, pp.7 and 8). Theoretically, this is true so far as temporary relief to prolonged pressure of poverty is concerned. But the political and material gains different groups (including politicians and administrations) get and rampant corruption and dependency that result thereafter create serious doubt as to whether governmental machinery can really be effective in providing solution for poverty. Rather a particular section of population is often benefited by the policies of the government at the cost of certain specified intended group of the district. The ability to command (basic) resources vary amply with the nature of the regional economy. Though the district has been successful in raising the foodgrains production, mal-distribution has caused serious food scarcity in various pockets. The state should provide infrastructure basing on which people can raise their purchasing power through self-employment.

Existing data shows the district has become self-sufficient in foodgrains and even supplies surplus grains to the neighbouring districts, nevertheless social and economic disparities has remained acute here throughout. Menon (1989) rightly mention that the conditions of relative prosperity and acute hunger have coexisted within the same region. The state has played a pivotal role not only creating new social stratification but also legitimizing the economic inequalities that are created with developmental endeavours (Mohanty, 1990). Various processes of resultant deprivation spring up almost simultaneously. It is a known fact that governmental measures for prevention of starvation deaths has resulted in failure, periodic hunger is largely unseen and mostly found among deprived sections of all micro regions of Kalahandi.

There is a spatial variation in consumption expenditure and purchasing power (entitlement) along with distribution of means of production. And this variation across sub-micro regions is a function of not simply household (economic) and community (social) characteristics but also of regional (geographic) characteristics. This has already been partly established in the previous chapters.

Here, we shall test whether the difference in success rate due to implementation of anti-poverty programmes and plausible increase in purchasing power are associated with regional characteristics, apart from household and community characteristics.

Justice B.N. Misra Commission Report reveals that despite huge governmental investment there had been hardly any perceptible change in the economic condition of the poor of Kalahandi* over the last ten years. The report after investigation holds that rampant corruption among administrators and various governmental and non-governmental agents is the root cause of failure of most of the schemes.

In the following paragraphs we analyse regional controllers apart from other factors in differential implementation of governmental schemes and utilisation of public resources in the form of loans, subsidies, assets etc. The assistance offered by the government has no doubt, helped relieving the agony of hunger and deprivation temporarily.

Assuming the finding of Misra Commission report (that there has been no change in poverty level of the poor over last ten years) true, let's first verify whether high equi-poverty

---

* The field observation, by and large, confirms this state of affairs.

villages (villages with high percentages of equal poverty) have been selected for poverty alleviation with equal force of implementation. In this respect Bhairajpur and Tentulipada villages have 50 percentage of poor households each. In Bhairajpur only 26.31 percentage of households and in Tentulipada 22.22 percentage households received the benefits under poverty alleviation schemes.

Similarly, in Kusumjore (66.66% poverty) and Basantpada (68.42% poverty) respectively 38.9 per cent and 47.3 per cent households have been provided with anti-poverty benefits. Matia, Chandpura and Kulihariguda have 38.88 per cent of poverty each. Percentages of beneficiary households are 50, 52 and 38.8 per cent respectively. These statistics show that poverty alleviation schemes have been implemented by not considering the level of poverty.

From the villages surveyed it is clear that each village whether tribe dominated or general caste dominated has more than one scheduled caste household. The omnipresence of SC families explains how other people have general consciousness about corruption and local level politics. Of course, general caste people are also politically conscious. Out of total 17 villages only Mahulpatana is SC dominated (in terms of number). In other villages though SCs are low in number they have, by and large, an important role in production relation and exploitation nexus.

In terms of economic (village economy) and social (mixed caste population and literacy) indicators, Degam and Bakharmal should exhibit similar results in 'poverty alleviation', as the schemes implemented there are the same. But there is marked variation between the two villages which is perhaps due to certain geographic factors. For example, the two villages have 40 per cent poverty each both belong to high economic village indicator, *i.e.* they have low non-working to working population, low marginal farmers to total farmers and high percentage of irrigated area per farmers. SC to ST to General Caste households ratios are 8:11:1 in Degam and 9:7:5 in Bakharmal. (The former has 40 per cent and the later has 5 per cent of literacy). The success rate of the anti-poverty schemes is 50 per cent and zero in Degam and Bakharmal respectively. In Bakharmal, though 12 households have received governmental assistance none of them is reported to be successful.* The geographic causes may be noted as follows :

Bakharmal is in Nawapada Forested Upland. It is situated in the rain shadow zone of Sunabeda plateau. In other words, it is a drought prone area. Looking to the weighted score of land and soil we find the low performance of the village can be explained in terms of local causes. About 20 per cent households are landless. Another 25 per cent have low scoring and 40 per cent household have moderate scoring, 25 per cent families work outside to supplement either their meagre income or zero income from land (as in case of landless).

Because of its location in the Tel Valley (of high development) and high village level indicator, Degam exhibit partial success in anti-poverty scheme implementation. Otherwise, the weighted scores of land and soil of the village are poor. Eight out of twenty households have scoring 3-4, six families are without any land. Rest six households have higher scores out of which three households have scoring value 5 only. (Appendix 8, p.370-371) Poor scoring is due to not simply landlessness but also poor quality soil of the fields, which is sand cast due to flood every year. Being landless few families go for outside labour. However they have not been able to utilise government loans successfully.

Village pairs with similar economic indicators and identical caste structure, which have been brought under common poverty alleviation scheme, exhibit wide range of results. The following paragraphs attempt to find out geographic causes, which can reconcile such contradictions.

High Economic Indicator and Backward (SC and ST Dominated) Villages

Kulihariguda of Golamunda, Degam of Kesinga and Barabandha of Madanpur Rampur fall under such category whose results after implementation of poverty-alleviation scheme (ADAPT) are the following :

---

* Success cases are those where the loan or assets received under the poverty schemes have been utilised properly by the recipients to their own advantage that enable them to attain certain degree of self-reliance.

Table 8.1: Success rate of the poverty alleviation scheme

Villages	Success rate of the poverty Alleviation
Degam	50.0 %
Barabandha	37.5 %

Source : Fieldwork data.

The following paragraphs explain the varied success rate in Degam and Barabandha. (Appendix 8, p. 356).

Degam is situated in the Tel Valley of high development. Besides, local geographic conditions are favourable. However, the weighted scores of land and soil of the village are poor. Forty per cent households have scoring 3-4, six households are landless. Remaining households have higher scores out of which three households have scoring value 5 only. Landlessness and poor quality of soil is partially responsible for partial failure of asset utilisation.

The very physiographic region in which Degam is located has undulating flood plains, fertile lands of alluvial and sandy loam soil, high ground water potential, agriculturally prosperous tracts of Tel and its tributaries. Further use of high yielding variety of seeds modern implements, chemical fertilizers and irrigation facilities. Double cropping, poultry farming, livestock rearing and surplus rice production; enable the farmers to repay the bank loan.

On the other hand "Barabandha" which is situated in Madanpur Rampur Forested Upland has 23.5 percentage household having weighted score 2 to 4 and 17.6 per cent households score value 5. (See Appendix 8, page 370-371) Madanpur Rampur Forests is known for bamboo supply. Local people earn wage through bamboo cutting. The Forested Upland which lies 1000 m above sea-level has more than the 65 per cent of the area forested. Here, available forest products includes *mahul, kendu, tentuli* and sal leaves. The soil of the area is sandy laterite and sandy loam, local and long duration paddy apart from maize, ragi, millets, *bajra,* and pulses are grown. But due to frequent drought farmers suffer badly. Food scarcity is common during pre-harvest season. Barabandha people have relatively less exposure to the outside world as compared to those of Degam. They have less political, educational and administrative access. Degam area is better linked with block headquarter. So it has higher success rate than Barabandha.

Evaluation of Loans and Schemes

First of all at the implementation stage we find only less than half of the total programmes are implemented. And out of those implemented programmes very less proportion show any sign of real success. This would be evident from the data analysis. The reasons for such a state of affairs could be many. But scarcity of funds is definitely not a strong cause to account for the long failure.

Post-Famine Labour Intensive Schemes have been implemented to avoid food shortage. Mainly road construction work was taken up for this purpose as a principal means to self-employment. Famine history shows, that the construction of (Visakhapatnam-Raipur and Raipur-Dhamtari) railway lines, roads, projects, irrigation bunds lift irrigation points, dug wells and boreholes have been carried out through out. Recent famine of 1986-87 and 1988-89 took up similar kind of employment generation post-famine rehabilitation works. The incomes generated from these short-term programmes do ensure better living due to rise in purchasing capacity. However, its result is again area specific and time specific.

Loan and Success Rate

Various schemes advance governmental loans to poor households in the district. Few of the beneficiaries have utilised the loan while most others have failed to use it successfully. By success rate we mean, the percentage of households who utilised the loans or the assets properly, provided under anti-poverty schemes. Mathematically,

$$\text{Success rate} = \frac{\text{No. of HHs utilizing loan or assets of poverty}}{\text{Total number of HHs Surveyed}} \times 100$$

Agriculturists Loan Act provides credit in cash as well as kind (seeds etc.) with a purpose that the affected people would be able to raise crops once again. Agricultural loans are advanced after drought. No doubt, they meet the immediate need of the farmers. But in most cases beneficiaries turn out to be defaulters and fall in the debt trap. Moreover, landless labourers for whom there is no provision for such loan suffer the problems of food scarcity more.

The primary survey reveals that out of total 309 households only 164 (*i.e.* 53 percentage) got loans from different sources. 34.95 per cent got governmental loans only and 18 per cent received loans from private sources. In other words, one-third of the total households received government loans and one-fifth of total households received private loans. Fifty-one per cent of the total poor households received governmental loans (34%) and private loans (17%). Under different poverty alleviation programmes total number of beneficiary households are 105 (*i.e.* about 34%). Out of them only 29.52 per cent of the HHs reported success.

Thus, about one-third of the total HHs received governmental assistance and from them another one-third successfully utilised the benefit. In other words only one-tenth of the total households of the Kalahandi are successful beneficiaries of the government's poverty related schemes. So the result of governmental effort to alleviate poverty is very limited. From among the successful beneficiaries 32.3 per cent are SC families, 38.7 per cent are ST families and rest 29 per cent belong to General Caste families. The rate of proportion of successful cases to total beneficiaries are 22.2 per cent for SCs, 36.4 per cent for STs and 33.3 per cent for General Caste households. Thus the success rate is the lowest among the SCs and it is highest among STs. So, caste has an inverse link with success rate.

Out of total twenty-two 'paid back' cases only 36.4 per cent are successful. Again from same number of 'partly paid cases' 40.9 percentage cases are successful. Out of 25 'yet to be paid' cases 36 per cent are successful. All the 'unable to pay' cases reported to be unsuccessful under poverty alleviation schemes. Even if loan has been waived in 7 cases only 42.9 per cent cases of the total 7 cases were successful in poverty alleviation scheme.

Table 8.2 : Caste and Success/ Failure of Poverty Alleviation Schemes

Caste	0	Success	Failure	Total
SC	36	10	35	81
ST	76	12	21	109
Others	92	9	18	119
Column	204	31	74	309
Total (%)	(66.0)	(10)	(23.9)	(100)

Source : Fieldwork

Table 8.3 : Loan Repayment and Success of Poverty Alleviation Scheme

Loan	Scheme Successful	Scheme Unsuccessful
Paid	8	14
Partly paid	9	13
Yet to be paid	9	16
Unable to pay	0	2
Loan waived	3	4
Total (%)	31(10)	74(23.9)

Source : Fieldwork data.

In the cross table of loan and livestock income we find there is very strong correlation between the two variables.

Those households who received loan and have some income from livestock are 88 in number. Out of them twenty-five received private loan and 63 received government loans. Among those households who received government loans, 49 households have less than Rs. 5000 annual income. Seven HHs have medium income and another 7 HHs have high income, *i.e.* income more than Rs. 1001 from livestock.

The tabulated data shows out of 66 cases of HHs, which received government loan for poverty alleviation, only 40.9 per cent were successful in utilising the loan.

Those who received government loan and failed to utilise it successfully are 35 in number. Of them 28 HHs used the loan for household consumption, 6 HHs complained of inferior breed being provided to them, a lone HH complained that he did not receive any assistance.

Thus the main reason for failure of the government's poverty alleviation programme is the use of loan for domestic consumption. The other reason is inferior breed. In fact, often the lack of infrastructural facilities and the very poor economic condition of a HH result in the death of domestic animals (such as goats, cow, chicken, bullocks etc.) provided under the poverty alleviation schemes. However, beneficiaries complain the above death cases are nothing but the result of inferior breed.

In fact, the failure reason could be either poor breed or lack of infrastructure or both. The cross table of 'Loan' and 'Poverty failure reason' shows that 70 per cent of paid cases did not get loan and in 1 per cent case no application form was submitted. This contradiction is due to fact that few HHs received private loan only and paid back the same.

Reasons for failure of poverty were enquired. From among the 45 responding HHs 60 per cent showed household consumption as the cause for both misuse of loan and failure of intended objectives of poverty alleviation.

15.5 percentage complained that the breed were of inferior quality. Twenty per cent did not get loan. Rest come under others ('spend in own repayment', 'did not apply' etc.) category.

In 'yet to be paid' category and 'partly paid' category most say that they need the governmental loan for HH consumption. This reflects acute poverty of the people who literally grab governmental money or resources in the form of assets to satisfy their hunger, the most urgent impulse.

Some utilise governmental loan for earning from 'sale of various products' (like *mudhi,* rice etc.). Of the total 108 households who received governmental loan just 26.9 per cent had some income from sale of products. Almost 50 per cent of the borrowing families selling products have less than Rs. 500 income per annum. 27.5 per cent borrowers have earning between Rs. 500-1000 and rest have more than Rs. 1000 earning from the selling of products.

Table 8.4 : Annual Income from land and loan repayment

Loan	Low	Low-Med	Med-High	High
Paid	32.1	38.2	60	44
Partly paid	25	11.8	20	28
Yet to be paid	30.4	41.2	15	28
Unable to pay	54	0	5	
Loan waived	7.1	8.8		
	56	34	20	

Source : Fieldwork data.

There is an inverse correlation between 'annual income from land' and varied response in loan repayment. Out of 135 respondents (family heads), 54 or 40 per cent paid off the loan, in seven cases loan was waived and rest (54.8%) were defaulters. Out of the 74 defaulters three different categories of responses were recorded. 39.2 per cent, 55.4 per cent and 5.4 per cent belong to 'partly paid', 'yet to be paid' and 'unable to pay' categories respectively.

In Table 8.4 we find the percentage of households which could pay back the loan is more among higher land income families.

Similar relationship is found among partly paid groups. Thus, in general there is a direct correlation between land income and loan repayment. Total beneficiaries were 88. Out of them 37.5 per cent of the total beneficiaries returned the loan. 23.86 per cent were able to make part payment. 30.68 per cent belong to 'yet to be paid' group. 2.27 per cent were unable to pay. In 5.68 per cent cases loan was waived

Four-fifth (80.68%) highest amount of the total beneficiary HHs earn only less than Rs. 400 (lowest amount) annually from livestock. In this lowest earning group 38.02 per cent, i.e. about 2/5th paid off the loan. 26.76 per cent, i.e. 1/4th could partly clear their debt. Few more HHs (28.16%) said that they were yet to clear the loan.

All these shows only very limited success of poverty alleviation scheme under which loan was disbursed to different households.

Total number of HHs who worked at some place and received private loan is 49. Out of them 14.28 per cent 7 HHs worked at multiple places. Number of HHs worked at some place and received government loan are 85. Out of them 16 per cent or 14 HHs work at multiple places.

Thus, almost equal proportion of HHs from among borrowers of private loan and from among the borrowers of government loan go to work at multiple places.

Table 8.5 : Labour and loan source

	0	Received from Private	Not received any loan	Govt. source Received
	17	7	–	23
Own village	105	42(1)	8(0)	80(2)
District	5	5(3)	(3)	3(4)
Outside district	70	2(3)	(1)	–
Column	137	56(7)	8(4)	108(14)
Total	44.3	18%	2.6	35.0

Source : Fieldwork data.

And the proportion is only 1/6th or 1/7th of the total HHs. Fifty per cent of the HHs who worked at multiple places and received no loan. Forty-nine HHs received private loan and worked at some place. Out of these 42 HHs 85.71 per cent HHs worked in the village. Out of the 85 HHs who received government loan and worked at some place 80 HHs 94 per cent worked in the village.

It follows, majority of workers who work in their own village or in the neighbouring villages can readily avail the government loan on their door step (through their) block office. About 14 per cent of the HHs worked at multiple places and received private loan and 6 per cent of the HHs worked at multiple places and received only government loan. Thus place of work has some influence on the choice of borrowing :

Poverty Alleviation Programmes

In the past different anti-poverty and employment generating schemes have been implemented in the district. These include:

(i) Integrated Rural Development Programme.

(a) IRDP (New)
(b) IRDP (Repeat Assistance)

(ii) Economic Rehabilitation for Rural Poor.

(a) ERRP (Pure)
(b) ERRP (Destitute)

(iii) Integrated Tribal Development Programme.

(introduced in 1974-75 in the district)
(a) Infrastructure Development Works.
(b) Beneficiary Oriented Programme

(iv) Bonded Labour Scheme

(v) Prime Minister's Massive Programme

(vi) Housing Programme:

NREP (National Rural Employment Programme)
RLEGP (Rural Labour Employment Generating Programme).

Infrastructure Development Programme

(vii) Jeebandhara Dug well/Millions wells for SCs and STs only.

(viii) Development of women and children in Rural Area.

(ix) Feeding and Immunization Programme lay Integrated Child Development Scheme (ICDS)

(x) Opening of Sevashrams, A/s and H/s and Primary School Hostels (Numbering 10) for providing residential education.

(xi) Jaladhara Scheme for energizing Dug wells.

(xii) Restoration of tribal land from SC and other caste unauthorized occupants.

(xiii) Allotment of homestead land, government waste land, mud ceiling surplus land to SC/ST persons.

(xiv) Supply of subsidized rice, wheat through ration cards.

(xv) Eradication of *podu* cultivation and persuasion for settled cultivation.

(xvi) Land Development work to prevent soil erosion.

(xvii) TRYSEM (Training Rural Youth for Self-Employment).

(xviii) Mulberry Cultivation, Sericulture.

(xix) Disability pension.

(xx) 'Kutir Jyoti' Programme.

(xxi) Insurance of Landless Agriculture Labourer.

(xxii) Hut Insurance Scheme.

(xxiii) DPAP (Drought Prone Area Programme) introduced in 1974-75 in 11 blocks (including Nawapada, Komna, Boden, Khariar, Sinapali, Golamunda, Kesinga, Narla, Madanpur Rampur, Th. Rampur and Lanjigarh).

(xxiv) IAAP (Intensive Agricultural Area Programme).

(xxv) ADAPT (Area Development Approach for Poverty Termination).

Employment generating schemes provide facilities for cultivation, small shops, vegetable vendors and household industries etc.

Keeping the repetitive drought condition and crop failure in the district the government introduced ADAPT as a special programme in Kalahandi. A number of earlier schemes such as IRDP, ERRP have merged with the ADAPT programme. It was specifically implemented in Thuamul Rampur and Lanjigarh Districts in April 1988. Under the scheme facilities like irrigation, short-term credit, social infrastructure, minor millets and groundnut cultivation etc. are provided to the poor people (Pattnaik:1991).

There is governmental provision for pre-matriculation scholarships for SC and ST students. Since the literacy rate is low, high schools often do not get enough students for providing such stipends. In case of old age pension, widows and disabled persons sometimes suffer starvation because of unnecessary delay in pension delivery.

Loans are advanced to purchase seeds, cattle, bullocks, plough and different agricultural implements for the construction of wells, tanks and storing water, irrigation, levelling and reclamation of land for agricultural purposes. The schemes under which such benefits are provided are – Land Improvement Loans Act, Agricultural Loans Act, Land Development Bank and various state aids and subsidies. Apart form other problems the loans are in most cases untimely and inadequate and are given through complicated procedures. The credit institutions, banks, cooperatives etc., which have been grown up in recent years, do not have any provision for lending labourers. Consequently almost all the landless labourer and marginal and small farmers borrow from private moneylenders who demanded high interest and purchases their crops in turn of loans at much lower prices. In most cases they (borrowers) become defaulters for years together and fall in the debt trap and hence in abject poverty. (Rajashekar and Vyasulu, 1990, p. 10)

Dairy farming, poultry farming and different agricultural schemes have little success because they lack local market with high purchasing power in the people. [Agricultural Department Production Data (1975-76) District Gazetteer (1981) pp.145,147]

State Tribal Development Agency (STDA)

STDA has been implemented in tribal dominated blocks like

Lanjigarh (10 villages) and Thuamul Rampur (15 villages) to provide better techniques and organisation in agriculture.

State Developers believe that *podu* (shifting cultivation) is a menace to agricultural development. Various measures have been adopted to curb *podu* related problems like deforestation, soil erosion and reduced Soil Conservation Department has prepared management plans for different villages as part of anti-*podu* campaign. The STDA programme provides for weaning away tribes from shifting cultivation to settled cultivation. [Directorate of Soil Conservation (STDA), Village Management Plan (1989 - 90)]

Village Management Plan 1989-90 mentions about the provisions of irrigational facilities and land development for sustained agricultural production. The Department of Agriculture introduced short duration, drought resistant and HYV seeds of paddy, maize, millets, vegetables, fertilizers, pesticides, insecticides to encourage farmers taking to double cropping, multi-cropping. Through various demonstrative and training camps farmers made acquainted about adoption of modern agricultural methods. The survey reveals that these efforts have not been successful only except a handful of rich cultivators. The tribes and scheduled caste people have not been able to adopt the new agricultural inputs easily because of their inherent socio-economic handicap.

STDA has not been very successful in shifting the tribes from *podu* cultivation to settled cultivation. Even some of the STDA villages do privatise shifting cultivation. There is no legal prohibition of *podu*. Apart from this other reasons of continuation of *podu* are involvement of less labour and its suitability to tribes' physiological, natural and socio-cultural conditions. The more important causes are less availability of plain land and the institutional constraints obstructing equal distribution of sufficient fertile land. According to the Directorate of Soil Conservation (1989-90) the Department of Soil Conservation has taken up dry land farming, utilisation of residual moisture, conservation and rational utilisation of water resources through excavation of dug well and economic use of water harvesting structure. As a part of the soil reclamation work the Central Coffee Board has selected the Thuamul Rampur Coffee Plantation. Despite local protests against the plantational effort on ecological and economic grounds, Government is set to go ahead with his plan on the belief that the plantation would boost the economic development of the area as well as the nation.

Government under STDA has provided backyard plantation facilities for raising vegetable and various kinds of local fruits under the land based irrigation scheme, each family gets 100 per cent subsidy to the maximum of Rs. 5000 for dug well and tube well facilities. However, the scheme has many limitations. Firstly, it is confined to just few countable villages, which are relatively more accessible to the agency. Interior villagers live as they did in the past. Secondly, weaker sections of the society (Scheduled castes and Scheduled tribes) fail to avail the facilities since most of them are landless.

Industry and Animal Husbandry

The Department of Industry has provided loans for *siali* leaf plate making, carpentry or making of bamboo baskets, ropes, beekeeping, rice-husking, *mudhi* making etc. It has also supplied sewing machines. The Integrated Tribal Development Agency has been training the tribes in small scale and cottage industry.

Integrated Tribal Development Agency (ITDA) provides training to the tribes in Animal Husbandry. Tribal beneficiaries having land have been given pairs of bullocks.

Similarly, in the field of Social Forestry the Social Forest Department afforest large areas, to meet the fuel and fodder needs of the people. The vacant patches of land left after *podu* cultivation are brought under vegetation cover by planting economically valuable and environmentally suitable species. However, the basic criticism raised against the control and management of forest by the Central Forest Department is that instead of providing sufficient and assured sources of permanent income to the landless labourers it has taken away their forest entitlement, which has been an alternative source of subsistence.

In case of Industry and Animal Husbandry the governmental facilities have remained confined to interior areas and to very small section of landed or economically and politically better off population. As a result the social inequality has been widened especially between the landless labourers and the land owning farmers. The special disparities, *i.e.* the gap between interior villages and the ITDA villages on the outskirts of the Block Headquarters has also increased.

Poverty Alleviation Programmes in Nuapada Forested Upland (High Underdevelopment)

Under Integrated Rural Development Programme (IRDP) beneficiaries groups are provided with buffalos, bullocks, goats, pigs, bullock carts, sewing machines, dug wells and tank facilities for land improvement and pottery. The target groups include small farmers (having land holdings less than 5 acres), marginal farmers (land holdings less than 2.5 acres) agricultural labourers, several artisans and others below poverty line. In more developed village Bakharmal (with high economic development indicator) 40.67 per cent and in low economic development indicator village, *i.e.* Bhairajpur only 52.25 per cent households have been benefited by IRDP. (Based on field work survey.) Area Development Approach for Poverty Termination (ADAPT) were implemented in this block in 1988, as a remedial measure to combat against poverty resulting from repeated drought. The earlier schemes like IRDP and ERRP were merged with the schemes which took up the following project :

Table 8.6 : Implementation of ADAPT Scheme Nuapada Block

Programmes	Achievements
1. Flow Minimum irrigation	3 Projects.
2. Jiwandhara dugwell scheme 5000 (in the subdivn.)	
3. Agriculture and allied non-traditional crop	
Ground nuts	30 ha.
Arhar	30 ha.
Mung	20 ha.
Biri	20 ha.
Minor Millets and ground nuts	1,510 ha.
Kharif	5,200 ha.
4. Village Programme	190
5. Social Infrastructure	I.C.D.S. Project
6. Short-term credit	Rs. 8.79 lakhs (Target) – Rs 20 lakhs

Source : National Bank of Rural Development.

In the study villages of Nawapada, *i.e.* Bakharmal and Bhairajpur different households have been benefited in a number of ways. Old disabled person and widows are given pension and to encourage education among backward casts, SC and ST students are provided with pre-matric scholarships of (ranging between Rs. 10 to Rs. 60).

Evaluation of Poverty Alleviation Schemes in other parts

Field observation shows that the subsidy generates a sense of dependency among the poor. People become less sincere in repayment (which rather becomes more difficult).

In the construction of dug wells village headmen interfere. Instead of providing work to each family they engage the families of their choice. Local politics is really strong even in small villages. While working in the field (Barabandha) it was found a contractor blackmailing the poor labourers for voting in favour of his *sarpanch* candidature.

In Kesinga common people beneficiaries were complaining of bad quality livestock provided to them. Very often the animals offered under IRDP scheme die out. Hence, they were unable to repay the loan. Moreover, the loan money is grossly misused in various ways, such as adjustment of the previous loans, bribing bank employees and household expenses. Poor people look upon it as 'aid' or 'free assistance' provided by the Government.

Beneficiaries taking loans under anti-poverty schemes are found unable to repay bank loan and many complain that because of compound interest their department burden increases. Banks cannot be blamed for charging compound interest which they themselves pay to their depositors. In public interest, banks must recover the loans even resorting to coercive process of law which may cause harassment. Hence government may devise a policy to liberalize recovery of socio-oriented loans either by reducing rate of interest or increasing rate of interest or increasing number of instalments, reducing their quantum providing a longer period for repayment.

To make repayment easier poor borrowers are allowed benefit of subsidy under various loaning schemes. Half of the total land is provided as subsidy to ST and SC and one-fourth of the advanced loan sanctioned as subsidy to agricultural labourers, rural artisans, marginal farmers and small farmers. However, for non SC/STs the subsidy limitation mark stands at Rs. 3000 and for ST families the subsidy limit is Rs. 5000. In selection of beneficiaries procedural complications and corruption are involved. Quite a often middlemen and influential persons take full advantage of the loans meant for the poor through manipulation.

Impact of the Anti-poverty Scheme

Looking to Table 8.7 and the appendix to Chapter 7, pp.370-371, 351 - VIII (of sample villages and sub-micro regions under different sub-regions of Kalahandi) let us examine if the variation of results of poverty alleviation schemes is a function of geographic characteristics.

Firstly, barring Bhairajpur all other representative sample villages exhibit success rate less than 50. Except Degam, Jariguma, Basantpada and Kusumjore rest of the villages Mankadasola and Bhangabari and Tentulipada and Mahulpatna have equal percentage of success rate. Matia exhibit lowest success rate. In Bakharmal, Chandpura and Padepadar the poverty alleviation schemes record utter failure. Not even a single HH found to have utilised governmental resource to benefit itself.

All the poverty alleviation schemes provide resources (loan and assets) to selected poor households to raise them above poverty line. Beneficiaries after receiving governmental packages or inputs have been able to repay the governmental loan after creating financial or economic bases for family's improvement. They have not used the assistance for household consumption, repayment of past loan, drinking liquor, gambling, marriage, festivals or any other unproductive or wasteful purposes.

The following analysis seeks regional, local and other household causes to explain varied degrees of success in poverty alleviation.

The geographic circumstances of Bhairajpur area, viz. forested upland character, rain shadow condition and other physical constraints do not help in explaining the high rate. The high poverty would have been a definite constraint in loan repayment.

Table 8.7 : Evaluation of poverty alleviation scheme

	Name of sample Villages	Poverty level in % of HHs below poverty line	Numerically Dominant	Success rate* of Poverty Alleviation Scheme (in %)
1.	Bakharmal	40	Mixed Population	0
2.	Bhairajpur	50	General Caste	57.5
3.	Ghantiguda	27.77	Scheme not implemented	-
4.	Kusumjore	66.66	General Caste	42.9
5.	Tentulipada	50	Backward Caste (equal number SCs and STs)	20
6.	Bhangabari	26.31	General Caste	33.33
7.	Matia	38.88	Mixed population	11.11
8.	Degam	40	Backward Caste (SC+ST)	50
9.	Tejipada	46.66	Mixed population	16.6
10.	Barabandha	23.52	Backward Caste (SC+ST)	25
11.	Basantpada	68.42	Mixed Caste	44.44
12.	Dumerpadar	44.44	Not surveyed	
13.	Jariguma	52.63	ST dominated	46.15
14.	Chandapur	38.88	Tribe dominated	0
15.	Padepadar	55.55	SC + ST (backward caste dominated)	0
16.	Mahulpatna	64.70	SC dominated	20
17.	Mankadasola	21.05	Mixed population	33.33
18.	Kuliharigud	38.88	Backward Castes (SC+ST)	28.57

Source : Fieldwork, 1993.

* Success rate = No. of HHs utilizing loan or assets of poverty (x)/Total number of HHs Surveyed × 100

Table 8.7 shows (as it is evident from case of Bhairajpur and Kusumjore) probably the general caste households are more sincere in input (loan or asset) utilisation. This seems not true in case of Bhangabari where despite low poverty HHs show only 'moderate' success rate. The nearness of Bhangabari to Bhawanipatna makes people conscious negatively. In other words, the better access to outside society has probably a negative effect on the people since the political consciousness has encouraged them to misuse the government assets and assistance. Degam comes in 'high success rate' group. The geographic causes behind it have already been mentioned. The predominance of backward class (especially scheduled tribes) is another cause for better utilisation of governmental resources. Jariguma is purely a tribal dominated village. It is located in the interior part of Kalahandi, which is a depositional basin of the Hatti-Behera and the Motter. The area is fertile.

Basantpada though located in a tribal dominated belt, has mixed caste population. The backward people, *i.e.* tribes have been made politically conscious by a voluntary organisation named FARR (Friends Association for Rural Reconstruction). As a result of which the people are better aware of their rights and obligations, the reason for which the governmental activities have a good record of success with ample cooperation and understanding from people.

Low success rate in rest of the villages are accounted for by specific local reasons. For example, in Tentulipada dug wells and shop loans have not been successful. People have received loan with some ulterior motives. Once they receive direct cash, they forget the noble purpose of building a permanent asset for themselves for self-reliance. In addition to that poverty is a genuine cause, for misappropriation of loan. Matia, which has mixed population has lowest success rate. The lands are flood prone. Because of poverty most of the households admit that they have spend the loan money and sold out assets for household consumption. A single household complains of inferior breed.

Tentulipada and Barabandha both are situated in Madanpur Rampur Forested upland. This part suffers from acute drought. Most of the population belongs to backward category. Forty per cent of the Barabandha's beneficiaries bluntly complain that they did not get any assistance from the government though they deserved for and applied for it. Another 40 per cent who received the benefits confess of using the loan, assets etc. for household consumption. Rest 10 per cent did not apply for any governmental help. The wells wherever dug, have not been utilised to their best capacity or fullest potentiality. In Tejipada the failure reasons are mostly 'household consumption' one of the household has an additional complain of 'inferior breed'.

Mahulpatna is SC dominated. The group behaviour of SCs is well known. They are shrewd, less labourious than tribes, trying to lead a life of easy going. They are more conscious and exposed to the outside world. They now easily avail governmental help. But at time of loan repayment or in successful utilisation of public help they show less interest and more pretence. More than 60 per cent of the families complain outright that they did not get any governmental assistance though they applied for it. More than 20 per cent say that goats, chickens, sheep and cows whatever provided by the government officials are of inferior breed, only 10 per cent complain that they used the loan for meeting their day-to-day domestic expenses.

In Kulihariguda, 20 per cent express their insincerity towards governmental help. One household makes an absurd complain of automatic damage to the well. Other have received loans for bullocks, for rope making, cot making and agricultural purposes, but they expect that government should completely waive their loans, since no more the assets are with them due to some reason or the other.

For inter-regional and intra-regional comparison two sets of identical villages were taken for comparison. They are (a) Bakharmal (Nawapada Forested Upland) and Matia (Tel Valley); (b) Kulihariguda (Tel-Hatti Basin) and Degam (Tel Valley).

The first pair of villages have mixed (SC, ST and General Caste) population, almost equal level of poverty and high economic indicators. The success rate of the two representative villages are expected to be the same. Instead there is 11.11 per cent variation between them, Bakharmal showing complete failure. There could be certain geographic factors, which explain such variation. Bakharmal is in the north-eastern margin of Nawapada Plateau while Matia is in the flood plain of Tel Valley. The geographic advantages and disadvantages of the two regions have already been mentioned in the previous chapter and they need not be repeated here.

Uniformity in geographic conditions should produce equal or

at least similar results in success rate of poverty alleviation programmes. One wonders to find the high unequal results. Kulihariguda has 28.57 per cent of successful households, Degam has as high as 50 per cent such households. The variation would be partly explained by the fact that the former is the sample village of Tel-Hatti Basin whereas the later is of a valley. However, geographic similarities is more than the dissimilarities. The gap between the success rate accordingly should be less.

Reviewing Developmental Activities

According to official survey the number of rural households and families below poverty line are 2,98,706 and 2,20,001 respectively. And the number of families covered under various developmental programmes till 1990-91 are 143,017. The expenditure incurred to implement those developmental activities is 76 crore 41 lakhs and 56 thousand rupees.

The Area Development Approach for Poverty Termination Programme was implemented in this district for two years i.e. 1988-89 and 1989-90 in Nuapada, Komna, Khariar, Boden, Sinapali, Golamunda, Lanjigarh and Thuamul Rampur blocks. The official report mentions that 571 water harvesting structures were constructed at a cost of Rs. 845.21 lakhs, 32 lift irrigation points were installed with an expenditure of Rs. 81.32 lakhs, 7 medium irrigation projects were completed at an expenditure of Rs. 29.00 lakhs. Work of 2521 dug wells were taken up. A Dairy Development farms has been established for more than 200 villages of Komna and Nawapara, Pisciculture facilities has been provided to 391 ERRP beneficiaries. D.F.O. Khariar has spent twenty-four lakhs for afforestation. Village wood lot has been done in 700 hectares of Nuapada Sub-division. Medicines and vehicles have been provided through mobile Health Centres in eight blocks where old and infirm destitutes were being given feeding. One lakh ration cards are being supplied and in the *hats* of eight blocks various essential commodities are being supplied through mobile vans.

Many needy poor get employment at upper Jonk Project and Upper Indravati Project. Until the beginning of 1991 1,97,469 beneficiaries have been covered under different schemes, such as

IRDP, DRRP, Bonded labour, ITDA, MADA. 21 crore 15 lakhs and 26 thousand have been provided. This shows that both Central and State Governments have financially done their best to assist such a small district like Kalahandi to combat drought and poverty. Despite this people have suffered hunger and starvation deaths. So, it is not directly the Central and/or State government but the district administration responsible for such state of affairs.

Generally speaking, it will not be correct to say that Government is apathetic to the misery as the Government has placed substantially large funds for developmental works and poverty alleviation schemes. Administration also has done a lot to generate employment to combat the calamity. But huge amounts appear to have been spent hurriedly without proposed planning and also faulty execution of projects resulting in wasteful expenditure as in case of water harvest structure made by Soil Conservation Department some of which serve no purpose. Leakage of funds and fraud cannot also be ruled out. Similarly, there are instances of non-use and misuse of funds in anti-poverty schemes. Government is aware of such shortfall as is evident from reports of evaluation of IRDP, ERRP programmes made by government (Planning and Coordination Department, Bhubaneshwar). Poverty continues as before, the misery being aggravated by droughts. Population explosion and high rise in prices raising limit of poverty line may also be contributory factors (Misra Commission Report of inquiry in O.J.Cs. No. 3517/88 & No. 525/89).

9

SURVIVAL STRATEGY

Barring the previous chapter on 'Governmental Programme Evaluation' where we found too low is the impact of the programme to meaningfully conduct a study on space variation in 'success rate', rest other chapters exhibit interesting linkages.

Amongst the three broad ecological micro regions, we have three corresponding sets of :

(a) Levels of Development,
(b) Varieties of Production Relation, and
(c) Levels of Poverty.

The current chapter is no exception to the pattern explored previously. We, similarly notice three separate strategies of survival in the district, they are :

(i) Survival Strategies for forested hilly areas.
(ii) Survival Strategies for plain land.
(iii) Survival Strategies in the region of mixed physical character. (Appendix 9, p.356)

The earlier analysis and observation shows that STs and SCs are the poorest social groups of Kalahandi. The poverty of STs is, however, not manifested in outmigration unlike SCs. The reasons are simple. The resource base (especially forest) of STs is vast. The affinity of tribes to the native place is more. Their cultural inertia fixes their life in a very limited geographic area. At present there is conspicuous change in this very tribal behaviour. Certain tribes have greater tendency towards migration. In case of SCs, however, the situation is completely different. This is evident from Table 9.1.

Table 9.1 : Population Growth rates, 1971-81

	India	Orissa	Kalahandi
Total	25	20.07	15.06
SCs		16.75	6.00
STs		16.62	23.01
Others		22.33	13.55

Source : Census of India, 1981.

The low growth rate among SCs is due to their greater outmigration. Outmigration is a clear indication of low land-holding. To quote Anil Mahajan, "among castes where average landholdings per family are low there is greater intensity of circular or even permanent migration to neighbouring district".[1]

Non-SCs (and STs) were having lands because *Gauntias* were mostly from those castes and tribes. So traditionally, *Harijans* had lesser land as compared to tribes and general castes. Though ceiling system has distributed surplus land among SCs, the impact is much less and the size of land-holdings is often uneconomic. It is for this reason there is higher intensity of SC mobility or outmigration.

The Traditional System of the Economy of Kalahandi

The traditional system of the economy of Kalahandi district can be divided into two kinds, viz. (i) Food gathering, and (ii) Cultivation.

Hunting, selling of forest products was the occupation of food gatherers. *Adivasis* (tribes) were by and large depending on local *gountias* (village headmen and the 'reference group' in their traditional economy). They were not permanent agriculturalists unlike plough cultivators of plain.

A community of peasantry naturally grew in plain areas. It has an economy of self-dependence and self-sufficiency. Barter (exchange of goods) and exchange of labour were deciding the interethnic relationship. The collected forest products like *Kendu leaf, Char, Lac,* Firewood, Bamboo, were sold in the villages and the tribes in turn were taking their necessary commodities for daily living. The interaction between the labour class in the periphery surrounding the peasant society was based on social reciprocity. The case of *Kutias, Paharias* and *Bhunjias* can be cited to explain the above interaction and exchanges. The forest collection was the primary basis of the economy. The village boatmen used to ferry in the rainy season and receiving paddy, *mung* in return of his service. So, also were the cases of black-smith, carpenter, barber, fishermen, *kallar* (liquor seller) and milkman, tattoo artist and oilman. Money had hardly any role in the traditional rural economy built on or founded on service organisation.

The interdependency between the peasants group of plain land and the tribes of hilly region and that between the rural people and urban people was comprising the whole net of traditional economy of mutual benefit in a rather stable state.

The Harsh Changes

Since Independence rapid changes occurred in the district with the decline of forest cover. Many tribes who were dependent on forests, had to adopt cultivation and manual labour.

The self-sufficient rural economy has become integrated with urban centres each expanding its exchange connection and economic dominance over fifty to hundred villages. Further all *panchayats* started serving the surrounding villages through weekly markets *(haat).* Tribes came to sell their products in these *haats*. Their lifestyle evolved in a new way.

One of the most undesirable and surprising changes occurred in the method of practice of traditional cultivation. Ecologically valuable crops such as *mandia, kodo, sua, guruji chhot dhan* (yielding paddy within sixty days) etc. are no more in use. A variety of paddies (fifty) which were existing earlier are now hard to find. All tribes except *Kutias, Dingrias, Bhunjias, Paharias* etc. have adopted agriculture to earn their livelihood, the output from which seem grossly inadequate.

The suction of agricultural products and forest products by local businessmen and *dalals* (middlemen) took place in an unhindered manner. Deforestation, rejection of traditional cultivations, unintelligent adoption of modern agricultural systems and constant crop failure due to irregular and untimely rainfall worsened the situation of Kalahandi.

The custom of private loan, mortgage of gold, silver, brass metal, house, land etc. and that of labour (in the form of *halias, bahabandha, kulibhuti, lag, thika* etc.) have distorted the normal way of tribal life.

The "present orientation" (lack of sense of awareness for future) of Kalahandi people in general and *sukhbasis* (landless agricultural labourers) in particular is one of the important cause of prevailing misery. It is said that to meet some petty need, a tribe can go ahead with little hesitation to sell his personal *mahul* tree or *kendu* tree (which earns rupees three hundred to four hundred annually to the owner), at a throw away price.

The subsidy and bank loans provided under various schemes have not a very significant role in changing the economic condition of the people. But what has definitely occurred is that various skills, artisans and traditional extra agricultural occupations have been saved from eminent danger of extinction. (Based on S. R. Das's article on the Traditional and Current Economic System of the Tribals in Kalahandi.)

Methods of Adjustment to Cope with Natural Change in Plain Region

In the past, just like a family head kings used to come to save their own people during critical periods such as drought, famine etc. This moral duty and natural sympathy for the subjects, however, should not justify the *Rajatantra* as an effective system for development.

Jitamitra Prasad Singh Deo in his book "Glimpses of Orissa" mentions, "His granaries throughout the state were the centres of relief operations". He helped the *kisans,* the backbone of the village economy with substantial loans, opened free kitchens at central places to provide cooked food for the disabled and emancipated persons, till the duration of toil and 'turmoil' and as long as government help was not made available. Works were provided to the able bodied unemployed. As a result of this, several tanks were excavated or renovated throughout the estate and people heaved a sign of relief.

Arnapurna Granary still existing at Khariar was the chief centre of relief operation. The only help that was rendered by Deputy Commissioner of Raipur was that the purchased paddy worth Rs. 1,000 from the Granary of Raja Brajaraj Singh Deo, at a very cheap rate for distribution to the cultivators, [known from the thanks giving letter of Deputy Commissioner dated 28th May, 1897 in Hindi to Brajraj Singh Deo (p.11)].

From 1985 onwards there was a series of droughts. The condition of landless labourers was miserable. From newspaper report it was learned that affected people sold away their properties to avoid starvation. For example, in Khasbahal village (which has best quality low lying *bahal* / lands) of Khariar about five hundred villagers left the village to seek work outside during 1985-1990. Some people, however, returned home after the government took up the work of Minor Irrigation Project and Water Harvesting structures in the area after the visit of the then[2] Prime Minister Rajiv Gandhi. During fieldwork in Tentulipada (of Sadar block) it was observed that the *Harijans* of Kalahandi are cunning for basically two reasons : (1) Government should not stop pumping easy money and other material allocations into the area under various schemes. (2) They should not be deprived of benefits. They frequently go outside to work and earn handsome wages (as compared to the local level economics). The places they visit are Nagpur, Bhilai, Bhopal, Raipur, Bombay etc. The labour rate was Rs. 25 per person per day then. One *Harijan* explained that by mortgaging his lands (which are not saleable under ceiling rules) he could arrange some initial cash to travel outside cities to find out a work for himself after learning from his neighbours about the availability of work outside.[3] On his return he saved required amount to recover the land.

Same way normal year outmigration is a sign of progress for the people of Kalahandi. Because wage earned through '*kuli*' often supplement their income. In cities they lived a better life, by and large. Drought may not be initial cause but not the one and only cause of outmigration. Dama Bhoi of Jhikimiki (Bhawanipatna) states that drought occurred in the year 1989 and prolonged for three consecutive years, during which 235 persons migrated outside the state to look for work. He himself managed selling his gold, utensils, belongings and somehow arranged funds for travel.

Harijans of this kind are benefited in different ways. Firstly, after harvest they stored the grains from their cultivating lands and then went in search of outside *kuli* labour for rest of the six months of the year. Again within the village they fully availed the government assistance (loan, subsidies, etc.). Few stay in the city slums for major part of the year with their families. The reasons for their not deserting the native place for ever are: Firstly, the grains (paddy, pulses) are raised from the field is a major support for the year round sustenance of family in normal years. Secondly, a hut in the village is enough to claim a government help for family, which in reality often act as a 'sink hole' of government allocation.*

The migration flow have been reported to have occurred from village like Udayapur, Chhatikuda, Deypur, Suhagpur, Khaibadi, Dongriguda, Khairmal etc. to various places of Madhya Pradesh, Andhra Pradesh, Maharashtra, U.P. and Delhi. Misra Commission Report (p. 26) revealed that the villagers who left comprised of landless labourers as well as land owners who could not get any employment here. He said that Kameswar

---

* From fieldwork experience *Harijan* as a caste has a number of qualities which help them manipulate a secured living. They make careful choice with respect to place of migration. In Waltier (A.P.), Madras, Western U.P., Punjab, Haryana the wage rate is higher than Sambalpur (Orissa) and Raipur (M.P.). So they prefer former than the later. SCs have greater awareness than STs and even many local general caste groups. They choose jobs which can provide higher wage with lesser hardship and little responsibility. Also due to higher literacy level among SCs they find jobs in government sector as well. If two works are available – one with higher wage and of heavier nature and the other with lesser money and of easier (lighter) kind, they would prefer the later, unlike their counterparts industrious tribals. Sometimes work on control basis is taken up by SCs. On interviewing, it was found that many of their households have fully availed loan from multiple sources (like Jeewandhara irrigation well, Indira Awas Yojna, Agricultural loan for plough and seeds etc.). Fortunately, due to increasing awareness they are less addicted to liquor these days. However, they are physically weak and numerically small in many villages, because of which in some areas, they are dominated by STs.

Mehar and also his own brother Gajapati who are considerably big land owners went outside to work as labourers. The economic misery is thus, a fact and so people selling away their property in distress cannot be ruled out. Kantabanji (of Bolangir) which is a commercial centre and railway station seems to be the exit point for migrating villagers. Similarly, the Kesinga station for the labourers of Tel Valley and Khariar Road station for the workers of drought prone Nawapada Forested Upland are the exist points for outmigrants suffering crop loss due to drought.

Jhikimiki has few large land holding families. Severe and continuous drought (like that of 1985-89 series) has strong impact on rich landed families and landless families alike. Many people including Kameswar Mehar and his brother who are the owner of about 20 acres of good cultivable lands left village and went towards Maharashtra, Rajasthan and Karnataka in search of employment. Kameswar Mehar's family members worked as labourer in Surat in Gujarat, in construction work on daily wage of Rs. 20 which has been now enhanced to Rs. 22. He says that Rs. 20 in Surat is an equivalent to Rs. 5 in the village and because he could not get Rs. 5 a day here he was compelled to leave village.[4]

The above account demonstrates that migration is not a preferred choice for more earnings rather under distress (*i.e.* due to lack of food) and survial people decide to migrate. Also, the lack of economic opportunities in the region prompt people to migrate for biological survival. Outmigration may save one from starvation death but not at all from the miseries and distress. Because different sort of exploitation and inhuman situation prevails outside where the poor works day and night just to earn his bread. The poor labourers know nothing except 'work and bread' in life. They do not have leisure nor a family life that a normal human being should have. Thus, a young man working outside can hardly save money to send back home. The choice left before the man of Kalahandi (during 1985-89 drought series) was not between a normal life and better life but between starvation death at village and wretched and exploited life outside. So, the outmigration during the acute drought is a distress migration for saving life.

Again during normal years since the grains produced do not go beyond six months the choice obviously is between half fed life in a village and the same harsh life outside. However, those who luckily manage to get a better work or go for rickshaw pulling or sending their women folk for prostitution or engage themselves in stealing, somehow lead a little better life. They become able to buy clothes, few consumable fancy articles or get little money saved to send home or to return with. Migration is a means to escape from economic distress. Poor go out to towns or dam sites, factory townships, rural industries like brick kilns, agriculturally prosperous areas during periods of harvests or before the cultivation season starts. The intensity, continuity and frequency of outmigration depends on :

(a) Intensity and duration of drought (which act like a push factor), and
(b) Job availability (which act like a pull factor).

When there is severe crop loss big farmers are compelled to reduce the number of agricultural labourers. Naturally, there is labour surplus due to worklessness in the local area. With landless labourers and marginal farmers, small farmers also join the stream of migration in search of employment. The strong affinity of the tribals with their birth place prevent them to move outside. Instead they prefer to live in their own villages and some how manage to live with minor forest collections and minor jobs in the neighbouring villages. Tribals and other caste people who stay back in the village look for opportunities outside agriculture which though few in number includes small business, grocery shops, tailoring, carpentry, selling out some processed products etc.

The 1987-89 drought had its impact in three successive stages.

Initial Stage of Drought

Large (rich) farmers have surplus grains saved from last (previous year) harvest, though there is a crop loss this year. Small and marginal (poor) farmers grow their favourite foodgrains Kodo and Ragi which can grow on inferior lands and under the conditions of relative dryness. Work availability in the rich farmers field is reduced. Landless labourers look for work outside. Here, nature, culture and structure balance each other. This is supported by P.K. Nayak's argument.

Second year of drought

Both poor and rich start suffering. Poor farmers suffer more than rich farmers do and so they start outmigrating first. Here, structure remains dominant. This explains how poor suffer more than the rich farmers even if the intensity of drought is the same. It is definitely a structural advantage for the rich. This view is supported by S. Roy and Prof. M. Mohanty in third work on the *Political Economy of Food Crisis in Kalahandi* (1990).

Third year of drought

If the drought continues for the third consecutive year crop loss becomes total. At last rich farmers join the migration stream and mass exodus starts. Rich farmers are the worst sufferers since they are compelled to take up manual labour which they are least accustomed to. At this stage nature is becomes dominant. This is supported by Justice B.N. Mishra's argument that both rich and poor farmers are affected by drought, (Mishra, 1989 Commission Report, pp. 35 and 38).

So, it is neither just natural calamity nor mere structural exploitation responsible for poverty and outmigration. Both contribute to it. And whether it is because of poor man's adaptation with specific natural condition or because of unintended structural advantage that occasional drought or dryness do not pose threat of any significant magnitude, to small and marginal farmers (SC and ST) in the initial year.

To quote the Mishra Commission finding –

> "......As a consequence of drought the economic condition of the rural population in both the districts of Bolangir and Kalahandi was severely affected. It is no wonder, therefore,

people somehow managed selling their properties in distress to avoid starvation and had to migrate to other states, for employment and bread. The worst suffers are well to do farmers and land owners, who also joined the exodus and went to other states to work as labourers to earn bread. There were starvation deaths in the district of Kalahandi only.

In village Singhibadi (Dharmagarh) villagers were engaged in Bamboo Corporation previously but as in the year the corporation ceased its operation, the labour class (public) were facing much difficulties to arrange their 'minimum meals' and so he moved the collector to provide immediate work to help the public for their 'minimum earn'.

There are the various methods of adjustments to natural change. Earlier there existed certain desirable cultural values such as religious and social customs, traditions, beliefs and myths that kept a balance between human need and ecological set-up.

Methods of Adjustment to Cope With Natural Change in Hilly-Forest Region

The symbiotic relationship between the tribals and forests of Kalahandi seemed to be total as later's dependence on forest food, fuel, housing, medicine and recreation etc. is integrative and exhaustive.

Irrespective of tribals and non-tribals most people depend on food from forests as a means of survival in the lean season. The forests food includes fruits (like *Kundra, Karil, Khatal, Sitaphal, Ramphal, Tendu, Amla, Jamun, Kabet, Kaith, Am, Sal, Imli, Bel* etc.), flowers (like, *Mahua,* August etc.), leaves (like *Poisag, Bathua, Hurvur, Chech, Nerisag, Palanga, Phan Bhegi* etc.) Roots (like, *Satmuli, Safed Musli, Agia, Kamal, Ram Datua) Rhizomes* Various *Kanda, Banahandi Kaseru, Tekhur* and now full of *Babul* and *Palas (Butea monosperma)* trees which thrive better in drought prone areas. This kind of situation is mostly prevalent in the eastern side of Nawapada and other drought prone areas like Lanjigarh, Narla, Madanpur and Rampur in the district. However, people also derive some benefits from these two species. The leaves of the Palas are used for making plates exclusively for domestic use. The flowers of the plant, besides their various decorative and ritual roles are also supplied after drying to the businessmen at prevailing market prices 25 paise per kg. in 1988-89 every year. The seeds of the plants are no less important. The villagers collect these and sell at the rate of Rs. 1.50 per kg. to the local businessmen. These are used in soap making. The forest having been denuded completely over exploitation some poor people are now regularly depending on the collection and sale of white soil (lime) stone chips from the forest area and wage labour in the nearby Nawapara town.[5]

For construction of houses (grass thatching, poles) building agricultural implements, furniture, ropes, mats, fences etc. different forest materials are used. Rope for *charpay* making, grass for mat making are procured from forests. Bamboos and branches of trees have been used for fencing, thatching and well erection etc. throughout. Twenty-five years back paper mills started monopolising bamboos trade. Branches of trees were clean felled for meeting industrial needs. They, at present, (both bamboo and branches) are in short supply for common men. They are forced to use small plants for fences etc. Like other areas forest dwellers of Kalahandi depend on firewood fuel but not for sale as it is done so widely today. Going for firewood selling in recent years is a sign of struggle for survival. Besides fuel, vegetative growth that decompose into partly or fully developed humus is used as fertiliser; green leaves, grasses, dry stems and leaves are used as fodder for milch cows and ploughing cattle.

In order to avoid the danger of over exploitation certain protective measures in the form of taboos, prohibitions, beliefs have been adopted. Tribals have some species of trees which are regarded sacred and so their cutting is prohibited as they are considered essential for survival. Example of such type of trees are sal, *mahua*, mango etc. Restrictions are imposed on also the quantity of forest products to be used by each household. For instance, in the district there are some areas where a single family is permitted only one cart load of firewood per month.

Mahua flowers are not plucked but collected from the ground once they fall down after ripening. Today, *Mahua* and

Tendu leaves being the major revenue earner restrictions are imposed on the poor tribals by the State Government. In the process the self-imposed restrictions which helped protection of forest resources have vanished today. Because people want to survive first. So many cultural values are abandoned. They realise that man must eat, drink, and live comfortably before he practises any ethics. However, despite governmental intervention and poverty few myths are still given due respect. Kond origin is mythologically linked with *salap* tree the juice of which is a favourite drink for every tribal. So, not even a single branch of *salap* is cut even on *donger* (*i.e.* shifting cultivation plot.)

With a sense of 'Live and let others live' we can see how for own sustenance people have been caring for the plants around them. It is believed that goddess dwells in the *Mahua* tree which is regarded as sacred. Wine prepared from its flower is offered to the gods and goddesses. The *bel* tree is the abode of Lord Shiva. The *sal* is that of forest goddess so also the case of *nimba*, *bata,* banyan and *peepal,* mango, tamarind, jack fruits etc. This belief protects various kinds of trees thereby protecting the protectors' native population themselves, from threats of starvation. The leaves, flowers fruits, seeds, bark and roots of *sal* trees used for food or leaf plates making or medicinal purposes. When the *sal* trees become old their trunks are used for house building. During the *Durbar* regime there was restriction on the felling of fruit bearing trees. This restriction has saved mango grooves and *Mahua* trees form reckless felling. Both these trees are important in the economy of the people. *Mahua* trees are very common in Mahulapatna and Madanpur Rampur area. *Mahua* flowers are used not only for feeding cattle but also for manufacture of liquor. The Kond tribals use these as their food during the rainy season when other kinds of food material are not available. After the flowers the kernels of the *Mahua* nut are gathered and pressed to get cheapest cooking oil. This is used by corrupt businessmen for adulteration of *ghee.* The poor labourers are employed in *Mahua* nut collection. Barring food, and oil Mahul can be used as medicine. *Tendu* fruits were taken as food item for at least two months a year. The *tendu* seeds of immature *tendu* fruits are consumed as substitution of rice. In 1965 drought year Kalahandi people could mange to live with this precious natural gift for a problem period.

Boiled *mahul* are eaten as food. Raw (unripe) *mahul* fruit provide sweet juices which is used as a favourite drink. *Gur* prepared from *Kaku. Gara* oil is extracted from *Mahul* fruits. *Sal* seed is used as medicine for dysentery or loose motion, stomach or headaching.[6] In the plain area of Karlapat adjoining Junagarh area one finds plenty of babul trees, the timber of which is used for making agricultural implements. Kusum trees are abundant in Mahulpatna *ex-zamindary* and are used for propagation of lac.[7]

Today, however, forest destruction by forest dwellers themselves has become a rule. The reasons are obvious. The primary cause is economic compulsion, the struggle people face just to fill their stomach. Outside intervention and gross destruction of rural ecology by foresters (forest officials), contractors, businessmen, industrialists and by government must itself have crossed all limits of sound ecology and sound economy. This has been elaborately explained in the previous chapter on 'Production Relation' and elsewhere. There is shortage of other timber after clear felling. So, people have no option but unwillingly join the crowd of annihilation. Myths and traditions are no longer followed especially when these are the cases of younger generations. Nevertheless, in quite a number of villages the traditional older people observe rituals as far as practicable. Asadi Jani of Jariguma (Jaypatna Block) says that they save economically useful trees such as *Sagun, Sargi, Chanar, Kendu, Kusum, Mahul on* the *dongar* before starting shifting cultivation. (Fieldwork)

The forest cover has a devastating condition. Villagers of Saripalli say, a few decades ago the area was full of *Sal* trees. The so called forest around the village is now represented by a few species, like *Kendu, Char, Pales, Mahul* and a few other species. The forest around the village Mahuabhata which is so named due to the presence of *mahua* trees has a similar story to tell. The forest cover is recklessly denuded through regular tree felling. In both the villages there are also numerous *Bahada, Harida, Mango* and *Neem* trees which constitute the significant component of the people's economy.[8]

Strategies to cope with Drought in the Region of Mixed Physical Character

People once affected by drought try to minimise the chances of death by adopting various means, such as by raising the use of forest products, seeking help from neighbours, rushing to use of forest products, seeking help from neighbours, rushing to find out work in Government Projects, outmigration for better wage etc. The opportunities for local work outside agriculture remains extremely limited. This does not mean employment with medium and big farmers available even during years of rain scarcity. In such a situation of seasonal abnormality marginal and small farmers either abandon their land uncultivated or try to lease out these agricultural lands. Large farmers try to optimise their production within the constraints of nature. Few of them look for help from their kith and kins. The majority of population struggle hard to ensure at least a belly full of meal a day.

In Nawapada Forested Upland, the traditionally drought prone region many rich farmers have adopted drought resistant crops, like early paddy varieties, groundnuts, millets etc. Some farmers from large and rich categories have started cultivating *kodo,* a drought resistant crop suiting worst lands (*i.e. Att,* inferior and infertile lands) *Kodo* can be cultivated in place of wetland, paddy which needs much higher dose of water. Earlier only small farmers cultivating *kodo* as a grain essential for survival during drought.

During the past decades and even today government has implemented a wide range of employment generation schemes, which are to be discussed in the next chapter. Moreover, work is now available plenty in big urban centres of India. Various NGOs are functional for common men in Kalahandi. Those includes BISWAS, FARR, AWARE, CARE, LOK DRISTI, AGRAGAMEE, RLP, CASA, Kalahandi district *Adivasi Sangha, Jana Kelyan Samiti,* Lutheran World Service, *Khet Majdur Sangha, Sarvodaya,* Tereds Home, Rotary Club etc. These organisations somehow moderate the intensity of unemployment and food crisis in the drought prone Kalahandi. Most of the middle class families in the village manage to take two meals of rice a day. Poor people not going for outside labour continue to remain half-fed during summer. Ragi *(mandia)* is their staple food. Outmigration is basically a response to worklessness and food scarcity. But there are other causes of outmigration too. Those are land ownership, group behaviour education, availability of opportunities, higher wage etc. Small and marginal farmers and landless labourers have a greater tendency for outmigration than large and medium sized well off farmers. The propensity to migration is less among tribals than among scheduled castes and other general castes. Among illiterate people migration found to be more than literates. These are few basic observations in Kalahandi. In his study, impact of drought on agricultural production, forest utilisation and migration. Dash (1991) observes that the big farmers under such conditions could manage to sustain because of their savings and other assets. The medium class farmers due to government service and necessary loan or help from their in-laws either in Kalahandi or Raipur district could also maintain their livelihood. Out of the rest (like small and marginal farmers as well as landless), some manage through the *Jajmani* System and labour intensive programmes, some try to cope through forest collection and others prefer to migrate to different industrial and project areas few in Kalahandi and Raipur[9], for employment. Sainath Reports Almost all the labourers are migrants from the Kalahandi (Nuapada) and Bolangir areas of Orissa, escaping complete marginalisation and unemployment at home by slaving for brick kiln owners in Andhra Pradesh. The complete destruction of wage employment in the Kalahandi-Bolangir area, alongside steady alienation from land, labour and produce is the driving factor for such migration... The average labourer had 268 days of work in a year – a decline of over 50 per cent leading to major migrations. The destruction of traditional irrigation systems, dismal prices for their products, unthinking development projects without popular roots, these have caused immense damage. Andhra provides only a few weeks of employment. Some of the same migrants even pull rickshaws in Raipur, Madhya Pradesh for somedays. On a good day in Raipur, says Ghasiram reminiscently, "I can be left with Rs. 15 in my hand at the end of the work".[10]

Who are those who leave their homes to travel 400 km for a pittance ? According to VIKALPA survey over 42 per cent are landless agricultural labourers. Another 31 per cent own an acre or less while a further 16 per cent hold under two acres. In short close to 90 per cent of the migrants are landless or marginal farmers. Therefore, it can be finally inferred that the severity of drought has been minimised both by different alternative strategies adopted by the people for earning and by labour intensive programmes as well as emergency measures implemented by the government.

Most of the medium and small farmers[11] cultivated *kodo* (a millet crop), *Khadi, Guruji, Ansi, Rasi* etc. in drought years. *Att* (upland) are left unutilised. Since the land quality is poorest water required by it is highest. It is prone to the maximum paddy crop loss especially when drought is continuous and hence it demands largest investment which poor can ill afford. The forms of mortgage like *Bandhak, Kalantaria, Bandhasaheji* and *Katti* and that of labour like *Goti*, *Halia* (annual servant) *Bahabandha and Kalibhuti, thika* etc. have debacle the normal way of peasantry life.

Along with these problems such as rural unemployment, non-industrialisation, growth of population and rapid deforestation are some of the major problems of Kalahandi. Man has found no other way of survival as a result of which either he has migrated from his motherland or lived in the wetland as a crippled soldier.[12]

Adhia (share cropping) and *Bandhak* (land mortgage) are the two common ways of land rent. In Barabandha (Madanpur Rampur) a Brahmin was given a piece of land under *Adhia* for a number of years. For fulfilling the terms and conditions, he has to pay half of the total harvest to the landowner every year.

Under *Bandhak* the land is usually given on mortgage to the interested person for receiving a loan. Risk is involved in this case as the landowner may loose land if he fails to repay the debt. Strict enforcement of Ceiling Act in recent years discourage most of the general caste to go for *Bandhak.* The lands of Scheduled Castes or Scheduled Tribes are restorable and non-transferable under the ceiling rule. So, the *sahukar* avoids *Bandhak* commitments in such cases.

Whether a person should go for *Regha, Adhia* or *Bandhak* depends on the economic status, bargaining capacity and the need of both the land giver and land receiver.

After marriage, the newly wed couple is supposed to shift to newly and separately built homestead. The agricultural land is usually equally divided among parents and sons. So long as parents are bodily able to work for themselves, land remains with them. Once they become old and feeble and think that they no more can cultivate for themselves, they offer the lands to another person or their own children who on receiving them become obliged to share part of the harvest with the old land owners (donors). In some cases old couple go for begging in absence of land or denial of harvest or justice. This is how very old people manage to live in their fag end of life.*

Like food, water is also life. Scarcity of rainfall, uneven, unequal and untimely nature of it demand artificial storage of water for different purposes like irrigation, bathing, drinking, cooking etc. Traditionally, local people have been dependent upon *Sagar, Nala, Chuha,* streams, river etc. *Gauntias* with peoples' participation help build them. Construction of tube wells and dug wells seems to be a success of the government and voluntary organisations. During the fieldwork it was found that tube wells exist in villages even in remote areas, providing good drinking water. Through 'Jeevandhara Programme' and 'Indira Awas Yojana' villagers are provided not only irrigation facilities but also work.

Methods of Adjustment to Cope with Human Change in Difference Micro Regions

In the previous chapter we noticed how institutional change have occurred in various spheres of society which has a direct impact on the regional economy. In congruence to the cultural and economic patterns various methods of adjustments have been evolved to cope with drought and extreme poverty situations. Presented below are the cases of adaptation adopted by native

* Based on fieldwork experience of Ghantiguda (Sinapali).

people in different micro regions as evident by the sample (village) survey.

In Plains (Valleys)

Tentulipada (of Bhawanipatna block) is located in the Tel Valley. About one-fourth of the either labourer, gatherers or hunters but they are good sellers (traders) who by pass middleman *(dalals)* and sell their agricultural products directly in the market.

Dhubal Rana though a potter depends upon cultivation. He is perhaps among the very few beneficiaries who has successfully utilised the Jeevandhara Scheme loan (amounting to Rs. 6,000 to dig a 'dug well' the water of which is now utilised for drinking purpose as well as watering the kitchen garden to produce *brinjal,* pepper etc.

Kultas, the traditional agriculturalists are relatively more prosperous. They use bank loan sincerely and properly like backward caste they are not addicted to kind of intoxicants. They raise various kinds of crop on *dongar* (*podu* plots), consume *Jhari, Kodo* during pre harvest and harvest season. *Ragi* constitutes a popular diet among tribals during summers season.

In Hilly Forests

Mahulpatna (Thuamul Rampur) of Dharamgarh plateau is located in forested area. But unlike them tribal villages of forested region here the inhabitant's dependence on tendu leaves and *tola* or *mahul* seeds etc. seems to be limited. The reason is because wage earners are attracted towards "Indravati Projects" works which provides them high wages (Rs. 25 per day/labour). Shifting cultivation is a common practice. Labi Muduli, a *podu* cultivators explains he cannot quit *podu* as he possesses no land for plough cultivation. (Most of the valley lands are in the hands of non-STs). He produces a variety of products such as *Niger, Kango, Koshala,* Ragi *(Mandia), Arhar, Kating* on freely available *dongar.*

Shifting cultivation constitute an integral part of tribal life. *Adivasis* are relatively more sedentary in nature. They don't migrate outside their native place like SCs whose migration is based on "more wage for less hard work". They instead find out work down the *dongar* once they are free from the year round engagement of *podu* work. Given choice tribals would prefer *podu*. Even if a ploughing land is provided to them they would still retain *podu*. This shows that *podu* is part and parcel of tribal life. Hill forest tribals believe that ragi eating during summer keep their stomach cool, physically fit and efficient which is true due to ragi's high nutrition value. Gond tribes who are more integrated in plan area caste system. They neither grow nor consume ragi. Rather they have developed different tastes and food habits, like Hindu caste people and so have their own method of adaptation.

Because of *podu's* ecological suitability, multiple crop raising capacity, and economic necessity even few non-STs (including SCs and Sundhis) do practise *podu*. Rabi Sahu, a Mahulpatna Sundhi complains that most of the plain's cultivable lands are in the hands of village headman, which are capable of producing paddy only (mono crop). Moreover paddy is insufficient to support all the economic needs like households consumption, selling or bartering to procure clothes, oil, salt etc. The *sukhbasi* (landless labourers) find free land on *dongar* (hill sides) which are devoted to 'slash and burn method' of cultivation. Sixteen different varieties of crops* have been noted from shifting cultivation by the author. Part of the produce is kept stored for household consumption and part of it is sold out in the market. Since the cultivation requires large number of labourers for which non-STs often find them least capable less skilled, the later employs hired labourers from among scheduled tribes. Tribals grow mostly minor millets like *Jhari, Kodo, Gurji, Kongo, Khosla* in the hill slopes and uplands. Though those crops are not remunerative and yield less but the tribals cultivate them as it is cultivated with much less labour. They grow those crops as they are harvested in August and immediately cater to their needs at a time when the food stock gets exhausted (*District Gazetteer,* 1981, p. 130). They don't have any staple food item

* *Podu* crops include Ragi, *Koshla, Kango, Kerjandri, Kating, Judung* (beans), cucumber, *Bada, Kumunda, Dongar brinjal, Kandul,* pulses), Ladies finger, *Jada,* Horse grams (Pulses), till, Black grams.

as such and mostly take Ragi, *Kodo,* Beans, *Gurji Kosala,* boiled green leaves, vegetables, *Kandamula* and *mushrooms* (*ibid.* 99). In addition a large number of tribals fall back upon numerous species of fruits and roots obtained from forest as their main source of subsistence. For half of the year, particularly when their food stock is over they live on the powder of tamarind seeds, mango stones, edible roots and tubers (*ibid.*). Though above minor millets are nutritionally good, they can only avail it for only five to six months in a year.

Mr. K. Sharma in his work on *The Konds of Orissa*, further writes Konds have irregular food habits and so it is very difficult to ascertain their nutritional status. They don't have any fixed timings of eating. They eat whatever food is available. Sometimes they just fill their stomach by stable forest products like wild fruits and edible fruits and wild animals, which they obtain by hunting. Staple food articles taken by them vary with the different seasons and the diet of the Konds is based on the availability of food... different cereals taken by Konds are Ragi, Rice, Maize and millet. The average adult allowance of cereals taken by Konds is 475 gm. Which is almost equal to the average Indian intake (*i.e.* 471 gm) but the value is higher than the I.C.M.R. recommended value (*i.e.* 400 gm).

Ragi is the staple diet taken through out the year and in winter seasons rice is used along with ragi. In summer Konds use mango seeds as their staple diet along with *mandia* or Ragi.

The most important pulses of this area and which is taken mostly by Konds is *Kulthi* (horse gram) and green gram but less frequently. The other pulse used is '*arhar*'. The average daily intake of pulses in 30 grams. The value is much less than the average Indian diet and I.C.M.R. recommended value (*i.e.* 68 gm and 85 gm respectively).

Konds take lot of green leafy vegetables but infrequently, *i.e.* whenever available. The different leafy vegetables are *Buhar* leaf, *Khera* leaf, *Gurdisag, Kulersag.* Bamboo shoots *(kardi)* and green leafy vegetables are mostly collected from the forests. Other leafy vegetables, those used by Konds are pumpkins tomatoes and number of wild roots available in forests like *bhat kanda, cherenga kanda, pita kanda, putogu kanda, kesa kanda,* oel *kanda...* All available tropical fruits are taken by konds, e.g.

mango, banana, guava, oranges, *sitaphal,* Papaya, *Mahua* fruits, *amaranth,* and wild fruits like *kendu, Bihi, Batquill,* etc. fruit products like mango seeds are also taken.

Today, the deforestation, food availability is largely reduced. Konds somehow survive but in malnourished form. The average calorie intake of an adult Kond is 1708.9 as against that of Indian adult *i.e.* 2100 calorie (*op. cit.* p. 44).

On social and religious festivals they take various kinds of meat in addition to their normal food items. Some of the lower castes and tribals eat meat of dead cows, buffaloes, pigs, pigeons, peafowl, rat, non-poisonous snakes and large reptiles like *godhi* (*ibid.* 141). However, the consumption of wheat and forest products have comparatively decreased in recent years after the nationalisation of forests. Earlier due to their forest entitlements the consumption of meat etc. was more among the tribals as they used to hunt birds and wild animals from the forests. Due to their social customs certain tribals share the meat of the hunted animals amongst themselves as a result of which the share of meat per person decreases in quantity (Roy, S.,1990, pp.131-33). But this points out the civilisation in uncivilised world.

In the past, the landless people as well as those having small landholdings, used to consume more of jungle products during the periods of food scarcity like bamboo flower, tender roots, mushrooms which are nutritious. After losing forest entitlements they have been advised to take leaves and drumsticks instead of wild plants.

Dongar chas (Kond nomenclature of shifting cultivation) is an ecologically sound method. While selecting site special attention is paid to surface conditions, site, direction of wind and rain, readiness of sun. The later eliminates the fear of unnecessary destruction of adjoining forest cover due to fire. Leaving economically valuable species like *(salap, mohua* etc.) which are protected by religious customs, only the branches of other bigger plants are chopped off. Bamboo is cut at certain angle above specified height avoiding damage to roots. These provide a partial cover to soil from being eroded. Fire is set to reduce the quantity of weeds, which threaten to suck the fertility of soil. The mixed cropping pattern of *podu* unlike mono-cropping of plough cultivation has an in-built insurance against vagaries of nature. As such famine and death due to hunger is unknown among many Konds practising '*dongar chas*'. No doubt *podu* is less productive but this is essential for tribal survival. Relaxation, leisure and labour intermingle here.[13]

Food crops of *podu* has not been replaced by new outer variety of commercial crops. Instead cash crops of traditional varieties have been linked with business of the outside traders. As a result cash crop varieties of *podu*, which has low yield are increasingly demanded. The only way tribals meet such growing demand is by bringing more and more areas under *podu*. Which lead to larger forest cutting.

Subsisting on *Bhat Kanda* and *Cherenga* (local roots) has a circumstantial origin. Perhaps, people starve eating them when there is severe crop loss all round but, gradually they become accustomed to root consumption which later constitute the part of tribal culture. Surprisingly Krusna Chandra *Harijan* (Mahulpatna) a scheduled caste though save money by not taking to liquor also subsists on *Cherenga* roots, which shows that forest root eating has become a part of their food even in normal economic condition.

Giridhar Naik with his three other brothers of Mahulpatna cultivate 22 acres of land. The production is shared. Still then they frequently depend on labour. Preference of labour over land may be due to

1. Less capital or seeds.
2. Insecurity or uncertainty in production due to vagaries of nature.
3. Productivity (output to input ratio) is less.
4. Unnecessary botheration.

In Plains (Basins)

Mankandashola (Tel-Hatti Basin) is a caste dominated village. People mostly produce vegetables (such as tomato, papaya, onion etc.) in their kitchen garden. Recently, under the horticulture programme, the ITDA has taken up backyard plantation and therefore, the tribals who have small backyards, grow vegetables like papaya, banana, pumpkins and drum-sticks... Few tribals who grow vegetables consume very less of it and sell the rest at lower price to the landlords or go to the *haats* and exchange it with either essential commodities like oil, salt and clothes. (Roy, S.,1990, p.134)

People do not use *tola* oil in place of mustard oil. *Muthi sag* fried with oil, turmeric, salt and pepper is a favourite food item. Borrowing from neighbour is a common practice. Work is available in plenty here. So, the labour charge is high. If 5 persons of a family are engaged in labour 2 members' income is enough to support the entire family. Often the *sahukar* (who has resource, capital, material but not labour) receives labour is turn of his lending. Dambarudhar of Kesinga (Tel Valley) borrows in advance by promising the *sahukar* his labour. Brass utensil, golden and silver ornaments etc. are kept as security with the *bandhak.* The workers sometimes lose their material on failing to repay the debt in time. These days aluminium and steel utensils are mostly used in place of brass utensils which are expensive also. (In other words, earlier the poor men after being unable to recover the gold, silver and brass materials from the village moneylenders have started purchasing aluminum and steel utensils.) Dambarudhar narrates that through a *dalal* (middleman/contractor) he had been to Dehradun to join a canal construction work. He had to engage himself in dangerous work of stone breaking. He used to earn Rs. 500 to 700 per month and after working two to three months there he could save only Rs. 2000 with which he gave his daughter in marriage.

In Bhangabari (Bhawanipatna) village Karmukanda and meat pigeon and duck flesh eating (especially by women) are popular.

In Forests

Podapadar (Thuamul Rampur) is located is Dharamgarh plateau. Here, none of the tribal family, the author is found dependent. (In other words, all the persons were above 10 years old.) Every one works at least on the *dongar.* Many items the villages consume are not purchased from market. Instead those are prepared by hand after being procured from the freely available material of forest. (For example *Kusum oil, tola oil,* dried mango stones, leave fry, root curry, fish curry, *chakhna* etc.) Household expenditure are done on 'daily earn and consume basis'. Villagers do not have the concept of 'monthly expenditure'. *Kanda* are available plenty, hence eaten during the month of scarcity.

In Chandpura of Jaypatna when sufficient labour is .ot available* people look upon forest and *dongar* as their source of income.

Paru Majhi belongs to Kond tribe. He carries a pair of wood bundles on his shoulder to the nearby town of Jaypatna and earn sixteen rupees once in a week. Besides he depends on *podu* products, viz. *kangu, koshla,* ragi, castor or *jhurang.* He borrowed paddy and ragi seeds for his *dongar* during shortage period.

It is important to note that many poor see the Government loan as free donation to meet their monthly family expenses. Pre-harvest borrowing and post-harvest repayment of loan is a common phenomenon. Loan recovery and loaning itself often takes place in the form of kinds (foodgrains, other agricultural products). The village moneylender ensures first that borrower has the capacity (mainly in the form of land) to repay the loan. Mortgaging is no more popular. Loan is advanced against production or labour. In Chandpur there is labour scarcity. So land is given the prime consideration. After nationalisation of forests poor people somehow collect *tola* seeds from *mahul* trees standing on private lands.

In Plains (Valleys)

In Degam of Kesinga Block tribes have become acculturated. Savar and Mahar tribes of this village unlike other areas seek work outside the state. This is partly in response of poor cover of forest resource in the area. After strict enforcement of 'Ceiling law' *Gauntias* have become poor. The reasons for which they

---

* Only for three months agricultural labour is available (once) in a year. Rest of the months people rush to the project area.

make half yearly migration to work in agricultural areas of more prosperous Sambalpur.

Availability of work in the agricultural fields is less in Jariguma because the field themselves are less than the tribal dominated village where most people depend on *podu chas*. After the severe drought of 1965 the economy of the entire district suffered miserably. The famine was so intense that it reduced the large farmers into medium farmers and small farmers into *sukhabasis*. These *sukhabasis* entirely depended upon labour during pre-harvest scarce period of July to December. Again during the two months of summer, the labourers engage in road building (soil carrying). Rest six to seven months of the year the landless labourers look for external labour. The time duration taken to consume the foodgrains harvested in six months for small farmers, eight to nine months for medium farmers and hardly twelve months for large farmers.

Barring day-to-day consumption extra resources are also needed for fairs, festivals, marriage birth, death (funeral) rituals etc. So farmers of all category for some period or the other depend on wage labour. There are many kinds of 'work for a labourer.' These includes *Kalantaria Bahabandha, Kalibhuti, Katti, Sahaji Bandha* etc.[14]

The natives have been using local varieties of paddy crops suiting micro-environment. There are many varieties of paddy but all fall into three main categories, the early, the medium and the late. The early varieties of paddy are sown on *Mal* and *Att* lands, the medium varieties on *Berna* lands and the late varieties on *Bahal* lands. Among *Bahal* paddy the *Jhilli puagi* and *Chinamali*, among *Berna* paddy the *Majhilli, Jhilli* and *Kakudi manji* and among the *Mal* paddy the *Kusums, Karni* and *Bausabati* are the most common in this part. The recently introduced 1,242 paddy has been found very suitable for the *Bahal* lands of the area. Kusum is a drought resistant wild variety of seed. Given during sowing and transplantation period it requires less rainwater. It can grow in dew condition.

In the hilly area of Karlapat the stream beds are cultivated with summer paddy. This is locally know as *Amdhan* as its period of cultivation corresponds with the season of mango crops. The stream beds are converted into terraced fields when the flow of water goes down and the plants are transplanted towards the end of February. The crop is generally harvested towards the end of May, the period of general food scarcity.[15]

The main sources of irrigation in this area are *Sagar, Kata, Munda, Bandha,* Wells, natural streams or springs. The undulating nature of the tract is very suitable for execution of irrigation project like *sagars* and *katas* which are formed by putting an earthen embankment across drainage area.Wells are used mainly for irrigating sugarcane fields and *baris* where vegetables are raised. The water is lifted by means of *tenda.* In specific geographic location of hill areas, natural streams and springs are used for irrigation.

Prior to abolition of *Gaunti* system, the *Gauntias* had a special responsibility with regard to construction and repair of irrigation projects their respective villages. Clause 23 of the old *Gauntia patta* enjoined on the *gauntias* to maintain the tanks and reservoirs of their village in proper, repair and distribute water to the tenants free of any charge. In practice peasants of the village communities remained responsible for the constructions, maintenance and renovation of the irrigation project (tank and wells etc.).

More or less construction of new tank or improvement of an existing one was a condition precedent to conferment of protected status on a *Gauntia* at the time of execution of agreement after the expiry of term of a settlement.[16]

The traditional sources of irrigation are thus tanks, wells etc. The District Gazetteer reports that tanks occur in almost every village. Apart form private tanks a large number of tanks are in government possession. These tanks vary from less than a hectare to about forty hectares in area. They are generally classified as *Kata, Sagar, Bandh* and *Sara.* The tanks are chiefly used for bathing, drinking, pisciculture, and irrigation purposes depending on the popular needs of the locality. The organisation of water reservoirs for drinking and irrigation purposes witnessed a major change after the incoming of Britishers. With the different sources of irrigation being owned by government and with the creation of private property in land, the construction and maintenance of water system was left with the government.

In the absence of reinvestment of the revenue collected by the government for developing such water sources and with the changing property relationship within the village preventing the organisation of village community as a whole for the development of these sources of water, the existing sources were left in the bad shape and were no longer able to come to the rescue of the community in conditions of scarce rainfall, leading to recurring drought and famines.[17] Let's now prepare the village profiles for knowing villagers adjustment in specific villages. Though the following approach seems to be sociological, it engulfs geographical circumstances. It presents gloomy picture of poverty and the way different village communities strive to overcome the difficulties.

Village Profiles

Rengopali lies nearthe tall Niyamgiri hill, which is densely forested. The village is home of forty families (about 450 people), of which only six are scheduled castes. The rest are Manjhi *Kandha* tribes. Ten families own about eight acres of land each. The rest have two (given by the Government). Almost all the land is rocky and unfit for cultivation. There is no irrigation, not even tube wells. Whatever little, paddy is coaxed out of the stones with the help of the rain is enough for barely two months. This, *mandia* and *Kusala* the villagers grow see them through three months. For about a month every year work is available in the farm of Lanjigarh landlords. The wage is either Rs. 10 in cash or 1.5 kg. of rice a day. For the rest of the year, *i.e.* eight months Rangopali folk depend on the forest for food roots, tubers bamboo shoots, leaves *(kaler sag* and mushrooms come in handy).

The government's Kutia Kandh Development Agency (KKDA) has tried to make showpiece of the village by giving seeds and fertilisers to a few who own land beside the approach road (actually a cart track). The small potato patches and a papaya tree are two reminders of the KKDA bounty create a false impression of agricultural prosperity.[18]

Maskapadar village of Lanjigarh has 68 households. 19 of them are of SCs, five Lahura and rest belong to Kandha tribe.

Twelve families do not own any land. The rest do, but the maximum with any family is 10 acres (about 4 hectares). This is only equivalent to two acres of cultivable land, for the soil is rocky and for every acre that can be farmed, four are fallow. There is no irrigation ... There is a single rice crop. Some *mandia* (a variety of millet known as ragi in some part of the country) and vegetables such as *Biri* and *Kusala* are grown.

The rice lasts two months at the most. The other crops are sold for a bit of hard cash. This fetches between Rs. 100 and Rs. 200 an acre. Another source of income is forest from which firewood is cut (illegally) and sold at Lanjigarh, 5 km away at Rs. 10 for a 20 kg load. Road repairs and other work under contractors, when it is at all available fetch Rs. 15 a day against the statutory minimum wage of Rs. 25.

Cash earned thus, is used to buy a bowl of rice. While a family of 10 needs 5 kg a day, one kg is all that can be afforded, that is when there is cash at all. It is eaten with salt, a little turmeric and home made *tol* (*mahua* seed) oil. Even this is not available for the later of the year, and the people of Maskapadar subsist on *mandia* gruel and boiled *kanda* (wild roots) taken with salt. Of course, they cannot dream of milk, eggs, fish or meat.[19]

Bengaon lies 26 km. from Biswanathpur (the block headquarter of Lanjigarh). The area which falls under four *panchayats* with a total population of about 30,000 remains cut off from the block headquarters for about four months every year because of the swollen hill streams.

The people are predominantly Kutia Kandh (tribals) who own no land. The area is hilly, but whatever land is there in the valleys and plains is in the hands of about a dozen landlords. The tribals have to depend on *podu* (shifting cultivation on hill slopes) for survival. This leads to endless harassment from the Forest Department *Podu* has destroyed much of the forest in the area. Mandia and certain indigenous vegetables such as *Kusala, Kating, Kandul* and *arhar* are grown. These sustain the Kandhas for four months – September through December as different crops mature at intervals of two weeks to a month in this period. These crops are also source of cash.

Some people get work with a landlords, each of whom employs 50 to 60 labourers for a month and a half, for a kilogram of rice or Rs. 5 in cash a day. Work under IRDP, RLEGP and so on is negligible. As for contractors they pay Rs. 20 against the government rate of Rs. 31.05 per 100 cubic feet of earth dug. But this work is also hard to get. As a result, there is no work of any kind for about eight months a year.

In the four good months of the year, the daily consumption of a typical Kandha family of the area comprising nine adults and six children of varying ages is rice 2 kg, *mandia* 1 kg (one of the local), *dals* 200 gms, mahua seed oil 150 gm, 50 gm of salt and some Mahua liquor. In the lean season jungle roots such as *bhat kanda* and *cherenga* are boiled and eaten with salt.

Nigjhari is under Sagada *panchayat*, about 14 km form Bhawanipatna, the district headquarter. The village has 70 families, of which 10 are scheduled caste and the rest Gond tribals. All but seven families are landless. The *Gauntia* that is, village headmen who stays at Bhawanipatna owns 150 acres (according to the villages). They sell firewood from the forest. Three days of hard work yields between Rs. 10 and Rs. 20. They also work as farm labour. Sometimes when they have cash, they cook 2 kg of rice for a day and eat it with salt, turmeric and leaves picked from forest. There is no oil, *dal* or spices. When such luxuries as rice cannot be afforded, they starve or eat boiled roots.

Half of the people of Borda migrate to Sambalpur (Orissa), Raipur and Durg (both in M.P.) and even as far as Kota (Rajasthan). The reasons are simple. Farm work is available only between July and September and again for a month (of harvest time) in December. No other employment is available in the area. In nearby Borohata village 45 of the 60 families have migrated in search of work.

Khasbahal is a large village in Khariar block of Nawapada sub-Division. It has about 400 Shahar (a hunting tribal families) 38 tribal Kond families, 60 scheduled caste families, 30 Patel families (General caste), one Gour family (General caste) and three Brahmin families. Here, half the families are landless of the rest majority have one or two acres each. The *gauntia*, Nimananda Shabar, has 10 acres. Here, too people are without work for eight months a year. The hills around Khasbahal are bare. They provide no sustenance. Hence, sometimes as many as

400 families migrate to Raipur, Bhilai, and other place, either the bread winner alone or entire families. But not all migrants are landless. Most plots are too small to feed, their own families. So, 'landed' people also have to look for work in distant cities.

Conclusion

Forest is well known for the resource base of food, fuel, shelter, fodder and medicine. When nature is harsh (especially when there is drought) people take refuge in it. When the situation becomes normal, *i.e.* monsoon is favourable people supplement their living with forest produce in the region of mixed physical base.

In the plains, people's dependence on agricultural lands is almost total since land is the major resource base here. Unlike forests the serious problem here is late outbreak or failure of monsoon, which is a hindrance for good cropping. The farmers of small land holding depend on the big landlords and offer their labour. The landless labourers outmigrate in search of work. Experience shows that through the adoption of traditional varieties of seeds, suitable for less watered lands and conventional methods of water utilisation, people can easily overcome the impact of dryness. However, due to some reason or the other, Kalahandi farmers have abandoned the traditional methods of farming.The conventional village tanks which were once major source of irrigation are left in derelict condition.

In hilly areas of rich forests, tribals dependence on forest is absolute. From daily food, fodder, fuel to materials for home construction, medicinal herbs and in numerous other ways they are dependent on the natural vegetative growth. The study enumerates a number of ways in which people's life is intricately associated with the nature. *Podu,* though less productive is essential for tribal survival. Our arguments go in favour of shifting cultivation, though its large scale practice had definitely negative environmental repercussion. Today, since the deforestation is widespread, forest policy is anti-tribal, afforestation remains a mere paper exercise, restrictions on the age old users are more stringent. So, the natives have been forced to quit their own adaptive methods of survival.

Because of man-made chaos produced by the so called development and outside agencies, all the survival strategies have in fact, turned into suicidal strategies.

NOTES

1. Nayak, P. K. and Mahajan, A., *Human Encounter with Drought, op.cit.*, pp. 21 and 31.
2. *Misra Commission Report, 1989, op. cit*, p. 25.
3. *Harijan* young men who are intelligent and travel outside lure the unemployed local labourers to go outside the state, and these *Harijan* boys work as *dalals* and during the drought period when people find no employment they left their villages in groups and wnt to other states for work accompanying the *Harijan* boys, *ibid.*, p. 36.
4. *Ibid.*, p. 36.
5. Dash, J., *Impact of Drought on Agricultural Production, Forest Utilisation and Migration, op.cit.*, pp. 74-76.
6. Behera, B., *Gadajata Kalahandira Kathamali,* Kalahandi Utsav Service Centre, Rourkela.
7. *Final Report on the survey and settlement of the Kashipur, Karlapat, Mahulpatna and Madanpur Rampur Ex-zamindaries in the district of Kalahandi,* 1963 by Sri Sundarrajan, I.A.S., settlement officer, Sambalpur Major Settlement, p. 5.
8. Dash, J. (1991), *Impact of Drought on Agricultural Production, Forest Utilisation and Migration, op.cit.* pp. 74-75.
9. About 1 lakh residents of Kalahandi district of Orissa, most of them *Gaurs,* SCs and STs have settled down in Raipur town of M.P. cr eating a slum which is known as *Raipur Ki Narak* (the hell of Raipur) Mishra, M. K., *Drought picture in the folklore of Kalahandi., op.cit.*, p. 21.
10. Sainath, P. "Carry 2 tons of bricks, take home Rs. 9 : Faces of Poverty", article published in *The Times of India,* New Delhi, 26th April, 1994, p. 22.
11. Dash, J., *Impact of Drought on Agricultural Production, op. cit.* pp. 52-90.
12. Mishra, M. K., *Drought picture in the folklore and folklife of Kalahandi.* II, *op.cit.*, p. 4.
13. Jenamani, S. (1992), "Environmental ethics and development : Experience of forest dwellers of Kalahandi", paper presented at the National symposium on environmental ethics and development styles, New Delhi, 1st to 3rd March. pp. 3-7.
14. Mishra, M., 'Kalahandira Sampratika Samasya', 1989, an Oriya article in the local daily, *'The Samaj'*, 19th February, 1989.
15. *Final Report on Survey and Settlement,* Kalahandi, *op.cit.*, pp. 28 and 29.
16. *Ibid.*, p. 35.
17. Hutasan, P., Rao, R. S. and Tripathi, P. K., "Drought and Poverty a Report from Kalahandi", *Economic and Political Weekly,* 2 November 1985. Vol. XX, No. 44, p. 1860.
18. Ray, T. (1992) : "Kalahandi's trauma, starvation and death yet again", in *Frontline,* 10 April, 1992, p. 77.
19. *Ibid.*

10

SUMMARY AND CONCLUSIONS

That there is a paucity, even of efforts to evolve theoretical constructs, is borne out by the review of literature with which the author initiated this presentation. The attempt of this thesis has been to highlight backwardness and explore causes of deprivation and its interfaces in a geo-analytic framework in drought prone Kalahandi. This concluding chapter offers a general model, with a fundamental concern for the well-being of people especially, the poor and intends to engineer socio-regional change for them. The work uncovers that given the variations in location, topography, soil quality, water availability and vegetation etc. which prevail among and within micro regions, even equal socio-economic conditions can go with very unequal levels of deprivation. Hence, poverty is not merely a function of socio-economic characteristics but also that of geographic characteristics.

At the outset, we have depicted how the district continues to remain a backward area in a backward state of Orissa despite its large quantities and fine qualities of soil, water and forest wealth. It ranks far behind the major regions of India in terms of economic development. This is indicated by the following points which includes : (i) place of Orissa in Indian Economy, (ii) state level development gap between the Eastern and Western Orissa, and (iii) Kalahandi in the socio-economic milieu of the state. Existing data shows that the state continues to be one of the poorest and extremely underdeveloped regions of India even after fifty years of planning era. Within Orissa there is gross disparity in development. Its western parts comprising districts of Sambalpur, Bolangir and Kalahandi has been neglected by the powers of the state. The inter district and intra district comparison further shows the aggravated condition of backwardness.

The chapter on conceptualisation is devoted to the meaning, approaches and literature review of poverty and underdevelopment. Comprehending the relationship between the two main concepts, the author defines poverty as a condition of relative deprivation measured in terms of assets, income, food intake (nutrition), clothing, housing, education, health, infrastructure and social participation which arise within a static geographic unit of natural resource distribution and due to a dynamic process of production relation, supported by strong institutional foundation.

The third chapter on 'Area of Study and Methodology' describes the physical and human attributes which are related to the issues of underdevelopment. It mentions how the study has been conducted at two levels, viz. (a) Development zones in the districts, and (b) the poverty regions within the district. The researcher relies on secondary sources of data and composite development index for the delineation and analysis of the former zones.

The poverty analysis has been performed through region-delineation by superimposition, village selection by stratified systematic random sampling method, questionnaire survey, computerised tabulation, chi square test and correlation, field observation, secondary source-materials' interpretation and above all, logical derivations.

The major findings of the work with their chapterwise sequence are the following:

The least developed part is the thickly forested, mountainous and tribal dominated South Eastern Kalahandi. The most developed part, on the other hand is a fertile and well cultivated tract, occupied by prosperous cultivators, businessmen and traders. The sub-micro region which lie in between the regions of high and low underdevelopment has medium developmental index conforming to its mixed natural character (partly hilly, partly forested and partly plain). This transitional strip is also a geographic belt of class interaction.

Institutional structures are conducive for a very small group of higher stratum of society and restrictive for a large chunk of weaker population. The present day Kalahandi still retains the basic mechanism and characteristics similar to colonial economy, though outwardly, the agents of its interacting groups have changed completely.

About a century ago, rice along with millets and pulses of varied kinds were raised on the hill slopes and the plains. The systematic production of rice was started in the late nineteenth century when the local king encouraged *Kulta* agriculturalists to migrate from the plains of Sambalpur. The tribes were pushed into hilly forested uplands. The marginalisation of tribals was aggravated with the arrival of caste people from costal Orissa (who were to man the official machinery of the royal administration in pre-Independence period and state government during post-Independence period).

The costal Orissan people who turned to be landlords, moneylenders, distillers and governmental officials constituted the new ruling elites of the districts.

During the sixties there was influx of less competent group of population of more developed and higher density areas of India in Kalahandi to occupy free and abundant resources with purely exploitative purpose. They deprived and exploited the native habitants who in turn were gradually pushed out of their own region.

The non-farm sector is, by and large, left unexploited or neglected and thus the rural regions were rendered incapable of absorbing the work force. As a result of this there was increase in propensity of horizontal migration of the work force. It was noticed that each of the large outmigration streams of weaker section follows drought and extensive crop failure.

What causes one category of region rather than another to command larger resources and what enables one group of population not another to control the economy and destiny of rest of the weaker sections of the region, is that what constitute the other theme of the chapter on 'Production Relation in Rural Kalahandi'. Class relationship and socio-political power influence access to materials of life (food, clothing etc.). The political economy over space throws light on the concealed issues of structure and culture and provides an compromising explanation of the contradictions in the development process of the district. No doubt there is spatio-temporal inadequacy of food from the so called plough cultivation. But the food and other life materials collected from the forest and *dongar* by and large compensate the scarcity. Extensive accumulative – export/out-flow system of foodgrains or other natural resources (forest and *dongar* products) coupled with absence of any systematic distributive system create a general condition of food crisis in Kalahandi. Whether in the form of facilitating resource drain off or in the form of preventing resource distribution or in the form of deep rooted traditions and customs that restrains tribes from being beneficiaries of government programmes, institutions play a major role in controlling the intensity of poverty.

As the purchasing power of a person depends on his socio-cultural status as well as mode of production in the economy one has to take into account political economy of production and distribution relations. We have found that the poor landless SCs and STs pass on their life in hunger. There are food surplus as well as food scarcities in the same district, thus exposing regional disparities and the unequal distributive system. Amongst the three broad resource regions, the 'predominantly hilly-cum-forested region' and 'predominantly cultivable plain region' have high and low poverty areas respectively. The region of mixed resource base exhibit varied intensities of poverty. That means extent of poverty and its operating factors varies within a single administrative unit.

In the 'predominantly hilly-cum-forested region', we find the son of the soil is treated as a secondary citizen in his very forest habitation. Elitist approach rather blames him for deforestation. Whether it is governmental or non-governmental institution the protectors have always been open exploiters. Natural vegetation belongs to the local inhabitants, first. But their natural as well as statutory rights have been snatched away by various institutional elements in production relation. The traders, contractors, forest department remain at the root of this system siphoning off the forest products through various mechanisms and processes.

A particular caste-class group has never retained plain land, the basic resource. What invariably has occurred in the 'predominantly cultivable plain region' is that there is no change in the status of the 'deprived' sections (scheduled tribes and weaker scheduled castes) who suffer persistent hunger. Though through institutional interventions attempts have been made to improve the economic conditions of the district and the poor, the efforts have only altered the agents of exploitation without changing the very process of exploitation. Thus, we find in the early period Konds were replaced by *Kultas* who became the traditional *Gauntias* after Gonds and Majhis. Other subsequent castes and religious groups (such as *Brahmins,* Muslims, local *Gauds* and *Malis)* enjoyed the privilege of being *Gauntias*. The historic events like *Kulta* inmigration, Land Ceiling Act of the government did not bring radical change but merely changed the ownership without providing the poorer section their legitimate powers. The whole process also gave birth to not only marginal and small farmers but also landless labourers and created vulnerable situation for new land holders of SCs and STs. The outlet for some poor and SCs was outmigration. But for the rest of the low landed and landless group it remains a sad tale of continuing deprivation.

The transitional area of mixed geographic properties possesses varied population groups. The typical and tenure system assumed importance because of constant influx of population both from within and without. Rich class has better adaptation in the event of a drought and crop failure since they possess better quality and big holdings. The poorer class become the worse sufferer as they face the problem of both crop failure (somctimes even land loss) and reduced work availability. Areas with its double resource base (land and forest) and varying population types exhibit multiple production relation and so less intense poverty.

Because of inaccessibility exploitation is minimum in the deep interiors of hilly-cum-forest region. (However, suction is high in accessible parts of the region). It is maximum in plain land, which produces bulk of the foodgrains, with better transport facilities. The exploiters in the former are mainly forest employees, contractors , SCs *(doms),* while those in the later are traders, politicians, government employees, village headmen. Obviously, the mixed resource region has both categories of exploiters.

Our study has shown nearly one-half of the total families of the district are poor. There is a positive and significant relationship between land size, quality of land, income from land and magnitude of poverty. This is specifically true for scheduled tribes. Households having low land income depend upon marginal earnings of sale of manually processed agricultural products and sale of forest products. This necessitates involvement of family members in labour and higher wage earning works. This reduces poverty. Larger nonworking-member families engage themselves in more labour intensive works outside the region and work at more than one place of work. Again, we have noted that higher dependency increases poverty. Thus, for some poor families it becomes a vicious circle. Poverty breeding poverty. Further higher dependency compels more family members to go for labour. Sex ratio is high in the district. So, more and more females join the wage labour as the number of dependent children increases in the family. Unfortunately, with increasing income more spending is incurred on liquor or other intoxicants. Thus, these three variables, *viz.* dependent persons, working members and intoxicant expenditure keep the per capita food expenditure at a level of stability. For poor labourers per capita food expenditure becomes lower and it becomes higher for better off labourers.

Poor households in general spend less on intoxicants and clothing. However, as there is rise in their income, expenditure on these consumption items also increases.

Land and labour constitute the single most important controlling variables of poverty.

Conventional economists strongly believe that gross economic controllers, *viz.*, land ownership, water supply and labour are central to the issue of poverty and as such poverty is basically an economic phenomenon. It is true that the basic facts or figures used to measure poverty and its fundamental correlates such as non-working population, proportion of marginal farmers and irrigation facilities (as used for this very study) are organically economic. But these factors themselves do not exhaustively explain serious deprivations leading to situations like starvation and starvation deaths.

The present study establishes that certain geographic factors, directly or indirectly, impinge upon poverty through regional or local conditions. It is noticed that the size of landholding and percentage of marginal farmers are important variables of poverty. However, in this study geographical factors such as location, terrain (or topographic conditions), site, slope, water availability and soil quality explain production relations and regional poverty in a better and convincing way.

Again, it is neither non-working population nor labourer to dependent population ratio but accessibility of the area to place of work, migrating distance, relative wage rate and soil productivity are another set of dominant factors of poverty.

Along with government provided irrigation facilities, local level topographic-drainage conditions, underground water availability and their exploitation through traditional and informal methods of irrigation, *i.e.* tanks, ponds, *chuha,* wells, *nalas,* streams, springs, *bandhas, katas,* have special significance for a backward and drought prone district like Kalahandi. Moreover, forests, which are region and location specific, also contribute towards income generation of a family in the forest and hilly region of Kalahandi. They change the nature of poverty by easing its severity and breaking its perpetuity. Thus, it is geographic and local ecological set-up which makes a cultivating and labourer class vulnerable to the unfulfilment of primary human needs (food, clothing and shelter) before the basic economic aspects influence acute starvation or poverty.

Sixth chapter looks into economic laws, which are independent of space whereas the seventh chapter establishes spatial law, independent of economics. Both the types of laws have validity only in a limited ways. Neither of them is absolute.

Governmental effort to encourage plough cultivation in plains replacing *podu chas* which is multi-cropped (growing millets, pulses, *niger* and local oilseeds), ecologically suitable, culturally compatible and economically viable for local inhabitants, has proved to be counter productive.

No doubt, the measures taken by the government and NGOs have improved the conditions of the poor but their benefits are limited to specific accessible regional and social groups. Hundreds of crore of money have been poured into Kalahandi through a plethora of special projects apart from normal development programmes. Central and State Governments have done their best to assist Kalahandi to combat poverty. Despite this people have suffered hunger and starvation deaths. So, it is not directly the Central and State Governments but the district administration responsible for such state of affairs. Investigation of improper planning hurried and wasteful spending, faulty execution of projects further reveal the fund leakage, fraud, and misuse of funds in anti-poverty schemes. There is hardly any perceptible change in poverty.

Barring the previous chapter on 'Governmental Programme Evaluation' where we found too low is the impact of the programme to meaningfully conduct a study on space variation in 'success rate', rest other chapters exhibit interesting linkages.

Amongst the three broad ecological micro regions, we have three corresponding sets of : (a) Levels of Development, (b) Varieties of Production Relation, and (c) Levels of Poverty.

In chapter 9, we describe how forest is well known for the resource base of food, fuel, shelter, fodder and medicine. When nature is harsh (especially when there is drought) people take refuge in it. When the situation becomes normal, *i.e.* monsoon is favourable people supplement their living with forest produce in the region of mixed physical base.

In the plains, people's dependence on agricultural lands is almost total since land is the major resource base here. Unlike forests the serious problem here is late outbreak or failure of monsoon, which is a hindrance for good cropping. The farmers of small land holding depend on the big landlords and offer their labour. The landless labourers outmigrate in search of work. Experience shows that through the adoption of traditional varieties of seeds, suitable for less watered lands and conventional methods of water utilisation, people can easily overcome the impact of dryness. However, due to some reason or the other, Kalahandi farmers have abandoned the traditional methods of farming. The conventional village tanks, which were once major source of irrigation are left in derelict condition.

In hilly areas of rich forests, tribals dependence on forest is absolute. From daily food, fodder, fuel to materials for home construction, medicinal herbs and in numerous other ways they are dependent on the natural vegetative growth. The study enumerates a number of ways in which people's life is intricately associated with the nature. *Podu,* though less productive is essential for tribal survival. Our arguments go in favour of shifting cultivation, though its large scale practice had definitely negative environmental repercussion. Today, since the deforestation is widespread, forest policy is anti-tribal, afforestation remains a mere paper exercise, restrictions on the age old users are more stringent. So, the natives have been forced to quit their own adaptive methods of survival.

Because of man-made chaos produced by the so called development and outside agencies, all the survival strategies have in fact, turned into suicidal strategies.

The author, before conceiving a model would like to give the following suggestions to the district and State Government.

Poor and landless people who depend on 'market economy' for their basic requirement are not directly benefited by the programmes emphasizing on increasing productivity of food crops. Any policy that raises their purchasing power must be encouraged.

Therefore, poor should be empowered. Kalahandi experience says that this is not possible through mere distribution of resources among the poor. State aided cooperative self-organisations could be the right way for not only building a survival strategy but also for preserving human dignity.

Kalahandi like other underdevelopment parts of India presents a picture of plenty amidst poverty. Access to productive assets and food is not uniform over the region. This demands a comprehensive plan for equitable and balanced development. The long process of underdevelopment and short-term determinants of famine must be dealt with separately but organically. Neither increase in production alone nor mere "distribution is the ultimate solution. Diversification of the economy (*i.e.* development of various sections of the economy) would not only increase production but would also ensure better distribution by raising employment (work) generation. By acquiring higher purchasing power, poor can get better access to basic needs (like food, clothing and shelter).

Merely 9.22 per cent of the net sown area (NSA) of the district is under irrigation. One hopeful and encouraging fact is that the ground water table in Kalahandi is only 15 to 30 feet deep under the earth. However, irrigation through village tanks has been left in derelict and abandoned condition in many villages. No longer they receive any care by village or *Panchayats* or the Government who earlier used to look after them. There is an urgent need of large number of small dams to optimize the use of a surface and underground water.

Government should take appropriate measures for the effective implementation of projects and programmes in providing service infrastructure. Officers of proven good records, dedicated to public services be placed in the administration and they should have fixed tenure of at least 4 years to effectively oversee the implementation of schemes. What we need today is committed political animators, responsible scholars, dedicated activists, extension workers, imaginative pedagogues and best professionals. Self-transformation will bring transformation in the whole population and the whole area. It is not the ecological degradation but the moral and ethical degradation seems to be the root cause of the problem of poverty and underdevelopment.

Mere generation of labour employment by projects would not control poverty. There must be generation of economy. Improved irrigation, a change from mono cropping to double cropping, with a second crop that does not require much water, detailed soil survey, improved transport may be prescribed for the districts development. There is no industry in the districts capable of absorbing the vast labour force. From agriculture and agricultural wastes, agro industries must be set-up in such a manner so that the people of an ecological area becomes self-sufficient in food and work. (Based on Misra Commission Report, *op.cit.*, p.75.)

There is always a big gap between 'Inner intention' and 'Outward practice'. This explains why all the noble institutions made so far has ultimately acted against man and have turned into means of anti-development rather than development.

The economy of these districts would continue to depend on agriculture for a long time to come.

Following methods may be adopted to ensure access of poor to productive resources and work.

Expansion of privileged minority would provide gradual access to ever larger sections of society, who are poor and deprived.

This can be possible if we diversify various sections of the economy looking to local geography, local resources and local knowledge. The over dependence of poor on land and forest, concentrated power of the landed gentry and forest traders can be gradually reduced.

Kalahandi's economy is primarily 'primary' in nature. The secondary and tertiary sectors have to be well flourished and integrated. They can provide more job opportunities to larger sections of various regions of the society. In doing so at least the problem of food scarcity and starvation can be solved. With diversification of the economy the purchasing power of the people can be increased, which in turn would enable them to buy food that is available plenty in the market. Infrastructure should be laid down thoroughly. However, all these technical solutions may not last long. For a permanent solution a kind of spiritual and ethical reform against exploitation seems to be the need of the hour.

The new model envisions 'Entitlement to the Poor' and 'Diversification of the Economy' as the two essential entities for "Area specific target group oriented Human Resource Development" (see Fig. 10.1). The focus is here, on the poor, who should not be viewed as objects of pity requiring charitable handouts, but as dis-empowered folk needing empowerment. The lines dividing common property, individual property and property for governmental use must be demarcated. Peoples right to own common resources (land, forest and water) must be recognised before diversifying economy. Once the deprived gains direct and uninterrupted control over the basic (developed) resources, he ensures not only food but also employment (work) for himself. Employment raises purchasing power and thus poor is empowered. From here other vital spheres of life such as education, health, leadership training through political consciousness and NGO building can be improved.

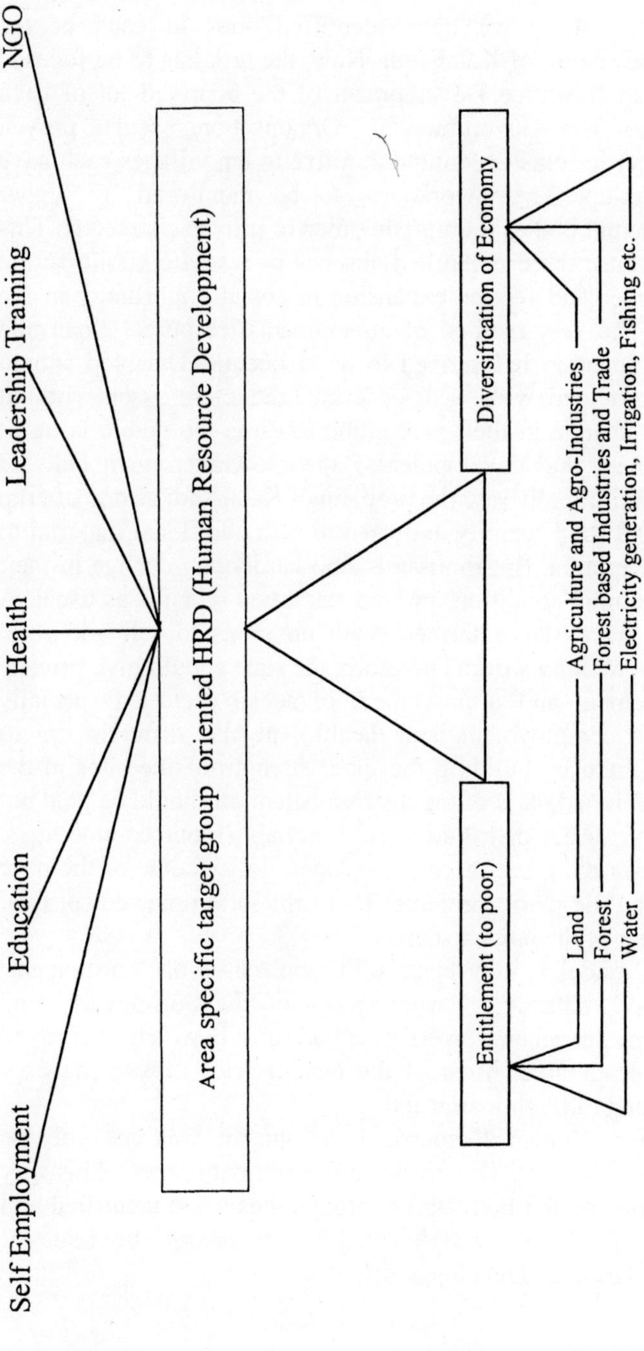

Fig. 10.1 : Development model prescribed for poverty-stricken and under-developed regions

In this study we have identified poor in each of the ecological region of Kalahandi. Now, the task has to be focused on Human Resource Development of the deprived lot of each eco-area. Non-Governmental Organisations (of proven efficiency) for clusters comprising five to ten villages each have to be set-up. Their work has to be monitored by higher governmental bodies (comprising men of proven character). This is so because there is marked absence of resolute public action for the poor and for the expansion of social opportunity in the district. The very method of governmental resource ('loan and asset') allocation has proved to be erroneous. Disabled should not be provided with cash or even productive assets without ensuring change in their perception towards the whole issue of development and developmental agency. Government and aid donors traditionally saw the problem of Kalahandi as one of crop failure and food scarcity and tried to rush additional material to the stricken area. But thousands find hardly any change in their own economic condition, instead starvation remains as usual. A drought leaves large farmers with no crops to sell and rural labourers with no work. Therefore, the state should give priority to entitlement and improvement of social sectors (especially education, employment and health) in the different micro regions, there by building the inner strength of the poor in the underdeveloped parts of the district. Attention should be paid not merely on direct distribution of materials (food, commodities, assets, loan etc.), but more on replacing lost income of the poor through public works projects. This calls for a renewed spiritual awakening of the human society.

This model is new because it emphasises on 'entitlement' instead of 'subsidy'. Earlier, most of the anti-poverty and developmental schemes were based on subsidy which has proved counter productive. Most of the beneficiaries misuse the easy cash gained through loan waiving.

Earlier, Human Resource Development was part of the whole development. There was no specificity of 'area'. This very model intends that both 'target groups' has to be identified and 'specific area' has to delineated before taking the issue of 'Human Resource Development'.

APPENDICES

APPENDICES

APPENDIX TO CHAPTER - 1

COMPARATIVE DEVELOPMENT INDICATORS

Indicator	Kalahandi	Orissa	India
DEMOGRAPHIC			
Urbanisation (%)	6.0	11.8	23.3
Decennial Growth Rate (1981-91)	16.7	19.5	23.5
Sex Ratio (1991)	1,000	972	929
Child Mortality Rate (Q2)	148	148	123
SOCIAL			
Literacy Rate (T)	19.4	48.5	52.1
Literacy Rate (F)	7.7	34.4	39.4
S.C. Population (%)	15.7	14.7	15.7
S.T. Population (%)	31.2	22.4	7.8
S.T. Female Workers	–	–	–
Participation Rate	14.9	19.8	28.8
Beds/lakh population	48	50	74
AGRICULTURE			
Agriculture Laboureres (%)	35.6	27.7	–
Consumption of Fertilizer Per hectare of Gross Cropped Area (kgs)	5.4	21.7	–
Percentage of irrigation Potential created to net area sown	13.1	30.5	–
Percent forest area	48.9	35.4	–
ECONOMIC			
Population below poverty line (%)	–	44.7	29.9

Source : Government Documents, 1991.

APPENDIX TO CHAPTER – 1

IMPORTANT VARIABLE SOF DISTRICTS OF ORISSA
ANIMAL HUSBANDRY

Sl. No.	Name of the Districts	Hospitals & Dispensaries (No.) (2000-01)	A.I. Centres (No.) (2000-01)	Live Stock, 1995 Census (in number)									Production 2000-01		
				Buffalo	Cattle		Cows		Sheep	Goat	Poultry	Pig	Milk (in '000 MT)	Egg (Mil. No.)	Meat (in MT)
					Crossbreed	Indigenous	Crossbreed	Indigenous							
		(1)	(2)	(3)	(4)	(5)	(6)	(7)	(8)	(9)	(10)	(11)	(12)	(13)	(14)
1.	Angul	16	40	51269	25521	495925	19332	254965	58865	195151	246040	1863	16.82	15.24	3219.38
2.	Balasore	21	78	7180	47879	864952	28866	399551	7407	332059	782114	13794	50.59	35.63	2268.20
3.	Baragarh	19	37	39191	69370	443822	41844	174027	47607	111264	377842	7456	46.80	21.45	635.65
4.	Bhadrak	13	57	14213	21295	528840	12971	240945	6756	152121	312667	3348	34.18	30.83	2332.22
5.	Bolangir	21	49	117014	23937	575146	14293	253439	161596	269796	741613	1894	21.80	27.37	2117.29
6.	Boudh	7	35	35609	4835	227045	2974	110441	59027	69612	203905	3053	10.45	14.95	315.54
7.	Cuttack	25	125	62516	79000	561966	61575	299434	108303	190181	302821	3856	61.12	48.70	9836.50
8.	Deogarh	4	4	21094	1648	179691	1330	83517	6029	87450	181943	5870	7.79	13.10	265.23
9.	Dhenkanal	18	39	75075	19621	467597	13673	239350	55883	154198	215575	3996	29.21	25.48	1179.83
10.	Gajapati	11	15	18140	5163	267608	2515	103913	11773	106364	346164	19680	14.37	8.12	457.30
11.	Ganjam	37	98	151874	17721	1011646	11911	558043	135735	216375	1470193	11944	56.15	142.40	1838.34
12.	Jagatsinghpur	13	77	15804	75160	362671	54948	166307	49765	91805	246701	3933	72.70	8.10	1527.38
13.	Jajpur	19	32	11932	10828	623194	8242	328091	45360	210037	421958	6539	30.43	14.12	2588.31
14.	Jharsuguda	9	13	21209	5866	187478	4484	81810	6630	46577	176264	5212	18.55	11.35	855.15
15.	Kalahandi	21	38	125945	14505	525785	10404	229415	112588	217303	692683	7582	26.16	29.72	576.20
16.	Kandhamal	20	29	76230	2435	306332	1693	124212	7336	193685	540833	56293	9.59	29.75	1083.80
17.	Kendrapara	14	36	22148	20630	450472	14720	232995	42644	110644	159255	2053	18.32	16.37	2419.11
18.	Keonjhar	23	41	37851	32307	663632	22761	284157	172280	360044	1096976	27255	37.95	51.18	2707.21
19.	Khurda	20	98	25452	53293	513672	41478	297949	67234	82923	595165	3195	39.50	123.00	1266.72
20.	Koraput	25	59	143271	8846	415898	7040	186221	106317	150930	717705	63276	41.13	45.81	1088.37
21.	Malkangiri	13	4	39039	1297	365499	938	163478	18513	134582	403072	57152	12.16	6.89	361.27
22.	Mayurbhanj	42	54	31233	26460	868081	19312	322851	169790	484293	2649686	70222	29.43	73.64	1431.35
23.	Nawarangpur	17	30	106961	5041	375337	3517	147294	75120	127663	595502	38870	11.48	11.68	521.32
24.	Nayagarh	16	33	62358	6876	383753	5468	213415	44974	109787	139332	172	37.44	7.52	82.31
25.	Nuapada	8	45	70232	5247	284436	1638	126021	44316	99766	183323	1254	6.01	7.17	123.47
26.	Puri	15	104	26232	106191	355191	79573	171479	87378	98012	330628	1484	53.10	19.53	379.56
27.	Rayagada	16	25	115385	2890	402549	2308	181489	35006	122952	393093	40143	26.96	29.28	576.20
28.	Sambalpur	18	63	36578	15844	413609	10766	180473	16278	151284	374055	21857	26.34	23.10	1225.88
29.	Sonepur	10	21	30086	13378	244964	8642	99329	43441	81684	202853	2545	6.70	7.27	82.31
30.	Sundargarh	30	58	60929	20756	655365	16006	268933	60863	653475	908466	86463	30.34	34.65	2638.81
	Orissa	**541**	**1437**	**1652050**	**743840**	**14022156**	**525222**	**6523544**	**1864814**	**5412017**	**16008427**	**572434**	**883.52**	**933.40**	**46000.00**

INDUSTRY – 1998-99 **FISHERY 2000-01**

Sl. No.	Name of the Districts	Annual Survey of Industries: Registered reporting factories (No.)	Total employees (No.)	Productive Capital (Rs. in'000)	Net Value added by manufacture (Rs. in lakh)	Production of fish in MT: Fresh Water	Brakish Water	Marine Water	Total
	(15)	(16)	(17)	(18)	(19)	(20)	(21)	(22)	(23)
1.	Angul	22	5308	9368333	200	5370	-	-	5370
2.	Balasore	99	8487	2071907	16932	7653	1922	34915	44490
3.	Baragarh	61	4838	6664382	4703	5956	-	-	5956
4.	Bhadrak	37	1005	2511536	(-)573	5187	1048	9350	15585
5.	Bolangir	38	2343	625718	(-)1596	3631	-	-	3631
6.	Boudh	1	23	1256	6	2475	-	-	2475
7.	Cuttack	165	10020	1505511	1428	5883	-	-	5883
8.	Deogarh	-	-	-	-	3042	-	-	3042
9.	Dhenkanal	29	3675	1800892	(-)1441	3968	-	-	3968
10.	Gajapati	2	13	727	7	1770	-	-	1770
11.	Ganjam	70	2693	197381	1010	14170	1504	6778	22452
12.	Jagatsinghpur	21	2734	5786980	3986	3784	1918	33899	39601
13.	Jajpur	24	2392	265367	438	4435	-	-	4435
14.	Jharsuguda	27	5573	2759328	(-)11453	3368	-	-	3368
15.	Kalahandi	28	1392	620317	(-)193	6812	-	-	6812
16.	Kandhamal	1	147	20091	61	745	-	-	745
17.	Kendrapara	15	172	2233026	79	3729	1167	13206	18102
18.	Keonjhar	25	3682	2381724	5732	3576	-	-	3576
19.	Khurda	211	8552	5582305	3111	4014	4251	-	8265
20.	Koraput	36	5301	1556	7862	1630	-	-	1630
21.	Malkangiri	6	92	927483	(-)28	2204	-	-	2204
22.	Mayurbhanj	41	1988	476461	(-)4379	10313	-	-	10313
23.	Nawarangpur	8	450	(-)17389	149	2013	-	-	2013
24.	Nayagarh	5	331	30486	(-)6	2100	-	-	2100
25.	Nuapada	15	417	3590	154	1361	-	-	1361
26.	Puri	24	506	59590	467	4271	1537	22940	28748
27.	Rayagada	26	4240	6294352	4287	653	-	-	653
28.	Sambalpur	93	4512	1519860	5196	3947	-	-	3947
29.	Sonepur	-	-	-	-	2906	-	-	2906
30.	Sundargarh	195	39638	70557287	60273	4148	-	-	4148
	Orissa	**1325**	**120524**	**124253057**	**96412**	**125114**	**13347**	**121088**	**259549**

OGP-MP-PTS(D.E. & S.) 26-5.000—18-12-2001

ADMINISTRATIVE SET-UP

Sl. No.	Name of the Districts	Geographical area in Sq. Kms.	No. of Sub-Divisions	No. of Tehsils	No. of CD Blocks	No. of Munici-palities	No. of NACs	No. of P.S. including Mahila P.S.	No. of G.S.P.	No. of Fire Stations	No. of Assembly Constituencies
	(1)	(2)	(3)	(4)	(5)	(6)	(7)	(8)	(9)	(10)	(11)
1.	Angul	6375	4	5	8	1	2	20	209	6	4
2.	Balasore	3806	2	7	12	1	3	19	289	7	7
3.	Baragarh	5837	2	8	12	1	2	14	248	2	5
4.	Bhadrak	2505	1	6	7	1	1	12	193	4	5
5.	Bolangir	6575	3	6	14	1	3	13	285	3	6
6.	Boudh	3098	1	2	3	-	1	6	63	3	1
7.	Cuttack	3932	3	11	14	2	2	34	342	7	10
8.	Deogarh	2940	1	1	3	1	-	4	60	2	1
9.	Dhenkanal	4452	3	6	8	1	2	11	199	9	4
10.	Gajapati	4325	1	3	7	1	1	9	129	4	3
11.	Ganjam	8206	3	14	22	1	17	26	475	12	12
12.	Jagatsinghpur	1668	1	4	8	1	1	7	195	3	4
13.	Jajpur	2899	1	6	10	2	-	11	280	3	6
14.	Jharsuguda	2081	1	2	5	2	1	9	78	3	3
15.	Kalahandi	7920	2	7	13	1	2	12	273	3	6
16.	Kandhamal	8021	2	4	12	-	2	15	153	3	3
17.	Kendrapara	2644	1	7	9	1	1	7	230	4	6
18.	Keonjhar	8303	3	8	13	3	1	20	286	7	6
19.	Khurda	2813	2	7	10	3	2	22	168	8	6
20.	Koraput	8807	2	7	14	1	3	20	226	3	4
21.	Malkangiri	5791	1	3	7	-	2	10	108	1	2
22.	Mayurbhanj	10418	4	9	26	1	3	28	382	6	10
23.	Nawarangpur	5291	1	4	10	1	1	10	169	2	4
24.	Nayagarh	3890	1	4	8	-	2	9	179	5	4
25.	Nuapada	3852	1	2	5	-	2	6	109	1	2
26.	Puri	3479	1	7	11	1	3	16	230	4	6
27.	Rayagada	7073	2	4	11	1	2	12	171	4	4
28.	Sambalpùr	6657	3	4	9	1	4	19	148	4	3
29.	Sonepur	2337	2	4	6	1	2	7	96	4	3
30.	Sundargarh	9712	3	9	17	4	-	41	262	4	7
	Orissa	**155707**	**58**	**171**	**314**	**35**	**68**	**449**	**6234**	**131**	**147**

Rainfall — **Irrigation Potential Created up to 1999-2000 (Area in 'ooo hect.)**

S. No.	Name of the Districts	No. of villages			Normal rainfall (m.m.)	Act. Rain-fall 2000 (m.m.)	Deviation from nor-mal (m.m.)	Major & Medium		Minor (Flow)		Minor (Lift)	
		In-habited	Unin-habited	Total				Kharif	Rabi	Kharif	Rabi	Kharif	Rabi
		(12)	(13)	(14)	(15)	(16)	(17)	(18)	(19)	(20)	(21)	(22)	(23)
1.	Angul	1635	287	1922	1421.1	896.5	(-) 524.6	10.76	3.24	18.77	2.67	9.37	5.62
2.	Balasore	2586	385	2971	1568.4	1492.2	(-) 76.2	20.55	7.18	6.99	3.05	34.72	20.83
3.	Baragarh	1177	31	1208	1527.0	844.1	(-) 682.9	94.06	57.06	18.67	2.87	8.44	5.07
4.	Bhadrak	1224	83	1307	1568.4	1034.1	(-) 534.3	77.71	12.00	1.27	0.06	16.60	9.96
5.	Bolangir	1761	31	1792	1443.5	813.5	(-) 630.0	7.69	0.86	1.59	3.02	8.01	4.81
6.	Boudh	1101	55	1156	1597.1	981.5	(-) 615.6	19.87	2.02	9.39	0.96	5.25	3.15
7.	Cuttack	1865	102	1967	1501.3	980.2	(-) 521.1	87.17	53.71	16.71	3.43	19.62	11.77
8.	Deogarh	697	170	867	1527.0	813.3	(-) 713.7	8.10	5.70	3.47	0.13	1.37	0.82
9.	Dhenkanal	1060	161	1221	1421.1	1011.4	(-) 409.7	16.79	7.81	19.35	3.89	9.29	5.58
10.	Gajapati	1460	116	1576	1295.6	1166.5	(-) 129.1	-	-	20.40	2.35	4.85	2.91
11.	Ganjam	2762	409	3171	1295.6	1013.4	(-) 282.2	119.93	8.13	97.12	6.80	23.02	11.62
12.	Jagatsinghpur	1207	73	1280	1501.3	829.2	(-) 672.1	26.62	17.17	-	-	8.06	4.84
13.	Jajpur	1560	221	1780	1501.3	1014.3	(-) 487.0	61.53	32.92	5.32	1.36	26.43	15.86
14.	Jharsuguda	353	3	356	1527.0	620.0	(-) 907.0	-	-	4.15	1.12	2.68	1.61
15.	Kalahandi	2068	137	2205	1378.2	1291.8	(-) 86.4	74.90	2.43	19.69	4.50	10.00	6.00
16.	Kandhamal	2336	179	2515	1597.1	1278.9	(-) 318.2	2.39	1.20	8.08	3.43	3.03	2.99
17.	Kendrapara	1389	143	1532	1501.3	873.5	(-) 627.8	62.88	40.59	0.17	-	30.14	18.09
18.	Keonjhar	2067	58	2125	1534.5	1161.3	(-) 373.2	27.90	6.09	24.97	5.18	15.35	9.21
19.	Khurda	1355	212	1567	1449.1	1208.0	(-) 241.1	43.51	25.81	16.00	1.89	6.37	3.82
20.	Koraput	1915	82	1997	1521.8	1359.4	(-) 162.4	42.18	20.65	5.87	1.52	9.37	5.62
21.	Malkangiri	878	50	928	1521.8	1296.2	(-) 225.6	66.00	18.51	1.14	0.29	1.25	0.75
22.	Mayurbhanj	3718	227	3945	1648.2	1287.1	(-) 361.1	36.96	14.04	35.71	3.46	15.18	9.10
23.	Nawarangpur	880	17	897	1521.8	1311.8	(-) 210.0	4.25	2.25	5.54	0.60	6.52	3.91
24.	Nayagarh	1511	183	1694	1449.1	1182.1	(-) 267.0	10.93	3.02	16.28	4.33	5.48	3.29
25.	Nuapada	643	16	659	1378.2	642.1	(-) 736.1	14.31	4.42	5.41	1.56	4.09	2.45
26.	Puri	1584	130	1714	1449.1	939.6	(-) 509.5	109.93	66.56	0.18	0.01	11.06	6.64
27.	Rayagada	2445	222	2667	1521.8	876.8	(-) 645.0	8.80	2.00	20.03	5.34	13.17	7.90
28.	Sambalpur	1247	78	1325	1527.0	821.3	(-) 705.7	28.95	23.00	16.04	2.01	6.10	3.66
29.	Sonepur	808	151	959	1443.5	1008.2	(-) 435.3	57.54	21.51	5.68	0.48	6.57	3.94
30.	Sundargarh	1688	56	1744	1647.6	977.2	(-) 670.4	13.46	7.48	23.04	3.69	9.15	5.49
	Orissa	**46980**	**4068**	**51048**	**1482.2**	**1034.0**	**(-) 448.2**	**1155.67**	**467.36**	**441.34**	**70.00**	**330.54**	**197.31**

POPULATION, 2001 CENSUS (PROVISIONAL)

S. No.	Name of the Districts	Males ('000 No.)	Females ('000 No.)	Total ('000 No.)	%age of District Population to State Population 2001(P)	Decennial Growth Rate (Percentage)		Sex Ratio (Females per '000 males)		Population Density (per sq. Km.)		No. of Literates ('000 No.)					
						1981-1991	1991-2001(P)	1991	2001(P)	1991	2001(P)	1991			2001(P)		
												Male	Female	Total	Male	Female	Total
(1)	(2)	(3)	(4)	(5)	(6)	(7)	(8)	(9)	(10)	(11)	(12)	(13)	(14)	(15)	(16)	(17)	(18)
1.	Angul	587	552	1139	3.10	22.31	18.55	942	941	151	179	276	132	408	414	267	681
2.	Balasore	1038	985	2023	5.51	24.96	19.24	955	949	446	532	510	297	807	728	505	1233
3.	Baragarh	681	665	1346	3.67	16.93	11.47	979	976	207	231	329	158	487	464	291	755
4.	Bhadrak	675	657	1332	3.63	23.55	20.47	985	973	441	532	340	210	550	496	361	857
5.	Bolangir	674	662	1336	3.64	15.94	8.52	981	983	187	203	290	109	399	407	224	631
6.	Boudh	188	185	373	1.02	18.35	17.45	987	985	103	120	81	28	109	121	62	183
7.	Cuttack	1208	1133	2341	6.38	19.37	14.00	922	938	522	595	677	420	1097	912	662	1574
8.	Deogarh	138	136	274	0.75	18.50	17.02	982	980	80	93	58	28	86	86	55	141
9.	Dhenkanal	543	523	[illegible]	2.90	18.92	12.46	954	962	213	239	280	156	436	382	267	649
10.	Gajapati	255	263	518	1.41	13.04	14.02	1027	1031	105	120	76	33	109	116	63	179
11.	Ganjam	1569	1568	3137	8.55	19.25	16.01	1006	1000	330	382	709	337	1046	1039	641	1680
12.	Jagatsinghpur	538	518	1056	2.88	17.98	13.15	977	962	560	633	340	225	565	424	322	746
13.	Jajpur	823	800	1623	4.42	22.01	17.08	977	973	478	560	408	258	666	591	429	1020
14.	Jharsuguda	262	248	510	1.39	21.41	15.13	938	946	212	245	130	67	197	90	128	318
15.	Kalahandi	667	667	1334	3.64	19.48	17.99	999	1000	143	168	222	72	294	353	166	519
16.	Kandhamal	323	325	648	1.76	21.69	18.60	999	1008	68	81	121	44	165	85	97	282
17.	Kendrapara	646	656	1302	3.55	17.15	13.25	1007	1014	435	492	365	246	611	489	386	875
18.	Keonjhar	790	772	1562	4.25	19.95	16.79	974	977	161	188	329	162	491	485	306	791
19.	Khurda	986	888	1874	5.11	32.67	24.79	903	901	534	666	528	333	861	769	556	1325
20.	Koraput	589	589	1178	3.21	19.93	14.41	991	998	117	134	144	64	208	234	122	356
21.	Malkangiri	240	240	480	1.31	26.00	13.71	985	996	73	83	48	20	68	82	42	124
22.	Mayurbhanj	1122	1100	2222	6.05	19.14	17.89	979	980	181	213	400	179	579	624	355	979
23.	Nawarangpur	511	507	1018	2.77	24.22	20.26	989	992	160	192	96	30	126	199	88	287
24.	Nayagarh	446	418	864	2.35	14.52	10.39	958	939	201	222	247	132	379	323	212	535
25.	Nuapada	264	266	530	1.45	19.56	13.00	1002	1006	122	138	82	25	107	131	59	190
26.	Puri	761	737	1498	4.08	18.08	14.80	970	968	375	431	430	269	699	592	441	1033
27.	Rayagada	406	417	823	2.24	17.29	15.27	1012	1029	101	116	107	46	153	158	85	243
28.	Sambalpur	472	457	929	2.53	18.47	14.17	956	970	122	140	229	121	350	324	219	543
29.	Sonepur	275	266	541	1.47	19.99	13.39	979	966	204	231	123	46	169	191	108	299
30.	Sundargarh	935	895	1830	4.98	17.62	16.26	936	957	162	188	444	250	694	609	417	1026
	ORISSA	18612	18095	36707	100.00	20.06	15.94	971	972	203	236	8419	4497	12916	12118	7936	20054

POPULATION, 2001 CENSUS (PROVISIONAL)

S. No.	Name of the Districts	Literacy Rates					
		1991			2001 (P)		
		Male (19)	Female (20)	Total (21)	Male (22)	Female (23)	Total (24`)
1.	Angul	67.66	34.32	51.53	82.02	56.01	69.40
2.	Balasore	71.23	43.40	57.64	81.75	59.57	70.94
3.	Baragarh	63.78	31.21	47.65	77.93	50.03	64.13
4.	Bhadrak	74.62	46.35	60.54	85.44	63.62	74.64
5.	Bolangir	55.64	21.30	38.63	70.36	39.27	54.93
6.	Boudh	60.61	21.01	40.98	76.86	39.78	58.43
7.	Cuttack	77.41	52.44	65.46	85.46	66.19	76.13
8.	Deogarh	59.43	29.26	44.45	73.79	47.56	60.78
9.	Dhenkanal	68.80	40.33	54.91	81.31	58.55	70.11
10.	Gajapati	41.76	17.44	29.37	55.14	28.91	41.73
11.	Ganjam	63.88	29.87	46.72	78.39	47.70	62.94
12.	Jagatsinghpur	78.27	53.05	65.77	88.96	69.94	79.61
13.	Jajpur	70.50	45.29	58.00	82.69	61.45	72.19
14.	Jharsuguda	67.29	37.11	52.73	83.04	59.23	71.47
15.	Kalahandi	46.85	15.28	31.08	62.88	29.56	46.20
16.	Kandhamal	54.68	19.82	37.23	69.98	36.19	52.95
17.	Kendrapara	76.82	50.67	63.61	87.62	67.29	77.33
18.	Keonjhar	59.04	30.01	44.73	72.53	46.71	59.75
19.	Khurda	78.74	55.39	67.72	88.38	71.06	80.19
20.	Koraput	33.98	15.15	24.64	47.58	24.81	36.20
21.	Malkangiri	28.24	11.69	20.04	41.21	21.28	31.26
22.	Mayurbhanj	51.84	23.68	37.88	66.38	38.28	52.43
23.	Nawarangpur	28.10	9.01	18.62	47.37	21.02	34.26
24.	Nayagarh	73.00	40.74	57.20	83.23	58.10	71.02
25.	Nuapada	42.31	12.78	27.52	58.78	26.01	42.29
26.	Puri	76.83	49.41	63.30	88.73	67.80	78.40
27.	Rayagada	36.53	15.63	26.01	47.35	24.31	35.61
28.	Sambalpur	65.90	36.43	51.52	78.87	54.79	67.01
29.	Sonepur	61.48	23.38	42.62	80.30	47.28	64.07
30.	Sundargarh	65.41	39.60	52.97	75.69	54.25	65.26
	ORISSA	**63.09**	**34.68**	**49.09**	**75.95**	**50.97**	**63.61**

PRODUCTION OF MAJOR CROPS (2000-01)

(Production in Qntl.)

S. No.	Name of the Districts	Paddy	Wheat	Maize	Ragi	Mung	Biri	Kulthi	Til	Ground-nut	Mustard	Potato	Jute	Sugar-cane
(1)	(2)	(3)	(4)	(5)	(6)	(7)	(8)	(9)	(10)	(11)	(12)	(13)	(14)	(15)
1.	Angul	701515	1404	7236	1115	5501	6340	6609	8955	32482	449	42246	-	93834
2.	Balasore	5794820	508	-	-	5040	2028	-	736	28606	2954	34861	6338	93840
3.	Baragarh	5392759	4088	403	32	38944	15059	1115	4080	121797	627	25234	91	689527
4.	Bhadrak	3836764	1384	-	-	3790	4450	36	14	1734	187	8617	1817	179090
5.	Bolangir	1166465	2660	2881	4727	9263	7781	23070	6754	15182	206	3078	-	774518
6.	Boudh	533476	425	4220	83	2694	1225	6893	2338	234	141	3895	-	28472
7.	Cuttack	2872276	157	837	1291	29876	35028	15666	409	15051	85	149671	23848	802725
8.	Deogarh	308962	985	2092	21	3828	2288	1075	4010	2073	160	27399	-	35824
9.	Dhenkanal	1112010	238	1385	207	2149	4229	2383	1431	42010	21	32704	30	291709
10.	Gajapati	977870	1	65024	33431	3958	4136	1649	1803	3064	203	-	-	64923
11.	Ganjam	5085053	-	7193	64339	55121	9895	3739	1113	61265	39	16370	-	1659643
12.	Jagatsinghpur	1912292	132	-	-	34073	9004	4577	80	12264	39	44012	-	114326
13.	Jajpur	1745217	313	746	-	4108	23686	3833	2	85354	75	35818	15709	111520
14.	Jharsuguda	365707	8178	33	10	480	13	60	504	990	311	8844	-	42423
15.	Kalahandi	5181757	937	11158	13228	9784	6793	10040	2702	15388	560	41	-	503455
16.	Kandhamal	620552	31	60527	1208	119	446	2094	487	3065	2742	25267	-	-
17.	Kendrapara	2019099	271	-	8	21519	40201	4853	103	41025	326	104635	15301	71445
18.	Keonjhar	3187344	14919	56443	14	517	5749	7664	464	6465	1587	22811	2553	100940
19.	Khurda	2748169	-	47	2844	17440	4731	1888	1041	4432	94	28123	-	71960
20.	Koraput	3450385	445	49817	205515	421	2085	5969	277	1210	589	21877	-	1826589
21.	Malkangiri	953932	-	10660	20666	123	711	957	7975	21593	-	-	-	8280
22.	Mayurbhanj	5906345	17235	18372	42	2837	4669	2279	287	17815	593	10924	-	296
23.	Nawarangpur	2631368	414	332322	37766	397	41083	14425	308	897	519	10640	-	327241
24.	Nayagarh	1721901	311	5567	2416	27223	6411	3165	1951	2663	450	3038	-	1453930
25.	Nuapada	482495	758	2057	2820	1507	3946	3340	676	7843	4	1065	-	7329
26.	Puri	2717617	16	-	50	5258	17704	5129	2322	19033	128	101167	12	23156
27.	Rayagada	1106918	-	42061	71818	1329	3616	3220	7579	2036	1066	4023	30	63246
28.	Sambalpur	1492598	6921	945	113	2760	2873	3210	5127	1051	1094	34663	-	30842
29.	Sonepur	2038197	1374	74	5	2151	46	2145	154	1757	3	1288	-	45915
30.	Sundargarh	1836834	64924	6552	1746	689	6330	4830	3691	6366	1231	56398	-	122154
	ORISSA	**69900697**	**129029**	**688652**	**465515**	**292899**	**272556**	**145913**	**67373**	**574745**	**16483**	**858709**	**65729**	**9639152**

LAND UTILISATION PATTERN, 1999-2000 ('000 Hect.)

S. No.	Name of the District	Forest Area	Misc. Tree, permanent pasture, Land put to Non-Agrl. Use, Barren & Uncultivable land	Cultivable Waste	Current Fallow	Other Fallow	Net Area Sown	% of Forest area of the district to the State total	% of forest area of the district
		(16)	(17)	(18)	(19)	(20)	(21)	(22)	(23)
1.	Angul	272	127	5	7	8	219	4.67	42.62
2.	Balasore	33	59	9	26	10	244	0.57	8.73
3.	Baragarh	122	110	6	14	1	331	2.09	20.83
4.	Bhadrak	10	36	11	6	7	180	0.17	3.88
5.	Bolangir	154	126	22	4	18	334	2.66	23.48
6.	Boudh	128	54	7	6	32	83	2.20	41.23
7.	Cuttack	79	103	11	20	6	174	1.35	20.04
8.	Deogarh	156	49	5	-	12	72	2.68	53.07
9.	Dhenkanal	174	38	1	21	5	206	2.99	39.03
10.	Gajapati	247	99	3	-	3	80	4.25	57.09
11.	Ganjam	315	89	11	3	8	395	5.42	38.39
12.	Jagatsinghpur	13	18	6	25	5	100	0.23	7.97
13.	Jajpur	72	17	11	12	5	173	1.25	25.02
14.	Jharsuguda	20	84	15	9	4	76	0.35	9.73
15.	Kalahandi	254	156	4	23	7	348	4.37	32.05
16.	Kandhamal	571	24	30	33	10	134	9.82	71.19
17.	Kendrapara	25	43	7	23	14	152	0.43	9.38
18.	Keonjhar	310	154	54	2	10	300	5.33	37.30
19.	Khurda	62	74	5	-	3	137	1.06	21.99
20.	Koraput	188	346	29	2	16	300	3.23	21.34
21.	Malkangiri	336	5	76	-	21	141	5.77	57.95
22.	Mayurbhanj	439	131	10	35	21	406	7.55	42.16
23.	Nawarangpur	246	23	16	-	29	215	4.24	46.55
24.	Nayagarh	208	32	7	7	9	126	3.58	53.50
25.	Nuapada	185	7	12	-	3	178	3.18	48.02
26.	Puri	14	109	15	28	18	164	0.23	3.94
27.	Rayagada	281	197	12	31	14	172	4.84	39.76
28.	Sambalpur	363	82	10	-	17	194	6.25	54.56
29.	Sonepur	41	66	8	4	7	108	0.71	17.79
30.	Sundargarh	496	98	27	4	13	333	8.53	51.04
	ORISSA	**5814**	**2556**	**445**	**345**	**336**	**6075**	**100.00**	**37.34**

EDUCATION (1999-2000)

S. No.	Name of the Districts	Primary Schools			Middle Schools			Secondary Schools			General Colleges		
		No of Schools	Enrolment ('000 No.)	No. of Teachers	No. of Schools	Enrolment ('000 No.)	No. of Teachers	No. of Schools	Enrolment ('000 No.)	No. of Teachers	No. of Schools	Enrolment ('000 No.)	No. of Teachers
(1)	(2)	(3)	(4)	(5)	(6)	(7)	(8)	(9)	(10)	(11)	(12)	(13)	(14)
1.	Angul	1235	139	3569	323	37	965	191	29	1158	46	20	614
2.	Balasore	1815	352	4849	917	77	2501	425	66	3586	72	28	966
3.	Baragarh	1429	168	3917	404	43	851	209	28	1695	58	19	633
4.	Bhadrak	1239	228	3049	522	41	1284	275	40	2314	44	18	632
5.	Bolangir	1933	177	5085	389	35	1182	205	28	1619	63	21	808
6.	Boudh	591	45	1436	111	12	283	46	7	468	11	8	193
7.	Cuttack	2177	262	5761	667	57	2055	388	68	3273	96	39	1184
8.	Deogarh	421	32	1015	113	11	254	59	7	559	22	6	246
9.	Dhenkanal	1115	135	3173	377	27	1074	217	35	1863	54	15	755
10.	Gajapati	937	62	2291	108	6	369	53	10	471	10	6	176
11.	Ganjam	2936	387	8611	695	57	1976	402	82	3120	94	35	1264
12.	Jagatsinghpur	1179	136	3049	421	40	1296	219	40	1806	45	20	684
13.	Jajpur	1516	273	4243	678	86	2066	399	74	3290	63	29	878
14.	Jharsuguda	611	57	1550	165	18	444	80	10	735	19	9	333
15.	Kalahandi	1705	153	4444	365	30	1003	192	17	1660	50	15	544
16.	Kandhamal	1519	85	3690	244	16	682	82	14	753	20	10	245
17.	Kendrapara	1430	151	3676	583	41	1790	305	61	2546	57	25	772
18.	Keonjhar	1807	202	5002	631	38	1670	385	49	3238	58	21	808
19.	Khurda	1262	172	3745	415	49	800	235	46	1982	72	33	901
20.	Koraput	1853	91	4308	236	12	524	109	22	939	25	10	315
21.	Malkangiri	898	68	1970	103	9	235	29	6	324	10	4	123
22.	Mayurbhanj	2941	256	7577	795	43	2199	437	68	3638	98	34	1282
23.	Nawarangpur	1249	106	2701	206	14	504	55	37	431	14	8	175
24.	Nayagarh	826	96	2356	274	21	755	222	12	1867	37	17	527
25.	Nuapada	731	66	1810	166	12	398	85	7	724	14	6	193
26.	Puri	1432	185	4277	479	38	1324	279	61	2370	63	32	810
27.	Rayagada	1482	84	3203	186	10	361	83	14	711	19	9	245
28.	Sambalpur	1006	88	2626	238	33	565	159	20	1391	35	14	545
29.	Sonepur	761	71	1877	176	19	482	87	10	739	27	11	382
30.	Sundargarh	2068	178	4942	523	58	1371	248	63	2161	71	33	892
	ORISSA	**42104**	**4505**	**109802**	**11510**	**990**	**31263**	**6160**	**1031**	**51436**	**1367**	**555**	**18125**

CONSUMPTION OF FERTILISER (1999-2000)

S. No.	Name of the Districts	Nitrogenous (N) ('000MT)	Phosphatic (P) ('000 MT)	Pottasic (K) ('000 MT)	Total (N+P+K) ('000 MT)	Gross Cropped Area (in '000 hect.)	Fertiliser Consumption (kg./Hect.)	Cropping Intensity (%)
		(15)	(16)	(17)	(18)	(19)	(20)	(21)
1.	Angul	4.56	1.62	0.86	7.04	302	23	138
2.	Balasore	18.80	6.94	5.43	31.17	341	91	140
3.	Baragarh	30.47	11.39	8.52	50.38	428	118	129
4.	Bhadrak	14.07	6.37	4.03	24.47	234	105	130
5.	Bolangir	5.66	2.30	1.24	9.20	417	22	125
6.	Boudh	1.80	0.53	0.30	2.63	115	23	138
7.	Cuttack	8.89	1.92	2.37	13.18	318	41	183
8.	Deogarh	1.50	0.76	0.42	2.68	97	28	134
9.	Dhenkanal	3.13	1.41	0.71	5.25	298	18	145
10.	Gajapati	3.82	0.33	0.32	4.47	116	39	145
11.	Ganjam	22.35	3.51	2.34	28.20	648	44	164
12.	Jagatsinghpur	7.09	1.15	1.22	9.46	167	57	167
13.	Jajpur	9.36	3.61	2.48	15.45	278	55	161
14.	Jharsuguda	5.04	1.67	0.72	7.43	93	80	122
15.	Kalahandi	8.98	4.32	1.52	14.82	523	28	150
16.	Kandhamal	0.50	0.03	0.04	0.57	160	4	119
17.	Kendrapara	5.91	2.29	1.56	9.76	253	39	166
18.	Keonjhar	5.04	2.33	0.64	8.01	392	20	131
19.	Khurda	6.60	0.86	1.47	8.93	216	41	157
20.	Koraput	3.27	1.17	1.12	5.56	369	15	123
21.	Malkangiri	2.27	1.31	0.75	4.33	209	21	148
22.	Mayurbhanj	10.34	3.48	1.91	15.73	479	33	118
23.	Nawarangpur	9.88	1.57	1.56	13.01	278	47	129
24.	Nayagarh	5.96	0.47	0.42	6.85	208	33	165
25.	Nuapada	3.47	0.78	0.47	4.72	239	20	135
26.	Puri	9.94	2.48	3.52	15.94	309	52	188
27.	Rayagada	3.77	0.61	0.71	5.09	229	22	133
28.	Sambalpur	13.79	5.81	3.12	22.72	255	89	131
29.	Sonepur	3.42	1.56	0.71	5.69	155	37	143
30.	Sundargarh	4.27	1.93	1.00	7.20	398	18	120
	ORISSA	**233.95**	**74.51**	**51.48**	**359.94**	**8524**	**42**	**140**

MEDICAL AND FAMILY WELFARE, 2000-2001 (in Numbers)

S. No.	Name of the Districts	Medical College/ District Head-quarter Hospitals	Sub-divisional and Other Hospitals	Community Health Centres	Primary Health Centres (New)	Primary Health Centres Mobile Health Units	Beds in Hos-pitals	Ayurvedic Hospitals & Dispen-saries including Unani	Homoeo-pathic Hospitals & Dispan-saries	No. of Post Offices (2000-01)	% of Village Electri-fied	ALL SCHEDULED COMMERCIAL BANKS (As on March, 2001)		
												No. of Offices	Deposit (Rs. in lakh)	Credit (Rs. in lakh)
(1)	(2)	(3)	(4)	(5)	(6)	(7)	(8)	(9)	(10)	(11)	(12)	(13)	(14)	(15)
1.	Angul	1	5	3	27	7	322	14	16	238	79.69	69	49520	15763
2.	Balasore	1	5	6	66	8	473	24	30	501	91.49	117	57976	34902
3.	Baragarh	1	2	5	42	9	249	18	14	213	98.72	71	19165	20339
4.	Bhadrak	1	3	6	49	1	273	22	23	328	28.10	61	29158	11390
5.	Bolangir	1	5	5	38	11	438	30	23	283	92.56	69	22984	9505
6.	Boudh	1	2	-	10	3	70	10	4	117	60.13	22	4923	2890
7.	Cuttack	2	13	5	52	9	1942	16	18	365	58.36	171	155046	57412
8.	Deogarh	1	1	1	6	3	118	8	2	41	41.89	20	4614	1397
9.	Dhenkanal	1	6	6	31	4	385	21	17	230	93.11	63	36726	15730
10.	Gajapati	1	2	3	18	6	199	4	3	146	53.08	28	10583	3390
11.	Ganjam	2	11	10	83	15	1541	42	38	676	88.56	188	143843	44190
12.	Jagatsinghpur	1	1	4	36	4	148	7	13	239	96.43	71	88009	15303
13.	Jajpur	1	4	5	54	6	223	19	15	303	95.45	82	45569	16559
14.	Jharsuguda	1	1	2	14	4	108	6	7	92	98.87	33	25202	7714
15.	Kalahandi	1	7	6	39	9	491	18	13	303	62.96	78	21295	14046
16.	Kandhamal	1	6	7	34	8	406	13	16	273	57.15	37	1000	84608
17.	Kendrapara	1	1	7	44	2	268	12	14	268	90.50	67	36690	9117
18.	Keonjhar	1	9	9	57	8	502	49	30	443	85.39	85	42223	19391
19.	Khurda	2	8	5	60	6	565	19	23	295	94.10	186	323527	162773
20.	Koraput	1	4	5	46	9	349	12	11	249	66.74	60	35076	15135
21.	Malkangiri	1	4	4	25	5	286	4	3	84	52.96	19	6142	2664
22.	Mayurbhanj	1	10	13	74	17	794	35	36	709	69.55	132	59858	22888
23.	Nawarangpur	1	2	5	37	5	236	16	13	177	85.91	29	8219	6271
24.	Nayagarh	1	9	4	32	4	489	13	19	210	72.73	53	16466	8803
25.	Nuapada	1	1	4	15	2	158	9	5	111	89.47	28	7615	3736
26.	Puri	1	10	5	43	6	625	21	14	297	97.54	103	56555	24091
27.	Rayagada	1	2	6	34	6	225	15	10	201	54.23	47	19435	8064
28.	Sambalpur	2	3	5	29	6	1139	13	14	249	69.13	78	53920	20855
29.	Sonepur	1	2	4	17	2	153	12	4	97	87.75	27	6974	3373
30.	Sundargarh	1	8	8	54	11	611	31	23	407	88.51	118	113766	44199
	ORISSA	**34**	**147**	**158**	**1166**	**196**	**13786**	**533**	**464**	**8145**	**78.82**	**2212**	**1511087**	**626498**

COMMUNICATION (2000-2001)

ROAD LENGTH (in Kms.)									Railway Route length (in Kms.)	No. of Railway Stations
National Highway	State Highway	Major District Road	Other District Road	Classified village Road	Village Road	G.P. Road	Panchayat Samiti Road	Forest Road		
(1)	(2)	(3)	(4)	(5)	(6)	(7)	(8)	(9)	(10)	(11)
199	48	84	170	190	645	7332	799	408	111	12
118	31	141	210	61	1302	1682	787	59	117	19
97	124	113	135	45	1061	6560	1310	314	53	3
40	114	125	90	91	775	1572	476	-	28	6
83	198	126	190	205	1056	5827	878	250	177	14
-	224	-	29	41	297	3745	173	256	-	-
64	60	268	361	144	1104	2641	814	156	14	20
204	28	13	6	100	563	2891	279	98	-	-
164	5	119	124	211	516	5670	628	213	51	8
-	250	66	39	37	441	4253	301	107	50	7
87	770	158	487	200	2118	6717	761	480	86	11
10	109	41	197	188	619	1308	673	-	70	8
149	18	115	315	96	874	2656	798	36	99	13
105	25	-	33	105	485	2850	348	13	33	5
128	255	223	46	282	806	9955	517	309	38	5
-	289	133	63	279	853	5651	532	323	-	-
45	63	50	279	45	707	2512	684	20	-	-
275	111	78	189	289	1191	2436	926	228	36	5
121	58	466	209	129	809	4925	595	305	118	22
157	213	209	16	541	417	4973	986	210	234	20
-	252	54	56	152	728	2954	357	94	-	-
193	283	200	392	309	2156	6641	1383	799	150	20
65	122	-	-	226	827	5127	1305	113	-	-
-	144	125	235	99	422	5497	506	322	-	-
-	110	77	14	48	401	4133	504	270	32	3
47	55	193	204	59	873	7282	574	8	42	9
-	399	130	69	175	750	4032	751	183	208	14
209	92	62	135	43	398	6499	603	726	240	19
12	84	59	50	01	470	3032	313	50	13	1
179	218	296	84	279	1197	8620	801	680	285	30
2751	**4970**	**3727**	**4445**	**4670**	**24843**	**139973**	**20372**	**7030**	**2385**	**274**

APPENDIX TO CHAPTER - 3

QUESTIONNAIRE

Schedule filled by :

1. VILLAGE IDENTIFICATION
   - (a) Village Name :
   - (b) Location Code No. :
   - (c) Name of Police Station :
   - (d) Name of Block :
   - (e) Name of Tehsil :

2. HOUSEHOLD IDENTIFICATION
   - (a) House No. :
   - (b) Name of the Head of the Household :
   - (c) Sex M/F..........., Age ....
   - (d) Caste or Tribe
   - (e) Dialect

3. HOUSEHOLD CHARACTERISTICS
   - (a) Household Size
   - (b) Land Owned (in acres) [i. 0, ii. Less than 1, iii. 1-3, iv. 3-5, v.5-7, vi. more than 7]
   - (c) Land cultivated (in acres)
   - (d) Average monthly household income (in Rs.) :

4. HOUSEHOLD MEMBERS AND THEIR PARTICULARS

Sl. No.	Relation to Head	Sex M=1 F=2	Age	No. of meals consumed/ day	Yrs. of schooling 0=Illiterate 1=Class I	Marital Status	Occupation Main/ Subsidiary
1.							
2.							
3.							
4.							
5.							

5. LAND REFORM (*in acres*)

Extent of ....

(a) excess land lost to government :
(b) leased out lost to tenants :
(c) leased out acquired from tenants :
(d) land received from government (Surplus land distributed) :
(e) land received from the landlord :
(f) leased land lost to the landlord :

6. PRODUCTION AND MARKETING

Agriculture (during last year)

Sl. No.	Plot code (quantity)	LAND			Production (Quantity & Value) Kharif/Rabi	Quantity Used		Sold Whom/ Where price
		Type I/U *a/b/ c/d/e/f	Quality 1/2/3/4	Distance Km.<1/ 1-5/>5		Consum-ption	Loan Sale payment	
1.								
2.								
3.								
4.								
5.								

I : Irrigated, U : Unirrigated, 1 : Good, 2 : Bad, 3 : Suitable if irrigated, 4 : Agriculturally unsuitable

*a) Nala, b) Stream Diversion, c) Dug well, d) Tube well, e) Tank, f) Others.

Livestock (during last month ended on ....)

Sl. No.	Livestock Particulars	Maintenance cost (Feed'g/Graz'g/ Veterinary)	Production (Quantity)	Consumption (Quantity)	Sale Quantity/ Value/No.
	Cattle				
	Meat				
	Milk				
	Milk Pdcts.				
	Pig				
	Meat				
	Goat				
	Meat				
	Milk				
	Milk Pdcts.				
	Poultry				
	Meat				
	Egg				

7. FOREST (during last month ended on ....)

Sl. No.	Items	Collected per day, in which Season & for how long	Consumed		Sold		Selling	
			Qnty.	Value	Qnty.	Value	Terms	Place
(a)	Wood/Timber							
(b)	Minor Forest Produce							
	Kendu leaves							
	Mahua leaves							
	Sal leaves							
	Bamboo shoots (Kardi)							
	Siali leaves							
	Siali Fibre							
	Others							
(c)	Food :							
	Fruit							
	Roots							
(d)	Fodder							
(e)	Others							

8. SHIFTING CULTIVATION (DONGAR)

(a) How much land you cultivate?
Where ?
How often you change the land?

(b) Ownership status/individual household.

(c) Labour Input

	No. of labours M / F	How many hours work per day	How many days per month
Family			
Outside family			

(d) Material input
Seeds (in quantity)
Forest area burnt for ashes

(e) **Production and use**

Sl. No.	Products	Consumption			Sale			Value
		Qnty.	For how	Long	Qnty.	Value	Place	
(i)	Niger							
(ii)	Kodo							
(iii)	Kongo							
(iv)	Gurji							
(v)	Jhari							
(vi)	Koshala							
(vii)	Ragi (mandia)							
(viii)	Kandul							
(ix)	Kating							
(x)	Arhar							
(xi)	Koshala							
(xii)	Jhudang							
(xiii)	Blackgram							

(f) Why do not you adopt Settled Cultivation fully?
(i) Lack reqd. amount of land
(ii) Risk of partial/total crop failure
(iii) Cannot grow crops of own choice
(iv) Any other reason

9. LABOUR

A. Permanent Hired Labour or Bonded Labour (Goti)

Sl. No.	Perma. Hired Labour	Area of Work Normal Yr. Drought Yr.	Season of Work Kharif/Rabi Two Seasons	How long	Employing Agency	Wage/day	Food No. of Meals/ Day	Share in Output or Other benefits
	Men Women Children							

B. Temporary Hired Labour/Casual Labour (During last one year)

Sl. No.	Temp. Hired Labour	Area of Work N.Yr. Dr.Yr.	Season of Work Kharif/Rabi Two Seasons	How long	Employing Agency / Scheme Govt. / Private	Wage/day	Food No. of Meals/ Day	Share in Output or Other benefits
	Men Women Children							

10. HOUSEHOLD DEBT

Mention quantity (Local Unit) and value (Rs.) during this Nuakhati to last year's Nuakhai

Sl. No.	Source	Purpose		Principal This yr. / Last yr.	Interest & Other terms of payment this yr./last yr.	How much paid back this yr./ last yr.
		Original	Actual 1. Festival/marriage 2. HH consumption 3. Liquor/gambling 4. Any other			
(a) (b) (c)	Sahukar/Marwadi Bank/Coop. Other					

11. GOVERNMENT'S POVERTY ALLEVIATION SCHEME EVALUATION

(a) Whether you are aware of any government programme?(Y/N)
If yes, mention name (IRDP, DPAP, ADAPT, any other)

(b) Did you apply (try) for any assistance? (Y/N)
If yes,

(c) Did you get assistance? (Y/N)
If yes mention type of assistance (with scheme name)
(i) loan, (iii) productive asset,
(ii) subsidy, (iv) others

(d) What happened to assets/loan?
(i) retained, (ii) mortgaged, (iii) sold, (iv) any other

(e) Give reason (i) earning livelihood, (ii) loan repayment, (iii) household consumption, (iv) marriage or festival, (v) drinking, gambling, (vi) any other

12. HOUSEING SCHEME EVALUATION

(a) Did you get a house free of cost from the government (Y/N)

(b) If yes, under which scheme?
(c) Is this unsuitable for you? If so why?
 (i) Does not conform to environmental (local) need or comfort?
 (ii) Not in tune with cultural need.
 (iii) Away from place of work.
 (iv) Away from cultivated field.
 (v) Away from forest.
 (vi) Away from water source.
 (vii) Any other reason.

13. CONSUMPTION/EXPENDITURE
(during month ended on)

A. **Cereals**

Sl. No.	Items	Quantity (local unit)	Money spend (Rs.)
(i)	Rice		
(ii)	Chuda		
(iii)	Khai Lia/Mudhi		
(iv)	Jhari		
(v)	Kodo		
(vi)	Gurji		
(vii)	Kongo		
(viii)	Swan		
	Sub-Total		
(ix)	Wheat		
(x)	Ata/Maida		
	Sub-Total		
(xi)	Jowar/Bajra		
(xii)	Maize/Barley		
(xiii)	Ata		
	Sub-Total		
(xiv)	Small millets		
(xv)	Ata		
	Sub-Total		
(xvi)	Ragi (mandia)		
(xvii)	Ata (mandia gruel)		
	Sub-Total		
	Total		

B. **Milk and Milk Products**

Sl. No.	Items	Quantity (Ltrs.)	Value (Rs.)
(i)	Milk		
(ii)	Milk product (Dahi/Ghee/Butter etc.)		
(iii)	Milk & Milk Product Total		

C. **Cereal Substitute**

Sl. No.	Items	Quantity	Value (Rs.)
(i)	Tapioca		
(ii)	Pea		
(iii)	Bamboo shoots		
(iv)	Wild roots, tuber (cherenga, bhat kanda etc.)		
(v)	Tamarind seeds (powder)		
(vi)	Mango stones (powder)		
(vii)	Boiled rice-water (peja)		
(viii)	Salap		
(ix)	Cereals substitutes Sub-Total		

D. **Pulses**

Sl. No.	Items	Quantity	Value (Rs.)
(i)	Arhar/Tur		
(ii)	Gram (chana/sola)		
(iii)	Moong (Green gram)		
(iv)	Kulthi (horse gram)		
(v)	Biri (Black gram)		
(vi)	Bean		
(vii)	Any local dal		
(viii)	Pulses Sub-Total		

E. **Oil and Oilseeds**

Sl. No.	Items	Quantity (Ltrs.)	Value (Rs.)
(i)	Mustard oil		
(ii)	Till oil		
(iii)	Groundnut oil		
(iv)	Niger (Alsi)		
(v)	Mahua seed oil (tol)		
(vi)	Linseed oil		
(vii)	Oil etc. Sub-Total		

F. Vegetables

Sl. No.	Items	Quantity	Value (Rs.)
(i)	Potato		
(ii)	Onion		
(iii)	Mushroom		
(iv)	Brinjal		
(v)	Papaya		
(vi)	Root vegetables		
(vii)	Leafy vegetables		
	Sub-Total		

G. Fruits & Nuts

Sl. No.	Items	Quantity	Value (Rs.)
(i)	Banana		
(ii)	Mango		
(iii)	Guava		
(iv)	Pineapple		
(v)	Sugarcane		
(vi)	Groundnuts		
(vii)	Dates		
(viii)	Fruits & Nuts		
	Sub-total		

H. Meat, Fish and Egg

Sl. No.	Items	Quantity	Value (Rs.)
(i)	Mutton		
(ii)	Beef (cow meat)		
(iii)	Pork (Pig meat)		
(iv)	Buffalo meat		
(v)	Goat meat		
(vi)	Rat		
(vii)	Non-poisonous snakes		
(viii)	Large reptiles (Godhi)		
(ix)	Egg		
(x)	Poultry		
(xi)	Pigeons		
(xii)	Pea fowl		
(xiii)	Fish (Fresh)		
(xiv)	Fish (Dry)		
(xv)	Meat, fish, egg		
	Sub-Total		

I. Sugar

Sl. No.	Items	Quantity	Value (Rs.)
(i)	Sugar		
(ii)	Molasses (Guda)		
(iii)	Sugar, Guda		
	Sub-Total		

J. Salt

Sl. No.	Items	Quantity	Value (Rs.)
(i)	Sea salt		
(ii)	Rock & other salt		
(iii)	Salt		
	Sub-Total		

K. Spices

Sl. No.	Items	Quantity	Value (Rs.)
(i)	Turmeric		
(ii)	Black pepper		
(iii)	Dry Chillies		
(iv)	Green chillies		
	Sub-Total		

L. Beverages

Sl. No.	Items	Quantity	Value (Rs.)
(i)	Tea/Coffee (cups)		
(ii)	Others		
(iii)	Beverages		
	Sub-Total		

M. Pickles, Jams etc.

Sl. No.	Items	Quantity	Value (Rs.)
(i)	Pickles, Jams or sauce etc.		
(ii)	Total (other Food items)		

N. Tobacco and Products

Sl. No.	Items	Quantity	Value (Rs.)
(i)	Bidi		
(ii)	Leaf Tobacco (country cheroot)		
(iii)	Cigarettes		
(iv)	Tobacco		
	Sub-Total		

O. Drugs and Intoxicants

Sl. No.	Items	Quantity	Value (Rs.)
(i)	Mahua-Liquor		
(ii)	Opium/Ganja		
(iii)	Toddy/Handia		
(iv)	Bhang		
(v)	Drugs etc.		
	Sub-Total		

P. Fuel and Light

Sl No.	Items	Quantity	Value (Rs.)
(i)	Charcoal		
(ii)	Firewood		
(iii)	Dung cake		
(iv)	Kerosene		
(v)	Matches		
(vi)	Fuel & Light		
	Sub-Total		

Q. Clothing

How much expenditure made on clothes per year, for household as a whole.

14. HOUSE AND LIVING CONDITION

A. House Structure

(i) Built up area
(ii) Cost of Construction (with present values in Rs.)
(iii) No. of rooms
(iv) Material Used for
Roof – Reeds (Nada),Bamboo, Grass (Thatched/ tiled/asbestos)
Wall – Mud/Ribs, bamboo, leaves, cement, bricks
Floor – Mud, cement, bricks

B. **Amenities Available and Assets**

	Quality *1/2/3	Source **1/2/3/4/5
(i) Water (Drinking/Cooking)		
(ii) Power (Electricity) Y/N		
(iii) Vehicle – Bullock Cart/cycle		
(iv) Machine – Sewing/Plough/ hoe/arrow/spear		
(v) Furnitures–String cots (*Khatia*), Woodenbox, dibri (Lamp), Wooden-table-chair-cots, clock/watch, radio/transistor		

(vi) Utensils for	Material *** a/b/c/d	No.
Cooking		
Eating		
Storing		

* 1 – Good
2 – Bad
3 – Usable if boiled

** 1 – Well (individual)
2 – Well (common)
3 – Pond/Tank/Chuha
4 – Stream
5 – Any other

*** a – Clay
b – Wood, b(i) Leaf (plate/cup) b(ii) Bamboo (basket) b(iii) Jute Bag
c – Brass/bell metal
d - Aluminium

APPENDIX TO CHAPTER-3

Kalahandi : Selected Indicators

PHYSICAL

Geographical Area	:	11772 km^2
Forest Area	:	5660 km^2
Low Land	:	16%
Medium	:	34%
Hilly Land	:	50%

AGRICULTURE

Area available for Cultivation	:	52%
Net Area Sown	:	94%
Area sown more than once	:	35%
Area under rice of total cropped area	:	52%
Area under pulses of total cropped area	:	25%
Irrigation (Kharif)	:	12%
Irrigation (Rabi)	:	5%

INDUSTRY & MINERALS

Registered Factories	:	32
Employment in Factories	:	880
Small scale industries	:	1,770
Persons employed	:	12,162
Major minerals	:	Graphite & Quartz

POPULATION

Population (Total)	:	15,92,000

Rural	:	14,88,000
Urban	:	1,04,000
Density km^2.	:	135

SOILS

Red Laterite Soils (Least productive)	:	45%
Red and Yellow Soil	:	27%
Red and Black Soil	:	9%
Black Soil	:	13%
Alluvial Soil (Most productive)	:	6%

RAINFALL

Average Annual (1970-90)	:	1378 mm
June to September	:	85%
Average No. of rainy days	:	65
Rainfall variability	:	40-48%

OTHER

Road length	:	8,722 km
Surfaced roads	:	1,253 km
Credit-Deposit Ratio	:	120

Source : Orissa Gabeshana Chakra, 1991.

APPENDIX TO CHAPTER-3

Infant Mortality Rate of Kalahandi District of Urban Units for 1990

	Units		% of Registration	I.M.R.
1.	Bhawanipatna	(M)	46.80	32.18
2.	Khariar Road	N.A.C.	64.00	59.34
3.	Khariar	N.A.C.	44.50	4.48
4.	Kesinga	N.A.C.	55.14	57.62
5.	Junagarh	N.A.C.	44.83	109.37
	Average		51.05	52.60

Source : Civil Registation of Birth and Death, 1990, Kalahandi.

Infant Mortality Rate of Rural Units of Kalahandi District (Blockwise) for 1990

	Blocks	% of Registration	I.M.R.
1.	Boden	64.14	59.73
2.	Bhawanipatna (Sadar)	49.74	66.16
3.	Komna	44.26	59.46
4.	Lanjigarh	58.76	90.49
5.	Junagarh	57.20	76.15
6.	Golamunda	52.03	59.71
7.	Jaipatna	63.70	43.98
8.	Kalampur	63.65	83.51
9.	Karlamunda	42.81	77.60
10.	Khariar	70.10	60.77
11.	Nawapara	64.11	60.73
12.	Koksara	66.43	79.78
13.	M. Rampur	44.71	83.82
14.	Narla	45.52	54.11
15.	Kesinga	58.84	83.38

Blocks	% of Registration	I.M.R.
16. Dharmagarh	54.72	43.52
17. Sinapalli	60.74	73.42
18. Th. Rampur	44.97	72.50
Average	55.91	68.72

Source : Civil Registration Unit of Kalahandi.
IMR : Infant Mortality Rate, M : Municipality, NAC : Notified Area Council

APPENDIX TO CHAPTER – 3

MINERAL RESOURCES, KALAHANDI

Mineral/ Year	No. of Working Mines	Area Covered (Ha)	No. of Workers Employed	Output (M.T.)	Value ('000 Rs.)	Revenue Accruing to State Govt. (Rs.)
Graphite						
1979	4	48.9	213	1452	491	–
1981	6	171.4	104	385	169	–
1982	6	89	99	364	81	–
1985	–	–	10	–	–	–
1987	–	–	50	–	–	–
Quartz						
1979	1	17.3	24	1778	60	
1981	5	42.6	115	8870	309	
1985	9	54	104	25143	1755	
All Minerals						
1979	5	66.2	237	3230	551	11063
1981	11	213.9	219	9255	478	40485
1985	15	143	114	25507	1836	76525
1987	181			21577		11190

Source : District Gazetteer.

APPENDIX TO CHAPTER – 3 & 4

IRRIGATED POTENTIAL CREATED AND ACTUALLY UTILIZED

Year	Source	Type	Name of Project	Potential Created (in Hectares)			Actual Utilized (in Hectares)		
				Kharif Season	Rabi Season	Total	Kharif	Rabi	Total
1986	Surface Water	Major Irrigation Projects	Jonk Sandul Indra, Sagada, Rajva, Udanti Utei, Indravati	92930	45750	13680	51920	23790	75710
-do-	-do-	-do-	Upper Indravati			3840			
	Flow or Surface Water	Medium Irrigation Projects	Saraikele Utei, Sundar			14278			
	Surface	Minor I.P.	117			25736			
	Surface	Water Harvest-ing Structures	1298			17950			
	Under Ground			47370	25660	73030			
1979	Under Ground	Dug Wells	7436 Irrigation Wells / 18761 dug wells			2500 / 3741			
	Under Ground	Lift Irrigation	544	6255	3935	10190			

Medium irrigation Projects	3
Minor	181
Lift irrigation	434
Functionary	390
Wells sunk till 31st March 1991	6989

Source : Rural Development notes on District Activities 1991-1992.

APPENDIX TO CHAPTERS – 3, 4, and 5

Soil Type	% Area covered	Blocks covered	Fertility	Crops Grown
Red Laterite	44.5	Foothills of M. Rampur, Th. Rampur, Lanjigarh, Jaypatna, Nawapada, Division and Dharamgarh	Deficient in P_2O_5 and N	*Arhar*, Ragi, Maize, Millets, oilseeds
Red and Yellow	27.4	Narla, M. Rampur, Jaypatna, Koksara, Kalampur, Junagarh	- do - contains Fe. Oxide (Sesquioxide) Silica is leached	Paddy, Pulses, Oilseeds, Maize, Ragi
Red and Black	9.0	Boden, Kesinga, Karlamunda		Paddy, Pulses, Oilseeds
Black	12.8	Bhawanipatna, Khariar and Dharamgarh Tehsil, Golamunda, Koksara, Kesinga	Rich in K_2O N poor in P_2 O_2 high water retaining capacity	Pulses, Oilseeds, Cotton
Alluvial and Sandy loam	6.3	Along narrow river bank strips, of Udanti, Sagada, Tel, Jonk, Utei of Dharamgarh, Nawapada, Khariar and Bhawanipatna Tehsil	V. Fertile soil	Cash crops like Sugarcane, Groundnuts and Vegetables

Source : Deputy Director, Agriculture, Bhawanipatna, 1991.

APPENDIX TO CHAPTERS – 3 and 6

GENERAL INFORMATIONS ON ECOLOGICAL MICRO REGIONS OF KALAHANDI

Micro regions	No. of settlements	Area (in sq.km.)	Population
Nuapada Forested Upland	425 Villages 1 Town	2,727	255,531
Udanti Basin	233 Villages	1,192	133,921
Tel Valley	503 Villages 3 Towns	1,585	347,480
Tel-Hatti Basin	490 Villages 1 Town	2,167	411,093
Dharamgarh Plateau	833 Villages	2,827	112,363
Madanpur Rampur Forested Upland	356 Villages	1,274	78,804
Total	2840 Villages	11,772	13,39,192

Source : Cartographic Regionalisation of India, Census of India (1981).

APPENDIX TO CHAPTERS – 3, 4,5,7 and 8

ECONOMICS CHARACTERISTICS OF SAMPLE VILLAGES

Sample Village	Police Station	Percentage of Non-Working population to working population	Marginal farmers to total farmers	Irrigated area per farmer
Barabandha	M. Rampur	94.87	67.90	8.64
Tejipada	M.Rampur	207.86	55.71	9.71
Kulihariguda	Junagarh	152.48	51.08	16.61
Padepadar	Th. Rampur	157.14	75.53	5.31
Mankadashola	Junagarh	216.15	54.19	20.76
Mahulpatna	Th. Rampur	151.78	55.55	6.07
Jariguma	Jaypatna	149.79	52.00	2.71
Chandpua	Jaypatna	101.05	53.92	20.30
BasantPada	Lanjigarh	248.41	81.13	18.86
Jugarajpur	Th. Rampur	201.45	76.19	2.97
Bhangabari	Sadar	161.01	29.47	1.57
Tentulipada	Sadar	222.72	56.41	79.48
Matia	Kesinga	196.07	23.42	6.28
Degam	Kesinga	70.78	51.72	13.79
Ghantiguda	Sinapali	134.00	47.84	61.96
Bakharmal	Jonk	89.22	40.57	18.11
Kusumjore	Sinapali	98.53	57.43	11.48
Bhairajpur	Khariar	130.67	51.44	5.20

APPENDIX TO CHAPTER - 4

COMPOSITE DEVELOPMENT INDEX

Blocks	X_1	X_2	X_3	X_4	X_5	X_6	X_7	X_8	X_9	X_{10}	X_{11}	X_{12}
Bhawanipatna	1.30	0.91	1.49	0.93	0.80	0.31	2.54	0.98	1.49	1.08	1.04	12.87
Kesinga	1.17	0.94	1.49	0.92	0.69	0.84	1.15	0.95	1.32	0.62	1.14	11.23
Narla	0.93	0.92	1.08	0.94	0.55	0.34	0.44	1.44	1.27	0.74	1.28	9.93
M.Rampur	0.43	1.14	0.76	0.93	0.42	0.34	0.37	1.35	1.01	0.99	1.12	9.46
Karlamunda	1.00	1.09	1.84	0.97	1.28	5.14	0.39	1.19	1.08	1.04	1.13	16.15
Lanjigarh	0.71	0.69	0.61	1.13	0.96	0.59	0.42	1.12	0.66	0.95	0.78	8.62
Th.Rampur	0.76	0.64	0.54	1.13	0.85	0.24	0.38	1.08	0.44	0.98	0.85	7.89
Dharamgarh	1.21	0.95	1.64	1.03	1.23	0.64	0.71	0.84	0.91	1.08	0.95	11.19
Junagarh	1.20	1.15	2.64	1.06	1.33	1.97	0.64	0.85	1.36	0.98	1.38	14.56
Jaipatna	1.09	1.18	0.78	0.94	1.26	1.65	1.45	1.04	0.81	1.06	0.84	12.10
Koksara	1.16	1.08	0.91	0.99	1.38	0.93	0.80	0.90	093	1.08	1.14	11.28
Kalampur	1.33	1.06	1.15	1.08	1.68	1.20	0.58	1.27	1.04	1.08	1.04	12.59
Golamunda	1.01	0.96	1.14	0.93	0.97	0.68	0.60	1.02	0.72	1.04	1.03	9.80
Nawapada	0.75	1.21	1.28	1.01	0.69	0.82	1.09	0.84	1.28	1.08	1.03	11.08

(Contd.)

Blocks	X_1	X_2	X_3	X_4	X_5	X_6	X_7	X_8	X_9	X_{10}	X_{11}	X_{12}
Komna	0.75	1.23	0.66	1.10	1.14	1.03	1.23	0.80	0.75	1.05	0.91	10.65
Khariar	1.29	0.95	1.69	0.95	0.83	0.44	1.41	0.76	1.40	1.07	0.85	11.64
Sinapalli	0.96	1.29	0.98	0.93	1.07	0.29	1.53	0.77	0.82	1.06	0.73	10.43
Boden	0.88	1.27	0.72	1.02	0.85	0.16	2.26	0.85	0.73	1.04	0.75	10.53

X_1 – Population Density (Persons per sq. km.)
X_2 – Percentage of SC population to total population
X_3 – Percentage of ST population to total population
X_4 – Percentage of working population to total population
X_5 – Yield rate of paddy (quintals per hectare)
X_6 – Percentage are irrigated to NSA
X_7 – Population per medical institution
X_8 – Number of primary schools per '000 population
X_9 – Percentage of literacy
X_{10} – Percentage of villages with drinking water facilities
X_{11} – Number of cooperative societies per lakh population

$X_{12} - \Sigma(\frac{x}{\bar{x}})$

Base-Data Source : District Statistical Handbook, 1997 and Census of India, 1991.

APPENDIX TO CHAPTER - 4

COMPOSITE DEVELOPMENT INDEX

Blocks	X_1	X_2	X_3	X_4	X_5	X_6	X_7	X_8	X_9	X_{10}	X_{11}	X_{12}			
Bhawanipatna	0.60	0.79	1.00	1.01	1.02	1.04	1.28	0.73	0.36	1.12	1.09	1.03	1.27	0.52	12.86
Kesinga	1.24	0.97	0.48	1.03	1.03	0.89	0.79	1.39	0.86	0.88	1.33	1.87	2.04	1.74	16.53
Narla	1.21	0.96	1.21	0.98	1.00	0.97	1.22	0.50	0.75	1.25	1.39	1.15	0.37	1.38	14.34
M.Rampur	0.40	1.42	0.96	0.79	1.03	0.91	1.48	0.71	1.13	0.96	0.91	0.49	0.35	0.40	11.94
Karlamunda	1.34	1.30	0.46	0.85	1.02	0.92	0.91	4.18	1.55	0.88	1.09	2.26	0.35	1.70	18.81
Lanjigarh	0.28	0.79	0.67	0.99	0.99	1.21	0.50	0.22	1.49	1.13	0.60	0.38	0.96	0.52	10.73
Th.Rampur	0.26	0.72	1.49	1.01	1.04	1.16	1.53	1.21	1.46	0.99	0.31	0.00	0.00	0.28	11.46
Dharamgarh	1.49	0.97	1.94	0.98	0.95	1.02	0.90	0.47	0.77	0.70	1.13	1.83	4.03	1.65	18.86
Junagarh	1.29	1.00	1.71	1.02	0.95	1.13	1.16	1.36	0.60	0.84	1.13	1.28	2.71	0.49	16.67
Jaipatna	1.52	1.52	1.52	0.85	0.97	1.91	1.60	0.22	0.69	0.78	0.94	0.84	0.29	1.60	15.25
Koksara	1.36	1.16	1.52	1.05	0.99	1.08	1.12	1.00	1.78	0.77	0.56	0.97	0.96	0.57	14.89
Kalampur	1.62	1.06	1.78	1.06	0.82	1.06	0.88	0.22	0.82	1.08	2.02	1.17	0.66	0.73	14.98
Golamunda	0.73	0.54	0.86	1.67	1.01	0.96	0.70	0.73	1.70	1.42	0.97	0.55	0.47	1.03	13.34
Nawapada	0.63	1.38	1.20	0.99	1.04	0.79	0.63	0.95	1.45	1.20	0.83	0.59	0.89	0.74	13.31

(Contd.)

Blocks	X_1	X_2	X_3	X_4	X_5	X_6	X_7	X_8	X_9	X_{10}	X_{11}	X_{12}			
Komna	0.66	1.13	0.76	0.93	1.03	0.80	0.84	0.83	1.11	1.05	0.91	0.97	0.57	0.75	12.34
Khariar	1.40	1.07	1.22	0.94	1.02	1.24	0.83	1.32	0.94	1.03	0.98	1.49	1.48	0.57	15.53
Sinapalli	1.10	1.26	1.09	0.89	1.04	0.92	0.35	0.82	1.00	0.99	1.00	0.59	0.34	1.75	13.14
Boden	1.08	1.23	1.15	0.96	1.04	0.99	1.06	1.11	0.55	0.95	0.83	0.51	0.28	1.57	13.31

X_1 – population density
X_2 – % of SC population
X_3 – % of ST population
X_4 – % of working population
X_5 – cropping intensity
X_6 – % of area under HYV to NSA
X_7 – % of net irrigated area to NSA
X_8 – population/medical centres
X_9 – No. of primary schools/'000 population
X_{10} – % of literacy
X_{11} – % of villages with *pucca* road
X_{12} – % of villages electrified
X_{13} – % of villages with drinking water facility
X_{14} – No. of cooperative societies per lakh of population

X_{15} – $\Sigma(\frac{x}{\bar{x}})$

Original Data Source : District Statistical Handbook, Kalahandi, 1989-90.

APPENDIX TO CHAPTERS – 4, 5, 7, 8, 9

Sub-region	Plains			Hilly Forests	Mixed	
Sub-micro region	Tel Valley	Tel-Hatti Basin	Udanti Basin	Dharamgarh Plateau	Nawapada Forested Upland	Madanpur Rampur Forested Upland
Sample villages	Degam, Matia, Bhangabari, Tentulipada	Mankadashola, Kulihariguda, Padepadar, Mahulpatna	Kusumjore, Ghantiguda	Basantpada, Dumerpadar, Jariguma, Chandpura	Bakharmal, Bhairajpur	Tejipada Barabandha

Source : *Cartographic Regionalisation of India*, *Census of India*, 1981 and Field Survey.

APPENDIX TO CHAPTER - 5

QUINQUENNIAL AVERAGES FOR PER CAPITA FOOD PRODUCTION IN KALAHANDI

Period	Rice	Cereals	Pulses	Total
1961-65	257.02	277.02	24.66	319.73
1966-70	179.29	214.18	26.29	240.47
1971-75	184.90	224.09	34.81	258.90
1976-80	153.70	194.61	37.48	225.95
1981-85	166.43	230.82	67.11	296.56
1986-90	154.39	196.29	87.12	283.41
1991-93	183.99	208.26	91.79	300.85

Source : District Agricultural Office, Bhawanipatna.

APPENDIX TO CHAPTER – 5

MARKET AND MARKET DAYS IN NAWAPARA SUB-DIVISION, KALAHANDI

Sl. No.	Name of the Block	Name of the Market	Days in which the market sits	Periodicity
1.	Nawapara	Amethi	Thursday	Weekly
		Bisira	Thursday	Weekly
		Sarbanga	Thursday	Weekly
		Dharmabandha	Tuesday	Weekly
		Sisiraguda	Monday	Weekly
		Birimal	Sunday	Weekly
		Sunsunia	Thursday	Weekly
		Jumpani	Thursday	Weekly
		Parsuguda	Tuesday	Weekly
		Nawapara	Sunday	Weekly
		Parkod	Thursday	Weekly
2.	Boden	Boden	Monday	Weekly
		Parsulda	Saturday	Weekly
3.	Sinapalli	Niliji	Friday	Weekly
		Singijhar	Monday	Weekly
		Sinalpali	Wednesday	Weekly
4.	Khariar	Chaturpur	Thursday	Weekly
		Khariar	Friday	Weekly
		Sanmahasur	Sunday	Weekly
		Borgaon	Tuesday	Weekly
		Tukuda	Monday	Weekly
		Jhulpada	Thursday	Weekly

Source : District Statistical Handbook, 1989-90.

APPENDIX TO CHAPTER – 5

RECEIPT AND DISPOSAL OF ESSENTIAL COMMODITIES IN KALAHANDI, 1977-1981

Year	Total receipts (in Quintals)				
	Rice (in Ql.)	Wheat (in Ql.)	Wheat Product (in Ql.)	Sugar (in Ql.)	Kerosene Oil (in Kl.)
1977	11,196	549	Nil	39,729	2,618
1978	10,961	290	Nil	32,733	2,874
1979	5,287	150	Nil	Nil	Nil
1980	1,02,588	7,620	Nil	46,280	2,689
1981	2,27,924	22,963	Nil	56,947	3,111

Year	Total disposal (in Quintals)				
	Rice (in Ql.)	Wheat (in Ql.)	Wheat Product (in Ql.)	Sugar (in Ql.)	Kerosene Oil (in Kl.)
1977	1,252	525	Nil	39,729	2,618
1978	2,654	290	Nil	32,733	2,874
1979	2,073	159	Nil	N.A	Nil
1980	1,20,856	7,068	Nil	46,280	2,689
1981	95,775	22,585	Nil	54,009	3,111

Source : Civil Supplies Officer, Kalahandi.

APPENDIX TO CHAPTER – 5

Today Kalahandi and Koraput districts are, in fact, amongst the major contributors of rice to the Food Corporation of India. In 1996-97, Kalahandi district alone provided more than 38,000 tonne of rice to the central food kitty.

Kalahandi is an area of food grain "surplus" contributing a fourth of Orissa's share to the procurement agencies year after year. In 1993-94, Kalahandi provided 24,000 tonne of rice. The next year, in 1994-95, rice procurement was a little less at 22,000 tonne. And in 1995-96, procurement shot upto 37,700 tonne. The paradox of plenty, unfortunately, is not only confined to food stocks piling up at a time when more than 320 million hungry and poor do not have the means to purchase it.

For the poor, human bondage and surviving on the charities of moneylenders, is perhaps an inescapable route. The innocent, simple and illiterate tribals end up borrowing money at the time of distress only to find themselves slipping deeper and deeper into debt. Although the moneylenders vehemently deny it, the annual rate of interest they charge works out to 200 per cent !

The Tribal Development Corporation set-up to eliminate the middlemen in the trade, ironically operates through middlemen. One private company alone has the monopoly marketing rights over 28 items of non-timber forest produce. Every time the district administration tries to break the monopoly, the collector is transferred.

Such is the degree of exploitation that even the poorest of the poor are not spared. Tendu leaves fetch a price of 35 paise for 60 dried leaves. Orissa government has raised the price this year, by one paise. After several years, the price of broom stick has been raised from Rs. 4 to Rs. 10, an increase of 250 per cent. Bamboo is another major produce of Kalahandi, which brings employment to some 10,000 families for about five months a year.

And yet, the wage rate at Rs. 2.56 for cutting and tying a bundle of ten bamboo sticks has been deliberately kept low at the instance of a private paper mill. After a lot of persuasion the wage rate has this year been increased to Rs. 3. "Chiroungi" another edible forest produce, is purchased at prices varying between Rs. 5 to 12 a kg. At Raipur, in neighbouring Madhya Pradesh, it sells for a minimum of Rs. 300 a kg.

If development assistance is the lone measure of economic growth, Kalahandi has failed miserably. Not even 15 paise out of a rupee of development aid has percolated down to the people who needed it most. Fifty years after Independence, an average rural family in Western Orissa survives on an annual income of less than Rs. 5,000. Malnutrition, disease and even starvation are, therefore, inevitable. The immediate task for the powers that be is to go in for capacity building among the local communities.

Source : Newspaper cuttings.

APPENDIX TO CHAPTER – 5

EXPLOITING NEXUS IN LIQUOR – MAHUL TRADE

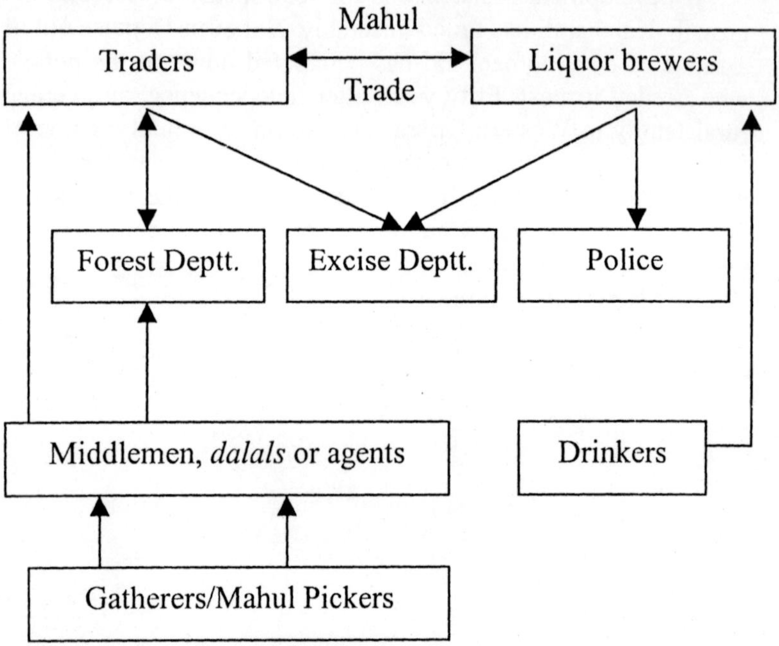

The table is self-explanatory. *Mahul* traders (*seth*) who live in big villages, or urban centres procure mahul directly by residing in villages or through mobile *dalals* deployed or engaged by them for such purpose. The middlemen collect the forest produce through exchange (barter) basis from *mahul* pickers who get only nominal wage. Often poor collectors in villages exchange one bag *mahul* to one bag salt. The measuring pots and local traditional weight systems have become a primary cause of unfair trade where obviously the poor is exploited.

The traders and liquor brewers have to satisfy to the Forest Department and Police respectively. Both the groups have to please the Excise Department. The monetary strength they require for such purpose is ultimately drawn from the common men, drinkers, labourer, pickers and *mahul* gatherers through various means of manipulation and muscle power.

APPENDIX TO CHAPTER – 5

GUESS ESTIMATES FOR NET AVAILABILITY OF RICE IN KALAHANDI (1983-93)

Year	Rice Procured by FCI (tons.)	Pvt. Export of Rice (tons.)	Total Export of Rice (tons.)	Per Capita Export of Rice (kg.)	Per Capita Net Export (kg.)	Per Capita Production of Rice (kg.)	Per Capita Net Availability (kg.)
Scenario I							
1983	10770	16155	26925	19.40	16.00	147.70	131.70
1984	14976	22464	37440	26.50	23.10	179.26	156.16
1985	15732	23598	39330	27.35	23.95	171.96	148.01
1986	25131	37696	69827	42.91	19.51	210.37	190.86
1987	9240	13860	23100	15.50	12.10	130.21	118.11
1988	3004	4506	7510	4.95	1.55	113.01	111.46
1989	4160	6240	10400	6.73	3.33	128.88	125.55
1990	16506	24759	41265	26.25	22.85	189.47	166.62
1991	18286	27424	45707	28.56	25.16	187.72	162.56
1992	19973	29959	49932	30.65	27.15	208.93	181.78
1993	30455	45682	76137	45.91	42.51	155.32	112.81
Scenario II							
1983	10770	20001	30771	22.17	18.77	147.70	129.93
1984	14976	27812	42788	30.29	26.89	179.26	152.57
1985	15732	29216	44948	31.25	27.85	171.96	144.11
1986	25131	46671	71802	49.04	45.64	210.37	164.73
1987	9240	17160	26400	17.71	14.31	130.21	115.90
1988	3004	5578	8582	5.66	2.26	113.01	110.75
1989	4160	7725	11885	7.70	4.30	128.88	124.58
1990	16506	30654	47160	30.00	26.60	189.47	162.87
1991	18286	33951	52237	32.64	29.24	187.72	158.48
1992	19973	37092	57065	35.03	31.63	208.93	177.30
1993	30455	56559	87014	52.46	49.06	155.32	106.26
Scenario III							
1983	10770	25130	35900	25.87	22.47	147.70	125.23
1984	14976	34944	49920	35.34	31.94	179.26	147.32
1985	15732	36708	52440	36.46	33.06	171.96	138.90
1986	25131	58639	82770	57.22	53.82	210.37	156.55
1987	9240	21560	30800	20.67	17.27	130.21	112.94
1988	3004	7009	10013	6.60	3.20	113.01	109.81

(*Contd.*)

Year	Rice Procured by FCI (tons.)	Pvt. Export of Rice (tons.)	Total Export of Rice (tons.)	Per Capita Export of Rice (kg.)	Per Capita Net Export (kg.)	Per Capita Production of Rice (kg.)	Per Capita Net Availability (kg.)
1989	4160	9707	13867	8.98	5.58	128.88	123.30
1990	16506	38514	55020	35.00	31.60	189.47	157.87
1991	18286	42657	60943	38.08	34.68	187.72	153.26
1992	19973	46603	66576	40.86	37.46	208.93	171.47
1993	30455	71062	101517	61.10	57.70	155.32	97.62

Note : Scenario I : 20% underestimation v Scenario II : 30% underestimation v Scenario III :40% underestimation

Source : Orissa Gaveshana Chakra, New Delhi.

APPENDIX TO CHAPTER – 6

MATRICES : POVERTY AND ASSOCIATED VARIABLES (in No. of Households)

Poverty category	Social Groups (in %)			Land Size Class (in acres)				Annual Income from Land			
House-holds	SC	ST	Other Castes	Marginal Farmers (0-2)	Small Farmers (2-7)	Medium Farmers (7-12)	Big Farmers (>12)	Rs.2000 (Low)	Rs.2001-4000 (Low medium)	Rs. 4001-6000 (Medium-high)	Rs. 6000 & above
Below Poverty Line	31	36	33	42.4	25.7	18.1	9.7	59.8	15.7	12.7	11.8
Above Poverty Line	22	35	43	29.1	27.9	24	10.9	42.4	28.0	12.9	16.7

Households	Labour Areas			Per capita labourer income from labour			% of dependent person			
	Within Village	Outside Village Within District	Outside District	< Rs. 1000	Rs. 1001-2000	> Rs. 2000	25	26-50	51-75	76-100
Below poverty line	110 [14]	6 [18]	5 [19]	6.5 (52)	39 (31.2)	21 (16.8)	10.4	40.9	36.5	12.2
Above poverty line	124 [1]	9 [11]	7 [8]	74 (57)	32 (23)	30 (25)	13.6	44.9	32.2	9.3

(Contd.)

Correlation : +0.1632 at +0.01 level

Poverty Category	Per capita food-expenditure (in Rs.)			Annual Intoxicant Expenditure (in Rs.)	
	1200 (low)	1201-2400 medium	2401 (high)	<1000	>1000
HHs below poverty line	44	56	0	87	13
HHs above poverty line	2	64	34	68	32

Correlation : .2343 at +0.001 level

Basic Data Source : Fieldwork.

APPENDIX TO CHAPTER – 6

MATRICES : LAND OWNING CLASSES AND ASSOCIATED VARIABLES (In %)

Land Owning Classes (with Land in acres)	Social Groups			% of literacy					Soil Quality			
(% of HHs)	SC	ST	Others	Zero	<25 Low	25-50 Low-Med	50-75 Med-High	>75 High	Bahal	Berna	Att	Bhatta
Landless (0)	56.79	28.4	26.9	41.3	34.5	34.8	6.9	22.2				
Marginal (0-2) Farmers	22.2	22.9	33.6	28.1	22.4	21.7	41.4	11.1	34.7	13.3	22.7	29.3
Small Farmers (2-7)	8.6	30.3	21.8	21.6	20.7	26.1	10.3	33.3	47.6	4.76	30.2	17.5
Medium Farmers (7-12)	7.4	8.3	5.0	5.4	15.5	6.5	31.0	22.2	63.3	10	10	13.3
Big Farmers (>12)	4.9	8.3	5.0	3.6	6.9	10.9	10.3	11.1	7.6	5.9	5.9	11.8

Correlation : 0.2256 at + 0.001 level. 0.4750 at +0.001 level

Land owning classes (with land in acres)	% of working members				Land Incomes (in Rs.)			
	Low	Low to Med.	Med. to high	High	1-2000	2000-4000	4000-6000	6000 and above
Marginal farmers (< 2.0)	50	49	46	31	67	24	6	3
Small farmers (2.0-7.0)	31	30	38	42	35	33	15	17
Medium farmers (7.0-12.0)	19	12	8	7	27	6	37	30
Large farmers (>12.0)	0	9	8	10	21	21		57

Correlation : -0.2846 at +0.001 level

APPENDIX TO CHAPTER – 6 (*Contd.*)

MATRIX : LAND INCOME AND ASSOCIATED VARIABLES (in %)

Land income sizes

Total Annual Income from land (in Rs.)	Annual clothing expenditure (Rs.)		Per labourers Annual Income (in Rs.)			% of working members			
	<1600 Low	>1600 High	<1000	1001-2000	>2000	<25	26-50	51-75	>75
1-2000	74.99	25.01	75.9	61.0	57.7	46	58	58	50
2001-4000	62.25	37.75	27.9	31.5	23.1	31	22	24	17
4001-6000	51.73	48.27	20.7	1.9	15.4	20	7	13	20
6000 & Above	21.21	78.79	10.3	5.6	3.8	20	13	5	13
Correlation :	0.4061 at 0.001 level		–0.3864 +0.001 level			–0.2247 at +0.001 level			

Basic Data Source : Fieldwork survey.

APPENDIX TO CHAPTERS – 7 and 8

HH No.	Wt. Score	HH No.	Wt. Score	HH No.	Wt. Score	HH No.	Wt. Score
		Village Kusumjore					
Village		39.	8	79.	6	120.	5
Bakharmal		40.	4	80.	5	121.	5
1.	8	41.	5	81.	6	122.	8
2.	4	42.	4	82.	7	123.	5
3.	4	43.	3	83.	6	124.	5
4.	5	44.	5	84.	3	125.	1
5.	5	45.	6	85.	2	126.	1
6.	5	46.	7	86.	5	127.	4
7.	5	47.	1	87.	7	128.	9
8.	8	48.	5	88.	5	129.	4
9.	5	49.	6	89.	7	130.	5
10.	1	50.	5	90.	3	Village Bhangabari	
11.	7	51.	7	91.	6	131.	1
12.	3	52.	4	92.	4	132.	1
13.	1	53.	3	Village Degam		133.	1
14.	1	54.	6	93.	1	134.	6
15.	5	55.	7	94.	5	135.	1
16.	5	56.	7	95.	4	136.	5
17.	1	Village		96.	3	137.	4
18.	3	Bhairajpur		97.	3	138.	6
19.	5	57.	5	98.	4	139.	7
20.	2	58.	3	99.	5	140.	7
21.	5	59.	3	100.	8	141.	1
		60.	5	101.	1	142.	9
Village		61.	5	102.	3	143.	8
Ghantiguda		62.	5	103.	4	144.	4
22.	3	63.	7	104.	6	145.	6
23.	3	64.	7	105.	1	146.	1
24.	7	65.	4	106.	7	147.	1
25.	5	66.	1	107.	3	148.	6
26.	6	67.	7	108.	1	149.	4
27.	4	68.	6	109.	1	150.	1
28.	6	69.	7	110.	1	Village Basantpada	
29.	4	70.	6	111.	4	151.	1
30.	5	71.	5	112.	6	152.	6
31.	4	72.	6	Village Tentulipada		153.	9
32.	4	73.	5	113.	8	154.	9
33.	4	74.	7	114.	7	155.	4
34.	4	Village Matia		115.	4	156.	1
35.	4	75.	5	116.	7	157.	3
36.	6	76.	6	117.	8	158.	1
37.	2	77.	9	118.	4	159.	3
38.	4	78.	5	119.	1	160.	6

HH No.	Wt. Score	HH No.	Wt. Score	HH No.	Wt. Score	HH No.	Wt. Score
161.	3	205.	5	245.	1	288.	1
162.	4	Village		246.	3	289.	1
163.	6	Mankadashola		247.	9	290.	1
164.	1	206.	8	248.	6	291.	1
165.	7	207.	7	249.	8	292.	5
166.	1	208.	5	250.	1	Village	
167.	6	209.	1	251.	3	Barabandha	
Village Chandpura		210.	1	252.	5	293.	5
168.	8	211.	1	253.	3	294.	1
169.	6	212.	1	254.	6	295.	1
170.	1	213.	1	255.	8	296.	1
171.	1	214.	1	256.	6	297.	5
172.	1	215.	4	257.	6	298.	3
173.	3	216.	8	258.	1	299.	3
174.	8	217.	7	259.	1	300.	7
175.	6	218.	7	Village		301.	2
176.	3	219.	7	Padepadar		302.	1
177.	2	220.	7	260.	1	303.	1
178.	3	221.	6	261.	8	304.	1
179.	3	222.	4	262.	3	305.	1
180.	6	223.	1	263.	1	306.	1
181.	3	Village		264.	1	307.	4
182.	6	Mahulpatna		265.	9	308.	7
183.	8	224.	1	266.	9		
184.	1	225.	1	267.	3		
Village Jariguma		226.	1	268.	4		
185.	7	227.	1	269.	1		
186.	6	228.	1	270.	4		
187.	5	229.	1	271.	4		
188.	6	230.	4	272.	3		
189.	1	231.	1	273.	3		
190.	5	232.	1	274.	3		
191.	4	233.	1	275.	1		
192.	5	234.	9	276.	1		
193.	4	235.	5	Village Tejipada			
194.	1	236.	1	277.	7		
195.	3	237.	1	278.	1		
196.	3	238.	1	279.	1		
197.	5	239.	1	280.	6		
198.	6	240.	1	281.	7		
199.	4	241.	6	282.	5		
200.	6	Village		283.	3		
201.	4	Kulihariguda		284.	1		
202.	6	242.	7	285.	1		
203.	5	243.	4	286.	1		
204.	6	244.	3	287.	4		

Note.

HH No. = Household Number

Wt. Score = Weighted Score (of land and Soil)

Landowner (land in acres)	Code assigned
Landless labourer (0)	= 0
Marginal landholder (0-2)	= 1
Small landholder (2-7)	= 2
Medium landholder (7-12)	= 3
Large-landholder (>12)	= 4

Soil quality	Code assigned
Bhatta	= 1
Att	= 2
Berna	= 3
Bahal	= 4

GLOSSARY

Adibasi	–	Tribe
Amdhan	–	Hill paddy
Att	–	Rocky or stony upland
Bahabandha	–	Mortgage of land, labour by giving advances
Bahal, Berna	–	Lands of higher grade
Bandha	–	Embankment
Bandha	–	Mortgage of land and labour.
Bandha Saheji	–	Mortgage of land with having a share in the produced paddy cultivated by both moneylender and mortgager.
Barchha	–	Sugar-cane plots
Bari	–	Homestead land
Bhata	–	Worst quality, dry and irregular land requiring more labour for less produce.
Bhat kanda	–	Root of rice substitute
Bhatti	–	Hut for liquor brewing and selling
Brahmin Sasan	–	Village or hamlet of Brahmin caste
Chakhna	–	Food prepared from *mahua*
Charpoy	–	Cot
Cherenga	–	Edible root of Konds
Chhotadhan	–	Drought resistant paddy variety
Chuda	–	Flattened rice
Chuha	–	Pond
Dalal	–	Middle man
Dom	–	Scheduled Caste
Dongar	–	Hill side plots prepared for shifting cultivation
Dongerla	–	Higher plateaus or hilly areas South Eastern Kalahandi. Also the portion of Eastern Ghats on the East to South East of Kalahandi, including Madanpur Rampur, Lanjigarh and Thuamul Rampur

Dongerla plain	–	Plain on higher plateaus
Gaer Hajir	–	According to which any SC student if remains absent in a school, his parents were required to provide free service as a form of punishment, in the king's palace
Gaud	–	A backward caste
Gauntia	–	Village head man commanding most of the cultivating fields
Goti	–	Free agricultural service to the village headman (*Gauntia*)
Haat	–	Market held at regular intervals
Halia	–	Annual agricultural labour in the master's house 15 to 25 'Puti' of paddy. (1 puti = 80 kgs.)
Judung	–	Bean
Kalantaria	–	Mortgage of land for money with compound interest
Kalibhuti	–	Purchase of labour giving a certain price before reaping paddy and collect double as labour during harvest
Kallar	–	Oilman
Kandul	–	A local variety of pulses
Kardi	–	Tender bamboo shoots which are gathered by tribals during the periods of food scarcity in rainy season
Kata	–	Stream diversion
Kating, Alsi, Gurji, Sua	–	Produces of shifting cultivation
Katti	–	Mortgage of land for a fixed period of time and fixed amount after the fixed period of mortgage is over the amount paid by the moneylender lapses. It is not returned by mortgager again
Kodo	–	A foodgrain the crop of which is a drought resistant. Grain suitable for inferior *Att* lands
Kulthi	–	Horse gram
Kusum	–	Local seed pressed to collect oil for domestic use

Mahajan	–	Moneylender
Mal	–	Clayey land suitable for Rabi crops
Mandia	–	Ragi
Muri	–	Puffed rice
Nala	–	Stream
Nuakhai, Toki Parab	–	Tribal festivals
Pahilpar	–	Plain tract of river valleys and basins.
Pita kanda	–	Root having a bitter taste
Pith kanda	–	Root obtained from deep soil, act as a cereal substitute
Podu	–	Slash and Burn cultivation in Kalahandi and other parts of the Western Orissa. It is a crude or primitive practice of farming or shifting cultivation.
Push Punei	–	Popular festival of Kalahandi observed on full moon day of late winter
Rasi	–	Til
Sag	–	Leafy vegetables
Salap	–	Juicy drinks which is tribal's favourite
Sukhbasi	–	Landless labourer
Tendu	–	Kendu
Tentuli	–	Tamarind
Thika	–	Contract labour where the labours may be in loss or gain
Tola	–	*Mahua* seed pressed to collect oil for domestic use.

Conversion Table

1 Mana = 4000 grams.(= 8 Sola = 16 Gida = 32 Bada = 4Ada)
1 Ada = 1000 grams. 1 Mana of rice = 4000 grams
1 Mana *Swan* = 2000 grams 1 Mana *Guruji* = 2000 grams
1Mana *Kang* = 2000 grams 1 Sola = 500 grams
1 Puda of rice = 4 Puti = 2 Quintals 1 Gida = 2 Bada = 250 gms.
1 Mana of land = 10 Decimals
1 Sola = ¼ Ada = approx. 250 grams (in some areas)
1 Puti of paddy = 80 kgs (in some areas)
Ada is considered a standard unit
Source : Fieldwork.

BIBLIOGRAPHY

Books

Baran, P., (1957): *The Political Economy of Growth,* Monthly Review Press, New York.

Bardhan, P., (1984): *The Political Economy of Development in India,* Oxford University Press, Delhi.

Bigman, D., (1982): *Copping with Hunger: Towards a System of Food Scarcity and Price Stabilisation.* Ballinagar Publishing Company Cambridge. The Hebrew University of Jerusalem, Massachusetts.

Castro, T.D., (1977): *The Geopolitics of Hunger,* Monthly Review Press, United States.

Dandekar, V.M. and N. Rath (1971) : *Poverty in India,* Indian School of Political Economy, Poona.

Dewey, C.J. (ed.), (1988) : *Arrested Development in India : The Historical Dimensions,* Manohar Publication, New Delhi.

Dreze, J. and Sen, A., (1989): *Hunger and Public Action.* Oxford University Press, New York.

Eisehans, H., (1991) : *Development and Underdevelopment: The History, Economics and Politics of North South Relation,* Sage Publication, New Delhi.

Frank, A.G., (1967) : *Capitalism and Underdevelopment in Latin America,* Pelican, London.

Frank, A.G.,(1981) : *Crisis in the Third World,* Heinemann Educational Books Limited, London.

Forbes, D.K., (1985) : *The Geography of Underdevelopment: A Critical Survey,* Select Book Service Syndicate, New Delhi.

Haimendorf, C.V.F. (1982) : *Tribes of India: The Struggle for Survival,* Oxford University Press, Delhi.

Kent, G., (1984) : *The Political Economy of Hunger:* The Silent Holocaust, Praeger Special Studies, New York.

Lipton, M., (1977) : *Why Poor People Stay Poor, A Study of Urban bias in World Development,* Temple Smith, London.

Marriam, M.W., (1984): *Rural Vulnerability to Famine in Ethiopia:1958-77,* Vikas Publishing House (P) Ltd. in association, Addis Ababa University.

Mishra,.P., (1979) : *The Political History of Chhatisgarh, 1740-1858,* Viswa Bharati Prakashan, Nagpur.

Misra, R.P. (ed.), (1969) : *Regional Planning: Concept, Techniques, Policies and Case Studies,* Prasaranga, University of Mysore.

Misra, R.P. *et. al.*, (1976) : *Regional Development Planning in India : A New Strategy,* Delhi.

Misra, R.P., (1985*): Rural Development: Capitalist and Socialist Paths,* Concept Publishing House, New Delhi.

Murdoch, W.W., (1980) : *The Poverty of Nations, The Political Economy of Hunger and Population,* John Hopkins University Press, Baltimore.

Nepak, B., (1984) : *Odissara Adibasi Samaj,* The Tribal Society of Orissa, K.K. Mishra and Co., Cuttack.

Pacey, A. and Payne, P., (1985) : *Agricultural Development and Nutrition,* Concept Publishing, Bali Nagar, Delhi.

Power, J. and Holenstein, A. M., (1976) : *World Hunger : A Strategy for Survival,* Maurice Temple Smith Limited, London.

Rath, R., (1958) : *Odissara Adibasi Samaj,* Cuttack Publishing House, Cuttack.

Reutilinger, S. and Selowsky, M., (1976) : *Malnutrition and Poverty: Magnitude and Policy Options,* John Hopkins for the World Bank, Baltimore.

Schineeder, H., (1984): *Meeting Food Needs: In a context of Change,* Development Centre of Organisation, Cooperation and Development, The OECD, Catalogue of Publication, Paris.

Sen, A., (1982) : *Poverty and Famines : An Essay on Entitlement and Deprivation,* Clarendon Press, England.

Sharma, K., (1978) : *The Konds of Orissa : An Anthropometric Study,* Concept Publishing Company, New Delhi.

Sinha, R., (1976) : *Food and Poverty: The Political Economy of Confrontation.* Ambika Publications.

Timberlake, M. (ed.), (1985) : *Urbanization in the World Economy,* Academic Press, Orlando, p. XIII

Wallerstein, I., (1974) : *The Modern World System I,* Academic Press, New York.

Wallerstein, I., (1984): *The Politics of the World Economy,* Cambridge University Press, Cambridge.

Warnock, W.J., (1987): *The Politics of Hunger: The Global Food System.* Methuen Publications, Toronto.

Washbook, D., (1990) : *South Asia, the World System and World Capitalism,* Oxford University Press, Delhi.

Articles

Agarwal, A., (1985): "Ecological Destruction and the emerging patterns of Poverty and People's protests in Rural India", *Social Action,* 35 (No.1 Jan.-Mar.,) pp. 54-80.

Ali, A., (1989): Background paper on Health Scenario of Kalahandi District (Memio) Orissa, Voluntary Health Association, Bhubaneswar.

Behura, N.K. and Das, P.K., (1991) : "Effects of Drought on Health Conditions and Nutritional Status of People", in Nayak, P.K. and Mahajan, A. (Ed.), *Human Encounter with Drought,* Reliance Publishing House, New Delhi.

Biswas, B.C., (1980) : "Effect of Forest cover on rainfall distribution in Andaman and Nicobar Island", *Mausam,* January 1980.

Blankson, C., (1987): "The Food Crisis in West Africa: An Examination of Theoretical Approaches" in *Rural African,* No. 27. African Studies Centre, Michigan State University.

Bollen, K., (1983) : "World System, Position, Dependency and Democracy: The Cross National Evidence", *American Sociological Review,* Vol. 48, August, p. 470.

Bose, A., (1983) : "The Mystery of Orissa's Low Growth Rate of Population : Tribal Development or Tribal Stagnation ?" in Mishra, S.N. and Singh, B. (Eds.), *Tribal Area Development,* Society for the Study of Regional Disparities, New Delhi.

Bradshaw, Y.W., (1985) "Dependency, Development in Black Africa: A Cross national study", *American Sociological Review,* Vol. 50. No.2, April, 1985, p.195.

Bradshaw, Y.W., (1987) : "Urbanisation and Underdevelopment: A Global Study of Modernisation, Urban Bias and Economic Dependency", *American Sociological Review,* Vol. 52, No. 2, April 1987, T. 226.

Bush, R., (1985): "Drought and Famine", in *Review of African Political Economy,* No.33.

Chandrasekharan, K. S., (1983) : "Forest and Tribal Development" in Koraput Seminar on *Development Prospects of Koraput Region,* Sri Jagannath Temple, Koraput.

Chaudhury, K., (1991) : "Stricken Kalahandi : Commission Confirms Deaths", *Frontline,* Sept. 28-Oct. 11, 1991, pp. 112-13.

Chazan, Noami and Shaw, Trimothy, M., (1988) : "The Political Economy of Food in Africa" in Chazan, N. and Shaw, T.M. (Eds.), *Coping with Africas Food Crisis,* Lynne Rienner Publisher, Boulder and London.

Choudhury, B., (1983) : "Agrarian Relation-Eastern India", in Dharma Kumar (Ed.), *The Cambridge Economic History of India,* pp. 131-32.

Chilcote, R.H., (1977) : "Dependency: A Critical Synthesis of the Literature" in Lughad, J.A. and Hay, R. (Eds.), *Third World Urbanisation,* Maquroufa Press, Chicago, p.131.

Christensen, C., (1978) "World Hunger : A Structural Approach in Hopkins, R.F., and Puchala, D.J. (Eds.), *The Global Political Economy of Food,* The University of Wisconsin Press, England.

Currice, B., (1992) : "Food Crises and Prevention : An analysis in the Indian context", *Contemporary South Asia,* 1(1), 93-111, University of Hull, Hull.

Dash, J., (1991) : "Impact of Drought on Agricultural Production, Forest Utilisation and Migration" in Nayak, P.K. and Mahajan, A., *Human Encounter with Drought,* Reliance Publishing House, New Delhi.

Deo, F., (1989): "Differential Response of Tribal Groups of Nawapada Sub-division to External Pressure", Paper presented in Orissa History Congress, proceeding of the XV Annual Session, Bhubaneswar, 4th-5th Nov.,1989.

Dwivedi, S., (1992) : "Mahua brewing, an alluring venture," in *The Times of India,* New Delhi, 14th July, 1992.

Evans and Timberlake, M., (1980) : "Dependency, Inequality and the Growth of Tertiary : A Comparative analysis of Less Developed Countries", *American Sociological Review,* Vol. 45, 1980, pp. 531-52.

Ford, M. and Frank, H., (1988) : "Crisis and State Reforms", in Chazan, N. and Shaw, T.M. (Eds.), *Coping With Africa's Food Crisis,* Lynne Reinner Publisher, Boulder and London.

Heinrichs, J., (1978) : "Political Economy of Hunger", in Harle V. (Ed.), *The Political Economy of Food,* Saxon House Teak Field Ltd., England.

Kentor, J., (1985) : "Economic Development and the World Division of Labour", in Timberlake, M. (Ed.), *Urbanisation in the World Economy,* Academic Press, Orlando, p. 26.

Lofchie, M.F., (1975) : "Political and Economic origins of African Hunger" in *The Journal of Modern African Studies,* Vol. 13 (4).

Lofchie, M.F. and Commins, S.K., (1982) : "Food Deficits and Agricultural Policies in Tropical Africa" in *The Journal of Modern African Studies,* Vol. 20(1).

Macyer, E.M.D. (1976) : "Protein-Energy Malnutrition" in Beaten, G.H. and Bengoa, J.M. (Ed.), *Nutrition in Preventive Medicine,* World Health Organisation, Monograph Series No.62.

Mahajan, A., (1991) : "Human Situation in Kalahandi : An Eco Developmental Analysis" in Nayak, P.K. and Mahajan, A. (Ed.), *Human Encounter with Drought,* Reliance Publishing House, New Delhi.

Menon, P., (1989) : "Ordeal in Orissa-Fighting the Drought" in *Frontline,* 29th April-l2th May.

Mishra, D. and Rao, R.S. (1992) : "Hunger in Kalahandi : Blinkered Understanding", *Economic and Political Weekly,* June 13-20, pp.1245-1246.

Mishra, M., (1989) : "Kalahandira Sampratik Samasya: Ekanuchinta", an Oriya article in *The Samaj,* Cuttack, 19th February 1989, pp.5-6.

Mishra, R.P. and Bhooshan, B.S., (1988) : "Rural Development: National Policies and Experiences" in Mishra R.P. (Ed.) *Rural Development,* Vol.4, UNCRD, Nagoya.

Mohapatra, P.C. and Patnaik, S.C., (1978) : *Tribal Development in a Forestry Framework: A case study of Koraput District*, mimeo.

Mohanty, M., (1990) : "Class, Caste and Dominance in a Backward State Orissa", in Francine R.F. and Rao, M.S.A. (Eds.) *Dominance and State Power in Modern India*, Oxford University Press, Delhi, pp.321-63.

Mohanty, M., (1990): "Political Economy of Development of Orissa since Independence", Abstract of the theme paper presented at V Indian Social Sciences Congress, Berhampur, 19-23, December, 1990.

Mohanty, M., (1992): "Kalahandi Awaits", *Mainstream*, 18th April, 1992, pp.7-9.

Panda, A.C., (1991) "Peoples Participation in the Management of Forests in Kalahandi", paper presented in the district level workshop on *Hunger and Underdevelopment : Is there way out for Kalahandi?*, Bhawanipatna, December 28-29.

Pattnaik, S., (1991): "Absolute Poverty and its Eradication in Rural Nawapara" in Nayak, P.K. and Mahajan, A. (Eds.), *Human Encounter with Drought*, Reliance Publishing House, New Delhi.

Pradhan, J., (1993): "Drought in Kalahandi : The Real Story", *Economic and Political Weekly*, July 29.

Purohit,.H., Rao, R.S. and Tripathy, P.K., (1986) : "The Drought Syndrome : A Report on Kalahandi District" in *Vigil*. Vol. VII, No. 40. October 1985, Vol. VII No. 42. November 1985, Vol. VIII No.10 March 1986.

Prusty, D., (1991) : "Karala Marudir Chhaire Puni Kalahandi", in *The Sambad*, an Oriya Daily, Bhubaneswar, 11th July.

Rajashekar, D. and Vyasulu, V., (1990): "The Credit Delivery System and the Development Process : The case of Kalahandi, A Backward District in a Backward State", Seminar paper presented at Institute for Social and Economic Change, Bangalore.

Ray, T., (1992) : "Kalahandi's Trauma: Starvation and Death, yet again," in *Frontline*, April 10th, pp.77-86.

Sainath, P., (1994) : "Nine years later Kalahandi remains the same: Faces of Poverty", in *The Times of India*, March 22nd, p. 22.

Sainath, P., (1994): "Surat's sorrow, Orissa's gain : Faces of Poverty" in *The Times of India,* New Delhi, April 12th.

Sen, A., (1973) : "Poverty, Inequality and Unemployment: Some Issues in Measurement" in *Economic and Political Weekly,* (Special Number, August).

Sen, A., (1982) : "The Food Problem : Theory and Policy" in *Third World Quarterly,* Vol. 4, No.3.

Sen, A., (1992) : "Anti Poverty Programmes: Who should benefit?" in *The Hindustan Times,* 22nd July.

Singdeo, J.P., (1986) : "Socio-Cultural History of Orissa : A case study of Khariar Estate" in Das, B.S. (Ed.), *Glimpses of Orissa,* Punti Pustak, Calcutta.

Thakur, D., (1991) : " They live with starvation in Kalahandi", *Indian Express,* 26th September.

Thrift, N., (1986) : "The Geography of International Economic Disorder", in Johnson, R.J. and Taylor, P.J. (Eds.), *A World in Crisis: Geographical Perspectives,* Basil Black Well, New York, pp.15-25.

Weisskopt, T.E., (1976) : "Dependence and Imperialism in India" in Blowers, A. *et al*. (Eds.), *Inequalities, Conflict and Change,* The Open University Press, Milton Keyness, p.275.

Yesilada, B.A. and Brocket, C.D. and Drury, B., (1987) : "Agrarian Reforms in Reverse : The Food Crisis in the Third World" in Yesilada, B.A. (Ed.), *The Impact of Dependency on Agriculture and Food Crisis in the Third World,* West View Special Studies in Agriculture, Science and Polity.

Yotopoulos, P.A., (1984): "Competition for Cereals: Food Feed Connection", *Ceres* XVII, No. 5, September to October.

Dissertations

Deo, F., (1984): *Tribal – Non-tribal Interaction with special reference to Nawapada sub-division of Kalahandi district in western Orissa,* M.Phil. (History) Dissertation, JNU, New Delhi.

Deo, F., (1990): *State Formation in Western Orissa,* an unpubliished Ph.D. Thesis, JNU, New Delhi.

Mohanty, B., (1988): *Famines and Agrarian Structure with special reference to Orissa division,* 1866 to 1921, Ph.D. Thesis, Delhi School of Economics, Delhi University, Delhi.

Mund, M.S., (1987): *Transportation Network, its Prospect and Problems in Kalahandi District (Orissa) – A Geographical Analysis,* M.Phil., Dissertation, P.G. Department of Geography, Utkal University, Bhubaneswar.

Sahoo, S., (1991) : *Land Reforms in Orissa,* M.A. Dissertation, Department of Political Science, Delhi University, Delhi.

Reports

Report on Supply of Controlled Commodities, 1989-90.

- *Gazetteer of Kalahandi (1981).*
- *Report on number of children malnourished in Thuamul Rampur and Lanjigarh in the month of October and November, 1990 (ICDS).*
- *Report on the Annual Administration of Scheduled Areas in Orissa for 1982-83.*
- *Human and Tribal Welfare Department, Govt. of Orissa, Bhubaneswar.*
- *Rural Development Administration Official Reports of Work Plan, DRDA, 1989-90.*
- *Statistical Data of Lanjigarh Block, 1989-90.*
- *Statistical Data of Thuamul Rampur Block, 1989-90.*
- *Statistical Handbook, 1989-90.*
- *Integrated Child Development Scheme, Work Plan, 1990.*
- Orissa Directorate of Agriculture and Food Production.
- Board of Revenue, Agricultural Census Commissioner, *Report on Number and Area of Operational Holdings in Orissa, 1985-86,* Rastrabhasa Corp. Press, Cuttack.
- Directorate of Health Service, *Number of Infant Deaths Registered in the District of Kalahandi*, 1981-87.
- Directorate of Soil Conservation, *Village Management plan of the two ITDA blocks – Thuamul Rampur and Lanjigarh.*
- Directorate of Economics and Statistics, Bhubaneswar, *District at a glance,* 1988.

- *State Electricity Board (East West Division), Bhawanipatna, Reports on Number of Villages Electrified in different blocks,* 1990.

Annual Administration Report of the Forest Department of Orissa for the year 1981-82, Department of Forest, Fisheries and Animal Husbandry, 1984.

Government of Orissa, *Annual Progress Report on Forest Administration in the province of Orissa for the year* 1936-37, Press Officer Cuttack, 1938.

Inspection Note of B. K. Misra, Director of Land Records and Survey on the *Settlement Operation, Nawapada Sub-division of Kalahandi District,* Kalahandi in Collectorate Office, Acc. No. XXIII, Sl.No. 94, April, 1961.

Selections from the records of Government of India (Foreign Department), published by Authority No.XXX, Report on the Bastar and Kharonde dependencies of the Raepore District, Calcutta, printed by C.B. Lewis, Baptist Mission Press,1861, Jhooamool, pp.1-30 (Raepore District), pp.31-57 (Kharonde), 28th July, 1856.

Centre for Science and Environment 1987 : *The Wrath of Nature: The Impact of Environmental Destruction on Floods and Droughts*, CSE, New Delhi.

"Hungerand Entitlements – Research for Action", A Report in *Frontline,* March 19-April l, 1988.

"Drought and Poverty : A Report from Kalahandi" in *Economic and Political Weekly,* November 2nd, 1985.

"Starvation Deaths Haunts Kalahandi", A Report in the *Times of India,* February 29th, 1992.

Report of the Commission on Kalahandi to Orissa High Court (Cuttack, 1991).

"Towards a Long-term Plan for the Chronically Drought-prone Region of South Western Orissa", draft prepared by Mohanty, B. *et al.* on behalf of Orissa Gabeshana Chakra for Kalahandi Support Committee, Delhi, pp.1-3, 1994.

INDEX